MEMOIRS OF
THE PEACE CONFERENCE

THE SIGNING OF PEACE

IN THE HALL OF MIRRORS, VERSAILLES, 28TH JUNE, 1919

Front: Dr. Johannes Bell (*Germany*) signing, with Herr Hermann Müller leaning over him.

Middle Row (*seated, left to right*): General Tasker H. Bliss, Col. E. M. House, Mr. Henry White, Mr. Robert Lansing, President Woodrow Wilson (*United States*); M. Georges Clemenceau (*France*); Mr. D. Lloyd George, Mr. A. Bonar Law, Mr. Arthur J. Balfour, Viscount Milner, Mr. G. N. Barnes (*Great Britain*); the Marquis Saionzi (*Japan*).

Back Row (*left to right*): M. Eleutherios Veniselos (*Greece*); Dr. Affonso Costa (*Portugal*); Lord Riddell (*British Press*); Sir George E. Foster (*Canada*); M. Nikola Pashitch (*Serbia*); M. Stéphen Pichon (*France*); Col. Sir Maurice Hankey, Mr. Edwin S. Montagu (*Great Britain*); the Maharajah of Bikaner (*India*); Signor Vittorio Emanuele Orlando (*Italy*); M. Paul Hymans (*Belgium*); General Louis Botha (*South Africa*); Mr. W. M. Hughes (*Australia*).

(Sir William Orpen, R.A.

Memoirs
of the
Peace Conference

By

David Lloyd George

VOLUME I

HOWARD FERTIG

NEW YORK · 1972

First published in 1939

HOWARD FERTIG, INC. EDITION 1972
Published in agreement with and by permission of
Beaverbrook Newspapers Limited.

Library of Congress Cataloging in Publication Data

Lloyd George, David Lloyd George, 1st Earl, 1863–1945.
  Memoirs of the Peace Conference.

  Reprint of the 1939 ed. of the work first published in 1938
under title: The truth about the peace treaties.
  1. European War, 1914–1918—Peace. 2. Paris. Peace Conference, 1919. I. Title.
D644.L55   1972   940.3'141   70–80566

PRINTED IN THE UNITED STATES OF AMERICA
BY NOBLE OFFSET PRINTERS, INC.

PREFACE

WHEN a man begins to acquire an entirely new art in his seventieth year, he cannot hope to attain proficiency in it. In these volumes, therefore, I am merely endeavouring to narrate simply, clearly and truthfully the story of the Peace-making as a man who was present at the Peace Conference and witnessed its proceedings throughout. I have set down the facts faithfully, without reference to their bearing on subsequent developments which may be held to condemn or justify the framers of the Treaty according as they may be interpreted by individual opinion. I have also written without any consideration of the effect which a plain statement of the truth may have upon present controversies.

Up to middle age I was a practising lawyer, whose business consisted largely in sifting, selecting and weighing evidence, both oral and documentary, with a view to presenting the case as a whole to trained judges and to a jury of citizens.

Any experienced lawyer knows that, in preparing a brief for a case, no more fatal error can be committed than the suppression or distortion of any relevant fact or document. Apart from the moral condemnation which such an act merits, it is a crime against professional discretion and efficiency. In that spirit, and with that experience in my memory, I have chosen the material at my disposal for the book.

But if an author, in recording events in which he personally took a prominent part, owes a duty to the public not to misinform or mislead them, the public also have their duty to discharge, in acquainting themselves with the real facts, lest they blame the framers of the Treaty for the way in which it has been disregarded and abused by others, or misjudge the action of men who honestly did their best to serve them in an emergency which would try the head and nerve of any man to the utmost limit.

Let the critics of the Treaties take the highest standard of right attained in any civilised community or between one civilised nation and another, and then measure the Peace settlement by that canon. As one of the authors of that settlement I protest against its being judged on the subsequent abuse of its provisions and powers by some of the nations who dictated its terms. The merits of a law cannot be determined by a fraudulent interpretation of its clauses by those who are in a position temporarily to abuse legal rights and to evade honourable obligations. It is not the Treaties that should be blamed. The fault lies with those who repudiated their own solemn contracts and pledges by taking a discreditable advantage of their temporary superiority to deny justice to those who, for the time being, were helpless to exact it. It is not fair to charge the authors of the Treaties with these abuses or their consequences.

For this reason, therefore, the intentions of the Treaty-makers, and their painstaking and honest efforts to carry them out, should be revealed to the public. It is right that these things should be known by a critical generation, which has been misled as to the truth by those who were anxious to shift the responsibility for their own failures from the shoulders that ought to bear them.

D. LLOYD GEORGE

Bron-y-de, Churt, Surrey,
  September, 1938.

CONTENTS

VOLUME I

CHAPTER III

CHAPTER IV

PRESIDENT WILSON AND COLONEL HOUSE

CHAPTER V

OTHER PERSONAL SKETCHES

CHAPTER VI

PROGRESS AT THE CONFERENCE

CHAPTER VII

CHAPTER VIII

lasting peace—Guarantee to France by Britain and U.S.A. against German aggression—Peace terms outlined: League of Nations—German frontiers—German Colonies—Reduction of armaments—Reparation—French exasperation with Fontainebleau Memorandum and their Reply—My answer to Clemenceau's reply—Further discussions on Rhineland—French insistence—King Albert's intervention—French give way—Temporary occupation of Rhineland demanded by French—Clemenceau persuades Wilson—Poincaré demands more —Permanent occupation indicated—Resentment of French Right against Clemenceau for his surrender—No voice raised for moderation of terms.

CHAPTER IX

Preliminary issues for Peace Conference—Muddled popular notions of the Reparations issue—The legal case—Its international validity—Precedents for exaction of Indemnities—Mr. Asquith's demand—Germany's deliberate devastation in France—German evidence of deliberate intent—Destruction of French coal mines—Declaration by Paris Conference, 1916—Appointment of Board of Trade Committee—The Ashley-Keynes Memorandum—Methods of collecting an indemnity—Keynes' authorship of instalment plan—Board of Trade's 1918 Memorandum—Claims will exceed capacity to pay—The Board's recommendations for Reparations in kind—My scepticism about hopes of big indemnities—The Treasury Committee's Report—Large immediate payment and small future tribute recommended—Business experts more optimistic than politicians—I appoint a Committee to assess Germany's capacity to pay—Difference between internal and external debt—The Committee's findings—Infallibility of the business man—My election statement—"The limit of capacity"—No large army of occupation—No dumping—Priority over German internal war debt—Immense cost of the War—All-party agreement to make Germany pay—Northcliffe tries to force the pace—Views of the *Economist*—Sanguine views of the French Finance Minister—British representatives on Reparations Committee—American estimates—Tardieu records my scepticism—Mr. Hughes defends his Committee's Report—Its findings criticised by the Cabinet—Mr. Long pleads business experts' advice—Sir George Foster distrusts the experts—Terms of Reference to Peace Conference Committee—Discussions of Interallied Conference—Reparations from Austro-Hungary—A system of priority for Reparation claims—Reparation Commission set up—Disputes about definition of scope of Reparation—War costs claim—Issue referred to Supreme War Council—I reject "cost of war" claim—"Injuries to civilians" restricted to pension claims—Claims for devastation of British trade impossible—Was the claim for Reparation legitimate?—American interpretation of Lansing Note—Lord Sumner's Memorandum—Argument for including War Pensions—The Smuts Memorandum—President Wilson convinced—Drafting the Reparations clauses—Klotz: "a heart stuffed with bonds"—Clemenceau bored by finance—American estimates—My Memorandum to the "Big Four"—Amount and method of payment to be left open—The Hughes-Cunliffe-Sumner Memorandum—Based on hope and assumption—Keynes submits a revised scheme—Reparation policy in my March Memorandum—Clemenceau and Wilson approve reference to a Commission—Text of the final Articles—Duties of the Reparation Commission—The initial payment—Wisdom of the policy adopted—Disaster of America's withdrawal—Consistent moderation of British view.

CHAPTER X

Unanimity against restoring Colonies—Disagreement on mandates—Interchange between Clemenceau and Hughes—I propose mandates—Annexation preferable in certain cases—Mr. Hughes opposes mandates for Australian conquests—Smuts for annexing S.W.Africa—New Zealand claims Samoa—Borden supports Dominion Premiers—Problem of raw materials for Germany—I propose Committee of investigation—The French view—France objects to mandates—Supports annexation—Would guarantee "open door"—Wilson provoked—I attempt conciliation—Wilson obstinate—Principle of trusteeship vital—Italy amenable—Clemenceau apprehensive of too wide powers for League—I urge an early solution—A deadlock—My draft proposals—The Charter submitted—Wilson difficult—Passage with Hughes—Botha as peacemaker—He supports my proposals—The crisis dissolved—Question of black troops—The Covenant and mandates—"A," "B," and "C" mandates—The "B" Category—The "C" Category—The claims of Belgium and Portugal—The Lost Turkish Possessions—Dominion responsibility.

CHAPTER XI

Lord Northcliffe's pride hurt—Press attacks—Discontent fomented in Parliament—Peace Delegates accused of breaking pledges—Bonar Law repudiates charges—Never said Germany could pay whole cost of War—Kennedy Jones' Round Robin—My reply: we stand by our pledges—I decide to meet Parliament—Reasons for delay in completing Treaty—The League's power of revision—I ask for fair play—Fear of Bolshevism—Folly to attempt to conquer Russia—I defend our action in Russia—Every pledge incorporated in Treaty—A stern but just peace—I demand confidence—Northcliffe the "Grasshopper"—Our opportunity—Opposition collapses—The situation eased.

CHAPTER XII

The issues that created trouble—French Press attacks on Wilson and myself—Confederacy against Clemenceau—Foch and Barthou critics of Clemenceau—Poincaré's sinister influence—Sham Republics in Rhineland.

CHAPTER XIII

Germany still formidable—Commission to draft military and naval terms—Clemenceau bitter—Foch against disarming Germany—Committee's Report—General disarmament mentioned—Foch's recommendations for Germany—No mention by Committee of general disarmament—My criticisms—Foch's explanation—What the proposals really meant—Foch disagrees with me—The debate adjourned—The counter-proposals—Generals obstinate—Principle of conscription for Governments to decide—French Staff go to other extreme—German Army to be 100,000—Allies' obligation to reduce armaments—German protest—Our guarantee.

CHAPTER XIV

First steps—British and French advocacy of the League—The Phillimore Committee—Wilson without a plan—Report of Phillimore Committee—Sanctions recommended—Wilson's hesitation—Bold Report of Bourgeois Committee—

CHAPTER XV

CHAPTER XVI

CHAPTER XVII

VOLUME II

CHAPTER XVIII

CHAPTER XIX

CHAPTER XX

THE NEW STATES

CHAPTER XXI

THE TURKISH TREATY

CHAPTER XXII

THE TURKISH TREATY (*continued*)

CHAPTER XXIII

THE TURKISH TREATY (*continued*)

CHAPTER XXIV

THE TURKISH TREATY (*continued*)

CHAPTER XXV

THE TURKISH TREATY (continued)

CHAPTER XXVI

THE TURKISH TREATY (continued)

CHAPTER XXVII

Importance of protecting minorities—Guarantees demanded from new Succession States—Bratiano objects to compulsory guarantees—Clemenceau's reply—Bratiano not satisfied—Poland's assurances—Czech statement—Yugoslavia lines up with Czechoslovakia—Wilson puts case for adequate guarantees in Treaty—Appeal to the objectors—Bratiano mollified but unconvinced—Polish Minorities Treaty serves as model—Special protection for Jews—League charged with responsibility for fulfilment—Terms of the Tittoni Report—League's decision in 1922—A breach of faith.

Bad record of Succession States—Poland's breaches of Treaty—Yugoslavia oppresses Macedonians—Terrorism and ruthless discrimination—Educational pledges dishonoured—A list of violations—Illustrations fail to show full oppression.

CHAPTER XXVIII

Infraction of Treaty by Signatories—Effect of Clemenceau's downfall—Poincaré's sinister influence—Defection of the United States—The League no longer impartial—Treaty not given a fair Trial—International law must prevail.

MEMOIRS OF
THE PEACE CONFERENCE

CHAPTER I

INTRODUCTORY

AS the World War of 1914–18 was the greatest clash of arms between nations ever waged on this earth, so was the Treaty of Versailles (with the ancillary Treaties of St. Germain, Trianon, Neuilly and Sèvres) the most far-reaching and comprehensive settlement ever effected in any international dispute. It was inevitable that so colossal a readjustment of national boundaries in four continents and of international relations in five continents, where feuds have been fought out between races for countless years, should be provocative of controversy and be responsible for a complication of misunderstandings. It will be many generations before the world settles down to a calm appreciation of the merits and demerits of the terms of these revolutionary compacts. Before they are finally accepted rough edges will have to be smoothed, inequities be set right and provisions which experience has proved to be unworkable as they stand will have to be amended and made more practicable and generally acceptable. But the first step towards a wise revision, where found to be imperative, is a thorough comprehension of the actual terms of the original text, of the reasons and motives which prompted the framers of the Treaty in their decisions, and a dispassionate and impartial examination of the soundness or the unsoundness of these decisions. To these studies must be added a stern investigation of the reasons why some of the most beneficent provisions of the Treaty have failed to take effect. Has the failure been due to any inherent defect in the Treaty itself, or was it attributable to a refusal to honour its provisions by the nations that were primarily responsible for drafting it and by many of those who signed it? A broken treaty is like a broken pitcher—it no longer holds water.

It is safe to say that ninety-nine out of every hundred of the critics of the Treaty have never made themselves acquainted with its stipulations. They have based their hostility on distorted versions of these stipulations written by partisans who disliked the Treaty because they either suffered its penalties or hated its authors. Most of the censors have had their minds poisoned by denunciatory phrases which they unwarily swallowed without examination. When world peace depends on questions arising out of this momentous settlement of a World War, it is essential that the actual stipulations should be mastered and comprehended. My endeavour will be to give a fair and authenticated account of the inexorable facts upon which the Treaty was based, of the aims of the men who were mainly responsible for drafting this momentous document, of the principles upon which they framed it, of the arguments and circumstances that moved them to take the course they followed, of the conditions which circumscribed their judgment, of the methods they adopted to achieve their purpose and to overcome their difficulties, and—most important of all— of the actual and not the suppositious provisions of the Treaty.

Before entering upon a narrative of the events, negotiations and conferences that led to the shaping of the Treaty, there are at least two fixed illusions that must be dispelled in order to obtain a clear perspective of events and conclusions. The first is the statement that the harsher conditions of the Treaty were determined when the nations responsible for its terms were intoxicated and ensavaged by victory over a foe that had slaughtered millions of their young men, devastated some of their fairest provinces and threatened civilisation with a servitude to be imposed and enforced by an unconquerable sword. Nations lacerated with wounds and grief-stricken by the loss of millions of dead were not unnaturally drunk with joy at their escape from a misery which threatened to terminate in an even greater and more unshakable catastrophe—the enslavement of mankind by a military despotism. If the terms were conceived in that state of delirium, then it can be said—and said with truth—that no human beings are in that mental condition capable of delivering a fair and balanced judgment on the terms to be imposed against foes who inflicted such hurt and inspired such dread before they were ultimately vanquished, or on the guarantees to be secured against the repetition of such a calamity. I propose to examine that accusation against the inherent justice of the Treaty.

The second misapprehension is due to the belief entertained and exploited in some quarters that all the harsh conditions of the Treaty emanated from one set of negotiators, whereas all its idealistic stipulations were inspired by a nobler mind. These two complete distortions of the actual historical facts are due to violent personal and factional prejudices inevitably roused by challenging events and to that kind of slipshod perusal of documents and of the course of events which invariably characterises most controversies where international political and personal antipathies are intermixed. There are multitudes of violent controversialists who have read versions of the Treaty only in epithets coined by its opponents, and who therefore persist in believing that it consists exclusively of the penal clauses they distort and thus condemn, and that the liberation of oppressed races, the Covenant of the League, the proposals for general disarmament and the establishment of an International Labour Office have no connection with the Treaty, but were carried over the heads of the statesmen they dislike by the influence and the insistence of others. The type of politician who feeds his convictions on these acrid and corrosive quackeries does not trouble to analyse their contents before he swallows them.

First of all I intend to deal with the fundamental misconception of the true history of the Peace Settlement which takes for granted that its provisions were determined in the frenzied hour of triumph. There are two salient facts about this war which are not applicable to any other war previously waged—certainly not in the same degree or in the same measure. The first is that it was not waged between mercenary armies but that the whole manhood of the combatant nations was engaged in the struggle—either in the fighting or in the preparations for it. All classes alike were drawn into the contest and all suffered alike. The sacrifices increased beyond any previous experience as the War continued. After the first impulse of zeal and anger died down the nations became too tired to feel or to feed enthusiasms and passions, and it is not a reflexion on the courage of any of the belligerents to say that a reasonable peace would have been welcomed by the majority of their people before the War was half over. Governments, in proclaiming their rival peace aims, were obliged to take full cognisance of this mood. Not only did death and wounds darken most households, but taxation and many irksome conditions which restricted habitual freedom had deprived the War of any popularity it ever enjoyed. The shoutings of the crowd which characterised the first days of the War in every country had been followed by a grim and sullen determination to see the struggle through to a just conclusion. No Government in any belligerent State could have prosecuted the War unless all ranks and grades of the nation were behind it. The Russian Revolution of March, 1917, and the events which followed it clearly demonstrate that fact. One Government after another in Russia did its best to continue the fight after the people had come to the conclusion that they had had enough of it. Czarist, Liberal and Socialist Ministries alike failed in their efforts because the peasants and workers were exhausted by the terrific strain of the conflict and disgusted with the shambles. They wanted to get out of them at any price. Governments in other belligerent countries had this startling development before their eyes eighteen months before the War came to an end. They therefore knew that it would be dangerous to exaggerate their demands beyond the acquiescence of their people. Naturally the tone and temper of public opinion had a readier response in official policy in a democratic country than in an autocratic State. But in no country were the people prepared to go on increasing their terrible sacrifices and burdens merely in order to extend imperial boundaries, or to inflict punishment on the disturbers of the peace.

There was another element which exerted a powerful restraint on the proclamation of extravagant or rapacious war aims—the effect such an exhibition of greed would have upon neutrals. Both the belligerent groups were anxious to secure the goodwill of neutral countries—notably that of the United States of America. In a moment of reckless exaltation over her victories in Russia and Roumania, Germany defied the censoriousness of

America on submarine warfare and paid the penalty of her rashness. Britain and France were sensitive to the importance of conciliating the United States. Allied statesmen were all conscious of the fact that a time would come when America could intervene with irresistible effect and that it would be unwise to antagonise its rulers and its peoples by an exhibition of greed or vindictiveness. Their peace aims were framed in such a way as to convince America, and especially the pacific and anti-imperialist American President, that their objectives were fundamentally just.

The slightest acquaintance with the long process of deliberating and conferring inside and between the Allied nations, by which ideas as to the kind of peace which ought to be aimed at gradually grew and developed, will show that the main outlines of the Treaty of Versailles were defined and fixed, not in the hour of victory, but during the years in which the struggle was going on and when the issue was still in doubt, when the nations saw ahead nothing but the prospect of the complete dissipation of their hard-earned treasure and the still darker outlook of the death or mutilation of myriads of their picked men in the flower of their youth. The negotiations in Paris after the War were—fortunately—directed and fettered by terms carefully discussed and determined by and amongst the Allies when they had the example of Russia before their eyes; when the fortune of war seemed to lean against the Allies; when the enemy was still confident of victory and could proudly refer to a series of resplendent triumphs in support of his confidence; when pacifists in Allied countries did not conceal their concurrence in this pessimistic estimate of Allied prospects; and when many advocates of the Allied cause, like Lord Lansdowne and others, whose patriotic devotion to that cause was beyond question, had reluctantly arrived at the conclusion that a stalemate was the best result attainable if the struggle were continued any farther.

The first notable summary of the war aims of the British Empire was made by Mr. Asquith on September 25th, 1914, in a speech delivered at Dublin in which he said:

Forty-four years ago, the time of the war of 1870, Mr. Gladstone used these words. He said, "The greatest triumph of our time will be the enthronement of the idea of public right as a governing idea of European policy." Nearly fifty years have passed; little progress it seems has yet been made of the great and beneficent change, but it seems to me now at this moment to be as good a definition as we could give of our ultimate policy. The idea of public right. What does it mean when translated into concrete terms? It means, first and foremost, a clear but definite repudiation of militarism as a governing factor in the relations of States, and in the future moulding of the European world, which knows that room must be found and kept for the independent existence and free development of smaller nationalities, each for the life of its history and corporal consciousness of its own. Belgium, Holland, Switzerland, and the Scandinavian countries, Greece, and the Balkan States, they must be recognised as having exactly as good a title as their more powerful neighbours—more powerful in strength and wealth—exactly as good a title to a place in the sun. It means the final, or it ought to mean, perhaps, by a slow and gradual process, the substitution for force, for the nourishing of competing ambition, for the groupings of alliances, and the precarious equipoise of . . . a real European partnership based upon the recognition of equal rights, established and enforced by common will.

In his famous Guildhall speech on November 9th, 1914, he used words which are now historic:

We shall never sheathe the sword which we have not lightly drawn until Belgium recovers in full measure all and more than all that she has sacrificed, until France is adequately secured against the menace of aggression, until the rights of the smaller nationalities of Europe are placed upon an unassailable foundation, and until the military domination of Prussia is wholly and finally destroyed.

The French Prime Minister, M. Viviani, associated France with these declarations, but added the further statement, "France will lay down arms only . . . when the provinces torn from her have been rejoined to her for ever."

This speech was delivered on December 22nd, 1914.

The war aims of the Allies promulgated at the commencement of the War might therefore be thus summarised:

(1) The vindication of international right against the tyranny of force used as an instrument not of righteousness but of arrogance, of greed and of national oppression.

(2) The complete restoration of the national independence and integrity of Belgium and Serbia.

(3) The defeat and destruction of Prussian militarism as a menace to the peace of the world.

(4) The establishment of the principle of international right on such firm foundations that the smaller and weaker nations could be guaranteed protection against the ruthlessness and aggressiveness of the strong.

(5) As far as France was concerned, the restoration of the lost provinces of Alsace-Lorraine.

These declarations of the purpose with which the Allied nations entered the War were accepted with virtual unanimity by the people in every Allied country without any distinction of party. In the British Empire young men volunteered by the million, from every continent where the flag of Britain waves, to attain these objectives and to establish these principles on a firm foundation in the world.

No attempt was made by any of the Allied Governments to elaborate and work out the detailed application of these general pronouncements until the beginning of 1917. Meanwhile four events had occurred which necessitated an extension of their previous declarations. First, the war with Turkey had assumed proportions and involved sacrifices which made it necessary to consider the application of the Asquith and Viviani pronouncements to the conditions of the Turkish Empire. The second event was the use made by the Germans of their colonies as bases for attack on the British Empire and its lines of communication and the considerable military operations which had consequently to be undertaken largely by the Dominion, Indian and Colonial troops in those colonies. In these two military undertakings alone the British Empire had been compelled to raise and maintain armies far more numerous and costly than those which Pitt and Castlereagh had to organise and equip in their colossal struggle against Napoleon. Allenby in his Palestine campaign and Maude in his march on Baghdad each had under his command an army more than twice as numerous as that which Wellington led in his peninsular campaign on his march from the Tagus to the Pyrenees. At the end of the War the British forces engaged in the

Turkish campaigns numbered not far short of a million men. General Smuts in his conquest of Tanganyika commanded four times as many troops as Wolfe led in the battle that won Canada for the British flag. The flotillas and the forces which swept the Germans out of Samoa and New Guinea were much more powerful than those which wrested the West Indies from the Spaniards or India from the French. These campaigns, waged in malarial jungle and across barren and burning deserts, attracted little attention in Britain during the World War. Considerable as were these enterprises standing alone, they sank into insignificance compared with the immense forces and the gigantic equipment maintained in France. Still, in life and treasure heavy sacrifices were incurred in these sideshows which wrenched from the hands of Germany an empire covering millions of square miles. These conquests created a new factor which was not in the minds of Governments when war was first declared, but of which peacemakers at the end of the War were bound to take cognisance.

The third event which introduced a new element into the settlement of peace terms was the entry of Italy into the conflict. Of all the Allied Powers Italy was the only one who, as a condition precedent to her co-operation, exacted terms which involved a substantial territorial gain for herself. She bargained tenaciously about the spoils of victory ere she committed herself to come to the aid of the Allies. For months her statesmen negotiated with both sides on the basis of territorial concessions. The Allies were in a position to offer better terms and the Italian Government decided to throw in its lot with them.

This is not the place to discuss the merits of the Treaty of London negotiated in 1915 between Mr. Asquith and Lord Grey on behalf of the Allies and Baron Sonnino for Italy. It cannot be denied that at least a portion of the geographical extension of territory promised to Italy in the Treaty of London was in distinct contravention of the principles laid down by the Allied Governments as a justification to their own people for calling upon them to face the horrors of a colossal war. It can be pleaded in extenuation of this descent of Allied statesmanship from the exalted level of the crusade they had launched for international right and liberty, that they were beginning to realise that the enterprise upon which they had embarked was beset with greater difficulties and perils than they had fully contemplated, and that success was not so assured as they had at first anticipated, and that they must seek—and if necessary, purchase—the assistance of an Ally which at the beginning of the War was bound by a treaty of alliance to side with the Central Powers.

Let those who condemn Mr. Asquith and Lord Grey for negotiating that bargain reflect on the situation in April and May, 1915, when the Pact was signed. Things were not going too well on the various battle-fronts. The effort to dislodge the Germans from France was not making any progress despite appalling losses of French and British lives. The Russian steam-roller was being pushed back with a greater velocity than it had rolled forward. Victory was tarrying heavily on the way and its chariots were not in sight on the distant horizon. The Allied leaders had therefore to weigh the chances and to deliberate whether they could hope to win without sacrificing something of the objectives which they had set before themselves and the people they represented, in order to achieve the rest. It was a hard choice and one with which men are confronted in all the affairs of life. It is easy to judge harshly when the impending disaster has been averted partly by the methods which are condemned. How many of those who denounce the Treaty of Versailles would have acted differently from Mr. Asquith and his Government when the choice was not impossibly between the triumph of Prussian militarism and a sure chance of its final defeat? This is no exaggeration of Mr. Asquith's dilemma. Had Italy not come into the War on our side in May, 1915, what would have occurred when Russia subsequently cracked up completely and left France and Britain alone to cope with the victorious armies of Germany and Austria? Whatever its motive or justification, the Pact of London was a bond which had to be honoured by the Allied treatymakers, for by that time Italy had paid the price to the full in blood and treasure. But those who framed the Peace Treaties (including President Wilson, who was no party to the London arrangement) were conscious that this engagement introduced new elements which affected any settlement with Austria and Turkey. It even modified prejudicially the legitimate interests of our Serbian allies. It must be admitted that the hacking of essentially Tyrolean villages and valleys from the rest of the Tyrol was incompatible with the principles of self-determination implicitly embodied in the original war aims of Allied statesmanship. When the time came to carry out the bargain, some of the terms almost caused a rupture amongst the victors. The trouble they are likely to make is not yet at an end.

A fourth element which the progress of this destructive war had brought into prominence was the devastation it wrought in the provinces where it was being waged. In the whole history of warfare up to that date there had been nothing to compare with it in the extent and thoroughness of the cost it incurred and the destruction it effected. It exceeded the worst anticipations of the students of modern warfare with its shattering weapons. The German march on Paris and the many sanguinary battles fought up to November, 1914, including the prolonged and fiercely contested battle of Ypres, hardly gave a foretaste of the indescribable havoc of which modern artillery was capable. The production of explosive shells on an immense scale on both sides began in the winter of 1914. By the end of 1916 the greater and more prosperous provinces of North-Eastern France were a scene of utter ruin and desolation. Factories had been demolished, considerable towns were in ruins, hundreds of villages and scores of thousands of farmhouses had been completely obliterated. The very surface of the ground over hundreds of square miles had been so scarred and churned up that no plough could find a few yards of level field for tillage of the tortured soil. Had Northern France been a virgin prairie, it would not have cost a pioneer a third as much in labour and material to bring it into cultivation as it did to restore this excoriated, pitted and poisoned wilderness to a condition which would fit it for production. Who was to bear the expense of that restoration—the invader or the invaded, the aggressor or his victim? By the year 1916 the question of reparation had assumed proportions unthought of in 1914. The principle of reparations had already been laid down in the category of Asquith and Viviani's war aims in reference to the wanton destruction of Belgian cities like Louvain. It was universally acknowledged amongst the Allied peoples that justice demanded the extension of that principle to the greater damage brought by German aggression in some of those provinces of France where the ceaseless toil of its workers for centuries had enriched the land and built up beneficent and prosperous industries.

When the War Cabinet at the end of 1916 came to review and to elaborate in detail the war objectives of the Allies, they had full cognisance of all these four factors which had entered into the struggle since August, 1914. Only two of them introduced considerations which were not covered in principle by the Allied pronouncements of 1914—the fate of the German Colonies, and such of the territorial claims of Italy as were not covered by the designation of Italia Irredenta: the Southern Tyrol, part of the Dalmatian slopes, the Anatolian coast and Libya.

In the autumn of 1916, when the highest political circles were sibilant with peace whispers, the Prime Minister issued instructions to the Foreign Office to prepare a memorandum as to a suggested basis for a territorial settlement in Europe. It was prepared on two alternative assumptions. One was an Allied victory —the other a stalemate. It is an impressive document, well-informed, bold and far-seeing. Some of its proposals are startling. They are all well worthy of a careful perusal in view of recent developments. It is the first official pronouncement in which what came to be known as self-determination constituted the principle of a readjustment of national boundaries. It is also the first official document which contains a declaration in favour of the establishment of a League of Nations and a reduction in armaments. It reads as follows:

His Majesty's Government have announced that one of their chief objects in the present war is to ensure that all the States of Europe, great and small, shall in the future be in a position to achieve their national development in freedom and security. It is clear, moreover, that no peace can be satisfactory to this country unless it promises to be durable, and an essential condition of such a peace is that it should give full scope to national aspirations as far as practicable. The principle of nationality should therefore be one of the governing factors in the consideration of territorial arrangements after the war.

For similar reasons we should avoid leaving any State subject to grievous economic disadvantage, as for instance by not providing it with the outlets necessary for its commercial development, since the absence of such facilities would necessarily affect the permanent character of any settlement.

In giving effect to the above principles, however, we are limited in the first place by the pledges already given to our Allies which may, as for instance in the case of Italy, be difficult to reconcile with the claims of nationalities. We must realise further that our Allies, apart from any promises which we may have made to them, may put forward claims conflicting with the principle of nationality. In such an event our attitude should be guided by circumstances generally and British interests in particular.

Lastly, we should not push the principle of nationality so far as unduly to strengthen any State which is likely to be a cause of danger to European peace in the future.

In dealing with Belgium, it declares emphatically in favour of her being largely indemnified by Germany for the losses she has suffered.

It will remain a vital British interest after the war, as it was before it, to prevent Germany from obtaining access to the Belgian coasts. Recent events have shown conclusively that that interest is not effectively safeguarded by treaties providing for Belgian neutrality under international guarantees; we submit that Belgian independence will be better secured by substituting a treaty of permanent alliance between Belgium, France, and ourselves in the place of the present safeguards. It is understood that Belgium herself would welcome such an alliance.

This proposal is open to the objection that it commits us to continental alliances and a probable increase of our military obligations. In our opinion, however, there is no alternative so long as it is a vital interest of this country to prevent the German invasion of Belgium, and so long as the latter is incapable of undertaking its own defence.

It declares in favour of the incorporation of Luxemburg into Belgium from which it was detached in 1839.

As to Alsace and Lorraine, it will be "mainly guided by French views." It would favour a further "rectification of frontier on strategic grounds, . . . provided the wishes of the population are consulted," but would "deprecate, as far as possible, any attempt on the part of France to incorporate any considerable extent of German territory on the plea of strategical exigencies."

As to the future of Heligoland and the Kiel Canal, it refrains from making any definite suggestions, leaving these questions to the Admiralty.

On Poland it mentions three alternative suggestions but declares finally in favour of the "creation of a Polish kingdom under a Russian Grand Duke."

This Kingdom would be merely connected with Russia by the personal link of its ruler, but would in every other respect enjoy complete independence. The grant of independence under such conditions would satisfy to the full the national aspirations of the Polish nation, and if it could be coupled with the acquisition of a commercial outlet for Poland in the Baltic, it would lead to the establishment of a State that, from the point of view of national feeling and economic interests, promises stability. Given the strong race antagonism of Poland to Prussia, which has secured during this war the open adhesion of the Russian Poles and the tacit support of what is best in Galicia and the Grand Duchy of Posen, there is every reason to expect that the future Polish State would become a buffer State between Russia and Germany in the best sense of the word, that is to say, it would secure for Russia a Poland that would be most unlikely to be found in league against Russia, as long as Russia remained faithful to the programme of the Allies, which is respect for the independence of small nations.

This new Polish State would be one of the most powerful units among the independent countries which are expected to come into existence upon the dissolution of Austria-Hungary. From the point of view of England and France this conglomeration of States would prove an efficient barrier against Russian preponderance in Europe and German extension towards the Near East, because these States would be happy and contented in the realisation of their national aspirations, and strong as regards their economic future, which would be secured by the possession of their natural commercial outlets to the sea. The Congress of Vienna attempted to secure a balance of power against France by the creation of kingdoms which were expected to prove a formidable barrier to any French aggression in the future. But these creations did not fulfil that expectation, because they were artificial and did not bring contentment and prosperity to the people who formed part of them. The solution we recommend has this in its favour, that it is based on more solid and lasting foundations than were obtained by the provisions of the Treaty of Vienna. We are quite alive to the opposition such a proposal may encounter at Petrograd; we also realise that it is not likely to be overcome unless the military situation should oblige Russia to require Anglo-French co-operation in order to secure the evacuation of her territory, which is now in the hands of the enemy. We do not presume for one moment, to offer suggestions as to how we can overcome any such opposition, but we should like to place it on record that the solution which we have submitted is the best in the interests of the Allies, as it will preserve for them the reputation of good faith, and constitute a great asset in their favour among the nationalities that are about to be created by their victory; it will seriously weaken Prussia by withdrawing from her a very capable and prosperous population, together with the loss of considerable coalfields in Silesia, and above all it will considerably add to the number of States in the future composition of Europe whose desires and interests will all tend in the direction of establishing the rule of right over the rule of might. In other words, we shall assist in creating nations that will be keen in their sympathy with our desire for a rule of peace, which shall materially decrease the burden of armaments that so heavily hampered the national and economic aspirations of the people of Europe.

We annex a map based on ethnological lines which, after enquiry regarding the distribution of the Poles, shows the frontiers a new Polish State might fairly claim. The figures of the population are taken from the German official census.

As to the Balkans, it is disposed to treat Bulgaria generously in spite of its defection and the trouble which that gave to the Allies.

Greece and Roumania, which at that time had refused to throw in their lot with the Allies, "deserve but little consideration at the hands of the Allies." But "as regards Roumania, the Allies are bound by the pledge given by Russia, under which Bukovina and the Roumanian portion of Transylvania were to be assigned to Roumania." Beyond that they are not prepared to go.

In dealing with the problems of Serbia, Montenegro and the Southern Slavs, it says:

The agreement concluded between Italy and her Allies on the 26th April, 1915, inasmuch as it concedes to the former the whole of Istria, a considerable strip of the Dalmatian coast with most of the islands, in which indisputably the population is predominantly Slav, unfortunately constitutes a very distinct violation of the principle of nationalities, and there is consequently no doubt that it involves the risk of producing the usual results, namely, irredentism, and lack of stability and peace. We understand, however, from competent and moderate judges of the situation, that there is every prospect of the parties reaching a satisfactory settlement by direct friendly negotiation.

This departure from one of our guiding principles need not, therefore, cause unnecessary alarm, and, in any case, we are precluded from suggesting any other solution in view of the binding nature of our engagements towards Italy.

It considers the question of the future of Montenegro:

Shall this country be revived as an independent State or be absorbed into Serbia?

Montenegrin policy, at no time of the most reliable, has since the commencement of the war surpassed itself in duplicity, and has proved distinctly unfriendly to the Allies. There is little doubt that King Nicolas and his Ministers were in direct communication with the Austrians, and that but for their treachery a far more successful resistance to the enemy's advance through the Sanjak of Novibazar and Montenegro might have been made. The King, therefore, deserves no consideration at the hands of the Allies, and in our judgment after such conduct his restoration or that of any of his family who were parties to his treachery is much to be deprecated, and, indeed, should be so far as possible opposed.

The resurrection of Montenegro as an independent State under another King must presumably depend on the wishes of the Montenegrins themselves, but it should be borne in mind that in any case such a State will serve no useful purpose; it will in the future as in the past not be self-supporting, and be dependent on the charity of the Powers. Its absorption by Serbia is therefore on the whole much to be desired.

As to the future of the Yugoslavs in Austria, it declares that:

The end which the Jugo-Slavs have in view is the liberation of all Serbs, Croats, and Slovenes from the domination of Austria-Hungary or any other Power and their union into one State. They desire, however, a free and voluntary union, not one imposed from without implying subjection of any one portion to the other. The Croats and Slovenes no doubt admire Serbia for her fighting qualities and look to her to assist their liberation, but on the other hand they consider themselves superior to Serbia in culture and education, and rely on this superiority to assume the leadership in the future confederation of Southern Slav States.

The statement made by Sir E. Grey to M. Supilo on the 1st September, 1915, that, provided Serbia agrees, Bosnia, Herzegovina, South Dalmatia, Slavonia, and Croatia shall be permitted to decide their own fate is therefore far more in accord with Jugo-Slav ideals than the assurance previously given, and should be the determining factor in guiding our policy on this question. We consider that Great Britain should in every way encourage and promote the union of Serbia, Montenegro, and the Southern Slavs into one strong federation of States with the view to its forming a barrier to any German advance towards the East.

. . . . .

The Jugo-Slavs desire that the boundaries of their prospective Confederation shall be determined on ethnological lines, and upon this basis they lay claim to extensive territories. These would include, in addition to Serbia, Montenegro, Croatia, Slavonia, Bosnia, Herzegovina, and Dalmatia, portions of Carinthia and Styria, the whole of Gorizia, Carniola, Istria, and the coast, together with islands down to the Albanian frontier. The northern frontier of their State would run approximately from Graz in a south-easterly direction along the Drave, then north of the provinces of Baranja, Backa, and the Banat, along the Moris River to Arad, thence south past Temesvar to the point where the Roumanian western frontier joins the Danube.

Although these claims may appear extravagant at first sight, the Jugo-Slavs maintain that in all these localities the population is predominantly Slav (*vide* Appendix III).

APPENDIX III

"The Jugo-Slavs claim that they form the compact population of the Kingdoms of Serbia and Montenegro (population, 5,000,000), of the Jugo-Slav provinces in Austria-Hungary (Jugo-Slav population, 8,000,000), and of the Italian district west of Gorizia (40,000 Jugo-Slavs), whereas 1,500,000 Jugo-Slavs live as emigrants in oversea countries.

"In Austria-Hungary the Jugo-Slavs are subordinated to two dominant State organisations, viz. the German and the Magyar. Their territory is broken up into ten provinces; they are politically oppressed, socially persecuted, and in every way hampered and menaced in their intellectual, economic, and national development.

"There are roughly 2,100,000 Jugo-Slavs under the German Administration in Vienna. Of these, 410,000 live in Southern Styria, 120,000 in Southern Carinthia, 490,000 in Carniola, 155,000 in Gorizia-Gradisca, 70,000 in Trieste, 225,000 in Istria, and 610,000 in Dalmatia.

"Under the Magyar domination there are 3,200,000 Jugo-Slavs, viz. 2,300,000 in Croatia-Slavonia and 900,000 in Southern and South-western Hungary (in the Medjumurje, along the Styrian frontier, in the Baranja, Backa, and Banat).

"A joint Austria-Hungarian Administration controls the 1,900,000 Jugo-Slavs living in Bosnia-Herzegovina.

"Finally, there are 400,000 Jugo-Slavs under Italian rule."

In so far as the Adriatic littoral is affected the Jugo-Slavs will have to conform to the requirements of the Italian Agreement, but outside of the regions referred to in this Agreement we see no reason why their claims should not be admitted to their full extent at the expense of Austria, though we suggest some reservations in respect of certain territories which they claim in Hungary. Our reasons for this recommendation appear below.

Then they come to deal with the future of Austro-Hungary and here they take a very bold line:

The future of Austria-Hungary will, of course, depend very largely on the military situation existing at the end of this war. If the situation should be one which enables the Allies to dispose of its future, there seems very little doubt that, in accordance with the principle of giving free play to nationalities, the Dual Monarchy, which in its present composition is a direct negation of that principle, should be broken up, as there is no doubt that all the non-German parts of Austria-Hungary will secede. The only objection that might occur to this radical solution would be the large accession of strength to the German Empire in population and in wealth by the inclusion of the Austrian provinces. We have, however, to remember that a solution favourable to the Allies will deprive Germany of a population considerably in excess of this Austrian increase. It will be deprived of Alsace-Lorraine, Schleswig, and the Grand Duchy of Posen. This will be a direct diminution of Prussian power. It will receive, it is true, the Austrian population, but this accession will add to the importance and influence of the non-Prussian States of the German Empire. Moreover, it will mean a considerable increase in the Catholic elements of Germany, and everything tending to decrease Prussian power will naturally tend in the direction of a more permanent settlement in Europe, as it will diminish the aggressive tendencies of the Central European Empires through the weakening of Prussia. We therefore

think that the drifting of the Austrian provinces to Germany need
not alarm the Allies, who are not out to crush Germany, but do intend
as far as they can to impair the hegemony of Prussia over other States.
The preparations for this war, the impulse to this war, the aggressive
designs connected with this war, are all traceable to Prussian enterprise, and it is not extravagant to hope that a defeated Prussia will
considerably lose its power for evil, and should it further be confronted
by a large, wealthy, and influential southern Federation within its
own borders, we shall not be far wrong in expecting to achieve the
diminution of its influence, which can only be brought about by the
play of political forces within the German Federation. Assuming the
Allies, for purely political reasons, contemplated the keeping alive of
an independent Dual Monarchy, they would have to consider very
seriously whether it would be possible to secure the real independence
of Vienna from Berlin. In the light of past events we do not hesitate
to come to the conclusion that whether the Central Powers are victorious or not, Austria-Hungary will remain, to all intents and purposes, subservient to its ally. A victorious Prussia would, as we have
already seen during the course of the war, still further absorb Austria-
Hungary within its political and economic orbit. A defeated Prussia
would equally be able to persuade Austria-Hungary that her only
future lies within a still closer amalgamation of the two countries.
There is no doubt that there has been in the past, and might be in
the future, a party both in Austria and in Hungary who are strongly
opposed to the German hegemony, but from all the information at our
disposal this party in both portions of the Dual Monarchy is a minority, and likely to remain one. An Austria-Hungary, therefore, at the
beck and call of Prussia is not a solution which the Allies should or
could contemplate; the survival of Austria-Hungary could not be
reconciled with the objects for which the Allies went to war, and even
if they decided to sacrifice these objects for political expediency, the
weapons they intended to forge, that is to say, a diminished but independent Austro-Hungary State, would fail to be effective for the purpose for which it would be intended. On the assumption, therefore,
that the solution which we recommend be adopted, we find no difficulty in disposing of those portions of the Dual Monarchy which
are likely to constitute the Slav State of the South.

As to Bohemia, they examined three different proposals: first,
the formation of an independent State; secondly, the linking of
Bohemia with a Southern-Slav State; thirdly, tacking it on to the
Kingdom of Poland. They are of opinion that the third solution
"is desired both by farseeing Czechs and Poles."

The latter realise fully that the addition of Bohemia to Poland would afford and promote very considerably the economic development of Poland. The Czechs, on the other hand, fully appreciate that they would benefit by the superior culture and civilisation of the Poles. At this stage we do not propose to go further than indicate what, in our opinion, would be the best solution for the Austro-Hungarian question.

Summing up their suggestions about the future of the Austrian Empire, they say:

Let the Slav provinces of Austria constitute themselves into a Southern Slav State; let the German provinces of Austria be incorporated in the German Empire; let Bohemia be linked up to Poland; and let Hungary be formed of the purely Magyar portions of the country into an independent State with the fully secured commercial outlets to the Adriatic at Fiume, and by means of the Danube to the Black Sea. This solution promises permanency, as it will be based on the national and economic elements of the countries affected by this settlement.

If Hungary is, however, to be an independent State with any chance of vitality it would be inexpedient to deprive it of territory beyond that which is necessary in order to conform to the principle of nationality. This boundary has the further recommendation of being in accordance with the Serbian strategical requirements for possession of the country on the north bank of the Danube opposite Belgrade, and of not conflicting with the Roumanian claims.

The above settlement may at first sight appear somewhat academic, being as it is mainly in accordance with national aspirations, but we quite appreciate that it may have to be modified in deference to the views of Russia, geographical configuration, military considerations, &c., our main object at present was to devise a scheme that promised permanency from the national point of view.

They have then a very searching study of the question of armaments.

In putting forward the above considerations we have endeavoured to approach the settlement, after the war, mainly from a political point of view. We have attempted to draw up a scheme which is not confined to the promotion alone of British interests as regards either territorial acquisitions or the establishment of British spheres of influence. We have tried to work out a scheme that promises permanency; we have aimed at a reconstruction of the map of Europe intended

to secure a lasting peace. We have been guided by the consideration
that peace remains the greatest British interest. The most direct way
to this end is, of course, to arrest the race in armaments, which has
gone on increasing for the last forty years. This object can be best
achieved by means of general arbitration treaties and the consequent
reduction of standing armies and navies. This ideal is doubtless common ground amongst all the Allies, but Great Britain would probably
be prepared to face greater sacrifices than other countries in order to
achieve that end. Public opinion in this country would be willing, we
think, to go very far indeed in this direction, but the danger we have
to guard against is that if we succeeded in persuading the enemy to
come to any kind of arrangement of the sort we must see to it that he
is both able and willing to abide by his pledges. In view of the attitude
which Germany has adopted in the past on this question we entertain
but little hope that the Germans will be willing to approach the subject in any sincere and serious spirit unless they have no option. If
we contemplate a condition of things which would force the Allies to
discuss terms of peace with the enemy on more or less equal terms,
we have no hesitation in saying that we should either be met by a
direct negative on the part of the German Government even to consider the subject, or we should be invited to submit proposals which
the German Government would either prove to be unworkable or
which they might accept with a mental reservation that they would
do their best to evade them. We have to consider that in the case of
a draw, the German Government would be able to persuade their
public that they had been successful in saving their country from invasion; we must remember that the leading people in Germany who
are mainly responsible for this war never allowed their countrymen
to suspect that their designs were aggressive; the German Government
have always officially dissociated themselves from pan-German propaganda. On occasions they have distinctly and publicly repudiated
pan-German aims. But in practice their policy, which remained carefully concealed from their countrymen, was dominated by ideas of
aggression in order to secure expansion of territory and spheres of influence. Territory was to be secured by the acquisition of additional
colonies in the possession of other Powers, and spheres of influence
were to be obtained by the policy of commercial penetration, which
has been so steadily pursued both in the Near and the Far East. The
same people will, in the case of a draw, be able to convince their country that it was due to their invincible army and navy that the integrity
of their country was saved, and they will have little difficulty in persuading them that for the future they must rely upon the same
weapons. This frame of mind would not readily respond to any invi-

tation on our part seriously to take in hand a reduction of armaments all round. On the contrary, it would be misrepresented as an insidious proposal to weaken the defensive forces of Germany for the purpose of taking it at a disadvantage, and thereby achieving the object which the Allies had in view when they went to war in the summer of 1914. The other alternative which promises more hope for the eventual reduction of armaments presents itself if the Allies are in a position to impose their terms. Even then, the matter will have to be very delicately handled so as to avoid all appearance of interference in what the Germans consider an essentially internal question which every independent State has a right to decide for itself. It is possible, however, that a substantial defeat of Germany may so shake the confidence of the German people in their rulers that they may be induced to listen to the voice of reason, and ask themselves whether it is an axiom that the safety of a State is exclusively secure in proportion to the extent of its armaments. It may be possible in those conditions to convince the German people that we do not confuse the military defences of a country with militarism. A German writer has defined militarism as a teaching of the dogma that might alone counts, and that right, which does not depend on might, is not worth consideration. If the Allies can succeed in substituting for this doctrine the principle that brute force is not entitled to override everything, that a country possessing the physical means to impose its will, irrespective of right or wrong, is not entitled to do so, but can promote in its stead the doctrine that no community can exist which is based on physical force alone, one of the main objects for which they went to war will have been achieved. In other words, one of the essential elements towards securing a reduction of armaments will be the conversion of the German people to these views. Another element, of course, but a less effective one, will be the creation of a League of Nations, that will be prepared to use force against any nation that breaks away from the observance of international law. We are under no illusion, however, that such an instrument will become really effective until nations have learnt to subordinate their personal and individual ambitions and dreams for the benefit of the community of nations. We have witnessed such a process in individual States with the development of what we call a civilised condition of things, but this process has been of slow growth, and we shall have to exercise considerable patience in watching and promoting a similar development among the nations of the world. This consideration brings up the question of whether it will be possible to secure the adhesion of the United States of America, a repetition of Canning's attempt to bring in the New World in order to redress the balance of the Old. There are signs in America that the more thinking people there are awakening to the fact that in the modern condition of things America can no longer cling to her position of splendid isolation. If America could be persuaded to associate itself to such a League of Nations, a weight and influence might be secured for its decisions that would materially promote the object for which it had been created.

We propose to confine ourselves to these general considerations, because we hesitate to discuss the question of reduction of armaments in a more detailed or technical fashion. We lack the knowledge, military, naval, and economical, which would enable us to submit recommendations of any value; such a task would be more properly and usefully entrusted to a committee representing the various national interests, acting on the advice of the most competent experts. In touching upon this question, however, we have been mainly guided by the consideration that no complete scheme for the settlement of Europe after the war is acceptable which does not seriously concern itself with this question and does not endeavour to formulate proposals that would secure the main object for which this country, almost subconsciously, went to war—for which it is prepared to pay heavily, and for which it is also prepared to carry on the war to the ultimate end in order to secure the triumph of the principle that right is superior to might.

They then proceed to discuss what would happen in the event of a stalemate and an inconclusive peace. It is rumoured that in that event Germany would have to be bought out of Belgium by concessions elsewhere. Most of these concessions would be at the expense of Great Britain.

To sum up, a peace the result of a draw such as we have endeavoured to sketch out in this report would imply that Germany will not have obtained all she wanted when she began the war, but will have obtained such an instalment of her ambitions as will enable her Government to justify themselves to their people for having gone to war in defence of their territory in 1914; in fact, they will have every reason to claim victory and to represent the Allies as having suffered defeat.

We have said enough to indicate that whatever concessions will be necessary in the event of a draw will have to be made by this country. Such concessions can only be made by the sacrifice of our colonial possessions. But this would have to form the subject of enquiry and report by a committee on which the Colonial Office would

be represented, so as to enable His Majesty's Government to decide
what price they could afford to pay for such a peace.

This remarkable document was prepared and signed by two
prominent officials of the Foreign Office. It was circulated to the
Cabinet without any covering recommendation or comment from
Sir Edward Grey. It was not considered by the Cabinet or by any
Cabinet Committee until after the War Cabinet and the Imperial
Cabinet were set up in 1917.

When I undertook the formation of a Government early in
December, 1916, the War had been raging for nearly two and a
half years: each year more destructive, more costly in life and
treasure than the last. We were now in the third year and the
end was not in sight. The contending nations were bleeding from
every artery. It was the blind and insensate fury of a struggle to
the death. Germany had thrown out certain signals in 1916 that
her rulers were willing to confer with their adversaries, but the
tone and substance of their proffers constituted no basis of hope
for a successful conference. It was merely a manœuvre designed
to propitiate the Pope and other powerful neutrals, including
America. The Asquith Cabinet had therefore decided with complete unanimity that the time had not arrived for discussing
peace with the enemy. They left it at that. They made no effort
to clarify their own ideas or to enlighten the public as to the aims
for the achievement of which this carnage was to continue.

When I became Prime Minister I was strongly of opinion that,
whilst not neglecting any legitimate means for prosecuting the
War efficiently (and thus calling upon the nation to make greater
sacrifices than ever), we should simultaneously devote some time
to working out, not in phrases but in concrete terms, the kind of
peace for which these sacrifices were to be made. Terrible losses
without appreciable results had spread a general sense of dis-
illusionment and war weariness throughout the nation. There
was a growing demand that the Allied peoples as well as those
dwelling in enemy lands should be told definitely and distinctly
what we were fighting for and the terms upon which we were prepared to settle. But no such conditions could be defined and

determined without calling into consultation the Dominions and India, who had been such loyal and valuable partners throughout the conflict. I therefore thought it was essential that an Imperial Cabinet should immediately be constituted and convened to exercise control and supervision over the direction of the War and to formulate the terms of peace which the Empire as a whole would regard as a reasonable and equitable settlement to be aimed at. This was the first Imperial Cabinet ever held in the British Empire.

Before the Dominion Premiers and the representatives of India could reach England there were two communications on the subject of peace which had to be dealt with immediately. One was a German Peace Note which showed that the German Government also realised the importance of convincing their own people at home, as well as neutral nations, that if this horrible and destructive war was being prolonged the responsibility for its continuance lay with their adversaries. The other communication was President Wilson's peace query addressed to all the belligerents, enquiring the terms upon which the rival confederations were prepared to terminate the struggle. The Allies thought it imperative to accord an immediate reply to these two important documents. Neutral opinion had been poisoned to an appreciable extent by enemy propaganda which represented our aims as selfish and imperialistic. We could not therefore afford to wait until the arrival of the Empire delegations before formulating and publishing some reply which would at least in outline indicate our policy. The Allied Governments met in London to consider the answer which should be made to the German Note and to President Wilson's interrogation. The Allied Conference first dealt with the German Note in brief terms. It reserved an elaboration of our conditions for the answer to President Wilson. In the reply to the German Note the Allies confined themselves to the assertion that "no peace is possible until assurances are given that reparation will be made for the rights and liberties that have been violated; that the principle of nationality and freedom of small States will be recognised: and that some settlement definitely eliminating the causes that have so long menaced the nations, establishes the only effective guarantee for the world safety."

In substance, that meant restoration, reparation, self-determination, disarmament and some means, other than war, of establishing and enforcing justice amongst the nations in their dealings with each other.

In examining the terms set forth in our reply to President Wilson, it is essential to bear in mind that the Allies were impressed with the supreme importance at this stage of reassuring President Wilson that we stood by the high purpose with which we had entered into the War, and that we had no intention of departing from the unselfish and elevated principles we then laid down as the foundation and incentive of our common endeavour. We knew that the attitude of America towards the belligerents might depend on the replies given by the Allied and Central Governments respectively to his interrogatory. It is equally important to recall the fact that President Wilson was satisfied with the character of our reply and that soon afterwards he brought America into the War on the Allied side without protest or expression of disappointment with any of the terms of peace we laid down in our considered answer to his enquiry. It will be found on examination and comparison that our reply to Wilson and the terms subsequently embodied in the Treaties were substantially the same.

For the benefit of those who believe that the Versailles conditions were dictated in the arrogant spirit engendered by a great victory, it will be helpful to give a hasty survey of the military position in the winter of 1916–17, when the peace aims of the Allies were considered in detail. So far from framing these terms in the unbridled insolence of a complete triumph, it is essential to recall the fact that when the Allied Governments considered this declaration of war aims, the War was going badly for the Allied cause. A powerful Government had fallen in Britain because of the almost universal feeling amongst the public that, so far from victory becoming nearer, the prospect of a triumphant termination for the War appeared to be receding. Belgium and Serbia were almost entirely in the hands of the Central Powers.

Roumania had been overrun by their armies and its great resources of oil and grain were in their possession. Turkey was not merely holding its own against all our concerted efforts, but had beaten off our attack on the Dardanelles and driven away helter-skelter a powerful army which had for months been seeking to force an entrance to the Marmora. We had been beaten in Mesopotamia, where a British army had surrendered to the Turks, and we were held on the Suez Canal by a Turkish force. All the immense armies of Russia had been beaten in the field and their brave spirit shattered. Vast tracts of Russia were occupied by the Germans and the Austrians. The Russian soldiers were seething with discontent. The supplies of food for the cities and towns of Russia had completely broken down and the country itself was on the brink of revolution. The repeated attempts made to release the German hold on French territory had all been driven back with a slaughter unequalled in the whole history of battles. The battle of the Somme, which failed utterly in its purpose, had cost the Allies upwards of 600,000 casualties. At sea, the one great naval battle of the War had just been fought off Jutland between the British and German high fleets. It was a muddled and drawn Trafalgar, where both fleets sailed at full speed from each other's range and each claimed victory as soon as they reached the port of safety. The actual losses in men and ships on our side were heavier than those sustained by the Germans, and all those who read the official reports of this battle issued by our own Admiralty were filled with dismay both here and in America. The revival of the submarine attack on our shipping was increasing the sinkings of our mercantile marine at an alarming rate, and threatening our island with a serious food shortage. Important Ministers who held key positions in the British Cabinet which resigned in December, 1916, were advising their colleagues that we could not carry on the War for many more months. Our principal naval adviser could see no remedy for the submarine attack. Discontent was spreading rapidly in our workshops. The pacifist movement was growing in the country. Crowded meetings were held in the towns and industrial centres demanding that the War should be brought to an end. At the

risk of some repetition it is worth recalling once more the noteworthy fact that at this juncture even distinguished statesmen
like Lord Lansdowne, the author of the Entente with France,
had come to the conclusion that we could hope for nothing better
than a stalemate, and were advising negotiations for an early
settlement. Men of high standing and of unchallengeable patriotism were privately urging the Lansdowne appeal upon the Government. Those who turned towards America with some glimmer
of hope that aid might come from that quarter were more than
ever discouraged by the fact that the Presidential election,
which had just taken place, had ended in a victory for President
Wilson who had fought on one issue—that he had kept America
out of the War. His rival in the Presidential contest was angling
for the German vote, and before and during his campaign
President Wilson had carefully refrained from uttering one word
of sympathy with our sacrifices, our cause or our aims. Not even
on the invasion of Belgium had he penned one word of censure
or protest.

These were not conditions where Allied statesmen could feel
that they were in a position to dictate ruthless terms to their
country's foes. Far from being depressed by any sense of discouragement and discomfiture, the German leaders were recounting
with jubilance and with justification the dazzling array of victories won on every front—land, sea and air. They were already
provisionally carving out of Russia an extension of the German
Empire on the Baltic and in Poland: in the West they were satisfied with the annexation of the Briey iron mines and a virtual
control over Belgium. Overseas, Britain and France were to be
let off with the surrender of a colony or two. That was the atmosphere and those the circumstances in which the chief Ministers of
Britain, France and Italy met in London on Christmas Day,
1916, to consider the conditions on which they were prepared to
advise the nations they represented to bring this devastating
conflict to an end. Bearing this in mind, let us now summarise
the conclusions come to at this eventful conference, and incorporated in the reply sent by the Allied Powers to President Wilson.

The joint reply of the Allies, which was dated the 10th January, enumerated the following demands as essential conditions of any peace settlement to which they could assent:

The restoration of Belgium, of Serbia, and of Montenegro, with the compensation due to them for damage done by the invaders.

The evacuation of the invaded territories of France, Russia and Roumania, with fitting reparation.

The reorganisation of Europe, guaranteed by a stable settlement, based alike upon the principle of nationalities, on the right which all people, whether small or great, have to the enjoyment of full security and free economic development, and also upon territorial and international agreements so framed as to guarantee land and sea frontiers against unjust attacks.

The restitution of provinces or territories formerly torn from the Allies by force or contrary to the wishes of their inhabitants.

The liberation of Italians, Slavs, Roumanians, Czechs, and Slovaks from foreign domination.

The liberation of the non-Turkish peoples who then lay beneath the murderous tyranny of the Ottoman Empire, and the expulsion from Europe of that Empire, which had proved itself so radically alien to Western civilisation.

The implementing of the Czar's proclamation as to the emancipation of Poland.

The rescue of Europe from the brutal encroachments of Prussian militarism.

With this message was sent a covering note which expanded the final point of the peace conditions. It emphasised the fact that a peace which left German military power still dominant in Europe would be no lasting settlement, and that treaties, however precisely drawn, could not maintain peace unless backed by a better order. The peace sought must therefore be based, first, on a clearing away of the international grievances which might lead to war, and secondly on a breaking and discrediting of the military imperialism of the Central Powers. Thirdly, it was necessary "that behind international law and behind all the treaty arrangements for preventing or limiting hostilities some form of international sanction should be devised which would give pause to the hardiest aggressor." By this was meant, of course, the establishment of a League of Nations to guarantee world peace by collective action against the threat of disturbance by any aggressor.

This Allied statement, sent to President Wilson on January 10th, 1917, clearly went much farther and in much more detail into the peace aims of the Entente than had any previous pronouncement; but in main outline it showed the same features as the original Allied demands: liberation and restoration of Belgium and Serbia; return of Alsace-Lorraine to France; reparation for damage done; settlement of territories and sovereignties generally on the basis, not of conquest and the might of the strong hand, but of the self-determination of their population; the overthrow of great military powers and the substitution of a concert of the nations obeying and enforcing international law and justice.

Within four months America had entered the War against the Central Powers without any qualifying declaration which would manifest any difference of opinion as to war aims. If President Wilson regarded some or any of the aims disclosed to him by the Allied Note as being contrary to right or justice, or as creating any misgivings in his mind on these principles, it is incredible that he should not have indicated dissent or doubt before he threw in his lot with the Allies. Not even in a confidential communication did he suggest disapproval or hesitancy. Thereafter President Wilson's utterances ran parallel with those of the Entente Powers as definitions of the objectives of the ultimate victors. This significant fact I shall confirm by reference to the President's subsequent declarations on questions of policy.

It will be observed that the conditions of peace laid down in this momentous document cover all the terms imposed upon Germany, Austria and Turkey by the Peace Treaties except the surrender of the German Colonies, the annexation of non-Italian territory in Austria, the arrangements for control of international rivers and the establishment of the International Labour Office. Nothing at this stage was said of colonies. No country was prepared to perpetuate the horrors of such a war merely for the sake of wresting the German Colonies from German control. Had Germany and her allies accepted in substance our terms, peace could have been established in the month of January, 1917, instead of November, 1918, without the surrender by Germany of one of her oversea possessions.

When the Dominion Premiers arrived in the early spring an Imperial Cabinet assembled for the first time in the history of the Empire. One of its first tasks was to institute a prolonged examination of the whole peace problem by general discussion of principles, reference of details to committees representing the whole Empire, and further deliberations by the Imperial Cabinet on the basis of the reports submitted by these committees. By way of showing the position taken up by the Imperial War Cabinet at this date on the problems of an equitable peace, I will quote one or two paragraphs from the statement I made at the first meeting in March, 1917:

Let us then consider the things which surely must be essential to any rational, acceptable peace. In the first place the Germans must be driven out of the territories which they have invaded. They must abandon the lands which they have overrun—in France, Belgium, Russia, Serbia, Roumania, Montenegro. The freedom and independence of those countries must be restored, and Poland must not be merely restored, but restored under conditions which will give freedom to its oppressed population, and the events of the last few days in Russia have brought that possibility nearer to realisation than it ever was before.* Compensation must be demanded for the damage done to these ravaged countries. It is undoubtedly desirable that there should also be such a geographical adjustment of the map of Europe, on the basis of recognising national rights, as will prevent trouble in future, secure a more permanent peace, and also make firmer and more solid the foundations of democratic freedom in Europe.

That surely is the very least which we ought to achieve in a peace. But if we only accomplished so much, we should have failed in some of the main purposes to which we have set ourselves in this terrible struggle. There are at least four or five other essential aims to be striven for, and the first is this: the conviction must be planted in the minds of the civilised world—a conviction that will ripen into an instinct— that all wars of aggression are impossible enterprises; that they accomplish nothing but the destruction of the aggressor. Men must in future be taught to shun war as every civilised being shuns a murder; not merely because it is wrong in itself, but because it leads to in-

* I was alluding to the Russian Revolution which had just occurred.

evitable punishment. That is the only sure foundation for any league of peace. Unless you drive that conviction into the human mind in every land, the league of peace will be built on a foundation of sand; and therefore the first thing to accomplish in this War is to make every country feel that in future, if it attempts to repeat the outrage perpetrated by Germany upon civilisation, it will inevitably encounter dire and destructive punishment. That, I think, is essential to the peace of the world.

The second aim that I hoped would be attained by this war was "the democratisation of Europe." I urged that "Liberty is the only sure guarantee of peace and goodwill amongst the peoples of the world. Free nations are not eager to make war."

Here, as in many other respects, the turn of events has clouded bright hopes. But temporary failure to attain ideals does not detract from their soundness as well as their nobility, or from the hope and certainty of their ultimate realisation. It only reflects on the defects of the human instruments which are responsible for disappointments in execution. When I come to deal with the Treaty of Versailles it will be my duty and pride to point to the clauses that embodied the lofty aspirations which sustained the spirit of great nations through years of anguish and discouragement. If they have not been attained it is not the fault of the Treaty but of the statesmanship that possessed neither the faith nor the courage to stand by all that was highest and best in its provisions.

When, in my statement to the Imperial Cabinet, I subsequently came to deal with the case of the Turk, I claimed that our aim ought to be the disruption of the Turkish Empire:

The Turks have been ruling, or rather misruling, the most fertile and the most favoured lands in the world. They have not ruled successfully any of the territories they have conquered, and I am not sure that they are not the only race in the world of whom that can be said unreservedly. They are ruling lands which were the cradle of civilisation, the seminary of civilisation, the temple of civilisation, and, from the material point of view, lands which at one time were the granary of civilisation; and now those fair lands are a blighted desert. . . . It will be a great achievement to restore these famous territories to the splendour they enjoyed in the past, and to enable them once more to make their contribution to the happiness and prosperity of the world.

I made no allusion to the settlement of the vexed question of the German Colonies. Personally I was not anxious to add any more millions to the number of square miles we already found much difficulty in garrisoning and a still greater difficulty in developing. But I knew the Dominions had with their own forces conquered territories adjacent to their own, and that they were not enamoured of the idea of retaining the Germans as their next-door neighbours in these domains. I therefore left the question of the destination of the German Colonies to the committees to be set up for a detailed examination of peace terms, and which were purposely unfettered by any instruction or suggestion from the British War Cabinet. The conclusion they came to on this subject was quite unanimous. The South African Republic was utterly opposed to the idea of continuing German proximity and intrigue in South-West Africa. The encouragement given by the Germans in that colony to Beyers and his fellow rebels against the authority of an Afrikander Government determined the attitude of Botha and Smuts. As to East Africa, the South African Union considered the presence of a vast territory in East Africa under German control to be a constant menace to Rhodesia and the Dominion and a block to the materialisation of the great Rhodes dream of a Cape to Cairo route. Australia disliked the prospect of Germany with a jumping-off ground so near to the Australian shores in New Guinea and the Solomon Islands. New Zealand took the same view about Samoa. I was always doubtful about the wisdom of stripping Germany of all the backward territories she had done much to open out and to equip. I was convinced that if Germany were prepared to come to reasonable terms at that stage of the War on the major issues on which the War was being fought, neither Britain nor the Dominions would have insisted on continuing the struggle merely in order to annex colonies they had conquered. We were naturally convinced that as between British and German rule the natives would have preferred the former with its less rigid and more indulgent traditions.

The natives were entitled to the foremost consideration in the determination of this issue. Their rights were considered when the Peace Treaty was framed by vesting the legal title to these German possessions in the League of Nations with such safeguards for native rights as were guaranteed by its supreme authority.

The committee set up to consider the question of a League of Nations accepted the principle not only without demur but with sincerity. Most members of the committee embraced the project with a genuine enthusiasm. Some of them were, however, very doubtful of the wisdom at this stage of establishing a supreme International Assembly with a rigid constitution claiming authority for its decisions over the independent nations of the world. The recommendation arrived at on this point I have already given in my "War Memoirs," but in view of its bearing on the actual terms of the Covenant and of the difficulties which have arisen and which partly account for the failure of the League to solve its most troublesome problems, it is worth quoting it textually in this narrative:

The Committee were deeply impressed with the danger of the complete destruction of civilised society which threatens the world if the recurrence of a war like the present cannot be prevented, and with the necessity of devising means which would tend, at any rate, to diminish the risk of such a calamity. They felt, however, that any too comprehensive or ambitious project to ensure world peace might prove not only impracticable, but harmful. The proposal which seems to promise the best results proceeds along the path of consultation and conference for composing differences which cannot otherwise be adjusted. The Treaty of Peace should provide that none of the parties who are signatories to that Treaty should resort to arms against one another without previous submission of their dispute to a Conference of the Powers. The Committee think that the details of such a scheme should be discussed with our Allies and especially with the United States of America, before the conclusion of the War.

The conclusions reached by the Imperial Cabinet in 1917 substantially represent the position taken in 1919 by the Empire as a whole on the question of the aims and objectives of a just peace settlement. And it is important to recall once more the fact that the decisions were arrived at when the military prospect was doubtful and even dark. When the Imperial Cabinet was in session over peace terms the submarine losses were at their peak, the Allied strength in Eastern Europe was crumbling under the disintegrating operation of revolutionary dissolvents and the Nivelles offensive in France ended in a sanguinary failure which drove the French troops into a serious mutiny. There was nothing to excite the arrogance of triumph in these depressing events.

During the winter of 1917 the War Cabinet deemed it desirable to restate Allied war aims in order to satisfy public opinion in the country and to refute statements which were being circulated not only by extreme pacifists, but by factionists who for one reason or another had a quarrel with the Government, that Germany was prepared to make peace on reasonable terms while bloodthirsty and ambitious Governments in Britain and France stood in the way of a termination of this horrible struggle. The constant and insidious circulation of these statements in the workshops was affecting the minds of the industrial population and interfering seriously with the output of essential war material and equipment. It was also clogging the machinery of recruitment for the forces in the field. The determination of the Russian workers and peasants to make peace on the basis of "no annexation and no indemnities" was also having its effect on public opinion amongst a considerable section of the industrial population in Britain and France. The Russian leaders were not concerned with redeeming subject races beyond their own frontiers. They were so absorbed in the urgent necessity for establishing peace with Germany and Austria in order to inaugurate in Russia the social experiments to which they had devoted their lives, that they were prepared to pay any price for its attainment. The attitude of the Workers' Government in Russia was having a very disturbing effect on the artisans in our workshops.

It was therefore deemed desirable to make a full, carefully prepared and authentic statement of Allied war aims so as to reassure the public, and at the same time to enable the Government to ascertain definitely whether the nation was behind them in the prosecution of the War until those aims were achieved. We were fully conscious of the fact that the impending campaign would be the costliest and the most risky upon which the Allies had yet entered. American preparations for taking an active part in the struggle were lumbering slowly and rather clumsily along. America had not yet put more than a single division into the battle line. There seemed no prospect that she could send many trained divisions to our aid when the impending German attack fell on the Allies in the spring. Our reserves of man power in Britain and France were approaching exhaustion. Unless the nation was united in purpose and spirit, the Government would not be justified in prolonging the conflict. With a timid and hesitant people failure was inevitable. Russia, with her immense army of brave men, was so completely out of the War as an effective combatant that Germany was able to withdraw all her best troops from that battle-front and for the first time since 1914 to establish an equality in numbers in the western theatre. The principal Allied army—the French—was only slowly and dubiously recovering from a serious mutiny in its ranks which had shaken its fine morale through and through. In the opinion of General Haig, expressed to the Cabinet only a few weeks before our January declaration of peace terms, the grand army of France—the heroes of a hundred desperate battles—could not be depended upon any longer for any sustained or major operation. I am not expressing any view as to the soundness of General Haig's estimate of the fighting value of the French troops at that crucial moment. I am only recording the fact that it had just been given to the Cabinet in writing before we sat down to frame our peace terms.

The British Army was sore, disillusioned, if not disheartened after the failure of the Flanders folly in which it never believed. It had lost hundreds of thousands of its picked officers and men in that enterprise. Italy had by no means recovered from the shattering disaster of Caporetto. Its army was in course of being re-formed, reconstituted and re-equipped. In the sequel of events it took no further effective part in the desperate decisive fighting

of 1918 until the very end, when the Austrian Army was disintegrating.

In these discouraging conditions a decisive battle was impending between a united army invigorated by victory on all land
fronts—the Russian, Italian, and French fronts—and a divided
army, depressed by a long series of futile operations ending in
colossal losses. The Allied leaders who were in control of the war
direction were convinced that the Central Powers, in spite of all
these advantages, would be beaten in the end, provided the
Allied nations remained united and resolute, and provided also
that Allied resources were wisely and effectively handled—a
proviso which contained many elements of doubt. But when they
indited the only terms of peace which they were prepared to
accept, they could not do so with the confidence of men who had
the enemy in the hollow of their hands, and who were only waiting for the crushing victory which was to place them in a position
to dictate terms to a vanquished and helpless adversary.

To test the feeling of the nation, I decided that it was essential
to publish a considered and challenging pronouncement of our
war aims. I took unusual measures to ensure that the pronouncement should have a national character and that it should represent every section of opinion. I gave it out in the form of an
address to a meeting of the Trade Union delegates on January 5th,
1918. The full text is given in Volume V of my "War Memoirs."
Every word of the declaration had been considered beforehand
by the Cabinet. It received the previous assent of the Liberal
leaders to whom also I had submitted it. No Trade Union or
Labour leader or delegate questioned the equity or wisdom of
any of the demands put forward by me on behalf of the Government. President Wilson and the French Foreign Secretary subsequently notified their approval. I shall not repeat here the category of the claims which the British Government then regarded
as essential to a just peace. Although this pronouncement was
the most comprehensive and detailed statement made up to that
date by any Government, it was simply an elucidation of aims
already put forward in previous declarations by Allied statesmen.
All these war aims were incorporated in the Peace Treaties signed

in 1919. What is more to the point is the unchallengeable fact that these Treaties did not go beyond the stipulations laid down in the January declaration.

Two days after my address to the Trade Unions, President Wilson gave utterance to his famous Fourteen Points. Although they are well known, the narrative of the developments that led to Versailles will not be complete without setting them forth categorically:

I. Open covenants of peace, openly arrived at, after which there shall be no private international understandings of any kind but diplomacy shall proceed always frankly and in the public view.

II. Absolute freedom of navigation upon the seas, outside territorial waters, alike in peace and in war, except as the seas may be closed in whole or in part by international action for the enforcement of international covenants.

III. The removal, so far as possible, of all economic barriers and the establishment of an equality of trade conditions among all the nations consenting to the peace and associating themselves for its maintenance.

IV. Adequate guarantees given and taken that national armaments will be reduced to the lowest point consistent with domestic safety.

V. A free, open-minded, and absolutely impartial adjustment of all colonial claims, based upon a strict observance of the principle that in determining all such questions of sovereignty the interests of the populations concerned must have equal weight with the equitable claims of the government whose title is to be determined.

VI. The evacuation of all Russian territory and such a settlement of all questions affecting Russia as will secure the best and freest co-operation of the other nations of the world in obtaining for her an unhampered and unembarrassed opportunity for the independent determination of her own political development and national policy and assure her of a sincere welcome into the society of free nations under institutions of her own choosing; and, more than a welcome, assistance also of every kind that she may need and may herself desire. The treatment accorded Russia by her sister nations in the months to come will be the acid test of their good will, of their comprehension of her needs as distinguished from their own interests, and of their intelligent and unselfish sympathy.

VII. Belgium, the whole world will agree, must be evacuated and restored, without any attempt to limit the sovereignty which she enjoys in common with all other free nations. No other single act will serve as this will serve to restore confidence among the nations in the laws which they have themselves set and determined for the government of their relations with one another. Without this healing act the whole structure and validity of international law is forever impaired.

VIII. All French territory should be freed and the invaded portions restored, and the wrong done to France by Prussia in 1871 in the matter of Alsace-Lorraine, which has unsettled the peace of the world for nearly fifty years, should be righted, in order that peace may once more be made secure in the interest of all.

IX. A readjustment of the frontiers of Italy should be effected along clearly recognisable lines of nationality.

X. The peoples of Austria-Hungary, whose place among the nations we wish to see safeguarded and assured, should be accorded the freest opportunity of autonomous development.

XI. Roumania, Serbia, and Montenegro should be evacuated; occupied territories restored; Serbia accorded free and secure access to the sea; and the relations of the several Balkan states to one another determined by friendly counsel along historically established lines of allegiance and nationality; and international guarantees of the political and economic independence and territorial integrity of the several Balkan states should be entered into.

XII. The Turkish portions of the present Ottoman Empire should be assured a secure sovereignty, but the other nationalities which are now under Turkish rule should be assured an undoubted security of life and an absolutely unmolested opportunity of autonomous development, and the Dardanelles should be permanently opened as a free passage to the ships and commerce of all nations under international guarantees.

XIII. An independent Polish state should be erected which should include the territories inhabited by indisputably Polish populations, which should be assured a free and secure access to the sea, and whose political and economic independence and territorial integrity should be guaranteed by international covenant.

XIV. A general association of nations must be formed under specific covenants for the purpose of affording mutual guarantees of political independence and territorial integrity to great and small states alike.

With the exception of the Freedom of the Seas, there is nothing in these points which is incompatible with the war aims already proclaimed by British and French Governments: the evacuation of all territories invaded and occupied by the Germans and the

return of Alsace-Lorraine to France, the liberation of all nationalities in the German, Austrian and Turkish Empires kept in subjection by force, the establishment of a League of Nations, the
reduction of armaments, reparations for damage done. The words
"restoration of the invaded regions" were somewhat ambiguous.
But they were understood to refer not only to the cost of restoring the invaded territories to the condition in which the Germans
found them at the date of the invasion, but to compensation for
damage inflicted on the civilian population. So that there should
be no doubt left on this point before the Armistice, President
Wilson was pressed by Britain, France and Italy for an explanation of this particular phrase. He instructed his Secretary of
State, Mr. Lansing, to reply on November 5th, 1918:

When the President formulated his peace conditions in his address
to Congress on January 8, last, he declared that the invaded territories
must be not only evacuated and liberated, but restored. The Allies
think that no doubt should be left as to what this stipulation means.
They understand by it that compensation will be made by Germany
for all damage done to the civilian population of the Allies and their
property by the aggression of Germany by land, by sea and from the
air. The President is in agreement with this interpretation.

This note, which was known as the "Lansing Note," was communicated to the Germans before they signed the Armistice.

Point V, which stipulates for the "impartial adjustment of all
colonial claims," is vague and capable of a variety of interpretations. But it must be recollected that I had already stated fully
the British view on this subject three days before the President
delivered his historic speech and that, so far from entering any
protest or reservation, he had prefaced his own statement of
aims by expressing approval of the moderation of my declaration.
It will be found, when we come to the actual disposition of the
German Colonies by the Treaty, that there was no difference of
opinion between him and his British and French colleagues at the
Conference as to the restoration of these colonies to their German owners and no irreconcilable difference as to their disposal.

The phrase about Freedom of the Seas led to some misunderstanding and a threatened rupture between the United States

and the Allies when negotiations for an armistice were opened up by the German Government with President Wilson. The Germans were prepared to make peace on the basis of the Fourteen Points.

The Allied Governments were firmly of opinion that the terms of the Armistice should be settled at a conference representative of all the Allied and Associated Powers. Such a conference was held at the Quai d'Orsay in Paris on the 29th of October, 1918. The discussion is very illuminating for the light it casts on the controversies which have surrounded the Paris Peace Conference. It shows that the Allies had no intention in the hour of complete triumph to exact any fresh and harsher conditions from the vanquished because of the completeness of their victory, but that they were determined to stand by the terms which they had settled and published when the balances of fate had given no clear indication of the side on which they would finally settle down. Here is an extract from a record taken at the time of the course of the discussion as to the terms upon which an armistice could be granted to the Germans:

MR. LLOYD GEORGE said that there were two closely connected questions which had to be considered. First, there were the actual terms of an armistice. With this, however, was closely related the question of terms of peace. If the Notes which had passed between President Wilson and Germany were closely studied, it would be found that an armistice was proposed on the assumption that the peace would be based on the terms set forth in President Wilson's speeches. The Germans had actually demanded an armistice on this assumption. Consequently, if the Allies agreed to an armistice, unless something definite was said to the contrary, they would be committed to President Wilson's peace terms. Hence, the first thing to consider appeared to be whether these terms were acceptable.

M. PICHON [the French Foreign Minister] read the actual note handed to the representatives of the British, French and Italian Governments by Mr. Lansing at Washington.

MR. LLOYD GEORGE asked Colonel House whether his interpretation of the situation was correct, namely, that the German Government were counting on peace being concluded on the basis of President Wilson's fourteen points and his other speeches.

COLONEL HOUSE said this was undoubtedly the case.

MR. LLOYD GEORGE said that unless the Allies made the contrary clear they themselves, in accepting the armistice, would be bound by these terms. Consequently, before they agreed to an armistice, they must make it clear what their attitude towards these terms was.

M. CLEMENCEAU asked whether the British Government had ever been consulted about President Wilson's terms? France had not been. If he had never been consulted, he did not see how he could be committed. He asked if the British Government considered themselves as committed?

MR. LLOYD GEORGE said that this was not the case now. But if he accepted an armistice without saying anything to the contrary, he would undoubtedly regard the British Government as committed to the terms.

M. PICHON said that the only question now put to us was the terms on which we would enter an armistice without prejudice to peace terms.

MR. BALFOUR said that, for the moment, unquestionably we were not bound by President Wilson's terms, but if we assented to an armistice without making our position clear, we should certainly be bound.

M. CLEMENCEAU agreed that this was the case, and asked that the fourteen points might be produced.

M. Pichon proceeded to read the Fourteen Points to the Conference. The only two clauses in them upon which any question was raised were the Freedom of the Seas and Reparations. As to the former (Point II), speaking on behalf of the British Government, I declared that I could not accept this clause. Had it been in operation during the War, we should have lost the power of imposing a blockade. Germany had broken down almost as much from the effects of the blockade as from that of the military operations. She was short of foodstuffs, copper, rubber, tungsten, wool, cotton, leather and many other essential materials. When Holland had been pouring foodstuffs into Germany and Scandinavia had been doing the same, we had been obliged to put a stop to it. So far as Clause II was concerned, therefore, I would like to see the League of Nations thoroughly established and proved before this issue was determined and even before any discussion took place.

COLONEL HOUSE said that the discussions were leading to this, that all the negotiations up to this point with Germany and Austria would have to be cleaned off the slate. The President would have no alternative but to tell the enemy that his conditions were not accepted by his Allies. The question would then arise whether America would not have to take up these questions direct with Germany and Austria.

M. CLEMENCEAU asked if Colonel House meant to imply that there would be a separate peace between the United States of America and the enemy.

COLONEL HOUSE said it might lead to this. It would depend upon whether America could or could not agree to the conditions put up by France, Great Britain and Italy.

MR. LLOYD GEORGE said that, so far as item II was concerned, it was impossible for the British Government to agree. If the United States of America were to make a separate peace, we should deeply regret it, but, nevertheless, should be prepared to go on fighting. (M. Clemenceau here interjected: "Yes.") We could not give up the one power which had enabled the American troops to be brought to Europe. This we were prepared to fight through and could not give up. Great Britain was not really a military nation. Its main defence was its Fleet. To give up the right of using its Fleet was a thing which no one in England would consent to. Moreover, our seapower had never been exercised harshly. He thought there was no serious complaint to be made by neutrals against the British, French, or Italian Fleets, or the American Fleet which was now engaged in close concert with them.

I then asked what the word "restoration" in the Fourteen Points implied, especially in respect of personal injuries. I gave as an illustration the loss sustained by the wives and children of the sailors drowned at sea. In the subsequent discussion this was extended to all who had been killed or maimed in the War.

MR. LLOYD GEORGE said that apart from this, he had no objection to the President's fourteen points. He suggested, therefore, that a reply should be sent to President Wilson, in the sense that the fourteen points must include reparation; that we believed reparation was included in the President's speeches; but that we wished to be perfectly clear about it. As regards freedom of the seas, we could not accept the interpretation which we understood Germany to put on it.

COLONEL HOUSE suggested the best plan was for the British, French, and Italian Governments to get together and make their exceptions to President Wilson's terms. This seemed to him to be the first step. Unless they did so it was no good laying down the terms of an armistice.

MR. LLOYD GEORGE expressed agreement. . . . He pointed out that

if we did not make any declaration on the subject, and we agreed to
enter a conference, we should be committed to the doctrine of the
freedom of the seas without definition of its scope.

M. Clemenceau said he could not understand the meaning of the
doctrine. War would not be war if there was freedom of the seas.

Mr. Balfour said that at any rate we must give Germany some
warning beforehand that some points were outside the armistice.

When Baron Sonnino raised the question of the inadequacy of
the reference to Italian claims in the Fourteen Points, Colonel
House gave a significant reply which has a much wider application. He made it clear that the President's peace terms were not
confined to the Fourteen Points, but that the subsequent speeches
he delivered on the subject must be incorporated in the conditions of the Armistice.

Colonel House said that the President's conditions were couched
in very broad terms. In the case of Alsace-Lorraine, for example, he
did not say specifically that it should go back to France, but he intended it positively.

M. Clemenceau said that the Germans certainly did not place
that interpretation on it.

Colonel House said that the President had said so much on other
occasions. He had insisted on Germany's accepting all his speeches,
and from these you could establish almost any point that anyone
wished against Germany. Reparation for Belgium and France, which
had been alluded to, was certainly implied in clauses 7 and 8, where
it had been stated that these invaded countries must be evacuated
and "restored." The same principle applied to illegal sinkings at sea
and to the sinking of neutrals.

As the War went on President Wilson had come more and more
into contact with realities, and each speech he delivered became
more and more an elucidation of principles he had laid down in
other speeches in the light of the grim facts which he now encountered for the first time in his dealings with the nations of the
world. He then realised that the conditions of peace after a war
which had so rent and torn the nations must be such as would
give a sense of security for the future to countries which had
suffered grievously at the hands of one of the most redoubtable
and relentless military confederacies that had ever menaced the
peace and liberty of mankind.

When we came to discuss the attitude of President Wilson on Reparations and the full meaning of his somewhat cryptic allusion to this subject in the eighth of his Fourteen Points, no real difficulty arose. Colonel House was prepared to accept the Allied interpretation of that phrase. The note received from Mr. Lansing on this subject during the course of the discussion, which I have already quoted, set at rest all our doubts on this point. The Wilson declarations covered compensation for all personal injuries sustained through enemy action. This satisfied the Allies, who had no intention of putting forward any demand which would include the costs of the War.

But as to the Freedom of the Seas, there still remained two antagonistic and apparently irreconcilable points of view. Mr. Balfour and I, for the reasons I have given, were quite resolved that we could not give in on the right of naval blockade, even if the War had to be prosecuted to the end without any further help from President Wilson. M. Clemenceau concurred. Colonel House appeared to have received instructions which were equally definite on the other side.

When, in negotiation with strong men, a point is reached where you have made up your mind that you cannot give in, I have always found it better to make this clear before the other side take up a position from which they cannot recede without public humiliation. President Wilson no doubt felt strongly about the interference by belligerents with neutral shipping. His experiences during the first two and a half years of the War had burnt into his consciousness a resentment, natural in the leader of a people with whom independence is the fount and origin of their national existence, against the notion of any foreign country stopping and overhauling on the high seas ships sailing under their flag, of which they are justifiably so proud. But during the year and a half in which he had participated in the War he had co-operated in the infliction of similar indignities on vessels sailing under other flags. What then did he mean by Freedom of the Seas? Did he mean to abolish all measures for effecting blockade of an enemy country? He had not committed himself to any definition of what he meant by the contentious phrase. It remained to find an interpretation which would provide an outlet consistent with his self-respect and our safety. The Conference of October 29th adjourned without coming to any conclusion in order to afford opportunity for informal conversations between Colonel House and the British representatives.

House communicated that evening with President Wilson, informing him fully of the tense differences which had arisen at the Conference. Wilson's first reaction to this communication was obduracy. On Reparation he experienced no difficulty in falling in with Allied ideas. But in spite of the recent record of his own navy, he would not give in on Freedom of the Seas, and he resorted to a threat which he tried with very indifferent results many times later on "to make the decision public"—that is, he would appeal to the public opinion of the countries represented by Clemenceau, Orlando and myself. There was no man who was in a less favourable position to take that step, for whereas British, French and Italian opinion showed itself to be overwhelmingly behind their representatives, America, in a very short time, practically repudiated its President. I need hardly say this unloaded blunderbuss did not intimidate either Clemenceau or the British leaders. The dangers of public sentiment in our respective countries came from exactly the opposite direction. We could not accept an interpretation of the Freedom of the Seas which would deprive Britain, who had no great army, of the only effective weapon in her armoury when challenged to the arbitrament of war. With Freedom of the Seas in the original Wilsonian meaning of the term, the Central Powers might have defied all the armies of the Alliance. The effectiveness of the blockade saved the Allies years of slaughter. Colonel House was wise enough to feel that there was nothing to be gained by a propagandist campaign engineered from America to rouse public resentment in Britain against a well-rooted conviction that the security of her island home was dependent on both the defensive and the strangling power of the fleet in any conflict that might be provoked. Gradually President Wilson was made to realise that he was up against a tradition that could not be overthrown by the blast of a single speech delivered from across the Atlantic.

Matters were eased by the interpretation which Colonel House ultimately placed upon the term "Freedom of the Seas." He insisted that "it did not mean the abolition of the principle of blockade"; for him it signified merely "that codification of maritime usage that would sanctify the doctrine of the immunity of private property at sea in time of war." This statement was not made at our first discussion on the subject. Colonel House was then inexorable in his adhesion to the full and unqualified Wilsonian doctrine. However, the conversations between us after the meeting improved matters and ended in an agreed declaration which was sent on November 4th to President Wilson, and which he practically accepted and communicated to the Germans before they signed the Armistice terms.

The agreed answer of the President to the Germans also placed on record House's and Lansing's assurance that the word "restoration" in the Fourteen Points meant compensation by Germany for all damage done to the Allied population as well as to their property.

The terms as conveyed to the Germans were as follows:

The Allied Governments have given careful consideration to the correspondence which has passed between the President of the United States and the German Government. Subject to the qualifications which follow they declare their willingness to make peace with the Government of Germany on the terms of peace laid down in the President's Address to Congress of the 8th January, 1918, and the principles of settlement enunciated in his subsequent addresses. They must point out, however, that clause 2, relating to what is usually described as the Freedom of the Seas, is open to various interpretations, some of which they could not accept. They must therefore reserve to themselves complete freedom on this subject when they enter the Peace Conference.

Further, in the conditions of peace laid down in his Address to Congress of the 8th January, 1918, the President declared that invaded territories must be restored as well as evacuated and freed. The Allied Governments feel that no doubt ought to be allowed to exist as to what this provision implies. By it they understand that compensation will be made by Germany for all damage caused to the civilian population of the Allies and their property by the *aggression of Germany* by land, by sea, and from the air.

As regards the Freedom of the Seas, the above declaration enabled the President to say that he had not given way, but had only postponed the settlement of the subject to the Peace Conference. I felt convinced that nothing more would be heard of the subject. My confidence was justified, for the topic was never alluded to in any of our discussions in Paris when we were framing the Treaty. On further examination of the President's various declarations it was found that there was no essential difference between the conditions he laid down for a just and honourable peace and those which had already been promulgated by the Allies. Apparent differences on the Freedom of the Seas and Reparations were thus reconciled before the Armistice was signed.

The impression left on my mind that President Wilson decided not to press the threatened point at our subsequent proceedings is confirmed by a statement made by M. Clemenceau in a speech defending the Treaty of Versailles delivered by him in September, 1919. Referring to the controversy which had arisen over the Freedom of the Seas, he said:

Mr. Lloyd George said to me: "Do you admit that without the British Fleet you could not have continued the War?" And I answered: "Yes." Mr. Lloyd George then added: "Are you disposed to prevent us, in case of war, doing the same thing again?" And I answered: "No." Well, now, I repeated this conversation to President Wilson. It did not in the least disturb him. President Wilson answered me: "I have nothing to ask you which could displease or embarrass either of you." *

An attempt has been made to create the impression that President Wilson experienced great difficulties in his endeavour to secure the adhesion of the principal Allied Powers to his Fourteen Points. Even Colonel House, who knew better what actually happened than outside critics, sought to foster that false impression. The objections to the Fourteen Points were confined to the matters I have indicated. They were confined exclusively to a question of interpretation of two out of the Fourteen Points. The explanations given to the Allies by or on behalf of President

* André Tardieu: "The Truth about the Treaty," p. 106.

Wilson of what he intended to stipulate in these two points were accepted in an unqualified manner by the Allied leaders. It turned out that when fully explained, the views of Wilson, Clemenceau, Orlando and myself on the dubious points were in essence identical. The nations we represented were surely entitled to ask for these explanations before we committed ourselves on matters of such concern to our respective countries. The sacrifices that made victory possible had been borne mainly by the European Allies. France had lost of her sons 1,364,000 dead and 3,740,000 wounded. Of the millions of young men under thirty who went into the line to defend the soil and honour of France, only 50 per cent. ever returned from the battlefield. The War also cost France the equivalent of £8,000,000,000; 4,022 of her villages had been destroyed; 20,000 of her factories ruined and millions of acres of her fertile land rendered uncultivable without complete reconditioning. France has a population which is one-third of that of the United States of America, whose dead numbered 60,000, and not one of whose villages had a single shack destroyed by enemy action. The British Empire had 900,000 of its young men killed and over 2,000,000 wounded; 8,000,000 tons of her shipping were sunk by enemy action. The War cost her directly £10,000,000,000. Italy sacrificed 2,000,000 of her youth in killed and wounded, and although a comparatively poor country, the War cost her seventy milliards of francs. Surely these sacrifices entitled these three countries to know to what kind of peace they were being committed by an associate that had made a truly notable contribution to victory, but whose sacrifices were not comparable to those made by the European States. We were entitled to ask a few questions about the meaning of two staccato phrases in a speech of President Wilson's which was to be made the basis of a peace settlement vitally affecting the future of the peoples who had trusted to us their fortunes. We did not mean to go back on any offer we made to Germany. Hence our insistence in clearing up obscurities before accepting her surrender. The main principles laid down by President Wilson were accepted without demur; and to taunt friends and colleagues with reluctance to accept the President's doctrines because they asked that two points which were vaguely expressed should be cleared up, is neither generous nor fair.

There are many explanations—mostly sinister and derogatory —offered of the indubitable fact that the peccant Four who were responsible for the Treaty of Versailles worked in friendly harmony and in the end reached unanimous conclusions. Those who view the Treaty as a cauldron of hatred, revenge and rapacity, but find it difficult to know where to place President Wilson on that assumption, picture him as the poor dupe of a couple of expert political gunmen who alternately bullied and cajoled, hoodwinked and flattered him until the poor man ultimately signed on the dotted line. Those who still consider that the Treaty was not a stern enough sentence on the culprits, having regard to the magnitude of their crime, and think we were lured into slosh by the apostle of idealist experimentation, adopt exactly the opposite point of view, and depict Clemenceau and myself as the converts of an American revivalist. Clemenceau was not the material out of which penitent forms are made. A perusal of the various declarations made by French, British and Italian statesmen long before the War had reached its climax, demonstrates beyond challenge that the European Allies who had borne the brunt of the struggle were in complete accord as to the main terms of the settlement; and a careful study of the Wilson war aims will also show that, as far as the determining principles of the Treaty are concerned, he also was in full agreement with his European colleagues. The two questions upon which any doubt remained as to his real views were cleared up during the Armistice discussions, before Wilson had been in contact with Europe and its antiquated and battle-scarred notions about what is right and wrong in international relations.

The Armistice was an intimation to friend and foe alike that the settlement which followed the War would be drawn up on lines with which the world had been familiarised by the repeated declarations of the men who spoke authoritatively on behalf of the victors. A peace conference would necessarily take time to define boundaries, but the principles upon which the map of Europe was to be redrawn had been repeatedly laid down by the

Allies and were not departed from. The amount of the reparations demanded, the machinery by which they were to be fixed and the methods by which payment was to be exacted and security established would require prolonged discussion, but the demand for damages in respect of destruction wrongfully inflicted upon persons and property had been proclaimed by all the victorious nations. The same thing applies to the other conditions of the settlement. The notion that President Wilson came to Europe a lonely crusader, to enforce his ideas about an Association of Nations upon hostile Governments, is a myth, and a foolish one at that. In the chapter on the League of Nations I propose to demonstrate, from quotations taken from contemporary documents, that the British and French Governments had not only committed themselves to the project before President Wilson ever entered the War, but that they had announced their intention of making it an integral part of the peace settlement and had actually set up expert committees to work out a practicable plan long before the President had given any time or thought to the subject in detail. One of these plans in substance constitutes the Covenant of the League to-day.

All the cheap stuff written by sensational economists about "the morass of Paris," "arid intrigues," "spoliation," "Carthaginian peace," is at best belated. These after-the-event critics ought to have made their protest when the Allied Governments repeatedly announced these terms during the War. Their criticisms would then have been timely and courageous. We went to Paris committed several times over to these terms, and on their strength secured the support and sacrifices of the nation which alone enabled us to struggle through to a complete victory. To depart from those pledges when the sacrifice and suffering had been consummated would have been a betrayal. We certainly would not have been entitled to do so in order to propitiate men who during the War did their best to discourage the efforts which averted defeat and ensured triumph. Those who led the attack on the Treaty of Versailles were the same futile and fainthearted "experts" who sought in 1916 to scare us into retreat by predicting that we could not keep fighting for more than a few months.

When we come to the position of Austria-Hungary, the Peace Treaty went beyond the original intentions of the great Allied Powers. The tearing up of the Austrian Empire into disparate and unconnected fragments was no part of the policy of France, Russia, Britain, America or Italy. We knew there must be a re-adjustment of frontiers in favour of Italy, Serbia and Roumania. As for the rest of the Austrian Empire, the idea that found favour was that which was expounded by General Smuts in his interview with Count Mensdorff (see "War Memoirs," Volume V): the conferring of complete autonomy on the component races who made up the Austro-Hungarian Empire, inside a federal consti-tution. Had that been found practicable there can be no doubt that it would have conduced to peace and stability in Central Europe. But when the Austrian Army collapsed, the fissiparous elements took charge of the situation. Czechoslovakia proclaimed its independence, and the Slavonic population of the South joined up with the Serbian kingdom. Hungary declared its inde-pendence and Austria became an isolated Republic. The Rou-mans of Transylvania had already joined their fellow-country-men. Ere the Powers came to consider the Austrian Peace they were confronted with accomplished and unreversible facts. I pre-dicted at the beginning of the War that it would end in a break-up of "the ramshackle Empire." The prediction was verified with startling suddenness and the most irreparable completeness. There was not an area in the whole Austrian Empire which had not been parcelled out amongst the various claimants and occu-pied by their troops before the Powers ever met in conference to consider the terms of the Treaty of Peace with Austria. The task of the Parisian treatymakers was not to decide what in fairness should be given to the liberated nationalities, but what in com-mon honesty should be freed from their clutches when they had overstepped the bounds of self-determination.

CHAPTER II

PREPARATIONS FOR THE TREATY: INTERALLIED CONFERENCES

M TARDIEU, in his very able book, "The Truth about the Treaty," seeks to dispel charges brought by French critics against the provisions of the Versailles Treaty on the ground of its undue leniency to Germany. When the draft of the Treaty was first published, all the serious criticism in the French Chamber and by French journalists was of that character. M. Clemenceau was accused of letting Germany off too lightly at the expense of French interests. As far as the majority of the British House of Commons and a powerful section of the British Press were concerned, the same observation applies. Such adverse comment as appeared during the course of the Peace Congress was all in the same direction. There was not an audible voice raised in Britain during the progress of the Conference in Paris urging a modification of the terms exacted by the Treaty from the vanquished. I was indeed at that time accused of breaking faith with the British electors by letting off Germany too lightly. The attack on the severity of the Treaty appeared at a later stage. It was only a long time after the appearance of the terms that allegations were made against the British negotiators that they were rushed at the General Election of December, 1918, into giving extravagant and foolish pledges from which they could not extricate themselves during the negotiations. The harsher provisions of the Treaty were attributed to the exigencies of the hustings.

The best answer to this charge is to be found, firstly, in my narrative of the declarations made during the War, with the full assent of every organised section of opinion, and secondly, in the official record, which I now propose to summarise, of the proceedings of Imperial Cabinet meetings, summoned immediately after the Armistice to consider the terms of the Peace, and of the transactions of the Interallied Conference, which met in London three weeks after the Armistice for the same purpose. At these gatherings—imposing conclaves of the principal statesmen of the Allies and of the British Empire—the most vital issues and, as far as British opinion is concerned, all the most controverted issues, were debated and dealt with exhaustively. The main lines of the Peace had, as I have already pointed out, been determined by the Allies when neither a victory nor an election was in sight. The deliberations of the Cabinet either immediately before or after the Armistice introduced no fresh conditions to be imposed upon the enemy except one: the demand for punishment of those who were responsible for the War or for atrocious offences against the laws of war. The assurance of victory effected no other change in the terms of peace. The Treaty itself conforms in essentials to the decisions of the Imperial Cabinet before victory was visible on the horizon, and these decisions were not altered when the triumphant goal was reached. These facts constitute an irrefutable answer to the suggestion that the British Government, prompted by electioneering motives, was responsible for stiffening the demands of the Allies.

Let us first review the meetings of the Imperial War Cabinet. This body had already played a very considerable part in the direction of the War, and afterwards in the shaping of the terms of peace. Between March 20th, 1917, when it first met, and the 31st December, 1918, it held altogether 48 meetings. In addition to these full meetings, Dominion representatives were placed on practically every important committee, and discharged important functions in helping the War Cabinet to investigate special subjects. I refer in Chapter I to the discussions on the terms of peace which occurred during the progress of the War at the Imperial Cabinet, and I have given a full account of them in my "War Memoirs." After the Armistice the Imperial War Cabinet was immediately called together to deliberate on the proposals for peace which should be submitted on behalf of the British Empire at the forthcoming conversations with Allied statesmen, and more particularly with President Wilson on his arrival in Europe.

It would occupy too much space even to summarise adequately

the whole of the discussions that ensued during these weeks. It is important, however, that an indication should be given of the opinions expressed on the most vital questions that were raised and more particularly on the more controverted issues, where misrepresentation is rife.

1. THE TRIAL OF THE KAISER

THERE has been so much foolish gibing on this proposal that it is necessary for me to state and document all the evidence. It was dealt with at the first meeting of the Imperial Cabinet held after the Armistice on November 20th, 1918. After a general discussion upon a variety of topics, Lord Curzon raised the specific issue of the trial of the Kaiser. This is the first occasion upon which any allusion had been made to this matter at any Ministerial consultations, and in view of the personal responsibility which has been attached to me for this proposal and the electioneering motive imputed to me as the instigation of my action, I must call attention to the fact that the subject was first introduced by Lord Curzon and that he definitely states that he was doing so as a result of a conversation in Paris with M. Clemenceau at which I was not present. I am not desirous of disclaiming my full share of responsibility in the matter. But in view of the reiterated sneers as to the origin and authorship of the idea which are constantly repeated in political speeches and articles of the cheaper and more repetitive kind, it is necessary that I should quote textually the statements made by those who inaugurated the discussion and first proposed the course of action adopted by the Allies.

During the last few months of the War there had been a growing feeling in France—which was the greatest sufferer—and also in Britain and in America, that punishment should be meted out to those who had been guilty of barbarities which exceeded the limits of atrocity held legitimate, because inevitable, in the waging of war under modern conditions. The French population in the occupied areas had suffered from these excesses. British feeling was roused to a pitch of irrepressible wrath by the cruelties inflicted on unarmed seamen by the sinking of merchant ships on the high seas in all weathers, and the crowding of the crew in frail boats where they would be left to the mercy of the waves in the tempestuous seas of the Eastern Atlantic. The losses through drowning and exposure were appalling. The Kaiser was held to be personally responsible for this cruel infamy. American opinion was also stirred to its depths by this outrage, which in fact had brought America into the War against Germany. There was also a growing feeling that war itself was a crime against humanity, and that it would never be finally eliminated until it was brought into the same category as all other crimes by the infliction of condign punishment on the perpetrators and instigators. The French in their draft Agenda for the Peace Conference placed "Responsibilities for the War" before "Reparation." They also informed us that they had collected evidence on the subject of war crimes and had referred the dossier to their experts for examination and report. Lord Curzon had paid a visit to Paris earlier in the month, and had spoken with Clemenceau about the trial of the Kaiser, amongst other matters. Curzon wrote me that Clemenceau

. . . thought that as an act of international justice, of world retribution, it would be one of the most imposing events in history and that the conception was well worthy of being pursued.

He prayed me to communicate with my Government on the matter and to let him have any papers or reports on the subject that we might prepare.

Curzon went on:

I pray you to consider it seriously. Public opinion will not willingly consent to let this arch-criminal escape by a final act of cowardice. The supreme and colossal nature of his crime seems to call for some supreme and unprecedented condemnation. Execution, imprisonment, these are not, or may not be, necessary. But continued life, an inglorious and ignoble exile, under the weight of such a sentence as has never before been given in the history of mankind, would be a penance worse than death.

I informed him that it was a matter worthy of consideration by the Imperial Cabinet and that he ought to raise it at the next meeting of that body. This he undertook to do.

This is how Lord Curzon opened the matter to his colleagues in the Imperial War Cabinet:

While in Paris last week I had a conversation with M. Clemenceau with regard to what the attitude of the Allied Governments should be towards the ex-Kaiser. I do not think I need argue the case about the desirability, still less the fairness, or the equity of trying him and the Crown Prince. We know the war was started by the Kaiser, and we have reason to believe that all the cruelty, the iniquities, and the horrors that have been perpetrated, if not directly inspired by him, have been countenanced and in no way discouraged by him. *In my view the Kaiser is the arch-Criminal of the world, and just as in any other sphere of life when you get hold of a criminal you bring him to justice, so I do not see, because he is an Emperor and living in exile in another country, why he should be saved from the punishment which is his due.* When I spoke to M. Clemenceau about the matter he said that, as far as he knew, the French jurists had not looked at it from the point of view of international law and of the questions that will arise in respect of internment and extradition, *but he said public opinion in France, as represented by the press, was strongly in favour of steps being taken for the trial of the Kaiser and that he himself shared that view,* although he would be very glad to hear from our Government what our ideas were on the subject. He then discussed the form which such a tribunal might take; I think he had the idea of an international tribunal, composed not only of delegates from Allied countries which have taken part in the recent war but of neutrals as well. He discussed the two conditions; first, of a successful demand for the person of the Kaiser himself and putting him up for trial before a body to which he himself could answer for his misdeeds; and the other was the question of the trial taking place in the absence of the Kaiser, supposing we were unable to get him from Holland. He did not think that would be a fatal bar. He thought the terms of indictment might be drawn up and that they might be sent to the Kaiser, if we could not get hold of him. *As regards punishment, the idea which he mentioned—I do not think he said much about execution; I do not think that entered into our minds—was that of treating the Kaiser as a universal outlaw so that there should be no land in which he could set his foot. These were the general views that he put forward, and he awaited further information from us.* There were two other points mentioned. One was that as we all hoped that a League of Nations would emerge from this war, would it not be really a great act of initiation if the first step that would really call the League of Nations in an effective manner into being, should be an act of justice taken by the world as a whole. I saw the

Attorney-General this morning on my way to the Cabinet. You will remember we referred to him some time ago the question of constituting a tribunal for the trial of all those persons who have been guilty of such acts of murder as that of Nurse Cavell and Captain Fryatt. I asked whether his Committee were considering the question of trying the Kaiser? He said they had not approached it yet, but that the majority of the Committee—and it is an effective Committee, as we know—were in favour of that course, and would submit a recommendation to that effect and put before the War Cabinet the scheme of a tribunal by which it might be done. On a point of law, I imagine that any action taken for getting hold of the Kaiser should be taken now; that is to say, it must be taken before the Peace Conference. He would be a prisoner of war now, but if you postponed it till after the Peace Conference you might not get him at all. That seems a reason why we should come to some decision at once. I have not thought it necessary to argue the case on its merits.

I followed and strongly supported M. Clemenceau's proposal with reservations:

I think rulers who plunge the world into all this misery ought to be warned for all time that they must pay the penalty sooner or later. I do not think it is sufficient punishment to this man that he should get away with twenty millions of money, as I see is stated, to Holland or Corfu, or wherever he goes. I think he ought to stand his trial. With regard to the question of international law, well, we are making international law, and all we can claim is that international law should be based on justice. If he was not responsible, he can make his case. The League of Nations is a Committee composed either of diplomats or statesmen, but this ought to be a judicial tribunal which should be set up by the Allies. Germany ought to be invited to join in it, and I have no doubt she will send men, in her present state, who will judge the ex-Kaiser very impartially. There is a sense of justice in the world which will not be satisfied so long as this man is at large.

The project led to a lengthy discussion in which a variety of opinions were expressed—some favourable, some doubtful and some definitely hostile. Ultimately on the motion of the late Lord Reading, who was also present, the matter was referred to the Law Officers of the Crown in the following resolution:

(a) To invite the Law Officers of the Crown to examine, from the widest point of view, the question of framing charges against the ex-Emperor of Germany and/or the ex-Crown Prince—(i) for the crime against humanity of having caused the war; and (ii) for offences, by one or both, against international law during the war—with a view to bringing home to one or both the responsibility for the acts charged;

(b) To invite the Law Officers of the Crown to consider the constitution of a tribunal to try the charges framed;

(c) To invite the Law Officers to examine with the Foreign Office the practicability of inducing the Dutch Government to hand over the ex-Emperor and the Crown Prince to such a tribunal for trial.

The Law Officers immediately took the matter in hand and investigated the case with the assistance of a very able and distinguished body of jurists whose names would carry conviction for their knowledge of international law and for their general soundness of judgment. Apart from the Attorney-General, Sir F. E. Smith (afterwards Lord Birkenhead), there was Sir Gordon Hewart, the Solicitor-General, now Lord Chief Justice of England. They were assisted in their study of the question by Professor J. H. Morgan, Sir John Macdonell, Sir Frederick Pollock, Sir Alfred Hopkinson, K.C., afterwards Chancellor of Manchester University, Mr. C. A. Russell, K.C., Dr. Pearce Higgins, Mr. Justice Peterson, Mr. C. F. Gill, K.C., the famous criminal lawyer, and Mr. J. F. More of the War Office. On November 28th, Sir F. E. Smith appeared at a meeting of the Imperial War Cabinet to give the views of the Law Officers and of this Committee of Experts. The late Lord Birkenhead was one of the most accomplished forensic orators of the day. In lucidity of exposition he was unsurpassed by any lawyer of his time. Few indeed were there who could rival him in this accomplishment. There was no man who wasted fewer words in the process of elucidation. The statement he made to the Imperial Cabinet on this case was an example of his style. As such, apart from the supreme interest of the subject, it is worth perusing and studying as a model of clarity and compression. It is a joy to read such limpid and vivid English. The experts had unanimously recommended a prosecution of the rulers who were responsible for the War, and in his statement to the Cabinet Lord Birkenhead set forth the arguments in favour of such a course with irresistible logic and cogency:

Prime Minister, Lord Curzon conveyed to the Law Officers of the Crown some days ago the desire of the Cabinet that they should give their opinion on this matter. The Law Officers pointed out the extreme importance, delicacy, and difficulty of the matter submitted to them, and the fact that they themselves were very much engaged in other matters, and asked what period of time could reasonably be allowed them to produce a written opinion adequate to the gravity of the topic. Lord Curzon at that time took the view that they might be allowed ten days. Well, of these ten days, only, I think, four or five have elapsed, and therefore the Cabinet will excuse any imperfection of form in the statement I am about to make. We have, however, arrived at a clear conclusion, otherwise we should have informed the Cabinet that we were not yet in a position to give definite and final advice. The matters involved here are partly legal and partly matters of policy. So far as they are matters of policy, the Cabinet will of course merely treat our views as the opinions of colleagues who are not entitled to, and who are not claiming, any special weight. The main question here which we, in common with our Allies, have to consider is whether the taking of proceedings against, or any punitive treatment in relation to, the Kaiser should become the declared policy of the Government. The Law Officers of the Crown answer this question in the affirmative. They point out to the Cabinet that the choice now to be taken is between two diametrically opposed courses, and that no half-way house is possible in the matter. The first is a decision in favour of complete impunity, an impunity which will be described as luxurious and wealthy; the second is in favour of punishment. We wish the Cabinet to consider very carefully how it will be possible for them to justify a decision in favour of impunity. The ex-Kaiser's personal responsibility and supreme authority in Germany have been constantly asserted by himself, and his assertions are fully warranted by the constitution of Germany. Accepting, as we must, this view, we are bound to take notice of the conclusion which follows: namely, that the ex-Kaiser is primarily and personally responsible for the death of millions of young men; for the destruction in four years of 200 times as much material wealth as Napoleon destroyed in twenty years; and he is responsible—and this is not the least grave part of the indictment—for the most daring and dangerous challenge to the fundamental principles of public law which that indispensable charter of international right has sustained since its foundations were laid centuries ago by Grotius. These things are very easy to understand, and ordinary people all over the world understand them very well. How then, I ask, are we to justify impunity? Under what pretext, and with what degree of consistence, are we to try smaller criminals? Is it still proposed—it has been repeatedly threatened by the responsible representatives of every Allied country—to try, in appropriate cases, submarine commanders and to bring to justice the governors of prisons? Is it proposed to indict the murderers of Captain Fryatt? In my view, you must answer all these questions in the affirmative. I am at least sure that the democracies of the world will take that view, and among them I have no doubt that the American people will be numbered. How can you do this if, to use the title claimed by himself, and in itself illustrative of my argument, "the All Highest" is given impunity? Must we not, at the moment of our triumph avoid the sarcasm: "Dat veniam corvis, vexat censura columbas"? In order to illustrate the point which is in my mind I will read to the Imperial War Cabinet a very short extract, which represents our view with admirable eloquence, from Burke's speech in the trial of Warren Hastings:

"We have not brought before you an obscure offender, who, when his insignificance and weakness are weighed against the power of the prosecution gives even to public justice something of the appearance of oppression; no, my Lords, we have brought before you the first man of India in rank, authority, and station. We have brought before you the Chief of the tribe, the head of the whole body of eastern offenders; a captain-general of iniquity, under whom all the fraud, all the peculation, all the tyranny in India are embodied, disciplined, arrayed and paid. This is the person, my Lords, that we bring before you. We have brought before you such a person, that, if you strike at him with the firm and decided arm of justice, you will not have need of a great many more examples. You strike at the whole corps if you strike at the head."

Prime Minister, in my judgment, if this man escapes, common people will say everywhere that he has escaped because he is an Emperor. In my judgment they will be right. They will say that august influence has been exerted to save him. It is not desirable that such things should be said, especially in these days. It is necessary for all time to teach the lesson that failure is not the only risk which a man possessing at the moment in any country despotic powers, and taking the awful decision between Peace and War, has to fear. If ever again that decision should be suspended in nicely balanced equipoise, at the disposition of an individual, let the ruler who decides upon war know that he is gambling, amongst other hazards, with his own personal safety.

For these reasons, we think the ex-Kaiser should be punished. If this view is accepted, the question arises: How is his person to be secured? And the question has been asked, and will be asked, whether or not he can be extradited. Now, Sir, the French have apparently expressed the view that he can. My own clear opinion is that that view is wrong, and I think my colleague, the Solicitor-General, is, on the whole, of the same opinion; but it is not necessary to argue that question, because we do not propose to involve ourselves in a doubtful technical argument when we have more powerful weapons at our disposal. Infinite vistas of litigious disputations are opened by an argument whether according to the law of Holland he can be extradited or not. And if, contrary to my opinion, he could be extradited, he could only be charged for the very offence (possibly a limited one) which had been successfully alleged as the ground in law of his extradition. I think it is unnecessary to ask whether in law we can extradite him, because it seems to me that Holland must, in effect, give him up. The League of Nations or the Conference of the Allies which will precede the formation of the League of Nations has, or will have, powerful arguments to address to Holland, and the internal condition of Holland seems to me to be such that it would be very difficult for her to reject arguments of the kind indicated. This is not a point of law, but my own conclusion is that the difficulty of obtaining control of the person of the ex-Kaiser from Holland will not be an insuperable one, though I should naturally defer to the views of the Foreign Office upon such a point. It may perhaps be assumed that the difficulty will not arise which would be occasioned in this connection by the ex-Kaiser's return to Germany. The taking of unnecessary risks has not up to the present been a distinguishing feature of his career. Different considerations might arise if the reconstitution of Germany should really bring with it an honest desire to deal with the Kaiser themselves.

The few observations, therefore, which I have still to make will be made upon the assumption that it will be possible to obtain control of his person. I have made it clear that in our judgment control should not be sought through the machinery of extradition. Supposing control of his person has been obtained, how is he to be dealt with? There are two alternative courses. In the first place, he might be treated by the Allies as Napoleon was treated, that is to say, by a high assertion of responsibility on the part of the conquering nations. The Allies might say: We are prepared, before the bar of history, to take upon ourselves the responsibility for saying that this man has been guilty of high crimes and misdemeanours, that he has broken the peace of the world, and that he ought either to be exiled or otherwise punished in his own person. That course may be recommended by powerful argument, and I do not myself exclude it, Prime Minister. I do not say more of it at this stage than this, that by its adoption we should avoid the risks of infinite delays and of a long drawn out impeachment. We should carry with us the sanction and support of the overwhelming mass of civilisation. And we are bold enough to feel that we have nothing to fear from the judgment of the future. It is even possible— as Austria and Germany will be reconstituted—that there will be few dissentients in the governing classes of these countries.

The second alternative is that he should be tried by a Court which must evidently be international in its composition. There are obvious advantages in this method upon the moral side if this method of dealing with the situation be carried to a logical conclusion. It is, of course, very desirable that we should be able to say that this man received fair-play, and that he has had a fair trial, but grave difficulties beset this course in its complete application. In this connection, how is the Court to be constituted? Are neutrals to be members of the Court? Are Germans to be members of the Court?

The only advantage of judicial procedure over the other alternative—a high exercise of executive and conquering force submitting itself to the judgment of history—lies in the fact that for all time it may claim the sanction of legal forms and the protection—in favour of the prisoner—of a tribunal whose impartiality can be established in the face of any challenge. This advantage, it must be observed, largely disappears if the fairness of the tribunal can be plausibly impeached. The Law Officers are not, indeed, of opinion that before a tribunal which consisted in part even of Germans, as Germany appears to be developing to-day, an indictment would necessarily fail. But it is unwise to ignore the difficulties. German and neutral representation would undoubtedly be claimed by the Kaiser. We can only qualify the consequent risk by saying that the German representatives would certainly be less German than they were, and the neutral representatives less neutral.

If a court be constituted, I confess that I myself incline on the whole to the view that the members of the court should consist only of citizens of the Allied countries. Grave judges should be appointed, but we should, as it seems to me at present, take the risk of saying that in this quarrel we, the Allies, taking our stand upon the universally admitted principles of the moral law, take our own standards of right and commit the trial of them to our own tribunals.

I cannot, because time is short, develop the matter as I should like now, and therefore I merely place it on record that I am well aware that the opposite view may be supported by formidable arguments.

The great question which I shall probably be asked—and here again inter-Allied discussion will be necessary is: For what offences, in your view (assuming the adoption of judicial proceedings), should the ex-Kaiser be made justiciable? The first charge which will occur to many persons is one which raises *in limine* the question of his responsibility for the origin of the war. Well, Sir, I can only say, without giving a decision, that the trial of such a charge would involve infinite disputation. We do not wish to become involved in a trial like that of Warren Hastings in its infinite duration. We do not wish to be confronted by a meticulous examination of the history of European politics for the past twenty years. It is very easy to see that no German advocate of the ex-Kaiser would find it difficult to enlarge the area of discussion, carrying it to what would be described in Germany as the "ringing round" system, and discursively spreading from the question of the origin of the war to a close discussion of the military significance of the Russian strategic railways. The view which I have at present is that it would not be wise to add so general a charge, but this provisional view might easily be modified if new and decisive documents were produced, like those recently disclosed by the Bavarian Minister, who was in Berlin in August, 1914. Such revelations are very likely to be made.

The second charge is extremely clear, and it is, in my judgment, a decisive one. A count should certainly be inserted in the indictment charging the Kaiser with responsibility for the invasion of Belgium in breach of International Law and for all the consequent criminal acts which took place. That is an absolutely clear issue, and upon it I do not think that any honest tribunal could hesitate. It is even possible, obscure as the present position in Germany is, that a partly German tribunal convened under existing circumstances in Germany would reach the same conclusion.

The next charge, in my judgment, which should be brought against him is that he is responsible in the matter of unrestricted submarine warfare. It may be necessary to associate other defendants in this charge. But it will, in my judgment, be absolutely impossible for us to charge or punish any subordinate if the ex-Kaiser escapes with impunity all responsibility for the submarine warfare. I wish to press most strongly upon my colleagues certain fundamental considerations in regard to submarine warfare, as it has been carried on since the incident of the *Lusitania*. Since then thousands of women and children, in our clear and frequently expressed view, have been brutally murdered. I am dealing with the case where a ship is torpedoed carrying no munitions of war, but which it is known must or may be carrying women and children, and where it is equally known that such passengers had no possible means of escape, and I do not in this connection deal with the vile cases of assassination when helpless boats, vainly attempting to escape, have been fired on and destroyed. Excluding the last class of cases, it is our view, and the view of the whole civilised world, that those acts amount to murder. It is surely vital that if ever there is another war, whether in ten or fifteen years, or however distant it may be, those responsible on both sides for the conduct of that war should be made to feel that unrestricted submarine warfare has been so branded with the punitive censure of the whole civilised world that it has definitely passed into the category of international crime. "If I do it and fail," the Tirpitz of the next war must say, "I too shall pay for it in my own person." How can we best secure that no one in future will dream of resorting to submarine warfare of this kind? You can best secure it by letting the whole world know that, by the unanimous consent of the whole of that part of the civilised world which has conquered in this war, the man responsible for those acts is responsible in his own person for that which he has done. To us of all people it is not possible to exaggerate the weight and force of these considerations. Nothing more vitally concerns these islands than that it should be recognised that these acts are crimes. The commission of such crimes, and their possible future development, menace us more directly than any other nation in the world.

The above are suggestions, and not necessarily exhaustive suggestions, in regard to the offences for which the Kaiser should be tried. There are other individual cases with which I do not think it necessary to trouble the Cabinet at this stage.

It is true that the Prime Minister authorised me to form a Committee to report upon these matters, but the Law Officers obviously cannot place their responsibility for advising the Government in legal matters in the hands of anybody else, and they have arrived at their conclusion independently of the conclusions of this Committee, and, indeed, before they were informed of them. I think I ought to point out who are the members who compose this Committee, which is the Sub-Committee on Law of the Main Committee.

Sir F. E. Smith then gave the Cabinet the names of the members of the Committee* and added:

Of these, Sir John Macdonell, Mr. Justice Peterson, and Mr. Gill are not members of the Sub-Committee on Law, but were called in for the special purpose of discussing the new issue as regards the ex-Kaiser.

I think the Lord Chief Justice will agree that it would not be possible in this country to form a stronger Committee for the purpose of arriving at a sound conclusion upon such matters. It is a source of satisfaction to the Law Officers that this Committee has unanimously and independently of them reached the conclusion that the ex-Kaiser ought

* These appear on page 58.

to be punished, either by way of trial or as Napoleon was punished. The Committee inclines to the first of those courses, namely that he should be tried. I am not at present wholly convinced upon this point, and, in the written opinion which the Solicitor-General and myself contemplate, we propose to discuss this matter in greater detail. Probably I have said enough to make the Cabinet aware of the views held by the Law Officers. I could, and would, have said much more if I were not concerned to be economical of your time. As chief Law Officer of the Crown, I say quite plainly that I should feel the greatest difficulty in being responsible in any way for the trial of subordinate criminals if the ex-Kaiser is allowed to escape.

I have rarely seen an assembly of Ministers so enthralled by the exposition of a case. Cabinet speeches are traditionally brief. The usual contribution lasts a maximum of five minutes. A Minister explaining a budget or a bill is necessarily allowed some latitude, but even then it never approximates the limits of Parliamentary indulgence. On this occasion Lord Birkenhead probably occupied three-quarters of an hour. He had no notes. He had no quotations. He therefore never read one sentence in his speech. It was indeed a masterly performance. The limpid clarity of the statement, the unerring choice of the apt word, the mellowness of a voice which had a great range but was subdued to the proportions and the quality of the audience, held every Minister, representing as they did between them the greatest Empire on earth, in complete bondage to the sway of one of the finest intellects and one of the most perfect speakers ever contributed by the British Bar to politics. It was a notable scene. Fortunately it was one of the few occasions when the written word conveys some idea of the power of the deliverance.

It is worthy of note that those who expressed doubts at the first discussion were all present on this occasion and all now concurred in the Attorney-General's recommendation. There was not a dissentient voice, and the Imperial War Cabinet carried unanimously the following resolution:

"The Imperial War Cabinet adopted the report presented by the Attorney-General, and agreed that, so far as the British Government have the power, the ex-Kaiser should be held personally responsible for his crimes against international law."

When I come to give an account of the meetings of the Inter-
allied Supreme Council held a few days later, it will be seen how
completely and emphatically the attitude adopted by the Imperial War Cabinet was endorsed by the French and Italian Prime
Ministers.

2. THE GERMAN COLONIES

Mandates

AT the meeting of the Imperial War Cabinet which dealt with
the trial of the Kaiser there was a general and somewhat desultory discussion as to the disposal of the German Colonies. Two
things however emerged from the conversations. One was that
the Dominions were not prepared to give up any of the territories
contiguous to their boundaries which had been conquered by
them during the War. On the grounds of security they did not
wish to have the Germans stationed near their respective countries, with the possibilities involved in submarine bases, air
stations, and organisation of black armies, all of which might be
a constant menace to their peace.

The second feature was the absence of any real desire on the
part of the representatives of Great Britain to add any more
territory to the vast areas of undeveloped land now under the
flag. There was not only a readiness, but even an eagerness to
bring in America and to hand over to her a mandate in respect of
some of these German possessions.

I had previously thrown out a similar suggestion to Colonel
House in a conversation which I had with him on the subject of
the disposal of the German Colonies. He agreed that they could
not be restored to Germany. But he was not disposed to regard
with favour the idea of an American mandate for any of these
colonies, his view being that "America could not run colonies.
Their experiment with the Philippines had not been a great
success. You required a special knack for handling colonies,
which did not interfere with the population, and which allowed
them to go their own way."

After some further talk it was decided to have a more formal consideration of the whole problem.

At a subsequent meeting the disposal of these colonies led to a prolonged discussion. All the observations made were on the accepted basis that not a single captured colony should be restored to Germany by the Peace Treaty. There was complete unanimity amongst the Dominion representatives, whose forces had conquered South-West Africa and German islands in the Southern Seas, that these should be retained by the particular Dominion whose armies had effected the conquest. There was a considerable difference of opinion as to how the remaining German Colonies should be disposed of. As I have already pointed out, there was no avidity on the part of the majority of the British Ministers to add to our Colonial possessions. The late Mr. Walter Long (afterwards Lord Long) was the only exception. I repeatedly urged that America should shoulder a part of the burden. I regarded colonies not as possessions but as Imperial obligations and I asked "why the Americans should not offer to take their share in any control that might be necessary. I see no reason why we should be asked to do it all."

I subsequently called attention to some wise observations made on this subject during the summer by the Canadian Premier, Sir Robert Borden, and remarked that there was a great deal to be said for the policy he then advocated:

"Sir Robert Borden had pointed out that it would create a very bad impression if the British Empire came out of this war with a great acquisition of territory, and if the United States undertook no new responsibilities. If America were to go away from the Conference with her share of guardianship, it would have a great effect on the world."

Sir Robert Borden (who was always in close touch with American opinion)

then read extracts from certain speeches made by President Wilson, in order to show the views which the President held. One of the most important assets that we could get out of the war would be assured goodwill and a clear understanding between Great Britain and the United States. There were very strong elements, such as the German and Irish, in the United States which were bitterly opposed to our Empire, and we must not put into the mouths of these people a plausible argument that we had gone into the war for territorial aggrandisement. He frankly said that, so far as Canada was concerned, she did not go into the war in order to add territory to the British Empire. In so far, however, as the colonies conquered by South Africa, Australia and New Zealand were concerned, he would be prepared to support their retention on one consideration, and one only, and that was that their acquisition was necessary for the future security of the Empire. As regards the remaining conquered territories, he was in favour of entrusting their control and dominion to whichever State was appointed as mandatory for that purpose by the League of Nations, on the lines suggested in General Smuts' paper. The mandate would be for the development of those countries in the interests of the inhabitants until they were capable of governing themselves. He assumed, of course, that the French and others who had occupied enemy colonies would agree to the same policy.

LORD CURZON suggested that we might be too ready to assume that the United States would be willing to accept these obligations. If she accepted any such responsibilities, she might have to accept them in Constantinople or Armenia before she accepted them in Africa.

MR. LLOYD GEORGE agreed that this was probable, but that by making the offer to America we would remove any prejudice against us on the ground of "land-grabbing." It was not a question of annexation, but of assuming a responsibility.

A short discussion followed as to the precise distinction between the occupation of a territory in a "possessory" and in a "mandatory" capacity.

It was generally agreed that "mandatory occupation" did not involve anything in the nature of condominium or international administration, but administration by a single Power on certain general lines laid down by the League of Nations. These lines would naturally include equality of treatment to all nations in respect of tariffs, concessions, and economic policy generally. Similarly, there would be no militarisation, or fortification of the territory in question. Finally, there would be a right of appeal from the mandatory Power to the League of Nations on the part of anyone who considered himself ill-treated, or claimed that the conditions laid down by the League of Nations were not being fulfilled. Subject to such appeal, which might involve the League of Nations withdrawing the mandate in the case of deliberate and persistent violation of its conditions, the mandate would be continuous until such time as the inhabitants of the country themselves were fit for self-government.

LORD MILNER pointed out that the mandatory principle was not altogether an innovation. Our administration of Egypt for thirty-five years was carried on on that principle, and subject to innumerable obligations which we consistently fulfilled, at one time even to the extent of giving a decided preference to other nations over ourselves. The more we had been able to get rid in Egypt of a condominium, the more satisfactorily were we able to carry out our duties as a mandatory.

.   .   .   .   .

MR. HUGHES suggested that, both as regards the Pacific Islands, which were in the immediate neighbourhood of Australia, and presumably in the case of German South-West Africa, the differentiating of their occupation from that of the adjoining Dominion would create insuperable difficulties in respect of customs, laws, coastwise trade, methods of economic development, labour laws, etc. He had made it perfectly clear to President Wilson that the demand for the Pacific Islands was being put forward in the interests of Australian security, and not in the interests of the British Empire.

LORD MILNER urged that the question of South-West Africa and the Pacific Islands should be treated quite separately from that of the other occupied colonies. We should make it clear with regard to them, from the outset, that we treated them as belonging to the Dominions concerned.

At this stage General Smuts put in an earnest and powerful plea for a British mandate in respect of German East Africa. He urged that:

. . . The British Empire was the great African Power right along the eastern half of the continent, and securing East Africa would give us through communication along the whole length of the continent— a matter of the greatest importance from the point of view both of land and of air communications. In his opinion it was not only on the grounds of our conquests and sacrifices, but on the obvious geographical situation, that we were entitled to make a strong claim to being the mandatory in that region. Personally he would give up very much in order to attain that. He was not putting in a claim to East Africa for the South African Union, but the view he had expressed would be very strongly felt in the Union, which had taken the main share in the conquest of East Africa. He would prefer to see the United States in Palestine rather than East Africa.

MR. BALFOUR suggested that the line of argument pursued by General Smuts was perhaps playing a little fast-and-loose with the notion of mandatory occupation.

After a few speeches of this kind, in which objection was raised by some speakers to parting with any of the captured territories in the East, West or the Southern Seas, Mr. Montagu made the very caustic observation that "it would be very satisfactory if we could find some convincing argument for not annexing all the territories in the world."

In a discussion about the particular African possessions which we were prepared to give to Italy by way of compensation under the terms of the Treaty of London, we had been confronted by a strong protest from the Navy against giving up any of our African conquests, on the ground that they were essential as naval bases. This egregious document recommended that French Somaliland would be a more suitable and valuable concession for the Italians.

Sir Robert Borden said that "if the chief result of this war was a scramble for territory by the Allied nations, it would be merely a prelude to further wars." Mr. Churchill said that "if we had to give up some territory he was strongly in favour of giving up German East Africa. We already had more territory in that part of the world than we had either the wealth or the capacity to develop. On the other hand, . . . an African colony used for purposes of investment would raise no strategic question."

When we came to discuss Palestine and Mesopotamia, Lord Curzon was opposed to the idea of an American mandate for either of these two countries. He said that the inhabitants of the country themselves were unanimously in favour of a British mandate.

He drew attention to a resolution in favour of British trusteeship, passed by a meeting of American Jews, which was reported in the previous day's *Times*.

The Emir Feisal had stated emphatically that while he was prepared to throw in all his influence with the British in Palestine, even to the extent of helping the Jews, he would oppose any other Power with all his might. On the other hand, Lord Curzon continued, there was Armenia, where the inhabitants themselves were asking for either French or American protection.

Lord Milner supported my views as to the desirability of securing the co-operation of America in the future control of the German possessions across the seas. He said "that he wished to get America in in any case. He considered that the future peace of the world depended on a good understanding between us, and regarded this policy of a mandate by the League of Nations not as a mere cloak for annexation, but as a bond of union leading to better working between the United States and ourselves. The essential thing was that we should survey the whole field from that point of view." In summing up the discussion, expressing agreement with Lord Milner, I said that "the first step was to find out if the United States were prepared to take their share of responsibility in a mandatory capacity."

No definite recommendations were come to by the Imperial Cabinet, but I gathered as a result of the discussions that the majority of the members of the Cabinet would be in favour of my sounding President Wilson on the question as to whether he was prepared to join the other Powers in accepting the position of a mandatory, and I certainly inferred from the course of the discussion that with one exception the Cabinet would not be averse to handing over the mandate for East Africa to the United States of America.

The outstanding feature of the conversations that took place was the complete unanimity with which the Imperial War Cabinet accepted the doctrine of the mandate in respect of enemy possessions, except in South-West Africa and the islands conquered by Australia and New Zealand.

One cannot appreciate the attitude adopted by the Ministers who represented the various parts of the Empire on the question of the restoration to Germany of her lost colonies without some understanding of the German colonial policy and the use to which German statesmen openly proclaimed they intended to put their colonial empire. German Ministers and publicists advertised their colonial aspirations with great frankness during the progress of the War. Their ambition was to found a black empire in

Africa extending across that continent from the Atlantic to the Indian Ocean. The territory comprised in their minimum claim would cover 7½ million kilometres (3 million more than the whole of India) and would include a population of 30,000,000. German publicists laid special stress on the fact that as a large proportion of the native population was Mohammedan, there would thus be a more formidable Mohammedan Empire in Africa than in Turkey and it would be all under German control. As one of the most reputable of the German writers put it, in a document issued during the War: "We are fighting . . . indirectly in order to get back our colonial territory *and to increase it. We are fighting for an Empire in Central Africa.*"

Portugal and Belgium were in the main the contributors to this enlarged empire, but France also was to yield her share. The German Colonial Secretary, a very able statesman and also one who, in comparison with some of his associates, was reputed to be a very moderate man, thus expounded the official German view:

(*a*) Africa is no longer the dark continent, but has become the fore-land of Europe, with a great part to play as the producer of tropical raw materials for European industries.

(*b*) The existing partition of Africa among the European colonising States is recent, haphazard, and accidental, with the result that weak and ineffective Powers are in possession of gigantic areas which they cannot develop, while Germany, in spite of her position and power, finds herself left in the cold with considerably smaller and far-scattered territories.

He therefore claims that when peace is made there shall be a repartition of Africa among the belligerent European countries. "In the treaty of peace there can only be the question of a *fresh partition.*"

(*c*) In this fresh partition Germany must receive a continuous domain, large in extent because the war in Africa has shown that defensive power is in direct proportion to the size of the continuous area; with frontiers on both oceans and fortified naval bases, the importance of which has been demonstrated in this war.

(*d*) This domain must be adequately defended by white and especially black troops, but conventions ought to be concluded between the Powers against the militarisation of the natives, who should not be employed in European or other campaigns outside their country.

Belgium was to be held as a pawn in this game. The Congo was to be the price of the evacuation of Belgium. The price of the withdrawal of German armies from French soil was to be the surrender of French colonies in Central Africa. Britain was to be told that unless she restored German East Africa and perhaps South-West Africa, Germany would retain her hold on Belgium and the Northern provinces of France. As one of their writers put it: "If the English are confronted with the choice of either allowing us to have these Colonies or of seeing us establish a direct or indirect dominion over Belgium, it will come easier to them to let us have the Colonial Empire." That was the peace strategy of the German leaders.

To what use were they intending to put their African Empire? The primary motive put forward by all the German writers is economic—"a domain for the production of tropical raw materials for German industry, with the help of black labour working under white supervision." That is a perfectly legitimate aspiration and the sooner it is met by some equitable and practical adjustment, the better it will be for the peace and well-being of the world. General Smuts thought that Germany's reasonable claim for a fair share of African products should be met by the setting up of an International Board of Control in Central Africa, made up of representatives of Britain, France, Germany, Belgium and Portugal, with an American chairman, whose functions would be confined to a distribution of tropical raw materials in Central Africa. But the aspect of German ambitions in this continent which alarmed Britain, the Dominions and India was of a totally different character. It was the avowed purpose of Germany's policy to use this huge African territory, which she contemplated demanding as the price of peace, for strategic purposes, inimical— and in certain contingencies possibly fatal—to the interests of both the British and the French Empires in tropical Africa and in tropical seas. A memorandum prepared for the German Imperial Cabinet in July, 1918, gives a summary of the aims proclaimed by German writers. The strategic case against the British

Empire was very bluntly put by Emil Zimmermann, an ex-Civil Servant:

For our present unfavourable position in the Far East England— apart from Japan—is chiefly responsible; the principal opponent of our expansion in the Pacific is Australia. But we shall never be able to exercise pressure upon Australia from a base in the South Seas; we might very well do so from East Africa. Australia needs for its exports (minerals, wool, meat, tallow, butter, cheese, wheat) an open road through the Indian Ocean. This road can be gravely menaced from East Africa. It is true Australian commerce might take the route round the Cape; but even on this route merchant ships would hardly be safe against attacks directed from East Africa. The policy therefore, both of Australia and of India, might be very strongly influenced by pressure from German *Mittel-Afrika*, and British policy, too, since England has as strong an interest in unimpeded commercial inter-course with India and Australia as India and Australia have in un-impeded intercourse with England.

If we have a position of strength in *Mittel-Afrika*, with which India and Australia must reckon, then we can compel both of them to re-spect our wishes in the South Seas and in Eastern Asia, and we thereby drive the first wedge into the compact front of our opponents in Eastern Asia.

He looked forward to a German Africa empire containing a population of 50,000,000 blacks and 500,000 Germans out of which "it will be possible at any moment to mobilise an army of 1,000,000 men." Sir Erle Richards, in the document he prepared on the subject for the War Cabinet, says:

Some writers [German] lay stress upon the idea that this army will be used in Africa in order to keep the armies of her enemies employed there. But the majority anticipate that these troops will be used in any war as an addition to the German forces, and indeed, it is hardly likely that if Germany possessed these large supplies of trained troops, she would not use them in future wars. . . . Great stress is laid by all writers [German] on the importance of the harbours as providing bases from which they will be able to strike at the world's trade.

Great stress is laid on the fact that this German Central Africa will completely dominate the strategy of the Indian and Atlantic Oceans, and will cut British land-power in Africa in two. Thus Oskar Karstedt (after describing the territorial limits of the new Europe):

"A German *Mittel-Afrika*, as it is here sketched in outline, would besides yield the great advantage, from the point of view of world-policy, that it would set a bar, once for all, to England's effort to become mistress of Africa from the Cape to Cairo. Within the territory, further, there would be enough places on the coast, which, when properly fortified and equipped, would be capable of furnishing Germany with the naval bases which it absolutely *must have* upon the Atlantic and the Indian Oceans. Such a German oversea Empire in Africa would be able to bid defiance to the strongholds of British power in Africa (Egypt and South Africa), the mainstays of the whole British world-power. It would give us, not only a great part of what we want in order to be economically independent of England, but it would also put the means into our hands of *striking England home* at any moment with the help of our navy and the man-power latent in this future dominion."

The smallest block mentioned . . . will comprise an area of between 7 and $7\frac{1}{2}$ million square kilometres (*cf.* area of India at a little over $4\frac{1}{2}$ million square kilometres), with a population of 30 million. This population will not only be capable of industrial exploitation on a large scale, but also of yielding an enormous black army under white officers, which will be a sufficient menace to French North Africa on the one hand, and Egypt and Arabia on the other, and will protect the southern flank of the Turco-German route to the East, through Asia Minor and Mesopotamia. When this great army, invulnerable in the vastnesses of Central Africa, is backed up by adequate submarine, destroyer, and cruiser bases on both Atlantic and India seaboards, British seapower in those oceans will be dominated, and Central Africa will become for Germany the stepping-stone to world-power. From Central Europe through Central Africa to world-dominion is the programme of these writers.

The development of German world-power from a great Central African base will be materially assisted by the influence of the Mohammedan religion. German Central Africa will be largely Mohammedan in religion, and will thus enlist on the side of the Germans the powerful Mohammedan influence in North Africa, in the Soudan, in Egypt, Arabia, and in Asia generally. Central Africa will thus be only another step in the union of German militarism with Mohammedan fanaticism towards the conquest of the world. Through its Mohammedan affinities the Central African system will make its influence felt over a great part of the globe.

As far as the Pacific islands were concerned, the case—from the point of view of Australian security and of restoring to Germany colonies which would enable her to establish submarine bases within 20 miles of the shores of Australia—was very forcibly put by Mr. Hughes in the course of the discussion.

The Imperial War Cabinet approached the problem of the disposal of the German Colonies with all these considerations in front of them. If they were reluctant to restore to Germany her lost possessions overseas, German Ministers and German writers were largely responsible for the attitude of suspicion and of anxiety with regard to the possible use that could be made by a hostile Germany of the opportunities which might be afforded her if she were once more put in command of large tracts of territory scattered here and there along the ocean shores of the world, on every line of communication between Britain and her Empire and the Empire and Britain. The encouragement given to the Boer rebellion from South-West Africa and the incidents of this war, such as shelter afforded to German raiders in the Indian Ocean, had taught Germany how unlimited were the possibilities provided by these possessions of inflicting dangerous wounds upon the British Empire. Fortunately for us it was too late for Germany to utilise her advantages when she first discovered them. But should there be any future conflicts between Germany and ourselves—which Heaven avert, but which all the same, Hell and its agents in all countries are doing their utmost to precipitate—Germany would be fully alive to the usefulness of these vast tropical territories with their numerous inlets, their great coastline fronting upon the East and upon the West, their submarine and air bases and the myriads of virile men who live in these lands, and whose aptitude for soldiering was so effectively demonstrated by General von Lettow in his memorable campaign against great odds.

In view, therefore, of the open and avowed intentions of German colonial policy for the future, it cannot be wondered at that there was complete unanimity amongst Allied statesmen that the German Colonies should not be restored to their former owners. If von Lettow could accomplish so much with a few thousand black troops led by a commander of genius, what could be achieved by a vast Negro army of 1,000,000 men? No reconsideration of mandates is conceivable except under conditions and guarantees which would make it impossible for Germany to convert her hold on an African colony into a formidable military, naval or aerial menace to her neighbours. She has shown us in Spain that she has no scruples about the using of a trained black army to destroy democracy in Europe and that she has no racial prejudices that will prevent her from sending German soldiers to co-operate with African legionaries against the liberties of a white race in its own country.

Inasmuch as the Imperial War Cabinet were more particularly concentrating on these aspects of the Treaty upon which a preliminary discussion with President Wilson was desirable in order to clear up any possible misunderstanding before the Congress formally opened, we devoted a considerable part of our attention to the Italian claims and to the composition of the League of Nations. The interchange of views at the Imperial Cabinet on these questions will be given in the chapters which deal respectively with these subjects.

3. THE INTERALLIED CONFERENCE TO PREPARE FOR THE PEACE CONGRESS

M. CLEMENCEAU and Marshal Foch arrived in London on the 30th of November and were given such a reception as I have never seen accorded to any foreign visitors to our shores. The dimensions of the crowd and still more the intensity of the enthusiasm displayed were beyond anything I had ever witnessed on such occasions. The King met the distinguished visitors at the station and drove Marshal Foch in his carriage through the crowded streets to Buckingham Palace. I accompanied M. Clemenceau to the French Embassy. I have never seen this hardened old veteran so much moved. He knew England and Englishmen well but he never thought they were capable of displaying such emotional warmth. It was to him a genuine and an agreeable surprise—a surprise which he expressed at every street through which he passed. The scene at Trafalgar Square was overwhelming.

The first meeting of the Conference which ensued was held in Downing Street that evening. The discussion was confined to the arrangements which had to be made for the occupation of the Rhine bridgeheads by Allied troops. The French were represented by Marshal Foch and General Weygand; the British Army by Sir Henry Wilson. I was accompanied by Mr. Balfour. M. Clemenceau had a social engagement which prevented his attendance. When I discovered the real topic which was to be raised, I realised why he was absent. The wily old politician, knowing our partiality for Foch and the debt of gratitude we owed him, deemed it advisable that the first introduction of French ideas as to the future of the Rhineland should be left to him.

This meeting is notable for being the first intimation given to the British Government that the French intended to secure control over all the territory on the left bank of the Rhine. As was his wont, Foch came straight to the point without wasting words:

. . . Considering, however, only military necessities, whatever the form of government on the right bank of the Rhine might be, namely, an Empire, Republic or Confederation, there would be concentrated there from 55 to 75 million Germans, and these, if they wished, might endeavour to repeat the experience of 1914. In such an event, what would be the means of defence? If there were no material barrier set up, and no special precautions taken, the invasion of France, Luxemburg, and Belgium, might again be undertaken. More particularly, the Belgian coast would be easier for the enemy to reach, for they now realised the importance of it, and would endeavour to cut England from France. The natural barrier against such an invasion was the Rhine.

MR. LLOYD GEORGE asked what Marshal Foch proposed?

MARSHAL FOCH said that Germany ought to be limited to the right bank of the Rhine. Even so, she would have a population of some 60 millions. We had to consider, therefore, what arrangements should be made on the left bank of the Rhine. It was perfectly useless to rely on neutral States as barriers. Belgium and Luxemburg as neutrals really constituted no effective defence. Hence, there was nothing for it but to have an armed State ready to fight, if necessary, against Germany. He then considered the States on the left bank of the Rhine. France, Belgium, Alsace-Lorraine and Luxemburg would give an aggregate of 49 million inhabitants. If to these were added the Rhenish Provinces on the left bank of the river, there would be a population of 54,900,000. Practically, therefore, in case of a coalition of all the countries on the left bank of the Rhine, there would be 55 millions against 65 to 75 millions on the right bank. With this agglomeration of countries, namely, France, Belgium and Luxemburg, properly organised in a military sense, it would probably be practicable to hold the line of the Rhine. If, however, the line of the Rhine were forced by a surprise attack there would be a repetition of the war of 1914, and in this case it was absolutely essential that Great Britain should lend her assistance. Otherwise Germany would become the master of the whole of the West. Hence it was essential that there should be a permanent mutual assistance between all the countries of the West. France, Belgium, Luxemburg, the Rhine lands left of the river, and Great Britain—all organised for the defence of the Western front. We ought to prepare an Alliance, *including the Rhenish Provinces*, whether they were in an autonomous organisation or not (a question which he did not wish to discuss) which would provide forces fully organised to safeguard the position. The control of the organisation should be under Great Britain, France and Belgium.

MR. LLOYD GEORGE asked what he contemplated would be the political condition of the German Provinces on the left bank of the Rhine? Would they be independent, or who would govern them?

MARSHAL FOCH said that they would probably be independent. They might consist of one State or several States. All that he insisted on was that they should be included in an economic and military system. His object was not to annex or to conquer, but merely to profit by our experience and provide proper defence against the 75 million inhabitants on the right bank of the Rhine.

MR. LLOYD GEORGE asked Marshal Foch how he reconciled his proposals with President Wilson's Fourteen Points?

MARSHAL FOCH thought it could be arranged. We could defend it on the grounds that we have before us a political organisation which, in spite of treaties, Hague Conventions, etc., has launched on the world the late tremendous war. The signature of this nation to any treaty could not be trusted. As this was the case, it was necessary to take material precautions. The military barrier of the Rhine was the obvious precaution to take.

MR. LLOYD GEORGE asked what would be the position if the inhabitants of the left bank of the Rhine did not like this scheme and declared in favour of being joined to Germany?

MARSHAL FOCH said that they must be brought to our side by the attraction of our economic organisation. There would be another attraction, that it was better to be on the side of the victors than of the conquered.

MR. LLOYD GEORGE asked whether Marshal Foch did not fear the danger of creating a new Alsace-Lorraine on the other side, which would in course of years result in a new war of revenge?

MARSHAL FOCH said that, of course, he would take precautions to conciliate the feelings and interests of these people.

MR. BONAR LAW pointed out that Germany had said exactly the same thing. We ourselves had tried for years to conciliate the Irish.

MARSHAL FOCH then handed Mr. Lloyd George a note he had himself prepared on this question, and asked him to read and study it. The whole problem was a very grave and large one and required mature consideration.

MR. LLOYD GEORGE said that he would study Marshal Foch's memorandum very carefully. Anything that emanated from Marshal Foch would start with a predisposition in its favour. Nevertheless, we must be very careful not to create new problems in Europe.

MARSHAL FOCH concurred in this consideration.

This is the first occasion when the differences between the British and French point of view about the future settlement of the territories on the left bank of the Rhine were revealed. But the fact that this was the first topic raised by the French at the first Conference held after the Armistice to discuss the Peace Settlement, shows the importance they attached to it.

The first full Conference was held in Downing Street the following day. France was represented by M. Clemenceau and Marshal Foch, and Italy by Signor Orlando, the Italian Premier, and Baron Sonnino, the Foreign Secretary. Colonel House was to have represented the United States, but a serious illness which incapacitated him for some weeks detained him in Paris. America was thus unrepresented at these important preliminary conversations. It is rather characteristic of President Wilson's suspicious nature that he would not depute the task of representing his views, or even of reporting the views of the delegates of other nations, to the American Ambassadors in France or in London.

The first subject discussed was that of Reparations. An account of this discussion is given in the chapter on Reparations.

The next subject that came up for consideration was the trial of the Kaiser for his supreme personal responsibility in precipitating the terrible calamities of wholesale murder and destruction upon the world. Lord Birkenhead's report on this subject was circulated to all the delegates at the Conference before the meeting. I opened the proceedings by calling attention to its purport. Up to that date I had made no public allusion to the subject. In fact I made no public reference to it until the 9th of December, a week after the Conference had come to a conclusion as to the action which the Allies had resolved to take. It has been suggested that this proposal was due entirely to my initiative and that, although the Allied Governments gave reluctant and lukewarm acquiescence to this idea, I was alone responsible for it and for pressing it forward. Let those who still think that, peruse extracts from the official record of the discussions that took place at the Imperial War Cabinet (which I have already quoted), and at the first Allied Conference after the Armistice. Here is a summary of the discussion which took place on the latter occasion as to the attitude to be adopted by the Allies towards the ex-Kaiser:

MR. LLOYD GEORGE referred to papers which had been circulated to all those present in regard to the ex-Kaiser. Those documents consisted of a statement made to the British War Cabinet by Sir F. E. Smith, Attorney-General, on behalf of the Law Officers of the Crown, and the recommendations of a legal committee of very highly expert jurists which had been appointed by the British Law Officers to the Crown to advise them.

The opinion of the British Law Officers had been that the ex-Kaiser ought to be punished, and that, if the ex-Kaiser was made justiciable, the charges on which he should be tried should be the following:

1. His responsibility for the invasion of Belgium in breach of international law, and for all consequent criminal acts which took place.

2. His responsibility in the matter of unrestricted submarine warfare.

3. Offences in the category of the execution of Captain Fryatt.

He then read extracts from the report of the Committee of Jurists who had advised that it is desirable to take proceedings against the ex-Kaiser personally, had suggested an International Tribunal composed of representatives of the chief Allied States and of the United States of America.

A closely connected question, MR. LLOYD GEORGE pointed out, was that of the responsibility of officers in charge of prisoners' camps. In some of the German prisoners' camps the treatment of British prisoners had been very good; in others their treatment had been very bad. In such cases we ought to demand the surrender of those responsible and try them.

BARON SONNINO said that he had read the reports, which were very well produced.

He felt, however, that the question must be considered from the general political point of view. Were the Allies desirous of making the ex-Kaiser a patriotic martyr from the point of view of Germany of the future? Were we to examine whether the Bundesrath were not equally responsible? Was it right to examine whether the leaders of a nation were responsible for the action of the nation? Was not the nation responsible as a whole?

In this connection he pointed out that a nation usually gets the Government it deserves. He questioned the desirability of making a scape-goat. Was not St. Helena useful to the Bonapartists? The answer was "Yes"; and the régime of Napoleon III had been the result.

M. CLEMENCEAU said that he thought it would show an immense progress if we could punish the man who was guilty of a great historic crime like the declaration of war in August, 1914. All the Governments represented here to-day were proud of the principle of responsibility. As a rule, it only meant responsibility in newspaper articles and books, which the great criminals of the world could afford to laugh at. He was not one of those who was sure we could immediately set up a League of Nations. A great step, however, would have been taken towards international understanding if the peoples of the world could feel that the greatest criminals, such as the ex-Kaiser, would be brought to trial. He therefore supported energetically the proposition of Mr. Lloyd George that the ex-Kaiser and his accomplices should be brought before an international tribunal.

BARON SONNINO asked who were the accomplices?

M. CLEMENCEAU said that the Court must determine this. The ex-Crown Prince would certainly be the first of them. The same could not be said of some of the great soldiers, who had merely obeyed orders. If, however, we could get seven or eight persons, and make them responsible before an international tribunal, this would be an enormous progress for humanity. Hence, he regretted to have to separate himself from his friend Baron Sonnino and rally to Mr. Lloyd George. The ex-Kaiser was the person really responsible for the war, and this case must be entirely separated from that of camp commandants and others who had been guilty of ill-treating prisoners. These latter ought to be court-martialled. (MR. LLOYD GEORGE interjected that he agreed.) Frankly, he himself had no other idea than to bring the ex-Kaiser to justice. The people everywhere would be satisfied if this could be done. They will feel that justice will in future be done in the case of Kaisers and Kings just as much as in the case of common men. If this could be achieved, it would be a magnificent advance and a moral revolution.

MR. BONAR LAW said there was no doubt that public sentiment was with M. Clemenceau.

M. ORLANDO (the Italian Prime Minister) said that the question was exclusively one of sentiment and it had nothing to do with interests. Therefore, no surprise need be felt if he differed from his colleague, Baron Sonnino. It was a great question of the universal conscience of mankind. It was not a question for examination by a small Committee of expert lawyers. It was a matter of universal sentiment which touched the highest moral laws. We had just witnessed the reaction of the world from a veritable crime against humanity. There was something to be said in the past for ideas that nations should be responsible for the faults of their Governments, and there were historical instances of this. In the present case, however, we were not dealing with mere blunders, but with crimes, and the ex-Kaiser ought to pay like other criminals. The ex-Kaiser, for example, had decorated, personally, captains of submarines which had come straight back from perpetrating murder. As to the method by which the ex-Kaiser should be brought to book, this was a question of detail. One plan would be to have a declaration by the Allied Governments pronouncing the ex-Kaiser to be a criminal. On principle, however, he was in accord with Mr. Lloyd George and M. Clemenceau. As to the idea that the ex-Kaiser might be regarded as a martyr, he personally did not believe that he ever would be. Anyhow, we could not calculate for centuries ahead, and we had to deal with a very strong sentiment in all countries at the present time.

MR. LLOYD GEORGE said that if the question of principle were accepted there were two questions of detail he would like to raise. The first was in regard to the time for action. Should we await the Peace Conference, or, in the event of the United States of America agreeing with us, should we demand the surrender of the ex-Kaiser?

M. CLEMENCEAU said we ought to await the arrival of President Wilson.

MR. LLOYD GEORGE agreed, unless President Wilson was prepared to accept the views of the Conference on the subject.

M. CLEMENCEAU agreed in this.

It was agreed that: "A communication on this subject should be made to President Wilson, and Mr. Lloyd George undertook to put forward a draft telegram at the afternoon meeting."

MR. LLOYD GEORGE said that the second question was as to whether the condemnation of the ex-Kaiser was to be effected by the decision of the Governments, or as the result of a trial. The latter course was much the more striking.

M. CLEMENCEAU said that he stood for trial.

M. ORLANDO said that the question of the constitution of the Court presented almost insurmountable difficulties.

BARON SONNINO asked what would be done if Holland declined to give up the ex-Kaiser, basing herself on her tradition of Liberal views.

MR. LLOYD GEORGE said that Holland would then be put outside the League of Nations.

M. CLEMENCEAU agreed. . . . He said that there would be no question of Holland standing against the opinion of all the Allied Powers.

MR. BALFOUR said that if the action against the ex-Kaiser were taken by administrative action, as in the case of Napoleon, it would be a clear and simple course, but it would lose the advantages of a legal trial. On the other hand, the plan of a trial had the disadvantage that it would probably be necessary to bring in neutrals, and the Allies would lay themselves open to all the delays of the law which would weary the whole world. There had been a famous British political trial which had lasted seven years. It would be possible to drag into the trial all questions such as to whether Germany was justified in anticipating the completion of the Russian railway system. There would be all the arguments of lawyers, which would draw attention off the main fact that this man was the ringleader in the greatest crime against the human race on which the eyes of the whole world ought to be fixed.

M. CLEMENCEAU said he knew nothing about the methods on which the political trials were conducted in England. In France, however, an important political trial was now being held. The case was before the Senate. The Senate made its own procedure and gave instructions. It was a sovereign body and made its own law. If this course were adopted, all Mr. Balfour's objections in regard to procedure would disappear. There would be no neutrals on the Tribunal. They had no right to it, they had not intervened in the war, and had undergone no sacrifice. The right of constituting the Court belonged to those who had made sacrifices. The Allies had secured this right by their immense losses in men and sacrifices of all kinds.

MR. BALFOUR asked if this course would not take away all appearance of impartiality? If the Allies set up the Court themselves, where would be the moral effect before the world?

M. CLEMENCEAU said that all justice was relative, and that the impartiality of all judges was liable to be questioned. It was a misfortune which could not be helped. But when a crime took place on a scale so unprecedented in history, he thought that France, Great Britain, Italy, and the United States must place themselves high enough to take the responsibility for dealing with it.

MR. LLOYD GEORGE pointed out that every judge tried an offence against the society of which he was a member. The same would be applicable in the present case.

At the end of the meeting the following telegram was sent to President Wilson on behalf of the Prime Ministers of Britain, France and Italy:

At a Conference of the Governments of France, Great Britain, and Italy, held in London this morning, the three Governments agreed to recommend that a demand ought to be presented to Holland for the surrender of the person of the ex-Kaiser for trial by an international court, to be appointed by the Allies, on the charge of being the criminal mainly responsible for the War and the breaches of international law by the forces of Germany by land, sea, and air.

During its deliberations the Conference had before it the opinion of a Committee of nine of the most eminent jurists of the British Isles, who recommended unanimously that the ex-Kaiser and his principal accomplices should be brought to trial before a court consisting of nominees of the principal nations victorious in the war.

In coming to the conclusion set forth above, the Conference were influenced by the following principal considerations:

(a) That justice requires that the ex-Kaiser and his principal accomplices who designed and caused the war with its malignant purpose, or who were responsible for the incalculable sufferings inflicted upon the human race during the war, should be brought to trial and punished for their crimes.

(b) That the certainty of inevitable personal punishment for crimes against humanity and international right will be a very important security against future attempts to make war wrongfully or to violate international law, and is a necessary stage in the development of the authority of a League of Nations.

(c) That it will be impossible to bring to justice lesser criminals, such as those who have oppressed the French, Belgians, and other peoples, committed murder on the high seas, and maltreated prisoners of war, if the arch-criminal, who for thirty years has proclaimed himself the sole arbiter of German policy, and has been so in fact, escapes condign punishment.

(d) That the court by which the question of responsibility for the war and its grosser barbarities should be determined ought to be appointed by those nations who have played a principal part in winning the war, and have thereby shown their understanding of what freedom means and their readiness to make unlimited sacrifices in its behalf.

(This clause is intended to relate only to the composition of the court which will deal with crimes committed in connection with the late war, and is not intended to prejudice the question of the composition of international courts under a League of Nations.)

The Conference hopes that the Government of the United States will share its views and co-operate with the Allies in the presentation to Holland of a demand for the surrender of the person of the ex-Kaiser and of the Crown Prince for trial before an international court to be appointed by the Allies.

President Wilson subsequently intimated that he was in agreement with the decision arrived at by the Allies on this subject.

A topic was then raised over which I had the misfortune to be somewhat at variance with one or two important colleagues in the War Cabinet, namely the representation of Bolshevik Russia at the Peace Conference. A full account of this discussion will be given in the chapter on Russia.

Then came a discussion on the future of Constantinople during which various suggestions were made to fill up the gap caused by the withdrawal of the Russian claim to that city. It is not without interest to note that it was not suggested by anyone that this ancient capital of the Greek Empire should be restored to the Turks.

Many questions of a temporary character arose out of the working of the Armistice terms. They were all adjusted, and thus ended this three days' Conference of the Ministers of the victorious countries. Its deliberations are worthy of examination, as they are a more reliable test of the temper and inclination of the victors in the hour of triumph than a few random phrases culled from the oratory of irresponsible persons who were still twirling their rattles to amuse and to please the naturally excited and delighted crowds in the street. In the passages I have quoted there is not a sentence which, twenty years after, any of the statesmen uttering it, had they all lived to this hour, would have wished to delete.

Throughout the whole of the discussions of the Supreme Council on the conditions of the Armistice as well as on the terms of peace, it was taken for granted that the establishment of a League of Nations would constitute an essential part of the settlement. It is true that neither M. Clemenceau nor Baron Sonnino took any special interest in the idea. Their minds were concentrated on the purely national issues affecting their own countries, and they were not convinced that an Association of Nations would achieve the purpose for which it was designed. They both took a somewhat cynical view of all idealistic projects. Clemenceau was by nature a man of little faith in human nature, and much has happened since to justify his distrust of international co-operation for peace. But both M. Clemenceau and Baron Sonnino realised that public opinion amongst their own people had been converted to the desirability of making the experiment, and they had committed themselves to supporting proposals which would be incorporated in the settlement. The best proof they gave of their good faith was that they chose enthusiasts for the League as their representatives on the committee that framed its Constitution.

4. PEACE CONFERENCE PLANS

IT was agreed that the Conference should be held at the earliest possible date. Paris was also finally fixed as the meeting-place. This selection was made in opposition to the view which had been previously expressed by the British Government and also by Colonel House, who were apprehensive lest the atmosphere of Paris—naturally excited and exasperated by the events of the past four and a half years—should not be conducive to that calm and detachment so essential to a durable settlement of highly controverted subjects. For that reason I had urged that some neutral city like Geneva should be chosen. But Clemenceau claimed that France, as the greatest sufferer and the scene of the fiercest struggles of the War, ought to have the honour of having its capital chosen as the site of the Conference. At first the Americans took our view strongly. But President Wilson during his recent visit to Paris was persuaded to give in to the French claim. No one had better reason to regret his surrender than he had. He became a victim of that untameable ferocity of hatred and disdain which is so characteristic of the Parisian temper when someone dares to challenge its cherished prejudices or aspirations. When America gave in we could not hold out. So Paris was adopted, with consequences that were unpleasant to all critics of the extreme French view of the settlement. However, it is fair to admit that I cannot point out that in the sequel the purely Parisian influence made any serious impression on the actual stipulations of the document finally agreed to, since I cannot discover a single particular in which it has departed from the terms of peace laid down by the Allies before the War came to an end.

It had been uncertain at one time whether President Wilson would come to Europe, but when his final decision was arrived at, I received the following telegram from M. Clemenceau:

President Wilson's coming naturally changes some of our arrangements for the preparation of the Conference. It seems to me that we cannot begin the work before the President arrives. We ought all to agree in this respect. Besides, I think it would not be a bad idea to let the German Revolution settle itself a little in order that we may know, before proceeding, whom we have to confront. I propose that we should draw up some preliminary documents (*travaux préparatoires*) on the procedure to be followed, either in Paris or London, just as you wish. If we acted thus, the President on his arrival could make his observations without any delay, and the work would have been advanced. I am to see M. Sonnino this afternoon. I do not doubt that he will agree. Rather a serious question is as to whether the President intends being present at the Conference. I do not mind telling you that in my opinion that seems neither desirable nor possible. As he is Head of the State he is not in consequence on the same footing as we are. It seems impossible to me to admit one Head of the State, and not all. Besides which, Colonel House tells me that he does not think this is the President's intention. I am telling you this for your information, but I greatly hope that you on your side will elaborate a plan while I have one prepared here. I shall invite M. Sonnino to do the same, as well as Colonel House, and this done, I think that in two or three days an agreement will be reached.

CLEMENCEAU.

In spite, however, of the opinion expressed in this message as to the desirability of Wilson's being present at the Peace Conference, we were later informed by Sir William Wiseman, a confidant of the President:

Dec. 16th, 1918.
The President is not anxious to sit at the Peace Conference. On the contrary he thinks it would not be wise. At yesterday's interview Clemenceau told the President that, although he had been opposed to the idea, he had changed his mind after meeting him and urged him to attend as the chief American Delegate.

This change of view on M. Clemenceau's part meant that the astute French Premier had found during his conversations with President Wilson that he was more amenable than had been anticipated.

It was agreed that the Peace Congress should begin at the earliest day on which it would be convenient for President Wilson to attend—making allowance for a reasonable interval for informal conversations with him before the official opening of the Congress. As to procedure, the Supreme Council was inclined to agree that the Allied delegates should thrash out all the vital issues amongst themselves, and prepare definite and detailed proposals before submitting them to the Germans for their observations. This decision has been adversely criticised on the ground that in every other peace treaty both parties were present at the discussions, and the vanquished as well as the victors were given a full opportunity to present their case in the presence of each other before even provisional agreements were recorded.

The justification of the course pursued by the Allies is to be found in the immense range of the subjects which had to be dealt with, and the urgency of a settlement. Had every proposal been debated between the parties concerned, peace would not have been reached for at least two years. Meanwhile the Allies would have been compelled to maintain on enemy soil and in reserve in their own countries, huge armies at enormous expense. The cost would not have been recoverable from the enemy lands. The financial burden of achieving victory was crushing enough, without adding hundreds of millions for the expenses of a military occupation of vast territories whilst statesmen were engaged in debating and deciding the details of peace. Moreover, men who were anxious to get back to their former vocations would have been kept under arms idling in improvised cantonments. President Wilson experienced great difficulty in keeping any considerable part of his civilian army in France after the Armistice. They were afraid of losing their jobs and of others taking them. He therefore had to send his men home as fast as he could find shipping to take them.

We also experienced great difficulties and ran grave dangers over the slowness with which demobilisation proceeded. There were threats of mutiny which were not easy to overcome. One contingent threatened to march on London, and Sir William Robertson at one critical moment had to contemplate the possibility of having to fire on the mutineers. So serious was the menace to order created by the discontent amongst the troops, that at one time I had to leave the peace discussions in Paris in order to deal with it. Sir William Robertson, who was in command of the Army in the Home Counties, afterwards told me that he was not certain that he could depend upon his troops to quell disturbances. He doubted if they would in the last resort fire on comrades who marched on London.

In Paris there were grave riots. The conscripts wanted to return to their homes now that the peril to their country was over and past. An early peace was imperative. Every week's delay was charged with danger. It was a choice of two evils, and in deciding on the course to pursue we chose the lesser. It gave the appearance of a dictated peace, without a hearing being accorded to the vanquished nations. But so in effect were the Treaties of Brest Litovsk and of Bucharest. They were both imposed at the point of the sword. Before Germany finally signed the Versailles Treaty she was afforded time and opportunity to present her criticisms and counter-suggestions. Her reply produced in several vital respects a substantial territorial alteration in the Peace Treaty in her favour, and a promise of general disarmament which, if it had been honoured, would have changed the history of the world.

5. THE TWO ELECTIONS: AMERICA AND GREAT BRITAIN

BEFORE I come to deal with the visit of President Wilson to London, it is essential to an intelligent understanding of the course of the negotiations to call attention to two events, one of which seriously impaired and finally destroyed the President's negotiating authority to conclude a peace in the name and on behalf of his own country, whilst the other considerably strengthened the position of the British Government in dealing with the problems of the peace.

First of all, to take the misfortune which undermined the prestige of the President and in the sequel ultimately proved to be a world catastrophe, for it severed America from co-operation with the victors in establishing the kind of peace which he himself had laboured so hard to achieve. In November, before the date of the Armistice, the biennial elections took place in America to fill vacancies in the Senate and the House of Representatives. The political complexion of these two Chambers depended on the result. The War was still on and every consideration of prudence and fairness enjoined on the President the wisdom of refraining from any party appeal to the electorate. His best and most sagacious friends entreated him not to antagonise a party which constituted half the nation, and which had given him throughout the War loyal, ungrudging and effective support. In further proof of the unwisdom of any interference in these elections which would antagonise the Republicans, I will quote a few sentences from a memorandum written about the elections by a distinguished Democratic lawyer who was personally attached to the President, and who did his utmost to dissuade him from plunging into a contest which did not affect his tenure of office. This gentleman afterwards urged the President to take with him to Paris one or two influential Republican leaders who were in general agreement with his policy on the League:

The War was drawing to a successful close and during its continuance thousands of Republicans and Independents had been working under Mr. Wilson's leadership and sacrificing their private interests and forgetting their political affiliations. Many had served without the slightest compensation. There were scores of Republicans in the Senate and House who had voted consistently for the President's policies and held up his hands during the struggle, at a time when many of his own party were doing their best to thwart him. Loyal Republicans and disloyal Democrats were candidates for re-election.

Nevertheless the President wrote and published a letter during the contest urging the electors to vote for Democrats only. It was a fatal error of judgment and of character. Without this message it is agreed that the President's supporters would have won the election easily, but this throwing over of men who had subordinated their party loyalties to the national interest and given him consistent support was regarded as an outrage on the chivalries which should obtain in public life, and the consequent resentment amongst fair-minded men and women who were not strongly partisan ended in a signal defeat for the party which the President had thus so shabbily sought to serve. The result was disastrous for his influence as the first delegate of the American Republic in the Congress of the Nations.

No treaty of peace signed by an American President has any validity until it secures the formal ratification of the American Senate. This august body works through a powerful Foreign Relations Committee which has always been jealous of its functions. It has a tradition of not allowing itself to be taken for granted. In parliamentary countries the Government of the day must necessarily represent a majority in the House that controls administration. In America the President may belong to one party and the majority in Congress to another. The Senate has therefore always displayed its independence of the Executive in matters specially delegated to its charge by the Constitution. The Chairman of this formidable Senatorial committee— Mr. Cabot Lodge—happened to have an insurmountable dislike of President Wilson which was haughtily reciprocated by the President. Each viewed the other with supreme disdain—for different reasons. Lodge regarded Wilson as a professorial sentimentalist who knew nothing of the realities of life at home or abroad. Wilson regarded Lodge as a narrow, pretentious and pompous Senator who was more bent on exalting his office than on discharging his duties. Apart from personal antipathies they were men who had an essentially different outlook on the great problems of the world. The first moment the President in a speech outlined his ideas as to a League of Nations, Lodge in another speech—by the way a very able critical deliverance—proceeded to tear it to pieces. As long as the Senate was Democratic, Lodge was powerless. Some of the most distinguished and respected of the Republican leaders sympathised with Wilson's views on the League, notably ex-President Taft, Elihu Root, the famous jurist and statesman, and Mr. C. E. Hughes, the present head of the Supreme Court. But the turnover at the November elections gave Cabot Lodge his chance. He had now a Republican majority in the Senate and consequently on his Committee, and a majority thoroughly exasperated against the President by the treatment accorded to them by him at the election. The whole situation was changed. The President as a delegate to the Peace Congress was subject to the veto of his most inveterate personal and political foe.

The President had still an opportunity to recover his lost power. Taft and Root were high-minded men and not the shallow type who change their opinions on vital issues from any considerations of partisan pique. They believed honestly in the League idea and were prepared to stand by it and work for it. Had the President taken both, or even one, of them with him to the Peace Congress, all would still have been well. Their influence on the Republican party was much greater than that of Lodge. At best Lodge might have split his party but he would not have carried the Senate. The Treaty would have been ratified by the Senate, America would have been a member of the League exercising an incomparable influence on world opinion, and the whole stream of international effort would have been diverted into the fertilising channels of peace. But in spite of urgent appeals from some of his best supporters, the President decided not to associate any of the Republican leaders with him at the Peace Congress. The delegation must for all practical purposes be a Democratic representation, entirely subordinate to the President's will

and direction. Neither he nor his party would share the renown
of this world settlement with any political rivals. The peace must
be a Democratic triumph, and not a single leaf in the laurel crown
should be placed on a Republican brow. The President thus threw
away both these chances, and he came to Europe to represent the
greatest democratic country in the world discredited by the universal knowledge that he was no longer the authentic spokesman
of its opinions, or the real accredited interpreter of its policy.

I was anxious that the President should visit our island. Had
he passed Britain by on his way to the Peace Congress it might
have seemed an unfriendly act. I had never been quite certain of
his real attitude towards this country. It had never, like Theodore
Roosevelt's, been undisguisedly cordial. In none of his speeches
had there been any warmth or generosity in his allusion to the
land from which his ancestors sprang. When he was playing the
part of the great Neutral, there was something to be said for that
cold aloofness, but when we were fighting what he at last acknowledged to be a righteous battle with gigantic losses to keep the
struggle going, whilst he was loitering on the way to the field,
he might have uttered one word of sympathy with our terrible
sacrifices and the gallant behaviour of our dauntless men. But
that was not his way. Not a word of generous appreciation issued
from his lips. I shall give some illustrations of this utter lack of
the human touch later on. We know how he distrusted Page—
one of the most beloved of the American Ambassadors—because
he thought him "too friendly to England." This was the tragic
defect which detracted from the renown of a man who had some
of the fundamentals of greatness in his gifts of mind and character.

The next important event which preceded the peace conversations with President Wilson was the British General Election.
Parliament had long exceeded the term of its natural life. Seven
years was the legal, and six years the traditional and accepted
limit of the life of a given Parliament. In 1917 that limit was cut
down by the Parliament Act to five years. The House of Commons had been elected in December, 1910, and it had thus exceeded the statutory span by three years. Its life had been twice

extended because it was thought impolitic and dangerous to have a contest of parties whilst the War was actually on. But now the War was over, and there was no reasonable pretext for a further renewal. There existed another factor which had always been regarded as a prelude to an inevitable election. The franchise had been considerably extended in 1917. On this occasion the numbers of the register had been trebled and for the first time millions of women had been given the Parliamentary vote. It would have been an outrage to decide vast issues which affected the lives of over 40 million men and women, three-fourths of whom had no voice in the election of the existing Parliament, without consulting them on the policy and plans of the Executive. Every argument of fairness, justice and genuine respect for free and democratic institutions demanded an early election. In France and Italy there had been no such extension of the franchise. There was no excuse for postponement, except the fact that the Opposition, which had done its best to harass and thwart the Government at every moment of difficulty and crisis during the past two years, considered the hour of victory an unpropitious one to challenge the opinion of the country on the record and efficiency of the Administration they had sought to turn out at one of the most critical hours in the conflict.

There was another reason for seeking the verdict of the country at this juncture on the question of confidence in the Government. Speaking at the commencement of the election at the Central Hall I said:

It is a moribund Parliament. It has not the necessary authority from the people to deal with the great problems with which we are confronted, and there is no time to lose. We must get the mandate immediately. Somebody will have to go to the Peace Conference with authority from the people of this country to speak in their name. There are problems which affect the world, problems which specially affect the people of this Empire, and whoever goes there must go with the authority of the people behind him. You must have authority immediately to begin on the task of reconstruction. Delay there is dangerous. . . .

I wish it had been possible to get every party, every section of the community, united for this task, the best brains of every party, the best traditions of every party. Every party has good traditions, and every party has traditions which it would rather forget. Let us each own up for the other party. I would like to see for the next four and a half years the two and the three parties together. In this election I want the best traditions of every party. I want the traditions that made Mr. Disraeli in his best days plead in that great book of his for a minimum wage, for better housing, for shorter hours, and for making the health of the people a national concern. And in the international settlement I would like to see the best traditions of Mr. Gladstone's life embodied in the settlement of Europe and the affairs of the world: regard for national liberty, national rights, whether nations be great or small. Let us have the best traditions of both and all parties.

I did not deem it practicable or desirable to aim at a permanent or a much prolonged coalition of parties. Differences in outlook and upbringing, and consequently of honest opinion on social and economic questions, were so fundamental that a merger of parties was unattainable and unworkable. It would be better for the working of democratic institutions that the issues should be argued out amongst the electors and decided by them. But a coalition during a period of emergency was essential to national security. A coalition which went beyond that term would be detrimental to national well-being.

There was a powerful Press combination—some of the papers Conservative, others Liberal or Labour—that had been conducting an active and persistent campaign of criticism against the Government. If this sniping went on during the Peace Conference, it would give the impression to the representatives of the Allies that the British people were not behind the British Government. Our opinions would not, therefore, carry the necessary weight at the Congress. Victory alone would not have endowed us with the necessary authority. The November elections in America, fought at a time when the Administration could claim that it had triumphed in the War, ended in a humiliating defeat for the President. That electoral disaster undoubtedly lowered his prestige and crippled his authority throughout the Conference. It also unconsciously impaired his own confidence. He could take no unnecessary risks in the way of insistence on his own point of view. His occasional threats to appeal to American opinion, when he did not get his way at the Conference, conveyed no real menace. There was no assurance that his country would support him in a break with the Allies on any issue.

There were times during the Conference when there was an exceptionally violent and pertinacious press attack upon the line I was taking. Had it not been that I had a resounding popular verdict behind me, I might have been overwhelmed. My temporary and precarious support in the old Parliament might have been intimidated with the prospect of a coming election as soon as peace was signed. I had no strong and well-disciplined party of my own to rely upon. I had at the outside a little over a hundred Liberal members pledged to support me. The leaders of the most powerful Opposition group in the House had, even whilst the fate of the War depended on complete national unity, displayed the greatest alacrity in taking advantage of disaffection in the Government ranks to conspire with the malcontents to manœuvre our overthrow. If they resorted to those tactics during the War they certainly would not hesitate to repeat the effort when the enemy had been defeated. The repeated Parliamentary attacks upon my endeavours to secure Unity of Command—and particularly the notorious Maurice onslaught—were a warning to the Government that we could not depend upon the united support of Parliament if trouble of any kind arose in the Conference on any issue. These attacks and intrigues were so formidable that they delayed the attainment of Unity of Command until disaster swept away the malcontent elements. The Opposition leaders resented with great bitterness of heart the events which turned them out of office in December, 1916. Their deposition involved the acceptance by Parliament and the nation of a suggestion that they had failed in their task. This gave a tang of personal resentment to the Opposition attitude towards my Administration, which differentiated it from the ordinary hostility of the old parties towards each other. It was so acrid and pervasive that it corroded the best judgments and the most equable tempers.

In view of this political situation I could not go to Paris without knowing where I stood in reference to the people as a whole. If the nation partook of the distrust with which I was regarded by the factions hostile to my Administration, it would be far better that this should be authoritatively recorded at the polls. Mr. Bonar Law and I therefore decided that it was essential for us to ask for a Vote of Confidence from the electorate to negotiate the peace and to carry through a comprehensive policy of reconstruction.

This is not the occasion for restating the programme which I laid before the country. As far as the terms of peace were concerned, I asked for a mandate to conclude a just, but not a vindictive, peace. I went so far in the first speech I delivered in the campaign as to appeal for a special mandate to resist the impulses of greed and revenge:

> We must not allow any sense of revenge, any spirit of greed, any grasping desire to overrule the fundamental principles of righteousness. Vigorous attempts will be made to hector and bully the Government in the endeavour to make them depart from the strict principles of right, and to satisfy some base, sordid, squalid ideas of vengeance and of avarice. We must relentlessly set our faces against that. A mandate for this Government at the forthcoming election will mean that the British delegation to the Peace Congress will be in favour of a just peace.

I placed the establishment of a strong League of Nations and disarmament in the forefront of my programme of peace:

> A League of Nations is an absolute essential to permanent peace A large number of small nations have been re-born in Europe, and these will require a League of Nations to protect them against the covetousness and ambitions of grasping neighbours. We shall go to the Peace Conference to secure a guarantee that the League of Nations is established and that it will be a reality. I am one of those who believe that without peace we cannot have progress.

I pointed out that there would have to be, of course, an efficient army to police the Empire, but I looked forward to a condition of things with the existence of a League of Nations "under which conscription will not be necessary in any country."

The policy of reconstruction which I sketched out in my various speeches, and in the Joint Manifesto issued by Mr. Bonar Law and myself to the nation, is the most comprehensive, thorough, and far-reaching ever set before the country by any political leaders. The formation of a League of Nations, reduction of armaments (including the abolition of conscription), self-government for India and for Ireland, the housing of the people as a national and not a local undertaking, larger opportunities for education, improved material conditions, the prevention of degrading standards of employment, the control of drinking facilities, the development of the resources of the country in such a way as to avoid the waste which had dissipated and depressed them, improved agricultural and transport conditions, measures for securing employment for the workers of the country—these were some of the reforms I indicated. One day I hope to give an account of the extent to which this comprehensive programme was realised, and wherein we failed and why. Our policy was summed up in a phrase which in a perverted form became historic:

What is our task? *To make Britain a fit country for heroes to live in.* I am not using the word heroes in any spirit of boastfulness, but in the spirit of humble recognition of the fact. I cannot think what these men have gone through. I have been there at the door of the furnace and witnessed it, but that is not being in it, and I saw them march into the flames. There are millions of men who will come back. Let us make this a land fit for such men to live in. There is no time to lose. I want us to take advantage of this new spirit. Don't let us waste this victory merely· in ringing joybells. Let us make victory the motive power to link the old land up in such measure that it will be nearer the sunshine than ever before, and, at any rate, that it will lift those who have been living in the dark places to a plateau where they will get the rays of the sun. We cannot undertake that without a new Parliament. The old Parliament has done its duty. I have not a word to say about it, but it has exhausted its mandate, and when you are beginning a great task of this kind you must get the inspiration which comes from the knowledge that you have got the people behind you in the business which you have undertaken. . . .

There is, as I never witnessed before, a new comradeship of classes, and I am glad, as an old political fighter, who has been hit hard and has been able to return the blows, always in a spirit of meekness, I am glad that we are approaching the new problems in a spirit of comradeship. Let us keep it as long as we can. I have no doubt human nature will prevail yet, but for the moment let us finish the task together, and when we have finished it, then let us play political football.

Mr. Bonar Law and I—and more especially I—have been censured because of the way in which we discriminated when we had to choose the candidates whom we supported. It is said that we were guilty of the same offence against judgment and fair treatment of political opponents as President Wilson was in his election appeal the preceding November, when he invited the electorate to vote against candidates who belonged to another party, although they had given loyal, helpful and steadfast support to his Administration in its efforts to achieve victory. As far as the Coalition leaders were concerned, that is a complete travesty of the truth. The American President urged the electors to vote for Democrats only, without reference to the fact that some of those Democrats had been unhelpful, whereas several of the Republicans whom he opposed had rendered conspicuous service to his Government. We, on the other hand, made a purely non-party appeal to the electors to support all those who had assisted the Government in its terrible task—whether they were Conservative, Liberal or Labour. We only opposed those who had embarrassed, hindered, and to the best of their opportunities, impeded, delayed and thwarted our war efforts. That is the general principle we applied in choosing the men in whose favour we exerted our influence or the men whose election we opposed. The application of that rule may have operated unfairly in two or three individual cases, but in the main no injustice was done. The Labour party by a majority decided immediately before the election that they would as a body withdraw their co-operation from the Coalition Government. There was a remarkably large dissentient minority, which proved that organised Labour was by no means unanimous in its decision to refuse its official assistance to a programme of social and economic reconstruction which went far beyond anything it could achieve alone. While 2,117,000 voted for severance, 810,000 voted for continued co-operation. Those who voluntarily withdrew from the combination that had so successfully worked together during the War, and decided to challenge and fight the comrades they left behind at the polls, could not fairly expect the support of the men they had deserted—and it is fair to acknowledge that they never asked for that support.

They even repudiated it, and therefore they had no complaint, and to the best of my recollection they made none. As a definite act of party strategy they placed themselves in battle array against the Government and thus deliberately chose all the risks of battle.

The section of the Liberal party which had declined to join the Coalition when Mr. Asquith ceased to be at its head was in a different position. They wanted it both ways. They wished to continue their rôle of a fractious opposition to the Government and, at the same time, secure immunity from opposition by the Government at the polls. In the House of Commons they numbered a little more than half the party—at the General Election they did not on any careful analysis poll one-half of the Liberals in the country. No one who followed the course of action they pursued in the House during the last few years of the War could possibly fail to observe that they regarded themselves as an Opposition, and a bitter Opposition, to the Government. They were in fact the only Opposition. Labour had by an official resolution authorised members of its party to join the Government. Several Labour members were in important positions in the Administration with the full approval of the Executive party. The group that came to be known as the Asquithian Liberals decided not to join the Government, but to discharge the functions of independent Opposition. Be it noted there was no Liberal opposition to the Asquith Coalition. It therefore meant that there was a definite change in the attitude of a large section of Liberals, not so much to the War or to the idea of national unity in its prosecution, but towards the particular Coalition that for the time being conducted the national effort in the War. And they left no doubt in anyone's mind as to the character of that change. It was distinctly—nay, it was venomously—antagonistic to the Government both in and out of Parliament. Whilst every ounce of my strength and every throb of my energy were absorbed in improving the position of the Allies in the terrible struggle which was then going against us, the Asquithian organisation was sending its emissaries to "confidential" meetings of Liberal Associations throughout the country, to poison the minds of the

Liberal workers everywhere against the new Government, and more particularly against its Chief. Even if the speeches delivered at these private conclaves had been reported, I had no time to reply. Had I done so, my mind would have been taken away from the essential tasks of a war which was not going too well for the Allies. Thus in the minds of active Liberals in every constituency, the impressions created were allowed two years to sink in and were then not easily removed. The suspicions and suggestions whispered at those underhanded gatherings stuck, and hundreds of thousands of Liberals became antipathetic—many of them irreconcilably antagonistic.

In the House of Commons no opportunity was missed by this new Opposition of embarrassing the Government. A small group of Asquithian Liberals kept up a continual sniping at Ministers— day after day and night after night. Anything that went wrong, or seemed to have gone wrong, was exploited to the discredit of the Government. Many matters, some of consequence, many trivial, which could easily have been adjusted by a talk with Ministers behind the Speaker's Chair, were broadcast as griev- ances and inefficiencies by questions and speeches in the House. There was a note of nagging querulity, often of personal spite, in these parliamentary activities. It may be said that the men who indulged in these unpleasantries were a very small gang drawn from the disgruntled who always hang around any party. But it was quite obvious to anyone who witnessed their perform- ances that they were approved and encouraged by more responsi- ble men in the party. There were consultations with leaders before the javelins were flung at Ministers—there were cheers from followers when there was an apparent hit. No real harm was done during the first few months. But when I entered into my difficult struggle with the military and their social and journal- istic adherents for the attainment of Unity of Command, then the Opposition threw itself officially as an organised force under its leader into the contest on the side of the reactionary and re- sisting Generals. They worked with these Generals and the Die- Hard Tory press to make unity of command unattainable, and for a dangerous while they succeeded. I had to face two or three serious parliamentary crises, fomented and organised by the Opposition in conjunction with hostile elements outside. The Generals were encouraged in their stubbornness. Serious delays occurred in straightening things out. What was still worse, measures designed to counter the impending German blow on our armies were not brought into operation. The grave defeat of the 21st of March was not altogether a triumph for German strategy—the parliamentary Opposition had a large share in compassing it.

The Maurice episode was a climax to these parliamentary manœuvres designed to intrigue the Government out of power. It is true that unity of commandment did not arise specifically on that issue. That had already been achieved; nevertheless, it arose out of the departmental divisions created by that conflict. Maurice was the champion of the military junta who fought against Unity. He had no judgment, but he had the advantage of being the only one amongst the military malcontents who could express himself coherently. That gave him a special position amongst them. When his Chief was dismissed, he remained. But, to quote a phrase of Ibsen's, the "tarantella was still in his blood," and when he and his political confederates thought that the March defeat provided them with a chance at last to upset the Government, they organised and delivered their coup. How much the politicians were in it was demonstrated by the efforts they made to bring the Irish Members back from Ireland, where they were conducting a campaign against conscription, to vote against the Government in what was practically a vote of censure. The vote on the Maurice resolution was an acid test of the members who were for and those who were irreconcilably opposed to the Government. During the General Election Mr. Asquith accepted the test when he said in one of his speeches:

If there has been a conspiracy to overthrow the Government I suppose I must have been the chief conspirator, for it was my motion to which reference is here made. It was a motion made by me, and I must say at once that there is no act in the whole of my parliamentary life, now extending for more than thirty years, for which I am less repentant or ashamed.

Mr. Bonar Law and I concluded that we must accept this challenge. In the reply I made to Mr. Asquith, which I quote from *The Liberal Magazine* of that date, I said:

. . . what happened in Parliament when I was working to secure unity in the Allied strategy—every step that I took was criticised, opposed, and worse. The difficulties were professional (i.e., from military sources); a section of the Tory Press was troublesome; there were men who said "Here are supporters of the Government who are against them—this is our chance." So they began to attack us, and a section of the Liberal Party took up the opposition to unity of command, and I say without hesitation it was because the Government were in difficulties in trying to put it through. It was challenged once or twice in Parliament. The Government were in a precarious position over it. Ultimately it culminated in the Maurice debate with a decision on a question of confidence. What was the occasion? At the time the German Army was in the ascendancy. One terrible, reeling blow had been delivered at the British forces. They had staggered back twenty miles under that terrible blow, and were awaiting another. The Germans had accumulated a gigantic army opposite the British Army, intended to renew the attack. We were engaged with all our power and strength in pouring men, munitions, and guns into France, and in getting men across the Atlantic. That was the opportunity that was chosen to move a vote practically of want of confidence in the Government, to overthrow them and to persuade the Irish members to come across the Channel from their task of refusing troops to help the British Army. Why? If they said the Government was incompetent, if they said we were not conducting the war properly, then we had to take that risk. But Mr. Herbert Samuel [who was a leading member of the Asquithian Opposition] said that in his judgment the Government was efficiently conducting the war, so that a Government which was efficiently conducting the war was, at the most critical moment of the war, to be flung out; confidence given to Germany, confusion created here, invaluable time lost. Mr. Asquith said last night there was no part of his career that he cared to apologise less for than that, and I am asked why I am opposing candidates who did that at a critical moment in the history of the war. Is any answer required beyond Mr. Asquith's statement that everything that he did in the last two years he would do again? *

I added that

the men whom we (the Coalition) have appealed to the electorate to support are the men who have given us constant support during the

* Newcastle-on-Tyne, Nov. 29th, 1918.

last two years—whether Unionist or Liberal—and those whom we cannot see our way to support are the men who were perfectly prepared at a critical moment to take advantage of temporary difficulties in order to overthrow the Government when they were undoubtedly carrying through the work of the nation. What guarantee have we that they will not again take advantage of our difficulties when we are endeavouring to carry through a great social reconstruction policy?

Asquithian candidates at the election promised "independent" support to the Government in carrying out its programme. They gave exactly the same promise when I formed my Administration in December, 1916, when they were apprehensive that I might then appeal to the electorate for a vote of confidence. I have given some indication of the way in which they redeemed that promise. We were not unnaturally apprehensive that, in practice, they would give a similar interpretation to their election pledges. As I put it in one of my election speeches:

We cannot accept the support of men who come in on the promise of supporting the Government and afterwards when they are elected begin to undermine and enfeeble us. I ask that the constituencies should ruthlessly examine the genuineness of their promise and satisfy themselves that where promise of support is given it is really meant. For the Government must have all the courage, all the confidence, which comes from knowing that there is a nation behind it.

In these circumstances, it is vain and irrelevant to compare Mr. Bonar Law's action and mine at the December election, 1918, with that taken by President Wilson in his electoral campaign in America in November, when he appealed for support for Democratic candidates only, without reference to the attitude which any of the candidates—Democratic or Republican—had adopted towards his Administration in the prosecution of the War.

There is another episode which has a bearing on the genuineness of our desire to secure complete national unity in the tasks of peace and reconstruction. When the General Election was impending, there was a real anxiety on the part of some of the more moderate supporters of Mr. Asquith, and also among the many Liberals who had not committed themselves to any faction inside the party, to avoid the spectacle of Liberal fighting

Liberal at the coming election, and if possible to re-unite the party once more. I received two deputations from influential Liberals who called upon me at Downing Street to offer their good offices to secure reconciliation between the contending sections. One of them came from the National Liberal Federation, and the other from Manchester. Mr. C. P. Scott, the famous Editor of the *Manchester Guardian*, one of the most respected figures in world Liberalism, was a member of the latter deputation. I welcomed both these deputations and expressed my deep sympathy with their aims. I was more than willing to agree that bygones should be bygones, and that a *modus vivendi* should be reached by which men who had all their lives worked together for the principles they held in common should resume that co-operation. After all, the split had occurred not over a question of principle but on a practical issue as to the best method of conducting a war to which the party was committed under the leadership of Mr. Asquith. Mr. Asquith himself had no objection in principle to a Coalition Government. His only claim was that he ought to be the head of it. That was hardly a question of principle.

I pointed out to the deputations the difficulty of securing any working arrangement unless the Asquith group were represented in the Government, and took their full share of the responsibilities that would fall upon us. I was asked whether I was prepared to give Mr. Asquith high office in the Government. One of the deputations suggested that Mr. Asquith might be given the office of Lord Chancellor. I told them at once that as far as I was concerned I should welcome him as a colleague, and that I thought he would fill that exalted office with distinction, and as such would be of great assistance to us in the formulation of the terms of peace. I then said that I was only expressing my own personal view and that I must necessarily consult my partner, Mr. Bonar Law, on the point. As I knew he would then be in his official residence next door, I told them I would see him at once on the subject, and if they waited a few minutes I would let them know. I left them in the Cabinet room and went in to see Mr. Bonar Law. Without a moment's hesitation he assented to the proposition. Lord Finlay was then Chancellor, but we felt that if Mr. Asquith would take the post his occupancy of that great legal office would be acclaimed not merely by the public but by the profession as well.

On my return to the Cabinet room, I informed the deputation of Mr. Bonar Law's willing acceptance of their suggestion. Another member of the deputation then very fairly suggested that it would be impossible for Mr. Asquith to go into the Government alone without carrying with him some of his immediate colleagues who had stood by him—although it would be more accurate to say that they had pushed him out. I concurred and said that I did not anticipate any difficulty in this respect. I left them once more to consult Mr. Bonar Law on this point. Both he and I agreed that it was a fair request, and I informed the deputation on my return of our acceptance of the amended proposal. They professed themselves to be very well pleased with the reception which had been accorded to their efforts, and said they would immediately see Mr. Asquith and report to me the character of his reply. Unfortunately for the Liberal party, he could not see his way to fall in with a plan which emanated from his own supporters, and which the two Coalition leaders were prepared to take the risk of carrying into effect.

The election had therefore to be fought out, with disastrous results not only to Mr. Asquith and his followers, but also to the party. Candidates who stood for full support of the Government received Government support in all constituencies without reference to their party labels. Members attaching themselves to Opposition groups were themselves opposed. All the Liberal leaders who belonged to the Asquith group were beaten at the polls. As far as Mr. Asquith personally was concerned, both Mr. Bonar Law and I refused to send a letter of support to his Conservative opponent. We went beyond that, and did our best to discourage his opponent's candidature through the agency of Sir George Younger, who had very considerable influence with the Conservative associations, particularly in Scotland. Nevertheless, so strong was the popular feeling about the part which Mr. Asquith had played in the Maurice debate, that he sustained a heavy defeat. His defiant speech, in which he said that he was proud of the part he took in that debate, finally wrecked his chances of re-election in a traditionally safe Liberal seat.

The effect upon the fortunes of the Liberal party was shattering. The split in the party was purely personal. There was no question of principle involved. Mr. Asquith formed and was the head of the first Coalition with the Conservatives, and the fallen leaders were all members of that Government. Some years later the same leaders all joined another Coalition in which Conservatives were predominant in numbers and policy. These Liberal leaders acquiesced in the reversal of an economic and fiscal policy which had for generations been regarded as an essential part of the principles of Liberalism. There was no such infringement of the essentials of the Liberal creed proposed by the Coalition programme of 1918. It was a bitter personal resentment which inspired that unfortunate schism. As long as it was confined to the men at the top, it was not irreparable. But the election sent the poison coursing through every limb and vein of the party. It cankered the whole body. There are traces of it still in the blood and tissue of the party. It frustrated the healing process attempted in 1923, when the leaders of the two sections came together.

I must now say a word upon the programme on which the election was fought. There have been fantastic tales related as to the character of the electoral appeals upon which millions of British men and women decided the issue. It is a calumny upon the intelligence of civilised democracy to suggest that any of its responsible leaders could have indulged in such fantasies, and that even if they had done so, any democracy could have been deluded by them. But as so far no one has thought it worth while to contradict these allegations, there is a danger that one day they may pass for the historical truth as to the level of British intelligence in the second decade of the twentieth century. There is no branch of knowledge where the impressionist has wrought greater havoc than in the realm of history. A few crude splashes of lurid paint pass for a true picture of a historical landscape. If the artists are of an inferior quality they not only paint an uninviting and an ugly prospect, but convey a thoroughly distorted view of the true landscape. The Treaty of Versailles and all its surroundings have suffered more from this pretentious school of artistic contortionists than any episode in the story of human enterprise. Anyone perusing these accounts would imagine that the electors went to the poll with one call in their ears from responsible statesmen who wished to be equipped with the necessary mandate to "hang the Kaiser" and to compel Germany to pay a sum of £24,000,000,000, or some equally astronomical figure, by way of indemnity. If these writers had thought it worth their while, before writing or repeating this kind of slanderous foolishness, to read the Election Manifesto issued by the two Coalition leaders to the nation, or the speeches they delivered at the election, they would have known that they were circulating falsehoods, and silly ones at that.

What was our appeal to the nation? There is not a word about Reparations in our Manifesto, and the only reference made to it by me was at Bristol in a speech which I quote verbatim in the chapter on Reparations, as my declaration there represented the considered policy of the Government.

As to the "hanging of the Kaiser," I never used the phrase. I said:

The Kaiser must be prosecuted. The war was a crime. Who doubts that? It was a frightful, a terrible crime. It was a crime in the way in which it was planned, in the deliberate wantonness with which it was provoked. It was also a crime in its action—in the invasion of a helpless little State, in the wicked and most brutal treatment of that little State. Remember the treaty of neutrality—the scrap of paper! Surely the war was a crime! The fact that all these iniquitous things were done in the name of war, and under the Imperial edict of an autocrat, does not change their nature. The war was a hideous, abominable crime, a crime which has sent millions of the best young men of Europe to death and mutilation, and which has plunged myriads of homes into desolation. Is no one responsible? Is no one to be called to account? Is there to be no punishment? Surely that is neither God's justice nor man's. The men responsible for this outrage on the human race must not be let off because their heads were crowned when they perpetrated the deed.

As both the Opposition parties and their leaders without exception took a similar line on both these questions, it can hardly be said that they affected the fortunes of the election. The Maurice affair was the line of cleavage. The electors summarily dismissed practically all those who voted for the Asquith motion of censure on the Government. He and his friends had deliberately chosen the issue. They stood by it at the election. And they had the answer.

The result was a sensational victory for the Government. It was much more complete than any of us had anticipated. All the leaders of the Asquith section were thrown out, and so were all the prominent anti-War leaders of the Labour party. The Government Delegation to the Peace Congress went there with the full authority of the nation behind it. It gave them greater confidence. It also added to their influence. It enabled them to ignore the elaborate efforts made by a section of the Press to work up a revolt against the Paris decisions on the ground of excessive leniency to Germany.

President Wilson was considerably weakened by an electoral disaster which indicated that his countrymen had lost faith in him. We were strengthened by the knowledge that the country trusted us.

6. PRESIDENT WILSON'S VISIT

PRESIDENT WILSON arrived in London from Paris on Boxing Day. We arranged the Foch and Clemenceau reception for a Saturday in order to give the workers a chance to see and welcome them. As I was most anxious that the President should be accorded an equally popular demonstration, I suggested a Bank Holiday in order to ensure that there should be an equally large crowd in the London streets to greet him. He was not exactly a popular hero with the ordinary citizen of our country. He did not make the same appeal to their combative instincts as Clemenceau and Foch did. They still remembered his "too proud to fight" speech, when their sons were fighting to the death for the ideas on which the President himself subsequently entered the War and delivered eloquent expositions. But still he was a great world

figure, and millions in every country looked to him as the man
who at that moment represented more than any other statesman
of his time the longing of humanity to put an end to the barbarity
of war from which mankind had suffered such afflictions the last
four and a half years. War leaders in every belligerent country
had to devote themselves to rousing and justifying the fighting
instincts of the people and to stimulating all classes to energetic
action in the prosecution of the War. When President Wilson
fought his Presidential election on the cry that he had kept
America out of the War, it was easier for him to make pacifist
speeches than for us who were actually engaged in a life and death
struggle against the most redoubtable army that had ever made
war.

The Royal Banquet at Buckingham Palace in honour of Wilson was a scene of unsurpassed splendour. It was noted at the
time that with the fall of the glittering Empires of Russia, Germany and Austria, there was no State pageant in the world which
could now compare with that which the British throne could display. It emphasised the revolution which the War had effected
in the government of Europe. Russia had become a proletariat
State, Germany was a republic, with a saddler ruling where the
bedizened figure of the Kaiser once radiated splendour. Austria
was broken up into fragments and Vienna was the capital of a
bankrupt republic. The grandeur of Britain dressed out around
the Royal table seemed more glorious than ever, not merely in
contrast to the bedraggled misery of its ancient rivals, but in
comparison with the gorgeousness of all its former displays. I
have never witnessed such a dazzling scene either before or since.
Field-Marshals and Generals who had commanded in the field
greater armies than Xerxes, Alexander, Caesar or Napoleon;
Admirals who had led into action Armadas which reduced those
of Philip of Spain, Rodney or Nelson into insignificance; Generals who had led the victorious armies of France, Britain, America and Italy; Princes and Ministers from every part of the Empire; Ambassadors of every land under the sun—except the few
enemy States and Russia—all arrayed in resplendent uniforms of
every cut and colour. It was a dream of magnificence. The most

outstanding figure there—the guest of honour—was clad in an ordinary black dress suit without a medal to adorn his breast. Apart from his intellectual features and his dignified mien, the stern simplicity of his garb lent distinction to his appearance amid such a brilliant assembly. He was welcomed by the King in a speech of cordial friendship for the great democracy he represented, and of warm appreciation of the services rendered by the American Army and Navy in the War which had just come to a triumphant end. These allusions to the American contribution to victory were enthusiastically acclaimed by the assembled guests. Wilson replied with the perfect enunciation, measured emphasis and cold tones with which I was to become so familiar in the coming months. There was no glow of friendship or of gladness at meeting men who had been partners in a common enterprise and had so narrowly escaped a common danger.

There was one particular blot on this deliverance which attracted general attention, and which caused many sincere friends of the President real distress at the time. It made no reference to the part played by the British Empire in the tremendous struggle just brought to a triumphant close and to the appalling sacrifices which had been sustained by the youth of that Empire in the cause of international right. The citizen Army that had stood firm against the most formidable trained legions that ever marched into battle, the sailors who had held the seas for America as well as for her Allies in every ocean on the face of the globe, were both represented at this banquet. Their leaders in the struggle were present in such numbers and were so apparelled that their presence could not have escaped the eyes of the orator. But not a word of appreciation, let alone gratitude, came from his lips. Our ships had carried half his troops across the Atlantic. The only allusion he had ever made to this fact was when he boasted of the numbers which had been transported to France: "and no lives were lost in the crossing except on one ship, and that was a British ship." It was felt that this was an occasion for making amends for that rude and ill-conditioned indiscretion. Not a word. So that when he sat down there was a perceptible chill of disappointment.

On my return to Downing Street I instantly wrote to Lord Reading to call attention to this blunder and to the mischief which might ensue to our relations with America, owing to the not unnatural resentment which such speeches would necessarily arouse. I told him that I was anxious to create a better atmosphere for co-operation at the coming Peace Conference, especially on subjects where we might have to take a more liberal view of the Treaty than Clemenceau was likely to adopt. Wilson was supposed to be well disposed towards Reading, and I was hopeful that he might persuade the President to rectify his unfortunate omission by making a cordial reference to the British efforts in the speech he was to deliver the following day at the Guildhall on receiving the freedom of the City. Reading at once put himself in touch with President Wilson and told me that he was assured that it was purely an oversight on the President's part—a curious oversight when in the circumstances the very nature of the spectacle organised to welcome him spread before his eyes the fact of the gigantic character of the British effort from the Rocky Mountains to the Himalayas, from the Northern Seas to the limits to the Antarctic. Reading was convinced that the mistake would be put right in the President's speech at the Guildhall. I was present at this other very striking ceremony arranged by the City of London to do honour to the President of the United States, but listened in vain for one word of generous allusion to Britain's sacrifices for, or achievements on behalf of the common cause.

A few weeks later I was to witness the same lack of human sympathy with France in her suffering when he addressed the French House of Representatives. It was an unprecedented honour. An address was presented to him by that Assembly in its own Chamber. It contained an expression of warm gratitude to America for the way she came to the assistance of France at a moment of accentuated peril. When President Wilson mounted the Tribune to reply, he was confronted by a considerable number of empty seats draped in black. They had once been occupied by young deputies who had gone to the front and there fallen in defence of their country in a struggle which was responsible for

1,400,000 French dead. Even the instincts of an orator would
have taught him that a reference to these grim reminders of
French heroism and sacrifice would have been an appropriate
prelude to any observations he might subsequently make. But
not even inferentially did he appear to have noted the existence
or the significance of these mournful vacancies in an otherwise
crowded Chamber. I never heard one sentence which would give
an impression that President Wilson was even cognisant of the
ravages wrought by the War in the homes of France. He was
indeed an incomprehensible character, but one can understand
why even among his sincere admirers in America he is not held
in that affectionate esteem which sheds a radiant glow around
the tomb of that great human character, Abraham Lincoln.

I will now give an account of my first business interview with
President Wilson. Mr. Balfour and I saw him in his room at
Buckingham Palace and had a lengthy conversation with him in
which the whole of the main conditions of a peace settlement
with Germany were passed in review. I found him extremely
pleasant. He was genial and friendly in his accost. He had none
of the professorial condescension towards young learners which
I had been led to expect. He was a clear and concise talker and an
attentive and receptive listener. I gave him a copy of General
Smuts' paper on the League of Nations and asked him if he would
furnish me with the proposals worked out on the same subject by
him, or on his instructions. He replied that he did not possess any
document of that kind, as he was desirous of establishing agreement on the general principles and outlines before framing a plan.
Neither he nor Mr. Balfour nor I took a *procès-verbal* of the conversations, which were an informal interchange of ideas. But
two or three days after the interview I gave a detailed report to
the Imperial Cabinet of what was said on both sides, and as I
have a full note of what I then said, I propose to give it here:

The President had opened at once with the question of the League
of Nations and had given the impression that that was the only thing
that he really cared much about. There was nothing in what he said
which would in the least make it difficult for us to come to some arrangement with him. His mind was apparently travelling in very

much the direction of the proposals advocated by Lord Robert Cecil
and General Smuts. He had no definite formal scheme in his mind,
and was certainly not contemplating anything in the nature of giving
executive powers to the League of Nations. The question of Germany's
inclusion had not been raised, but was not apparently contemplated
by him as a matter for the immediate future. What he was anxious
about was that the League of Nations should be the first subject discussed at the Peace Conference. Both Mr. Lloyd George and Mr. Balfour were inclined to agree, on the ground that this would ease other
matters, such as the questions of the "Freedom of the Seas," the disposal of the German colonies, economic issues, etc. The President,
having attained his object, could then say that these matters could
be left to be worked out by the League of Nations. There was also
the consideration that the President might have to go back to America
before the Conference concluded, and would wish to be able to say
that he had achieved his purpose of creating the League of Nations.

LORD CURZON added that the President had, on another occasion,
given to him as a reason for beginning with the League of Nations,
that the question of giving a mandate to certain Powers in certain
territories could not be settled unless there was a League of Nations
to give it.

MR. LLOYD GEORGE said that, as regards the Freedom of the Seas,
the President was very vague. He did not oppose his suggestion that
the matter could be left for further consideration after the League of
Nations had been established and proved its capacity in actual working. The impression he gave was that he might not resist that proposal,
provided the League of Nations had been actually agreed to before
the question of the Freedom of the Seas was raised.

As regards disarmament, the President had urged that a definite
decision should be arrived at before the Conference separated, and
before the League of Nations was actually constituted. He admitted,
however, that the intricate problems involved in relative disarmament
all round could not be settled during the Conference. Eventually they
agreed that the Conference should not separate before a definite provisional limitation of armaments had been imposed on Germany and
her allies, a limitation which would enable them to maintain order
in the troubled conditions of their territories but no more. Subsequently, Germany might raise at the League of Nations the question
of revising this provisional limitation. They felt that if the German
army was limited France would have to follow suit, and that she could
hardly maintain an immense army under those conditions. In discussing this matter they had not overlooked the question of reserves
and system of training, and he himself had reminded the President

of what Prussia had done when her forces were limited to a fixed figure by Napoleon. He had suggested that Germany should not be allowed to impose conscription in any shape or form until she had entirely failed by voluntary means to raise the army provisionally assigned to her, after which she might be allowed to make good the deficit by ballot. In answer to a question by Sir J. Cook, Mr. Lloyd George said that what he contemplated would prevent Germany from enforcing even the compulsory training of the young, such as they had in Australia.

LORD ROBERT CECIL raised the question of whether conscription was to be forbidden to the friendly new States created in the territories of Austria-Hungary, e.g. the Czechs and the Jugo-Slavs. He was inclined, with regard to them, to hold General Smuts' view, viz., that they should not be allowed to build up large armies.

MR. LLOYD GEORGE concurred and thought that this was one of the questions which the Chief of the Imperial General Staff might consider.

The Imperial War Cabinet instructed: "The Chief of the Imperial General Staff to make a provisional recommendation as to the strength to which the military forces of the various enemy countries should be limited, taking into consideration the need for maintaining internal order: and as to the manner in which they should be raised."

The Imperial War Cabinet similarly instructed: "The Deputy First Sea Lord, in the light of the same considerations, to revise the estimate which the Board of Admiralty had already made with regard to the strength to which the enemy fleets should be reduced."

Reports on the above subjects to be available early next week.

With regard to Russia, MR. LLOYD GEORGE explained that President Wilson, though not pro-Bolshevik, was very much opposed to armed intervention. He disliked the Archangel and Murmansk expeditions and would, no doubt, withdraw his troops from there. He was not very much in favour of the Siberian expedition, though as regards that his principal anxiety was as to the conduct of the Japanese, who were apparently taking the whole of Eastern Siberia into their own hands, sending sealed waggons into the interior, and generally behaving as if they owned the country. His whole attitude, in fact, was strongly anti-Japanese.

LORD ROBERT CECIL reminded the Imperial War Cabinet that the Japanese had just informed us that they were removing 30,000 out of the 60,000 Japanese troops now in Siberia.

With regard to the Western frontiers of Russia, MR. LLOYD GEORGE said that they had discussed the question, but had come to no sort of conclusion, as they felt the information was too defective. It was not clear, for instance, how far the so-called invasion of Esthonia or Poland was a direct invasion by Bolshevik forces from outside, or an internal Bolshevik rising in those countries. The President had not shown any keenness on the idea that Russia should be represented at the Conference. On the other hand he had suggested that we should ask M. Litvinoff formally and definitely what his proposals were. Mr. Lloyd George suggested that it might be possible to take more formal steps to ascertain exactly what the Bolshevik Government were prepared to do.

A short discussion followed with regard to the informal negotiations which had already taken place, arising out of the telegram from M. Litvinoff, transmitted by Mr. Clive from Stockholm where he had met Litvinoff. It was pointed out by Lord Robert Cecil that we could not definitely act on President Wilson's suggestion without communicating with our Allies, some of whom took a very strong line against the Bolsheviks. We ourselves had, in fact, asked our Allies and some neutral Powers to keep out the Bolsheviks. The discussion on this question, however, was postponed pending the production of M. Litvinoff's answer to our request for definite proposals.

With regard to the Near East, MR. LLOYD GEORGE informed the Imperial War Cabinet that President Wilson expressed himself in favour of the Turks being cleared out of Europe altogether, and of their place at Constantinople being taken by some small Power acting as a mandatory of the League of Nations. Mr. Balfour had told the President that the Eastern Committee had been in favour of the United States acting as mandatory at Constantinople. With regard to this, President Wilson had pointed out that the United States were extremely proud of their disinterested position in this war and did not wish to be deprived of that pride. It would be difficult to persuade them that such a mandate was not a profit, but really a burden. Altogether, he had shown himself very much opposed to any intervention on the part of the United States in these territorial questions. To this Mr. Lloyd George and Mr. Balfour had replied by asking the question who was to undertake the burden of finding the two divisions, or whatever troops might be required, to prevent the Armenians from being massacred. The President had not given a definite answer but had certainly not yet reached the point of accepting the argument.

LORD CURZON said that he had put the same point to the President himself, and that the President had replied asking that we should lead him a little more slowly up to his fences; that, if the League of Nations were once constituted and the Conference had been sitting some time, the United States might possibly be less reluctant to consider the question of mandatory intervention. As regards Constantinople, he reminded the Imperial War Cabinet that the Eastern Committee had only discussed the suggestion, and had not actually recommended that it should be entrusted to the United States.

As regards the German colonies, the President agreed that they could not be returned to Germany, and that they should be put under some Power acting as a mandatory. Mr. Lloyd George had impressed upon him the distinction between the German colonies conquered by the British Dominions and adjacent to them, and those in the conquest of which the forces of the Empire as a whole had shared. He had expressed our willingness to leave German East Africa at the disposal of the League of Nations, and to accept all the conditions imposed by the League if we were entrusted with a mandate for its administration. In the other category he had put German South-West Africa as the strongest case, pointing out that it would be quite impossible to separate from the South African Union what was essentially part of the same country. The President did not seem prepared to contest that contention, but of his own accord retorted that the position of Australia with regard to the Pacific colonies was not quite the same. Mr. Lloyd George and Mr. Balfour had endeavoured to put the case as strongly as they could for Australia, on the grounds of security, but the President had answered that a case on similar grounds might be made for every other captured territory. In answer to the argument that we had definitely promised to Japan the islands in the Northern Pacific, and that it would be impossible to deny to Australia and New Zealand what was given to Japan, the President had shown that he was by no means prepared to accept the Japanese treaty, and was doubtful whether Japan could be admitted there even in the capacity of a mandatory Power. They had not succeeded in moving him from that position.

MR. BONAR LAW, who was present at that part of the discussion, said that President Wilson had remarked in that connection that he regarded it as his function to act as a buffer to prevent disagreeable things, such as the Japanese retention of the islands, being carried out.

LORD CURZON suggested that President Wilson ought not to be regarded as a sole arbiter in these matters; he would be only one of a party round the Conference Table.

MR. LLOYD GEORGE agreed. He was only reporting the President's views, and had in no sense accepted them as final. With regard to the Colonies, he had left the matter by telling the President that the question would have to be fought out at the Conference, where the Dominions would be able to present their own case.

With regard to indemnity, Mr. Lloyd George reported that he found the President, on the whole, stiffer than on any other question. The utmost concession he seemed inclined to make was that the claims for pure reparation should be tabled first, and that then other claims might possibly be considered afterwards. Mr. Lloyd George had pointed out that that practically ruled the British Empire out in spite of the enormous burdens it had borne, and that France and Belgium, who had borne a lesser burden, would practically get everything. He had pointed out also that as a matter of fact our own burden of over £6,000,000,000 to a population of 45,000,000 was much heavier than that of Germany with a similar debt distributed over 65,000,000 of people. Similarly, he had pointed out that Australia at this moment owed £75 for every man, woman, and child of her population, a loss which was just as real as any loss represented by destroyed houses. He had, however, failed to make any impression upon the President.

In answer to a question by Mr. Hughes, Mr. Lloyd George said that with regard to the question of economic barriers, raised in No. 3 of the President's Fourteen Points, the President had shown no inclination to raise the matter. His opinion was that President Wilson meant nothing in particular by that Article anyhow, and since he had brought it forward he had lost the election in the United States.

With regard to Italy, Mr. Lloyd George reported that he found President Wilson distinctly anti-Italian, as the consequence of the conversations he had had with Baron Sonnino. He and Mr. Balfour had tried to do their best to state Baron Sonnino's case with regard to the strategical position of the Dalmatian coast, but the President's only suggestion was that the Power to whom the Dalmatian coast was given should be forbidden to have a navy at all.

MR. HUGHES said that, in other words, the President held the view that those Powers which had ports should have no fleets, and that only those Powers which had no ports should be allowed to have them.

MR. LLOYD GEORGE said that in any case it was clear that the President would strongly support the Jugo-Slavs against Italy.

With regard to France, he did not think the President was prepared to tolerate schemes for the control of the west bank of the Rhine, though he might be prepared to accept the French annexation of the Saar Valley.

With regard to the proposed Inter-Allied Conference, they had found the President entirely opposed to holding such a Conference, at any rate formally. He considered that the general Peace Conference would be a sham if definite conclusions were simply arrived at beforehand and then presented to Germany. He was quite prepared to hold inter-Allied discussions in Paris between the four Powers informally, and agreed that definite decisions would have to be arrived at there and presented to Germany at the Peace Conference. It really came to the same thing, but the President insisted definitely on his point of view.

LORD CURZON suggested that, unless the President got beyond the very loose talk he had had with members of the British Government in this country, the Peace Conference would be a dreary fiasco. In any case, France had a very different conception of what was to be done, as was shown by the French proposals for the representation of the smaller Allies at the Inter-Allied Conference.

With regard to the language to be used at the Peace Conference, MR. LLOYD GEORGE mentioned that the President proposed to insist that English and French should both be the official languages, and that the reports of the Conference should be published in both languages.

Lord Robert Cecil undertook to communicate with our representatives abroad, with a view to their supporting Colonel House's attitude in this matter.

With regard to the question of publicity, Mr. Lloyd George mentioned that President Wilson had been in favour of allowing the papers to publish what they liked, and to impose no restrictions.

MR. HUGHES said that if we were not very careful, we should find ourselves dragged quite unnecessarily behind the wheels of President Wilson's chariot. He readily acknowledged the part which America had played in the war. But it was not such as to entitle President Wilson to be the god in the machine at the peace settlement, and to lay down the terms on which the world would have to live in the future. The United States had made no money sacrifice at all. They had not even exhausted the profits which they had made in the first two and a half years of the war. In men, their sacrifices were not even equal to those of Australia. Relatively their sacrifices had been nothing like as much as those of Australia. America had neither given the material nor the moral help which entitled her to come before France. If M. Clemenceau took the line which President Wilson seemed to be taking, he (Mr. Hughes) might be prepared to say, "You have a right to speak." He hoped that Great Britain and France, which had both sacrificed so much, would defend their own interests, and not let their future be decided for them by one who had no claim to speak even for his own country. Mr. Lloyd George had received an overwhelming vote from his fellow-countrymen, not only in recognition of what he had done but because of their confidence that he would see to it that their sacrifices had not been made in vain. In taking up that line at the Peace Conference, Mr. Lloyd George would have not only all England, but more than half America behind him. He and M. Clemenceau could settle the peace of the world as they liked. They could give America the respect due to a great nation which had entered the war somewhat late, but had rendered great service. It was intolerable, however, for President Wilson to dictate to us how the world was to be governed. If the saving of civilisation had depended on the United States, it would have been in tears and chains to-day. As regards the League of Nations, Mr. Hughes considered that a League of Nations which was to endure and weather the storms of time would have to be a thing like the British Empire, framed in accordance with historical associations and practical needs. President Wilson, however, had no practical scheme at all, and no proposals that would bear the test of experience. The League of Nations was to him what a toy was to a child —he would not be happy till he got it. His one idea was to go back to America and say that he had achieved it, and that everything else could then be left for the League of Nations to complete. He (Mr. Hughes) did not consider that the peace of the world could be settled on the terms of "Leave it all to the schedule." Speaking for Australia, he wanted to know what Australia was to get for the sacrifices she had made. When he had secured what he wanted, the Freedom of the Seas, as we knew it and meant to have it, and necessary guarantees for the security and development of the Empire and reparation and indemnities, then he would have no objection to handing over other matters to a League of Nations. Such a League must, however, be properly constituted, and one in which the British Empire occupied a place corresponding to its sacrifices in the war and its position in the world. He insisted that in any case we should not commit ourselves to the League of Nations until the Conference had completed its labours. To start with a League of Nations and then continually refer everything to this League would mean giving up the substance for the shadow. The League of Nations should be the gilded ball on the dome of the cathedral, and not the foundation-stone.

As regards the German colonies in the Pacific, he thought that President Wilson was talking of a problem which he did not really understand. New Guinea was only 80 miles from Australia. In any case, whatever else the people of Australia differed on, they were united on two things: firstly their attitude towards Japan and the White Australia policy; and secondly, the retention of these islands. He asked above all things that the Prime Minister who now stood clothed with all power by the recent vote of the people, should resolutely insist upon such terms of peace as were necessary for the safety of the Empire, through whose sacrifices and efforts victory had been won.

MR. CHAMBERLAIN suggested that it might be made clear to President

Wilson that there should be a British Monroe doctrine for the Southern Pacific.

LORD CURZON considered that Mr. Hughes' views were shared by many members of the Imperial War Cabinet. More particularly he thought it was felt that Mr. Lloyd George should remember the power he possessed not merely in virtue of the recent election, but of all the sacrifices made by the British Empire, and of the interests which it had at stake all over the world. While holding the opinion that the future fortunes of the world must largely depend on co-operation between England and America, he did feel that if President Wilson persisted in the line reported it might be necessary, on some issues at any rate, for Mr. Lloyd George to work at the Conference in alliance with M. Clemenceau.

MR. LONG agreed cordially with the views expressed by Lord Curzon, adding that he did not think that President Wilson realised what the conquest of German East Africa had meant, or the extent to which every part of the British Empire had been involved in it.

LORD READING thought that it would be lamentable if the result of the friendly discussions which had taken place was to convey the impression that President Wilson and Mr. Lloyd George were acutely divided. He fully agreed that we could not give up our claims on any matter without fighting, but he did hope that we should not lightly abandon the position that, consistently with the maintenance of our rights, our main object was to bring about the closest co-operation hereafter between ourselves and the United States.

LORD CURZON explained that he placed as much reliance on the future co-operation of Great Britain and the United States as any member of the Imperial War Cabinet. All he had meant to imply was that at the Conference Mr. Lloyd George would go with an authority fully equal, and indeed superior, to that of President Wilson.

MR. CHURCHILL considered that the only point of substance was to induce the United States to let us off the debt we had contracted with them, and return us the bullion and scrip we had paid over, on the understanding that we should do the same to the Allies to whom we had made advances. If President Wilson were prepared to do that, we might go some way towards meeting his views in the matter of indemnity. For the rest, we should be civil and insist on our essential points.

SIR ROBERT BORDEN said that he would regret if we entered on the Peace Conference with any feeling of antagonism towards President Wilson or the United States. He considered that the recent conversations had, on the whole, been as favourable as he had anticipated. Future good relations between ourselves and the United States were, as he had said before, the best asset we could bring home from the war. With regard to the two points on which there had been a pronounced difference, namely the Pacific Islands and indemnity, there was no reason to conclude that we had yet got the President's final point of view. He agreed that with regard to these we should maintain our position strongly. He wished, however, to make clear that if the future policy of the British Empire meant working in co-operation with some European nation as against the United States, that policy could not reckon on the approval or the support of Canada. Canada's view was that as an Empire we should keep clear, as far as possible, of European complications and alliances. This feeling had been immensely strengthened by the experience of the war, into which we had been drawn by old-standing pledges and more recent understandings, of which the Dominions had not even been aware. He was in no sense reproaching the Imperial Government with regard to the past, and admitted—in answer to a question by Mr. Lloyd George—that since the Imperial War Cabinet had been set up the Dominions had not been committed to any treaty binding upon them without their knowledge.

With regard to Russia, he did not see how the war could be regarded as terminated if we left the Peace Conference with five or six nations and Governments still fighting in Russia. There were only two alternatives: one was to go and forcibly intervene in Russia itself; the other, which he preferred, was to induce the Governments of the various States in Russia to send representatives to Paris for conference with the Allied and associate nations. These could then bring pressure, if necessary, upon them to restrain and control aggression, and to bring about conditions of stable government under the power and influence of the League of Nations.

LORD ROBERT CECIL expressed his agreement with Sir Robert Borden's suggestion concerning Russia. He admitted that there were certain difficulties in dealing with the Bolshevik Government, but thought they were not insuperable. He suggested that all parties in Russia should be told to stand fast where they were till the Peace Conference was over, and that meanwhile Allied Commissions might clear up many disputed points in the situation.

LORD MILNER suggested that, if Lord Robert Cecil's proposal were accepted, there was no reason why all the Governments in Russia, including even the Bolsheviks, should not be invited to the Peace Conference. If the Bolsheviks really accepted the conditions and stopped their aggression upon their neighbours, they would, in fact, have begun to cease being Bolsheviks.

MR. LLOYD GEORGE agreed, but pointed out that it would be

necessary to stop aggression by General Denikin and the Siberian Government upon the Bolsheviks, and that measures might have to be taken at the Peace Conference to prevent the Bolsheviks using it for the purposes of propaganda.

LORD ROBERT CECIL said that he agreed with Mr. Hughes' view that the Empire would go into the Peace Conference in a position of enormous power, which, however, was also a position of prodigious responsibility. The vital thing was to secure a settled peace. The greatest guarantee of that was a good understanding with the United States, and that good understanding could not be secured unless we were prepared to adhere to the idea of the League of Nations. He agreed that the details of the League of Nations could not be settled at the beginning of the Peace Conference, but the general principles might be laid down as early as possible. His own idea would be that the Peace Conference should at the outset pass, say, three resolutions, laying down: firstly the desirability of a League of Nations; secondly the general functions of such a League; and thirdly the Powers which at present could be trusted to take part in it, the elaborating of these resolutions to be referred to a technical Commission, which could be working at the matter while the Conference was sitting. In answer to a question by Sir J. Cook, he agreed that indemnity and other main terms of peace would have to be settled by the Peace Conference itself, and could not be left to the League of Nations.

This account of the Buckingham Palace conversations with the President produced a worse impression on the minds of the Cabinet than the actual interview had on mine. Mr. Hughes' mordant comments on the speech are an indication of the immediate effect it produced on the Imperial Cabinet. The Cabinet were much impressed with the critical power of the Hughes speech. It was their first explanation of the reason why this man of frail physique, defective hearing and eccentric gesticulations had attained such a position of dominant influence in the Australian Commonwealth. It was a fine specimen of ruthless and pungent analysis of President Wilson's claim to dictate to the countries that had borne the brunt of the fighting. I wish there had been a verbatim report which would reproduce the stabbing sentences in the form in which they were delivered. As it is I am only able to give an incomplete summary.

Before the deliberations of the Imperial War Cabinet on the instructions to be given to our delegates at the Peace Congress came to an end, the representation to be accorded to the Dominions at the Conference was discussed.

7. DOMINION REPRESENTATION

THE Dominions were perturbed by the inadequate representation accorded to them at the table of the Conference by the French proposals, and they invited a decision upon the subject from the Imperial Cabinet. It was very difficult to induce foreign countries to understand the position which the Dominions occupied inside the British Empire. In foreign affairs, the Foreign Office in London constituted the executive and spokesman of the Empire, and therefore it was not unnatural that the friendliest Powers should assume that when a peace treaty came to be negotiated the British Government would represent the views, not merely of Great Britain, but of the whole Empire, just as the Quai d'Orsay represented the mind of France on foreign affairs. None of them quite realised that each of these Dominions was completely independent of any direction or control from Downing Street; that decision as to whether they would take part in a war in which Britain was engaged was entirely their own, and not subject to any order received from the British Government. They appreciated only vaguely, if at all, the fact that of the million men who crossed the seas from these remote territories, not one would have come in obedience to a command issued from Whitehall. It was the events of the War that began to bring home to the French and Americans the essential difference between the structure of the French Empire or of the United States on the one hand and the British Empire on the other. France could levy and command armies in Algeria, and the Federal Government in the state of New York, by orders issued respectively from Paris or Washington—but a decree issued in London could not raise a platoon in Canada. When I was Secretary of State for War in 1916, a special effort was made to raise more troops at home and throughout the Empire. Communications to the Dominions were couched in the form not of a direction to the Governor to take the necessary steps to secure recruits, but as an appeal to the Prime Ministers of the respective Dominions, calling attention to the grave emergency, urging the need and entreating their assistance in view of that need. Their decision in August, 1914, to throw their resources of men and material on the side of Britain was as much their own as was that of the United States of America in April, 1917. The part they had played in the struggle had been a notable one. Some of the most brilliant victories on every battlefield, East and West, had been largely due to the valour of their troops. They therefore felt that they were entitled to an official recognition of the part they played by at least equal representation with Allied nations who had not contributed anything comparable to their great efforts. They were thus incensed at what they regarded as the unfair and humiliating representation which the French proffered to them at a conference which would effect a settlement of world affairs made possible largely by their sacrifice. The change which the appearance of these formidable warriors, levied and equipped by their own Governments and fighting under their own commanders for the first time on the battlefields of Europe and Asia, had achieved in the status of the Dominions was not quickly understood even by British statesmen.

During the first two and a half years of the War the Dominions were not called to our councils to assist in the direction of the War. The first time they were invited to sit at the same table as British Ministers on equal terms at the Great Council Chamber of the Empire was when I set up the Imperial War Cabinet in February, 1917, and sent an official invitation to the Prime Ministers of the Dominions to join it. The meetings were no formal and perfunctory make-believe Sanhedrims of the elders and chief priests of the Empire, to give an appearance of consultation. There was a genuine discussion of all questions of policy bearing on the direction of the War, and decisions were taken which affected the conduct of the War and the settlement of the peace. But the Victorian attitude of Britain's hegemony still lingered.

It seemed as though the French and Americans harboured a slight suspicion that this plea of Dominion independence and separate nationhood was an artifice of the wily Englishman to increase his representation at the Congress. Foreigners always suspect us of advancing the most altruistic principles for any scheme that promotes British interests. All Empires have that knack. The French compromised by according separate representation, but on a scale which placed the Dominions below the rank of States that had contributed much less to the victory. Hence the indignation of the Dominion Premiers.

The question was raised by Mr. Hughes at the last meeting of the Imperial War Cabinet in the year 1918.

MR. HUGHES said that, under the French proposals, the Dominions would not be accorded representation equivalent to, say, Sweden. He called particular attention to the second of the two phases proposed, which referred to the eventual organisation of the League of Nations. If the League of Nations were to endure, it would be one of those questions at the Conference which would most vitally concern the Dominions. It was probable that in 25 years the white population of the British Empire overseas would exceed the population of Great Britain. He therefore suggested that, when the Conference discussed this question, the Dominions were entitled to representation equal to that accorded to neutrals. Australia had put and kept more men in the field than Belgium, and deserved as much representation at the Conference.

In reply to this, MR. LLOYD GEORGE pointed out that at a meeting on December 2, 1918, at which M. Clemenceau and Signor Orlando were present, it had been agreed by the representatives of the British, French, and Italian Governments:

"Inter-Allied Conference of each of the great Allied and Associated Powers, namely, France, Great Britain, Italy, Japan, United States of America: Representatives of the British Dominions and India should attend as additional members of the British delegation when questions directly affecting them are under consideration."

MR. LLOYD GEORGE pointed out that the Dominions and India would be in the same position as, if not better than, the smaller Allied Powers, because it had been agreed at the same meeting:

"That the smaller Allied Powers should have no right of representation at all the meetings of the Inter-Allied Conferences but that any of the smaller Allied Powers should have the right to be represented whenever questions concerning them were being discussed."

In all discussions on the subject, it had been intended to include in the five delegates representing Great Britain, one representative of the Dominions and India.

SIR ROBERT BORDEN strongly urged that the question of representation had a very serious aspect for the Dominions, and a peculiar significance for Canada, which had no special material interest in the war, and no claims to additional territory. It would be regarded as intolerable in Canada that Portugal should have a representation in the Peace Conference which was denied to that Dominion. Canada had lost more men killed in France than Portugal had put into the field. If the French proposals were adopted as put forward in Lord Derby's telegram, the result upon public opinion in Canada would be such as he did not care to suggest, or even contemplate. The status of the Dominions was not well understood by foreign Powers, and it would be not only proper, but necessary, for the British Government to set it forth fully. The British Empire had the right to define the powers and functions of the nations which compose it, and foreign Powers had no right to question that definition. He alluded to the unanimous resolution passed in the Imperial War Conference in 1917, which was accepted by the British Government, and which declared that the constitution of the Empire was based on the principle of equal nationhood and adequate voice in foreign relations. Each Dominion should have as ample a representation as Belgium or Portugal. There was no question on which the people of Canada were more insistent than their claim to representation at the Peace Conference which would settle the issues of a war in which they had taken so notable a part. He hoped that the Cabinet would appreciate, although it was almost impossible for them fully to appreciate, the strong feeling in Canada on this subject. To provide that Canada should be called in only when her special interests were in question would be regarded as little better than a mockery. It would be most unfortunate from the point of view of the Dominions that the British delegation should be selected entirely from the British Isles. That delegation had authority to represent not only the British Isles, but the whole Empire. He therefore strongly urged that the delegation representing the British Empire should be in part selected from a panel, upon which each Prime Minister from the Dominions should have a place, and that one or more of these Prime Ministers should be called from time to time, as occasion might require, to sit in the delegation representing the whole Empire at the Conference.

LORD ROBERT CECIL agreed with Sir Robert Borden as to the wisdom of creating such a panel, and suggested that its members might serve on a kind of rota.

THE PRIME MINISTER, who also approved of the idea of the panel, said that the real business of the Peace Conference would be transacted not at the formal conferences, but at the small informal con-

versations. The Dominions and India would have the same representation as Serbia, Belgium, and Roumania. He considered, however, that
it would be unwise to press for such a full representation of the British
Empire at the first big conference, as five delegates from Great Britain
and three each from the Dominions and India, because in that event
there would be no fewer than twenty-three representatives of the
British Empire at such meetings; and in attempting to get so full a
representation we might run the risk of losing more than we gained.

The Imperial War Cabinet decided that:

(a) Representatives of the British Dominions and India ought to
be present at the opening session and at any other session of the Peace
Conference or the Allied Preliminary Conference (should it be held) at
which Belgium and other small Allied States were represented.

(b) The British Dominions and India should in all respects have
the same powers as, and be on an equal footing at the Conference with,
Belgium and other smaller Allied States.

(c) Lord Robert Cecil should re-cast the telegram to Paris on these
principles.

(d) The Prime Ministers of the Dominions and the representatives
of India should be placed on a panel from which part of the *personnel*
of the British delegation could be filled, according to the subject for
discussion.

In the choice made by me of our colleagues to form the British
Delegation at the Peace Congress, I acted on the principle suggested by Sir Robert Borden, of choosing one delegate out of the
panel of Dominion Premiers to make up the five to which we were
entitled. The selection of the five was a difficult and delicate matter. We had to take into account the fact that we were a coalition
of political parties—mostly Conservative, but with a substantial
Liberal contingent and a faithful remnant of Labour members
representing a very large Labour and Trade Union vote cast for
us at the election. Mr. Bonar Law and I, as joint leaders of this
coalition, were necessarily selected. When vital decisions had to
be taken, often without much opportunity for consultation with
our colleagues, it was impossible to leave out the head of the
Government or the leader of the largest party amongst its supporters. The Foreign Secretary, Mr. Balfour, both by virtue of
his office, his experience and his fine intelligence, was indispensable. Mr. Barnes represented the views of organised Labour. His
long association with the Trade Union movement, the respect in

which he was generally held by the workmen of the country for his integrity, unselfishness, sympathy and sound judgment, constituted him a distinguished representative of his class. The fifth vacancy was filled from the rota of Dominion Premiers.

Personally I should have liked to see Mr. Asquith on the Delegation. But which of the others could we have displaced to make room for him? Had he joined the Administration as Lord Chancellor, Mr. Bonar Law, with his usual readiness to suppress all personal claims, would have gladly surrendered his position on the Delegation in favour of so eminent a member, especially as his presence in England was required as leader of the Commons. But the Conservatives would have resented his exclusion in order to substitute another Liberal, and thus have a representation of two Liberals and one Labour man to one Conservative. Had Mr. Asquith been a member of the Government, they might conceivably have made the sacrifice. But Mr. Asquith unfortunately refused that offer. And it would have been difficult to leave out Bonar Law and men like Lord Curzon and Lord Milner in order to find room for a political leader whose lead had been so emphatically repudiated by the people of this country.

CHAPTER III

ARRANGEMENTS FOR THE
PEACE CONFERENCE

PREPARATIONS were made on an unprecedented scale by all the Departments concerned to assist the British delegation in its share of the tremendous task of world reconstruction. Both the Foreign Office and the War Office examined all their records and reports in order to give the delegation accurate information about the pre-War position under then existing Treaties, about the statistics showing the racial composition of countries involved in the settlement, claims put forward for independence by provinces annexed by force, or proposals by Allied States for readjustment of boundaries on principles laid down by the great countries during the War. Every demand and suggestion for change put forward by rival claimants was given the most careful examination. The Foreign Office dug deep into its archives for the long, varied and blood-stained history of fluctuating frontiers. The Treasury were prepared with their information and advice on all financial questions, the Board of Trade with theirs on all matters affecting trade, navigation and labour conditions. The Intelligence Organisations of the fighting services constituted a storehouse of information on the position of affairs in the vast areas covered by the War. The facts gathered by them during the War and in the period of occupation of conquered territories that followed, supplemented and checked the information in the possession of the Foreign Office on ethnical and economic questions and was invaluable when strategical considerations entered into the fixing of boundaries.

The judicious selection and co-ordination of all this information involved prolonged and immense labour by every Department. It was executed with a knowledge, freedom from bias and a breadth of view which reflected great credit on the intelligence and impartiality of our Civil Service in all its branches. The

Departments were fully represented in Paris during the whole of the negotiations by their ablest officials, whose assistance and guidance the peace negotiators constantly sought.

The British Delegation had to decide the question of whether the arrangements for the Conference itself should be given to the Foreign Office or to the Secretariat of the War Cabinet. Lord Hardinge was at the head of the Foreign Office organisation in Paris. He was a man of unrivalled experience. He possessed a calm, clear and unprejudiced judgment which gave to his advice an authority which was invaluable. On the other hand, there were other Departments whose advice had to be sought on the most controverted subjects in the Treaty—such as reparations, the military and naval clauses, labour conditions, the German Colonies. Most important of all was the keeping in contact and consultation with Dominion representatives. The Secretary of the Cabinet, Sir Maurice Hankey, had been in close touch with the Dominion Premiers and with the various Departments at home during the whole of the War, and he had been present at all the discussions which took place in 1917 and 1918 on the terms of peace. It was therefore decided to appoint Sir Maurice Hankey as Secretary to the British delegation at the Conference. Lord Hardinge accepted that decision with an unreserved loyalty worthy of his magnanimous and unselfish nature.

M. Clemenceau, as President of the Conference, nominated to the position of General Secretary of the Peace Congress M. Dutasta, a young man whose affability and tact made the appointment acceptable to all and helped to carry the proceedings through to the end without any friction on points of procedure. Dutasta did not, however, possess the necessary experience to discharge the day-to-day functions of a Conference entrusted with an infinite variety of gigantic problems. It was soon discovered that there was only one man who possessed the necessary qualifications for such a position. Whenever there was any difficulty experienced in the arrangement of the proceedings, in the disentanglement of various topics and in the arrangement of the procedure, it was always Sir Maurice Hankey who came to the rescue. Every member of the Conference was impressed with the fact that he had made a profound study of all the issues and that all the relevant facts were at his finger ends. He generally brought with him to the meetings a load of documents, and when there was a discussion upon any subject where there was a difference of view, Sir Maurice Hankey could put his hand without the slightest difficulty upon a document which cleared up all the obscurities. Gradually the President of the Council began to depend upon him and turn to him whenever there was any confusion which could be cleared up by a paper that could be regarded by everyone as conclusive. No other delegation secretary had the same mastery of all the relevant facts, or counted as much in these matters. Sir Maurice Hankey's word was final on questions of fact. M. Clemenceau was very devoted to M. Dutasta, but that made him all the readier to take advantage of the services of someone who would avert the delays and the confusions for which the General Secretary might have been blamed. In the end, M. Clemenceau treated Sir Maurice Hankey as the actual Secretary, and when any question arose about which we were not very clear, he turned to the British Secretary and said, "Where is that bag of yours?" and the decisive document was soon forthcoming. Gradually, with some stiffness at first, but with complete acceptance at last, President Wilson took M. Clemenceau's lead in this respect, and when the Council of Four was constituted, Sir Maurice Hankey became the sole Secretary and kept all the minutes.

At first progress was slow and the discussions were inclined to be rambling and desultory. We were all feeling our way, and I had a sense that we were each of us trying to size up our colleagues, reconnoitring their respective positions, ascertaining their aims and how they stood in reference to the desiderata in which each of them was most deeply interested and involved.

The first few meetings at Paris on the Peace Settlement were composed of representatives of Britain, France, Italy and the United States of America. These were purely sittings of the Supreme Interallied Council. Japan was invited to join. The time was occupied in determining the numbers and allocation of the delegates at the Peace Congress, and their classification into those who should attend every meeting and those who were to be brought in when some issue arose which specially affected their respective countries. A second question which occupied a good deal of our time was publicity; and the third was whether Russia should be invited to send delegates to the Peace Conference, and if not, how she should be dealt with. Each of these questions necessarily absorbed much time. The first was not so easy to determine. It was agreed that the main duty of drafting the Treaty must be left to the Great Powers and submitted to the others for their approval. Had all the Allied nations been represented, the Congress would have been merely a debating society, and for at least a year it could not have come to a definite decision on all, if any, of the vast and varied issues which had to be determined. The main burden of the War had fallen on the Great Powers and the victory was almost exclusively theirs. Without their intervention the little nations would have been trampled to the ground and would have had to accept such terms as the conqueror vouchsafed to them. If Germany had rejected the terms, it would have been the Armies of the Great Powers that would have had to enforce the settlement to the utmost of their capacity. But the small Powers had made their contribution and some of them had endured sacrifices and sufferings greater than even those to which the Great Powers had been subjected; and they were entitled to a voice in the peace settlement. We had to decide the numbers which should be given to each of the Allied countries who were not in the rank of Great Powers: and whether the numbers should be fixed on the basis of population or of the contribution made to the struggle by each. China had a population of 400 millions; the assistance she rendered was insignificant compared to the efforts and sacrifices of Serbia, Belgium, Roumania or of Canada and the other British Dominions.

On behalf of the Dominions I pressed for a better representation and a higher rank than that which had been accorded to them in the proposals submitted to the Supreme Council by France after consultation with the United States of America. I proposed that each of the Dominions and India should have two representatives and Newfoundland one, and I claimed that they should have the same status as Belgium and Serbia as countries which should be called in on questions which affected them. President Wilson certainly had no feeling of hostility or jealousy towards the Dominions. He entertained a warm feeling of friendship towards Canada in particular. But he felt bound to enter a mild protest against my proposal, no doubt because he realised the difficulties that anything which looked like a doubling or trebling of the representatives of the British Empire might cause in America. I urged the independent nationhood of the Dominions and the enormous assistance which they had rendered in men and material to the Allied cause throughout the struggle. I pointed out that Canada and Australia had each of them lost as many men as the United States of America, and I quoted a remark made that day to me by Sir Robert Borden that "if he returned to Canada and confessed that Canada was getting merely half the number of representatives that had been allotted to Serbia, Roumania, or Belgium, there would be a feeling that they were being badly treated, especially when it was known that the Canadian losses during the War had been greater than those of Belgium." At last I accepted an amendment by President Wilson that Canada and Australia, South Africa and India should each have two representatives, New Zealand one and that Newfoundland should not be given separate representation. All other questions of representation were amicably settled; at least the settlement was an agreed one as far as the Great Powers were concerned. One or two of the more persistent little States continued to grumble—but outside the Conference room.

There was one interesting sidelight on the foreign relations of the United States with her American neighbours when Costa Rica claimed a representative and President Wilson declined to sit at the same table as a Costa Rican delegate. He said that:

When he first became President, revolutions had been fomented in Central America by people desirous of supplying arms and munitions, and anxious to obtain concessions. He had then issued a Note to the effect that the United States of America would not accept any Government formed for the purpose of furthering the ambitions of an individual. An example of this had occurred in Mexico, and for that reason America had refused to recognise Carranza. Later on, a similar instance had occurred in Costa Rica and the United States of America had refused to recognise the new ruler of that country. Costa Rica had made many attempts, without success, to renew relations with the United States of America. With this object in view, she had first offered to declare war on Germany and, finally, receiving no reply to these overtures, had actually declared war in order to force the United States of America to recognise her. In these circumstances he could not bring himself to sit at the same table as a Representative of Costa Rica. Naturally, if any question directly affecting Costa Rica should come up for discussion he would be prepared to reconsider his decision, but under present conditions he proposed that Costa Rica should not be represented at the Peace Conference.

The question of the publicity to be given from day to day to our deliberations occupied a great many sittings. There were swarms of newspaper correspondents from every part of the world clamouring for copy. As the eyes of the world were concentrated on this great assembly of the nations, which was to decide such momentous issues for the future of so many individual nations and for humanity as a whole, it was expected that each of these journalists should send daily messages to their respective papers as to the progress of events. On the other hand, there was a very strong feeling inside the Conference room that if the discussions were published each day before any decision had been arrived at, it would interfere materially with our efforts to reconcile differences and to arrive at a common understanding. It was pointed out that if it were known that the delegates of some particular country were putting up a fight on some special question on which opinion in that country took a somewhat different view from that which obtained in other Allied countries, it would be difficult for either side to give in or to compromise without an appearance of surrender. Ultimately after consultations between the delegates and by the delegates with the representatives of their own Press, an agreement was reached which on the whole and with a few notable exceptions worked very well throughout the whole of the Conference. There was no dearth of copy for the journalists. Nothing was withheld from the public which it was imperative they should know, and which had they known earlier would have caused them to insist upon a change in any of our decisions. On the other hand there were no premature and mischievous revelations (which often meant exaggerations) of the differences which often arose, and were bound to arise, in the discussions on the issues great and small which we had to determine before the draft Treaty could be formulated. My views on the question of premature publicity of our deliberations were thus summarised by the official note taken:

If at every stage of the discussion public and parliamentary agitation had to be pacified the discussions might be prolonged *ad infinitum.* What he (Mr. Lloyd George) wished to avoid was a Peace settled by public clamour. He had just had the experience of an election in England, during which the public was beginning to ask embarrassing questions concerning peace. Had the election lasted longer he might have come to the Conference with his hands tied by pledges, and deprived of his freedom of action. He wished to remain free to be convinced. If there were daily reports of the discussions, as soon as the representative of any country yielded on a point that he had maintained on the previous day there would be headlines in the Press: "Great Britain is betrayed," or "France is betrayed." . . . At a later stage it would be possible to show to the public that, if this or that had been conceded, other advantages had been obtained. He was not afraid of facing the Press, when its demands were not unreasonable. The Press was well aware that it was excluded from proceedings of Cabinets. This was a Cabinet of the nations. Furthermore, the enemy must not know beforehand what our decisions were, and still less what our differences were. Dangerous agitations might be aroused even in our own countries by premature publication of news, and he pointed out that in France and Italy the elections had not yet taken place.

I was specially anxious not to excite public opinion on the question of Reparations, concerning which such extravagant estimates had been formed by men who had a high standing as financial experts. Clemenceau was also anxious to avoid agitation in the French Press and Chamber on this question as well as on the vexed issue of the Rhineland.

Both the British Press and the delegates were very fortunate in the person who was selected with the consent of both to act as liaison between British journalists and the Delegation—Lord Riddell. He was a highly prosperous newspaper proprietor, whose

journal did not compete with any of the daily journals, and therefore excited no jealousy or suspicion in that quarter. He was a
man of exceptionally genial accost, who was on good terms with
most politicians of all parties and almost every newspaper owner
in the kingdom. He possessed tact, affability and ultimate firmness. He got on well with Northcliffe, whilst at the same time he
was a friend of mine. That was in itself a tribute to his tact and
dexterity. The success of the British Press arrangements at the
Paris Conference were largely due to him. But they were also
attributable to the type of journalist chosen by the British Press.
They were amongst the best representatives of their order. When
British Ministers came to know them, they felt the most implicit confidence in their patriotism and sense of honour. Nothing
was given away which had been revealed to them in confidence
for their guidance and not for publication.

CHAPTER IV

PRESIDENT WILSON AND COLONEL HOUSE

BEFORE proceeding to narrate the discussions and the business transacted at this historical conference, it might be well to give some idea of the personages who took a leading part in these transactions. In my "War Memoirs" I have already given my impressions of the veteran statesman who was President of the Conference, and also of Lord Balfour and Mr. Bonar Law.

All the European delegates were especially concerned to discover what President Wilson was like, what he was after and what he meant to insist upon. As to the rest of us, we had often met before and worked together harmoniously during the trials of the War. We could not always agree, but the disagreements were national rather than personal. We could only act within the limits permitted by the opinions of the people we respectively represented. Their exigencies, their difficulties, their aims, traditions and prejudices had to be taken into account. We all understood that perfectly well and allowed for it in our judgment of the stand taken by others. Clemenceau, Orlando, Sonnino, Balfour and I had conferred, conversed and consulted times without number on all the most important issues with which we would be confronted at this Congress. Clemenceau and I had gone together through the dark and depressing events of the 1918 spring-time. Orlando, Sonnino and I had spent anxious days together restoring the Italian front after the catastrophe of Caporetto, and we had all discussed round the same table Unity of Command during the winter and spring of 1918. We had also had many conversations on some of the main outlines of a peace settlement. But President Wilson none of us knew. He was the product, not, it is true, of a different world, but of another hemisphere. Whilst we were dealing every day with ghastly realities on land and sea, some of them visible to our own eyes and audible to our ears, he was soaring in clouds of serene rhetoric. When the Allied Armies were hard pressed and our troops were falling by the hundred thousand in vain endeavours to drive back our redoubtable foe, we could with difficulty even approach him to persuade him to view the grim struggle below, and to come down to earth to deal with its urgent demands before the accumulating slaughter should bury our cause in irreparable disaster. When he came to France, the French Government and people were anxious that he should visit the devastated areas so as to acquaint him with the demoniac actualities of war. He managed to elude their request and to ignore their hints right to the end. Once, under great pressure, he visited Rheims and, viewing the ruins that a few years ago were a glorious cathedral, congratulated the prelate on the edifice not being nearly as much defaced as he had expected to see it. He shunned the sight or study of unpleasant truths that diverted him from his foregone conclusions.

That is how Wilson appeared to those who met him for the first time, and they eyed him with a measure of suspicion not unmixed with apprehension. Clemenceau followed his movements like an old watchdog keeping an eye on a strange and unwelcome dog who has visited the farmyard and of whose intentions he is more than doubtful. There never was a greater contrast mental or spiritual than that which existed between these two notable men. Wilson with his high but narrow brow, his fine head with its elevated crown and his dreamy but untrustful eye—the make-up of the idealist who is also something of an egoist; Clemenceau, with a powerful head and the square brow of the logician—the head conspicuously flat topped, with no upper storey in which to lodge the humanities, the ever vigilant and fierce eye of the animal who has hunted and been hunted all his life. The idealist amused him so long as he did not insist on incorporating his dreams in a Treaty which Clemenceau had to sign. It was part of the real joy of these Conferences to observe Clemenceau's attitude towards Wilson during the first five weeks of the Conference. He listened with eyes and ears lest Wilson should by a phrase commit the Conference to some proposition which weakened the settlement from the French standpoint. If Wilson ended his allocution without doing any perceptible harm, Clemenceau's stern face

temporarily relaxed, and he expressed his relief with a deep sigh.
But if the President took a flight beyond the azure main, as he
was occasionally inclined to do without regard to relevance,
Clemenceau would open his great eyes in twinkling wonder, and
turn them on me as much as to say: "Here he is off again!"

I really think that at first the idealistic President regarded
himself as a missionary whose function it was to rescue the poor
European heathen from their age-long worship of false and fiery
gods. He was apt to address us in that vein, beginning with a few
simple and elementary truths about right being more important
than might, and justice being more eternal than force. No doubt
Europe needed the lesson, but the President forgot that the
Allies had fought for nearly five years for international right and
fairplay, and were then exhausted and sore from the terrible
wounds they had sustained in the struggle. They were therefore
impatient at having little sermonettes delivered to them, full of
rudimentary sentences about things which they had fought for
years to vindicate when the President was proclaiming that he
was too proud to fight for them. Those who suggest that anyone sitting at that table resented President Wilson's exalted
principles are calumniating the myriads who died for those ideals.
We were just as truly there to frame a treaty that would not dishonour their memory as was the President of the United States.

There was a memorable meeting where President Wilson's
homiletic style provoked from Clemenceau one of his most brilliant replies. It arose over the question of the restoration to
France of the 1814 frontier of the Saar Valley. The Allied Powers,
including Britain, Prussia, Russia and Austria, had after Napoleon's overthrow in 1814 determined the North-Eastern frontiers of France in such a way as to give to the French a part of
the Saar Valley. Clemenceau pleaded for the restoration of a
frontier thus accorded to France in the hour of complete defeat.
President Wilson retorted "that was a hundred years ago—a
hundred years is a very long time." "Yes," said Clemenceau,
"a very long time in the history of the États-Unis." Wilson then
diverged into his usual rhapsody about the superiority of right
to might: he referred to those great French idealists—Lafayette

and Rochambeau—whose names were held in immortal honour in the United States; and he ended an eloquent appeal to Clemenceau by quoting Napoleon's saying on his deathbed that "in the end right always triumphed over might." Clemenceau did not reply in English, of which he had a considerable mastery, but as was his invariable practice when he had something to say to which he attached importance, sent for an interpreter and then replied in French. He said: "President Wilson has quoted Napoleon as having said that in the end might was beaten by right. He says that he uttered this sentiment on his deathbed. Had it been true it was rather late for him to have discovered it. But it was not true. President Wilson alluded in glowing language to those idealistic young Frenchmen who helped to liberate America. However exalted the ideals of Lafayette and Rochambeau, they would never have achieved them without force. Force brought the United States into being and force again prevented it from falling to pieces." The President acknowledged the cogency of the reply.

But his most extraordinary outburst was when he was developing some theme—I rather think it was connected with the League of Nations—which led him to explain the failure of Christianity to achieve its highest ideals. "Why," he said, "has Jesus Christ so far not succeeded in inducing the world to follow His teachings in these matters? It is because He taught the ideal without devising any practical means of attaining it. That is the reason why I am proposing a practical scheme to carry out His aims." Clemenceau slowly opened his dark eyes to their widest dimensions and swept them round the Assembly to see how the Christians gathered around the table enjoyed this exposure of the futility of their Master.

Gradually we rubbed along to a better understanding of each other; we learned to make allowance for difference of tradition, antecedents, temperament and environment. This was President Wilson's first contact with Europe and its tangled and thorny jungle, for ages the favourite hunting ground of beasts of prey and poisonous reptiles springing and creeping on their victims. He discovered that he could not judge this old Continent, with its feuds dating from a time when the historical memory of man fades into utter darkness, as he would the relations of America with Mexico. Ancient races have been exterminated in America and their quarrels and wrongs have been buried with them. Emigration has settled the disputes about the righteousness of the conquests of Texas and California. The Rio Grande has not the tragic memories of the Rhine. There are no chronicles which record the savageries perpetrated on the banks of the Rio Grande. The annals of the sanguinary feuds which centuries of watch on the Rhine by Teuton, Gaul and Roman provoked are still preserved. On the other hand, we accepted the fact that the remoteness of America from the scene of our endless conflicts enabled her to take a more detached and therefore a calmer view of the problems upon the solution of which we were engaged.

When a man provokes angry controversy about himself, his theories and his actions and when it continues years after his death, then it is safe to assume that he was an arresting personality. I visited the States some years ago and came across many men and women in many States who accorded to Wilson a reverence which is reserved only for the most venerated amongst the saints of the calendar. On the other hand, I met a great number to whom I dared not mention his name because of the fury it engendered. It was as great a breach of good manners to mention him in certain circles as it would be to introduce the name of the Devil in refined society. A man who excited such a clash of passion in his day and after his day was done must have been a man of striking and powerful individuality.

What kind of man was he? With friends and foes alike his personality unbalanced judgment. How did he impress those who for the first time came into close personal contact with him without possessing any definite preconceived ideas, whether prejudices or predilections about him? To that class I belonged. His stern and dauntless Radicalism always appealed to me. He was disliked by Wall Street and feared by millionaires. I had not myself been a particular pet of financiers or of the ultra-rich except perhaps when they were in dire distress at the beginning of the War and they needed my help to extricate them from their troubles. I admired his oratory—his phrases which were like diamonds, clear cut, brilliant, if hard. On the other hand, I am not enamoured of doctrinaires who shrink from the audacious action which alone can make effective the far-reaching doctrines which they preach. Here I did not think him comparable to his great rival Theodore Roosevelt who curbed the oppression of concentrated wealth by measures which made him hated by the rich right up to and beyond the tomb. "How is it," said the great progressive, "that whenever I mention the Eighth Commandment, there is a panic in Wall Street?" The answer was: because he applied that Mosaic precept to some of the most profitable transactions of the more rapacious in that potent fraternity. The Wilson action was more hesitant and timorous. He did not hit as hard or as direct as the famous Bull Moose at the weak spots of the beasts of prey who infested the American financial jungle. That defect characterised Wilson's conduct before and after the War. He had an implicit faith in the efficacy of phrases. Diamond does not break glass; its impress has to be followed by adequate pressure.

When I first encountered Wilson it was with mixed feelings. I certainly felt no hostility towards him but I was very curious to know what he was like. At our first meeting at Charing Cross Station, the frankness of his countenance and the affability and almost warmth of his greeting won my goodwill and, as far as I was concerned, he never lost it. I sat opposite to him for months in the same small Parisian room. I conversed with him repeatedly in private, and I broke bread with him on a few occasions. I therefore had all the opportunity that anyone could desire for forming an estimate of this notable and towering figure in his day. The favourable personal impression made on my mind by our first handshake was deepened by my subsequent meetings. He was even-tempered and agreeable. He had the charm which emanates from a fine intelligence, integrity of purpose and a complete absence of querulity or cantankerousness. He was stiff, unbending, uncommunicative but he was pleasant almost to the confines of geniality.

When the Congress was drawing to a close, Clemenceau asked

me in his abrupt manner: "How do you like Wilson?" I replied:
"I like him, and I like him very much better now than I did at
the beginning." "So do I," said the Tiger. No three men, cooped
together for so many months discussing momentous issues bristling with controversial points, ever got on better or more agree-
ably together than did Clemenceau, Wilson and I. To quote
M. Tardieu in his book on "The Truth about the Treaty":
"Despite divergencies of opinion, the personal relations between
the three men during those forty days have never ceased to be
sincere, calm and affectionate. May their fellow countrymen
never forget it!" I gladly endorse this testimony to the good
feeling, goodwill and—towards the end—the really affectionate
relations that existed between the three men who took the leading
part in deciding the lines upon which the Versailles Treaty should
be framed. When I criticise Wilson it will be with genuine personal regret. It will be attributable to my resolve to write a
truthful narrative as to events and persons without reference to
my own personal inclinations.

He was a most interesting but not a very difficult study. There
were no obscurities or subtleties in his character—at least none
that an average student of human nature could not decipher
without much difficulty.

All men and women have dual natures. But Wilson was the
most clear-cut specimen of duality that I have ever met. The
two human beings of which he was constituted never merged or
mixed. They were separate and distinct contrasts but nevertheless on quite good terms with each other. It is not that he had
feet of clay. He stood quite firmly on his feet unless he was pushed
over entirely. But there were lumps of pure unmixed clay here
and there amidst the gold in every part of his character. And
both were genuine. There was nothing false or sham about him.
The gold was sterling and the clay was honest marl, and they
were both visible to the naked eye. He was the most extraordinary
compound I have ever encountered of the noble visionary, the
implacable and unscrupulous partisan, the exalted idealist and
the man of rather petty personal rancours.

Most men—perhaps all men in a greater or less degree—are

an inextricable mixture of good and evil motives and impulses—
some noble, some base. Wilson was no exception. He was not
only a mixture, but he was badly mixed. There must be sand in
all concrete: character depends on the proportions of the sand to
the cement and on the way they are mixed together. On the one
hand there were his idealism and his undoubted integrity. On the
other there were his personal hatreds, his suspiciousness, his
intolerance of criticism and his complete lack of generosity towards men who dared to differ from him. The result was that at
one moment you seemed to come up against a fine strong character which was a solid pillar upon which you could rest the weight
of any cause, however momentous; the next moment you found
patches of rather poor stuff in his attitude and actions which
destroyed your confidence and your respect. This was the President Wilson we were expecting in London, and with whom we
had to discuss the terms of peace on the official assumption that
he was speaking the mind of America and that what he said would
receive the full endorsement of the great country of which he was
the Chief Magistrate.

But Wilson's duality obtruded itself more and more as the
Congress proceeded. It was registered in his face, and any prac-
tised physiognomist could readily detect the imprint. There was
the lofty brow of the idealist, there was the fine eye now shining
with righteous passion, now remote and distrustful and hard
with suspicion; one moment faith kindling into a prophetic glow,
the next moment flaming from personal dislike into hatred.

There never were greater contrasts so conspicuously displayed
in the same person without any effort at concealment. He rose
naturally and without effort to great heights. He descended just
as easily to the depths. Spiritually he dwelt above the snow line
high above his fellows in an atmosphere pure, glistening and
bracing but cold. Suddenly he was precipitated like an avalanche
into the swamps of petty personal or party malignity down below.
His was rather an ecclesiastical than a political type of mind. He
had high ideals and honestly held them as a faith with a religious
fervour. He believed all he preached about human brotherhood
and charity towards all men. Nevertheless he was a bigoted sec-

tarian who placed in the category of the damned all those who belonged to a different political creed and excluded them for ever from charitable thought or destiny. His radiant charitableness towards mankind turned to flame when it came into contact with heretics.

He was also vigilantly jealous of all who seemed to dispute or even impinge upon his authority. He would not share or delegate the minutest particle of power.

His face was contorted with an unsightly hatred if you mentioned the names of two or three eminent Republicans who had criticised him or his policies. I shall always remember with a horrified pang the interview I had with him on the day when the news came of Theodore Roosevelt's sudden death. The late Mr. Wickersham had forwarded to me in Paris a letter of introduction written by Mr. Roosevelt from his sick bed. It was placed in my hand just after I had received the tragic news of his sudden death. I was naturally shocked, for I had a great admiration and liking for this great dynamic personality. I had been about to leave for a meeting at the President's house, and as soon as I entered Mr. Wilson's room I expressed my sorrow. I was aghast at the outburst of acrid detestation which flowed from Wilson's lips. He was a man of burning animosities—against persons as well as principles, and he took no trouble to conceal either. There was nothing of the hypocrite in his composition. I would not like to suggest that there is less reticence observed in the States on these occasions than in the Old World. There is the story of a famous American politician who, on being asked whether he proposed to attend the funeral of a rival whom he cordially detested, replied: "No, but I thoroughly approve of it!"

Unconsciously Wilson copied Lincoln—his stories, his vivid phrases, his human appeal. In spite of this unconscious imitation there never were two men who offered so complete a contrast in intellect and character. Lincoln's wit and humour were the natural flow of a gay and genial temperament and of a keen sense of the merry as well as the ridiculous. Wilson had no humour and his wit was synthetic. Wilson was a man of outstanding ability—highly cultivated and polished; Lincoln was a man of genius.

Lincoln had the practical common sense of a son of the soil. He was intensely human and therefore hated war with its abominable cruelty. Above all his heart was tortured with the thought that he had to kill and maim and starve and deny medicaments to tens of thousands of his own fellow-countrymen, and he did his best to avert it. I once read a biography of Lincoln which gave photographs of this resolute but warm-hearted humanitarian at the beginning, in the middle and at the end of the Civil War. By the last act of the tragedy anguish had chiselled deep furrows in his brow and countenance. Gaiety had been chased from the humorous eyes, and deep sadness and grief reigned in their depths. But once war was declared he went all legitimate lengths to achieve victory for what he conceived to be the cause of right. He did not haver and hesitate. He concentrated all his powerful mind on the most effective means and instruments for winning through. Wilson also abhorred the carnage and savagery of war— he also did his utmost to keep out of it—he also was driven by an irresistible current which he could not control to resort to it against his will, and after prolonged efforts to keep out of it. There the comparison ends and the contrast appears. When he finally committed himself to the struggle he did not, like Lincoln, put all his energies and abilities into preparing for battle. He continued to display his aversion to the war he had himself declared by failing to throw his strength of mind and will into its energetic prosecution.

He was genuinely humane, but he completely lacked the human touch of Lincoln. The hand was too frigid. It gave you the impression that Wilson's philanthropy was purely intellectual, whereas Lincoln's came straight from the heart.

There has been a vast amount of discussion as to whether Wilson ought ever to have crossed the Atlantic and to have taken personal part in the deliberations of the Peace Conference. Opinion has now definitely settled down on the side of declaring that it was a grave error of judgment. That opinion is by no means confined to Wilson's detractors. I cannot say that I took that view at the time. I was delighted to have an opportunity of meeting him and of entering into a heart-to-heart discussion with this remarkable man on problems affecting the settlement of the world. I am now convinced that his personal attendance at the Conference was a mistake. It would undoubtedly have been better if he had chosen a mixed team of Democrats and Republicans to represent his views. He would have wielded much greater authority and achieved his own purpose more surely. A cable from the President of the United States intimating that he disapproved of some particular proposition and that, if it were inserted in the Treaty, he could not sign it, would have made it much easier for the French and British representatives to persuade their respective publics to accept modifications. But it was essential that the delegation appointed should not merely be men of capacity and influence, but also persons in whom the President trusted, and unfortunately he was not of a trustful disposition. That was his most disabling weakness—his pervasive suspiciousness. He believed in mankind but distrusted all men. Trustful natures encounter many hurtful disappointments in life, but they get more out of it than the suspicious. Co-operation with their fellow men is to the former a constant joy; to the latter it is a perpetual worry. With ordinary prudence, vigilance and insight the former get the best help from the best helpers; the latter only get an uneasy and grudging service from the second best. The higher types respond to confidence and are chilled by distrust. For that reason Wilson never rallied first-rate minds around him and he did not always succeed in retaining the second-rate. That is why he decided that his personal presence in Europe and at the table of the Congress was inevitable. But the moment he appeared at our Councils, he was there on equal terms with the rest of us. His training had never qualified him for such a position. Whether as Principal of a College, as Governor of New Jersey, or President of the United States, he was always *primus*, not *inter pares* but amongst subordinates. He was not accustomed to confer with equals. He found it exceedingly difficult to adapt himself to that position. In the capacities he had filled he might have debated but he also decided. But when he came to the Peace Congress his decisions counted no more than those of the Prime Ministers with whom he conferred.

I had also an impression that this was the first occasion upon which he had entered into the rough and tumble of political life. He entered into politics late in life. Before he threw himself into the tumult and savageries of the political arena he had led a secluded and sheltered life as the Head of a College. As such he dwelt in a tranquil environment of implicit obedience from all who surrounded him and all who were subject to his rule. Outspoken criticism of the Principal was a breach of discipline. He was like an autocrat with a censored Press and a platform monopolised by himself and his subordinates. If you lead that kind of life well into middle-age, sensitive nerves are not hardened for the stinging and scorching arrows that burn and fester in the ruthless conflicts of a political career. Despite Wilson's apparent calm and his impassivity of countenance, almost Indian in its rigidity, he was an extremely sensitive man. The pride that prevented him from showing it made it all the more hurtful. There is no knowing what pain he suffered from the rancorous criticisms of his own opponents in America whilst he was engaged on his great task in Europe, or from the spiteful paragraphs and caricatures of the Parisian Press. Clemenceau and I had endured this kind of malignity all our days, so when the French Press attacked Clemenceau as a traitor for surrendering the rights of his own country, and both the French and English Press reviled me, neither of us lost a minute's sleep. There was nothing new in this experience for either of us. I once visited the snake farm at São Paulo, Brazil, where they have a shuddering collection of the most poisonous serpents in the Brazilian jungles. The head of the establishment explained to me how a few years ago these vipers destroyed thousands of horses and cattle every year, and something had to be done to protect the rancheros from their ravages. That was the origin of the snake farm. They were now able to inoculate the stock with a virus prepared out of the poisons extracted from snakes. A few injections in the horses or cattle when they were young made them immune. With the older animals it was rather late in life to begin the process. Old politicians like Clemenceau, and I claim the same for myself, had been from our early youth upwards working and hunting in the most snake-infested jungles

that politics can provide. We had been bitten and stung many a
time by every kind of poisonous reptile, and having survived so
long we were now immune. But Wilson had led a protected life
amongst well ordered and academic cloisters. There he had no
stings to fear except from the insects which you cannot keep
from buzzing in the best garnished edifice. Even against those he
was carefully netted around, and therefore he had not been thoroughly inoculated by the experiences which had made the old
horses of the political jungle indifferent to attack.

This accounts for his nervous and spiritual breakdown in the
middle of the Conference. He was received in Paris on his first
appearance with an organised adulation of applause in the streets,
and approbation in the Press which was intoxicating and intended
to inebriate. Streets were named after him, Senate and Chamber
of Deputies gave him an official welcome, a palace was placed at
his disposal, the picked regiments of France provided his escort
and their best bands played him through the most impressive
avenues of the city. Then came a blighting, withering blizzard
of criticism and calumny. Wilson's self-confidence wilted and
shrivelled under the ceaseless blast.

Many angry controversies have raged around his name in his
own country, and they have not yet died down, so that it will be
difficult there to secure a fair verdict on either side as to his rank
amongst the rulers of America. But no one can doubt that he was
a supremely able man. As to his character, outside the partisans
who still hold him in detestation, those who met him in Europe,
and had every opportunity of weighing and measuring his character, pay him the tribute of unreserved recognition of his sincerity
as an idealist.

His last spurt of will-power and energy at the Congress he spent
on a futile endeavour first to cajole and then to bully a gifted but
hysterical Italian poet out of Fiume. The more clumsily he cooed
or the more loftily he preached, the more vehemently did D'Annunzio gesticulate and orate defiance inside Fiume. After his pact
with Clemenceau which protected Woodrow Wilson from the
calumnious scribblings of the Parisian pen* dipped in gall his

* See chapter VIII.

interventions on the German Treaty were languid and his protests tepid. Things were not shaping themselves on the lines of
his dream. When he sailed for Europe he had a vision of arriving
in the Old World as a New Messiah to save it from its predatory
transgressions, and directing its feet along the paths of peace,
righteousness and fraternity. The diverse races and traditions of
America had been hammered partly in the fires of war into one
people with one common national patriotism. Wilson thought he
might persuade the warring tribes of Europe—no more numerous
than those of the States—to weld into one fraternity whilst they
were still soft and malleable after issuing from the glowing furnace
of the Great War. He had a habit of beginning his admonitions
to the statesmen of an old hemisphere whom he believed were
steeped in the spirit of rapine: "Friends—for we are all friends
here."

His experiences at the Peace Congress disclosed to him two dis-
concerting truths. One is a truth which has so often baffled all
of us in life: that our greatest difficulties come not so much from
deciding whether we should follow the dictates of a clear principle
or not, but in choosing the particular principle which is most
applicable to the facts or in ascertaining accurately the particular
facts upon which the principle is to be shaped. Thus President
Wilson discovered that the chronic troubles of Europe could not
be settled by hanging round its neck the phylacteries of abstract
justice. He found that abstract principles did not settle frontiers
so tangled historically and traditionally that no one could with
certainty unravel the title to lands on either side. He found that
strict justice required that compensation should be paid for all
torts, but that strict insistence on a right which every civilised
country recognised caused complications he was not prepared to
face. Everywhere he found that decisions based on his conceptions of right and wrong carried him away from a real settlement,
and that practical expediency demanded compromise on every
side and on every question. From his desk at the White House it
all looked so simple and easy provided he could persuade the
sophisticated diplomats of the Old World to stick to his revised
Decalogue. He found that he could not measure accurately with

his rigid yard-stick timber gnarled and twisted by the storms of centuries.

But another truth which came to him as a slap in the face was the discovery that war-ridden Europe was readier than were his own countrymen to enter into an Association of Nations to preserve peace. His bitterest disappointment came not from the greed and obduracy of the sinful Old World, but from the narrow selfishness of his own people bred on a soil not yet soured by ancient memories of wrong and strife. There was one part of the Treaty he claimed—not justly—as the work of his own hands—the Covenant of Peace. He had anticipated opposition and chicanery in Europe to defeat his cherished aim. When he met the men whose evil disposition he had crossed the seas to overcome, he found they were entirely of his mind on the subject of the League. He was almost abashed to discover that they had worked out careful plans to give practical effect to ideas which he had been satisfied to leave in the realm of undefined aspiration. His sycophants flattered him that when he presided over a committee which adopted those schemes, and when the full assembly endorsed them, it was his art and courage which had triumphed. He knew better. The bloodstained hands of European statesmanship had actually prepared the plan and had helped him to mould and to fashion the idea until it was perfected, as he thought, according to his own image. And then, his own fellow countrymen flung it into the gutter to rot. They would have none of it. That blow from his own kith and kin in whom he believed stunned and paralysed him. A disillusioned prophet is an abject spectacle. All Wilson's appeals had been in vain: the Heavens remained as brass and the false prophets were permitted to strike him down. He never recovered, but his fame will endure. He sacrificed his life for the attainment of a noble purpose. The immolation was none the less genuine that it was unnecessary, and that his aim could have been better achieved had he not taken steps which entailed a fatal breakdown in his powers. More tact and less pride would have enabled him to attain his end. A gentle bow on entering the portals of the Senate would have enabled him to get through. But he remained stiff and erect, and hit his head on the lintel and was for ever stunned and silenced by the blow. It was a double tragedy. The first was his ignominious failure to register a success which was already in his hands. The second was that, in taking the longest and most craggy road to reach a goal which was easily attainable by a shorter and equally honourable avenue, he fretted away the remnant of a strength which was already almost worn out by unnecessary toil. Had he conquered his stubborn pride, had he subordinated his personal antipathies for the sake of a great cause of which he was an outstanding champion, America would have been in the League of Nations and the whole history of the world would have been changed. Has there ever been a greater tragedy in human history?

The last time I saw him was when I visited America in 1923. It was shortly before his death. His health was then so precarious that his doctor warned me that the interview must be a short one. Physically he was a wreck. One side was paralysed, but the impairment to his powers of speech was not apparent. He was pleased to see me and his reception was cordial. He alluded with pleasure to his experiences at the Conference. Of Clemenceau he spoke in kindly terms. But when the name of Poincaré was mentioned, all the bitterness of his nature burst into a sentence of concentrated hatred. "He is a cheat and a liar," he exclaimed. He repeated the phrase with fierce emphasis. Poincaré disliked and distrusted him and the detestation was mutual. The name of Coolidge provoked another outburst. When I informed him that I had just left his successor at the White House, he asked me what I thought of him. I replied that I was not quite sure. He replied: "I will tell you what he is like. Oscar Wilde once saw a man who was giving himself great airs at a social function. He went up to him and putting on his eyeglass"—here Wilson took his glasses in his right hand and fixed them at his eye—"he said to him: 'Are you supposed to be anyone in particular?' Coolidge is no one in particular." Here was the old Wilson with his personal hatreds unquenched right to the end of his journey.

We shunned all reference to the League of Nations. The doctor signalled to me that the interview should be terminated. That is the last I saw of this extraordinary mixture of real greatness thwarted by much littleness.

Was he hero, saint or martyr? There was something of each in the struggles of the last years of his life and in the circumstances of his death, though not enough to warrant the claim made on his behalf to any of these noble appellations. But that he honestly consecrated an upright character and a fine intellect to the service of mankind, no one will deny who is not afflicted with a party spirit so charged with rancour as to have become an insanity of the soul.

THERE was no man who played as active, continuous and useful a part in President Wilson's dealings with Europe as Colonel House. He was the Claudius of this pacific American Caesar. He was one of the most subtle and successful political managers of his day. His manœuvres were largely responsible for Wilson's ascent to the Presidential throne. A Democrat from the southernmost of the Southern States, he was drenched with all the party fanaticism of that fierce breed. His natural suavity of demeanour and softness of speech concealed his real antipathy towards Republicans of all sorts and kinds. It was uncompromising and inexorable. I attributed Wilson's greatest blunder—the failure to take one or two of the more moderate and sympathetic Republican leaders with him to Paris—partly to House's encouragement of Wilson's instinctive dislike of all Republicans, if not to the actual counsel which he gave him to have nothing to do with any of them. But he was not only an intense Democrat; he was above all a devoted and devout Wilson Democrat. Wilson was his idol, but his in the sense that it was House who had picked him out, shaped him as a politician, built the altar for him and placed him there above it to be worshipped. As a party leader Wilson was not the creator of House, but his creation. All the same there could be no doubt of House's genuine admiration and worship for what was the work of his own hands. He recognised that he had chosen first-class timber. Judging from his Memoirs, he was under the impression that he not only chiselled and shaped the idol but also pulled the hidden strings that moved it. And he was ecstatically proud of it.

House was about the only man that Wilson really trusted amongst his associates and counsellors. He gave him that abnormal measure of confidence because House very adroitly gave Wilson the impression that the advice he gave was not his own but Wilson's idea. The President was exceptionally distrustful and full of lurking misgivings about men in general. He demanded the most exacting proofs of faith and attachment from all his subordinates. He was not satisfied with mere party loyalty. The incense offered must have a distinct aroma of personal adoration. House accorded it in full—not to say, fulsome—measure. Page, the well-beloved American Ambassador in London, was not a true worshipper; he was just a good Democrat at home and a faithful servant of his country in a foreign court—and no more. Hence his despatches on the course of events in England during the War were suspect and carried no weight in the White House. Secretary Lansing was a mere cypher—an amiable lawyer of good standing and of respectable abilities but of no particular distinction or definite personality. He just did what he was told, and was never told to do very much. He was not of the true faith; his Memoirs show that he had not assimilated into his system the Decree of Infallibility. But House had. So in foreign policy he became the trusted—and the only trusted—instrument and exponent of the President's ideas across the Atlantic. He visited Berlin, Paris and London during the War, saw every statesman who counted on either side and reported every interview that he had to the great chief. When the Supreme Council met in Paris to discuss the terms of the Armistice and afterwards the arrangements for the Peace Conference, House, with no official status, was the acknowledged spokesman of the American Republic. I think there were other Americans present, but I have forgotten their names, for they did not matter and took no part in the discussions. The voice of House was the voice of Wilson. He cabled to the White House every day messages setting forth how he had stood up to the unregenerate Europeans for Wilson's high ideals. He told the President how all the Allied statesmen dreaded his appearance in person at the table of the Peace Congress, and were pleading that he should not come.

When the President arrived in Paris, I saw less and gradually less of House. I thought it better to deal with Wilson direct. In spite of all that has been disseminated and believed to the contrary, I was more in sympathy with the President's ideas as to the main objectives we ought to strive for in the Peace Settlement, and particularly as to the things we ought to avoid, than I was with Clemenceau's one aim of keeping Germany down feeble and fettered. Wilson soon came to understand my attitude and therefore he realised that no intermediary was required between him and me. On the other hand, the astute French Premier saw the value of getting at House and using his influence over Wilson to mollify and mould the too idealistic President into the right frame of mind on the French policy. House and Clemenceau saw a great deal of each other behind the scenes. Whenever there were difficulties Clemenceau got at House. It was House who negotiated the nefarious arrangement by which the French Press were to be induced to withdraw their disreputable campaign of slander and spite against the President in return for an assurance that Wilson would modify his objections to the French demands on their eastern frontiers. It was a fateful and in some respects a fatal pact which did no credit to either party. Wilson crossed the watershed and henceforth the stream of American influence flowed downwards on the wrong side of the Mount of Beatitudes.

There is no man whose real character has always eluded one more than that of Colonel House. This genial, kindly, unpretentious, insignificant looking little man baffled analysis. That he was intelligent, tactful, understanding and sympathetic, all who knew him will recognise and gladly recognise. But how deep did his intelligence, comprehension, and sympathies go? He saw more clearly than most men—or even women—to the bottom of the shallow waters which are to be found here and there in the greatest of oceans and of men. But could he penetrate the depths of human nature or of human events? I have come to the conclusion that he emphatically could not. Intellectually he was nowhere near the same plane as Wilson. But he was sane, even-tempered, adroit and wise in all things appertaining to the management of men and affairs. He had a well-balanced, but not a powerful mind. He got his ideas from his chief and he accepted them loyally and manipulated them skilfully. But he gave one the impression that had he served a different type of leader with a completely different set of ideas he would have adopted his theories with the same zeal and put them across with the same deftness. He was essentially a salesman and not a producer. He would have been an excellent Ambassador but a poor Foreign Minister. In the sphere of law with which I am acquainted he would have been an accomplished family lawyer—prudent, courteous, courtly and thoroughly loyal to his client. In every transaction I had with him he was frank and straightforward. His methods were not without guile but there was no deception. When I recognise that he was honourable in all his dealings, it is not inconsistent with this characteristic to say that he possessed craft. It is perhaps to his credit that he was not nearly as cunning as he thought he was.

House was generally liked by all those who transacted any business with him and it is a testimony to his sterling quality that those who took to him at the beginning continued to like him. It is a tragedy that the only exception to that experience was President Wilson himself, whom House had helped to high office and who incidentally gave to House his one avenue to celebrity. They quarrelled at the end of Wilson's day when the shadows were falling on his brilliant career. A long and continuous friendship is a great strain, and with men and women of strong personality it hardly ever survives the wear and tear of incessant contact over a prolonged period in trying times. My impression of the break between these two men, each remarkable in his way, is that Wilson was primarily at fault. I was present on the occasion which caused the coolness. Wilson was at the time involved in a bitter dispute with the Italians over Fiume. He threw himself into the contention between Italy and Jugoslavia with an intensity which I had never seen him display over any other difference of opinion in the framing of the Treaty. It was distracting his thoughts from infinitely more important issues and it was fretting his own nerve. House realised this with

the eye of a devoted and tender friend and was anxious to find
some solution that would get the troublesome little matter out
of the way. He talked to Clemenceau and to me on the subject
and we found ourselves in complete sympathy with his desires.
One day an informal meeting was summoned at the American
headquarters at the Hotel Crillon to talk over one or two questions which needed straightening out. House invited M. Clemenceau and myself to come to his room half an hour before the
Conference to talk over the Fiume imbroglio, in order to see
whether we could find some way out that would on the whole
satisfy all the contending parties. We had not been in the room
very long before the door opened and Wilson appeared with a
rigid and displeased countenance and an unfriendly eye. I have
always thought someone must have communicated to him the
fact that House had the two Premiers closeted with him in secret
conference at his room in the Crillon. House had his rivals in the
American camp who were not too pleased with the position accorded to him. As soon as Wilson entered the room, he said in a
quiet but somewhat stern voice: "Hello, what is this about?"
He was clearly upset, and as we discovered afterwards irreconcilably angry—not with the two foreign Premiers but with House
for not informing him. He felt he ought to have been present
when a question was being discussed in which he had so supreme
an interest. It was undoubtedly an indiscretion on House's part
but it was done entirely in order to save Wilson from an annoy-
ing problem which was undermining his strength.

House was never forgiven. I saw little of him after this unpleasant interview. He was not charged with any more errands
from Wilson. The President was intensely jealous of his personal
authority. He had at least one divine attribute: he was a jealous
god; and in disregarding what was due to him House forgot that
aspect of his idol and thus committed the unforgivable sin. The
snapping of the golden thread of a tried and affectionate friendship over a trivial misunderstanding easily explained was one of
the premonitory symptoms of the fatal disease which soon after
laid the President low.

When Wilson was stricken down and became a helpless

paralytic, he refused to see Colonel House—once his most intimate friend—at his bedside. Although he lingered on for years and saw many of his old friends, Clemenceau and myself amongst them, House he would not receive.

CHAPTER V

OTHER PERSONAL SKETCHES

1. POINCARÉ

DURING the whole of the sittings of the Congress I saw nothing of President Poincaré except at official receptions. I was never attracted by his personality. He possessed all those gifts which enable a man to make a successful career either in law or in politics. He had a logical mind, definite and clear-cut opinions which never changed and yet therefore gave an impression of stern honesty of conviction. Moreover he possessed considerable courage and dour tenacity.

A man who changes his views, however honestly, is always suspect of doing so for personal motives. A man who sticks to them through all vicissitudes is acclaimed as a man of incorruptible sincerity. Poincaré never changed a single opinion he ever held. He was therefore trusted without question put.

When compared with Briand or Clemenceau, Poincaré's was a dull and sterile mind. He had no wit or imagination or play of fancy. He uttered the commonplaces that command respect and confidence. His was the triumph of commonplace qualities well proportioned, well trained and consistently well displayed; just the man to gain the trust of the numerous class he so adequately represented. He was a worthy chief of that populous and powerful clan. In competition for the high places with men of genius, a man like Poincaré wins in 99 cases out of 100. Such a personage is supposed to be safe, and most people place safety first. He held high administrative office in France on three occasions. On the first he was snatched to the heaven of the Elysée before he had an opportunity to exhibit his powers or defects. The second time he became Premier his only service to France was that by his melodramatic invasion of Germany in search of reparations he exposed the folly of trying to make the Germans pay debts out of an empty cash-box and an overdrawn account. His fame will rest on his third Premiership, when he persuaded France that by devaluing its franc to a fifth of its pre-war standard its real wealth was increased. That was a genuine triumph of common sense and courage. He was the only man who could have succeeded in inducing all classes to accept that humiliating estimate of French credit.

In business he was a fussy little man who mistook bustle for energy. When Barthou represented him at the Genoa Conference, he came to me one morning and said: "I have just received my nine-hundredth telegram this morning from Poincaré!" The Conference was then about halfway through. Clemenceau suffered a good deal from this fussiness, especially during the Peace Conference. Poincaré constantly sent for the aged and burdened Premier to bother him about the Rhineland and about Reparations. One morning Clemenceau, who was always punctual, kept the Congress waiting for nearly an hour. His Secretary explained that Poincaré had sent for him to the Elysée. When the Tiger arrived, he burst into the room blowing and puffing, apologised for his lateness and then, coming up to me, said in my ear: "Cannot you lend me George the Fifth for a short time?" Clemenceau loathed and despised Poincaré. That was also President Wilson's opinion of him. It was also Bonar Law's impression of the man. Clemenceau had a sincere admiration and respect for intellectual power, even when he disapproved of the use to which it was put. Jaurès, the great Socialist leader, was one of Clemenceau's most formidable parliamentary antagonists. But Clemenceau told me with pride that he thought him the greatest orator he had ever heard. Of Poincaré, on the other hand, he had no opinion as a speaker, a politician or a man. Speaking of him in the latter capacity, he once asked me: "Do you know what the word Poincaré means?—*Point:* not; *carré:* square!" He suspected him during the Peace negotiations of intriguing behind his (Clemenceau's) back with Foch and the Extreme Right to annex the Rhineland and afterwards to set up little republics there. At that time I had not had any direct dealings with Poincaré. I subsequently had and I now accept fully Clemenceau's and Wilson's estimate of him. An agreement with Poincaré simply meant that he thought an open break was inconvenient at that time. He was one of those men who, having acquired a reputation for honesty, can afford to be tricky.

I afterwards had an opportunity of measuring his intelligence when he visited London in 1922 to discuss the non-payment of Germany's reparation instalments. He actually proposed that we should demand payment in German marks. They stood then at 900 to the pound. I asked him who would take them, and what use could be made of them by the recipient. He replied that England would take them at their nominal value. How we were to cash them he did not explain. Nor had he considered what the effect would be on the value of the mark of placing milliards of marks on the money market.

The fact that he was a Lorrainer, born and brought up in sight of the German eagle waving over the ravished provinces of France, bred in him an implacable enmity for Germany and all Germans. Anti-clericalism was with him a conviction; anti-Germanism was a passion. That gave him a special hold on the France that had been ravaged by the German legions in the Great War. It was a disaster to France and to Europe. Where a statesman was needed who realised that if it is to be wisely exploited victory must be utilised with clemency and restraint, Poincaré made it impossible for any French Prime Minister to exert these qualities. He would not tolerate any compromise, concession or conciliation. He was bent on keeping Germany down. He was more responsible than any other man for the refusal of France to implement the disarmament provisions of the Treaty of Versailles. He stimulated and subsidised the armaments of Poland and Czecho-Slovakia which created such a ferment of uneasiness in disarmed Germany. He encouraged insurrection in the Rhineland against the authority of the Reich. He intrigued with the anti-German elements in Britain to thwart every effort in the direction of restoring goodwill in Europe and he completely baffled Briand's endeavour in that direction. He is the true creator of modern Germany with its great and growing armaments, and should this end in another conflict the catastrophe will have been engineered by Poincaré. His dead hand lies heavy on Europe to-day.

2. ORLANDO AND SONNINO

THE two Italian delegates—Signor Orlando, the Premier, and Baron Sonnino, the Foreign Secretary—were both men of distinction and capacity. But the antithesis between them was marked and occasionally developed into an antagonism of purpose and policy. Signor Orlando was a learned, cultured and eminent lawyer, possessing considerable oratorical gifts. As he had to express himself at our Conferences in French, his powers were never exhibited at their best. When he spoke in his own language, either in the Italian Parliament, or to great crowds outside, I am told he was exceedingly effective. This, coupled with the deep respect he had won by his integrity and genuine patriotism, was the secret of his strength. He had an amiable and attractive personality which made him an extremely pleasant man to do business with. His interventions at conferences were always sensible and to the point. His views were Liberal and democratic. There was no fundamental difference of outlook or principle between him and President Wilson, and I always thought that if the President had taken more trouble to talk things over with him on a friendly basis, instead of lecturing him from on high, the wretched quarrel that developed over Fiume and was never settled between the two could have been accommodated.

Baron Sonnino was a man of a totally different type. He was dour, rigid and intractable. He was not an Italian by race or origin. His father was a Hebrew. He told me his mother was Welsh. Both of them stubborn races, not easily persuaded. One parent may have accounted for his tenacity and toughness in a bargain—the other may have explained the obstinacy with which he held to his opinions. But whatever his racial origin, he was Italian through and through in his policy and patriotism. To him the War was not a fight for international right and human liberty. His interest in either of these two ideals was torpid and a little scornful. The victory was to him a supreme chance for extending the boundaries and increasing the security, the importance and the prestige of Italy. That is why he threw over the Triple Alliance and used the whole of his influence to induce Italy to join the Allies. He was shrewd enough to see that the Central Powers could give Italy nothing for either alliance or neutrality. Austria would not sacrifice valuable towns and sea-ports or formidable mountain bastions to enrich and strengthen Italy at the expense of the Austrian Empire. Germany could not persuade Turkey to surrender any part of the Anatolian littoral in order to placate Italy or purchase Italian support. And as to Germany herself, it was more than she could do to save her own colonies without helping Italy to acquire new African territories. Moreover Italian statesmen did not display any great eagerness for African territory. Neither during the War nor at the Peace Conference did they press for any share in the German Colonies. Sonnino, the diplomatist, knew he could drive a better bargain with the Western Allies, and he therefore plumped for them.

In the course of our discussions questions like the League of Nations, disarmament and international labour did not interest Sonnino much. At the Conference table he looked like a man waiting in bored sullenness for the only question that mattered to come up: that is, what Italy was going to get out of the spoils of victory. When he occasionally intervened in discussions on other questions, it had generally a direct or oblique reference to this paramount consideration. He had a nervous, jumpy manner of speech, all his own. He had one curious mannerism—to empha-sise his points he constantly jerked his right hand towards his breast as if he were pulling invisible levers. He did pull levers but they were not invisible. What he said was effectively and some-times picturesquely phrased. For instance, when Colonel House, in pressing the Wilson point about the Freedom of the Seas, seemed to be hostile to the British view as to our right to use our Navy to cripple an enemy, Sonnino said that different animals fought with different weapons: some used their teeth, some their claws, others their fangs. So with nations—some fought with their armies, others with their navies. I heard him at a great meeting at the Queen's Hall using a felicitous illustration to explain why, although he had a workable knowledge of the English language, he was unable to deliver a speech in that tongue. He said that a language of which you had no perfect mastery was like a tram— it took you near your destination but not right up to the door.

He was a resolute man, but too unbending to make a first-class diplomatist. He lacked suppleness. That is why he did not make the best use for Italy of the wonderful opportunity presented to her by the great part she had played—directly or indirectly—in the break up of the German, Austrian and Turkish Empires. There were certain concessions he had set his mind on securing. He would have no others, although they were much better from the Italian standpoint. The two Italian delegates were each in his way exceptionally able men, but they were not a good team. When trouble came Orlando was too emotional and not hard enough, Sonnino was too sulky and too rigid.

Mutual understanding between the Allied representatives ultimately ripened into goodwill, and goodwill into friendship. The only exception was the case of Italy. The lack of sympathy between the President and the Italian representatives widened into an unbridgeable chasm. But of that I shall have something to say further on.

3. BOTHA, SMUTS AND MILNER

THERE were three men whose names will ever be associated with the history of South Africa, who in 1919 stood for a peace out of which every punitive element should be purged—General Botha, General Smuts and Lord Milner. The three had sat at the same table once before to settle the terms of a peace which fashioned the destiny of vast territories on the African Continent. Milner was then all out for a ruthless settlement which would take cognisance of the fact—a fact by the way not too evident to the British Commander—that his foes in that war had been beaten in the field. He was in favour of basing the conditions of peace and the future government of South Africa on an acknowledgment by his Boer adversaries of the fact that their racial domination of the lands in which they had been the pioneers of white civilisation was for ever at an end. Kitchener's suppler and more practical mind saved the situation at that conference, and he and not Milner was responsible for the conciliatory character of the Treaty of Vereeniging. In Paris, Milner joined with his former antagonists in resistance to that spirit of relentlessness which would humiliate the vanquished foe and keep them down in the dust into which they had been cast by their complete overthrow.

They were three noteworthy men. Of the three Botha was the most striking personality in his physical appearance, in strength of character and in his general impressiveness. He was one of those men whose presence you feel in a room even when they are silent. He attracted attention without making any effort to do so. The first time I met him was when as President of the Board of Trade I attended an Imperial Conference in 1907. There he represented South Africa as Prime Minister of the Union. It was his first Imperial Conference as well as mine. Although Botha foresaw a war with Germany, neither of us had any vision of another Conference where we should both be engaged in helping to settle the affairs of four continents after a World War. Botha took hardly any part in that meeting of the Imperial Conference. He had not at the time acquired such a mastery of English as would enable him to take an active part in the discussions, and he left the handling of trade questions to others. Deakin, the Australian Prime Minister, a man who commanded that torrential flow of sonorous commonplace so often mistaken for eloquence, spoke for hours at a time. Sir Joseph Ward, the New Zealand Premier, was also a speaker of easy fluency.

But there were two men who fascinated me at these gatherings. One of them delivered a short speech—the other hardly uttered a word. The first was Sir Wilfred Laurier, the Canadian Premier, a man whose distinguished and graceful appearance, whose musical voice and short quivering sentences thrilled all to attention. The other was Botha himself, a born leader of men. The great head, the steady, dauntless, understanding eyes full of fire and light, the deep, husky, commanding voice—as I sat opposite him for hours I found myself drawn to gaze upon him. I thought of him leading his men in a charge and I felt I would rather be by his side than facing him. Afterwards I heard him speak in his own tongue. There was power, directness, conviction in his voice and manner. One could understand the sway he exerted over his rugged and valiant commandoes and why they followed him into battle without reckoning the odds. He was a more moving magnetic speaker than either Smuts or Milner. The timbre of his voice had an arresting quality and the way he used it had all the tokens of a natural artist. Its inflexions conveyed meaning better than when the words were translated by an accurate but toneless interpreter.

There was an amusing incident which occurred during the delivery of the speech I heard from him on the occasion to which I allude. It was at a banquet, over which I presided, given to him during the Conference. The suffragette campaign was then at its height. All meetings attended by Ministers were interrupted by female shrieks and screechings about "Votes for Women." The interruptions were indiscriminate. Speakers who sympathised with the movement were subjected to the same annoyance as those who were opposed. And although I was an ardent suffragist, that seemed to exasperate these ladies all the more. To avoid disturbance all women were now being excluded from functions of this kind. The suffragettes retaliated by organising groups of men sympathisers to pursue the same tactics. Arrangements had been made for expelling interrupters from the Botha meeting. Botha addressed the gathering in the Taal. After he had spoken a sentence or two a man rose behind him and began to interpret in English. No sooner had he uttered a few words than a stalwart attendant, mistaking him for a demonstrator who had crept in, took him by the scruff of the neck shouting: "Outside," and hustled him towards the door. No one was more amused at the incident than Botha.

Next time Botha came to England he spoke excellent English—idiomatic and vigorous. Later on I shall give an account of the impressive speech on the question of mandates which he delivered at the Peace Congress, and which moved us all—none more than President Wilson, to whom it was addressed.

When he came to Paris his health was precarious. The privations he had endured in the field as a hunted man, and the anxieties of one who had the fate of his race dependent on his leadership, had told on his powerful constitution. The fine physique was crumbling visibly, and soon after he returned to South Africa he passed away. I never met a man who seemed to be more of an embodiment of wisdom in speech and action. He was truly a great man. He was a great warrior, an even greater counsellor and conciliator. Throughout the Paris deliberations he stood for a settlement that would leave no roots of bitterness behind.

General Smuts and Lord Milner were utterly different types. Botha was pre-eminently a man of the great wide spaces where he communed with the vast distances of earth below and the infinite heights of the heavens above. That was his upbringing—that was his academy. Men thus trained, if they are well endowed with natural gifts of mind and character—and Botha was exceptionally equipped in both respects—develop a clarity of vision, a breadth of mind, a steadfastness of purpose which raises them to a level where they can confront all the problems of life with a steady nerve and a calm clear judgment. It enables them to discern the things that matter and determine their course with assured wisdom.

Smuts was also a product of the great African Veldt, and his experiences there account for the detachment with which he is able to judge world problems. They give his speeches a unique character which goes beyond their mere intellectual superiority. But he never struck me as being as much a son of nature at its greatest as did Botha. Smuts and Milner were "the fine flower" of the culture given by the old Universities. They both possessed an exceptional intellect, perfectly trained. I have had occasion repeatedly in these "Memoirs" to relate the great part they both played in our Councils during the War. It is difficult to overrate the importance of the contribution General Smuts made to our peace preparations. It is not easy to draw the line between genius and talent. I have seen and heard it attempted on many occasions, but never with satisfying success. Still, history bears witness to the fact that there is an unbridgeable chasm between the two. Botha was undoubtedly a man of genius—of intuitive, imaginative understanding.

What about the other two? They were both men of remarkable

intellectual capacity. I have no hesitation in saying that Smuts
was the ablest man that came to help us from the outside Empire,
and that Milner was much the best all-round brain that the
Conservative party contributed to our Councils. He had none of
Curzon's brilliancy or Carson's dramatic oratory—he was a poor,
dull speaker. He had no flow of words. He had no colour, his
voice had no resonance, his delivery was halting. In fact, he had
none of the qualities of an orator. Nor did he possess Balfour's
extraordinary analytical powers, nor Bonar Law's gifts as a de-
bater. But in constructive power and fertility of suggestion he
surpassed them all. The chief lack of his party to-day is that they
have in their ranks no statesman of Milner's calibre to handle the
economic problems with which they are faced. Up till the spring
of 1918 it is difficult to exaggerate his value as a counsellor. He
did not shine in general discussion. He seemed to find a difficulty
in giving expression in words to his ideas. He was at his best when
I invited him, as I often did, to a quiet talk in the Cabinet room
on the perplexing questions which constantly arose during the
War. He was dauntless; he never shrank from making or con-
curring in a proposal because it was original and might offend
party or professional prejudices. When we came to deal with food
production, his suggestions were revolutionary. When they came
up for discussion in the Cabinet I remember Balfour gaping with
astonishment. Looking at the clock, he turned to his neighbour
and said: "As near as I can reckon we have had one revolution
for every half hour."

When Lord Derby left the War Office Milner insisted on the
succession. Neither Bonar Law nor I could dissuade him from
undertaking so arduous a task. Physically he was not a strong
man, and the interminable variety of bothering detail which
came before him for decision soon wore out his limited reserves.
The result was a tragic change in his quality. His nervous power
was exhausted. His contributions henceforth were those of an
exhausted man. His powers waned and his usefulness in the consideration of great issues gradually disappeared. Now and then
we had a flash of his old powers of insight into the heart of a problem, but the lamp was flickering for the oil was running out. As

an elder statesman in Council he was resourceful; as an administrator he became limp, flabby and ineffective. The War Office
literally killed him. He undertook a task which would have tried
to the utmost the strength of a man in his prime. It aged him
prematurely, and he gradually faded away. When he resigned it
was too late to effect a restoration of his splendid faculties. But
I shall always recall with gratitude the Milner of 1917 who lent
me the constant aid of a mind rich in suggestion, resource and
courage.

He had no political nostril. He acquired the reputation of a
Die-Hard Tory on the strength of his appeal to the Conservatives
to reject the Parliament Act of 1911 and "to damn the consequences." There was no man who was less a reactionary. The
author of the Death Duties of 1906 could hardly be so described.
There was no man of his time who was less of an old Tory, in the
meaning of being an instinctive opponent of reform and reconstruction. He was by inclination and conviction a State Socialist.
In agriculture he was prepared to go greater lengths in the way of
State intervention, aid and action than any statesman I met in
any party. If his politics could be classified by any known ticket,
I should call him a Radical Imperialist. His belief in the British
Empire had the fervour and faith of a religious conviction. He
will rank with Disraeli and Rhodes as an apostle of Empire.
Their zeal led each of them into serious blunders, but no one can
doubt the sincerity of their confidence in the mission of the
British Empire. The Great War was a noble vindication of their
faith.

When Milner was in South Africa he gathered around him a
group of brilliant young men who in different spheres have since
justified his insight. To one of them—Philip Kerr (now Marquess
of Lothian) I must pay a tribute of grateful acknowledgment for
the priceless help he gave me during the greater part of my
Premiership, in peace and in war. When I became Prime Minister in 1917 he was introduced to me by Lord Milner as a young
man of conspicuous ability who was specially knowledgeable on
all Imperial questions and on foreign affairs. No man more completely justified his recommendation. Kerr had a thorough, wide,

and intelligent understanding of both. During the few years he was in my service he played an important part in my dealings with the Dominions, with India and with America. Kerr had considerable literary gifts which on many occasions I found of great service. An excellent example of the vigour and lucidity of his style is the reply given by the Allies to Brockdorff Rantzau's challenge of Germany's responsibility for the War, which he drafted. Both President Wilson and Clemenceau—who were excellent judges of literary style—admired it as a piece of cogent writing and agreed to its incorporation in the Allied Official Reply without a single alteration of sentiment or phrase.

He was particularly helpful to me in my difficulties with the Russian entanglement. It would not be fair to characterise him, as did some of my friends and his, as pro-Bolshevik. But he was just as strongly opposed as I was to the intervention of Allied forces in the internal affairs of Russia. So energetic were his protests that a prominent Allied diplomat sent a warning to me through one of my secretaries that Kerr was "the Bolshevik head centre in Western Europe"! When, on one occasion after the signature of the Treaty of Versailles, I left Paris for a few weeks, Philip Kerr remained behind to co-operate with Mr. Balfour in the drafting of the other treaties. He discovered that advantage had been taken of my absence—not, I need say, by Mr. Balfour but by another Minister—to make an effort to organise an Allied Confederacy to overthrow Bolshevik rule by force of arms. He promptly informed Mr. Balfour, who thoroughly disapproved of the project, and requested him to inform me at once as to what was happening. I wired immediately to Kerr instructing him to communicate with the French, American and Italian delegates my definite veto of this wild project so far as the British Government were concerned. That put an end to the scheme.

It was Kerr's activities, acting on my instructions, that gave rise to the legend that the Foreign Office had been transferred to "the garden suburb" at 10, Downing Street. That was an allusion to the wooden structure that had been built during the War to accommodate my staff in the tiny enclosure outside the Prime Minister's official residence. The arrangement worked well as long as Mr. Balfour remained at the Foreign Office, for they were in complete harmony. Mr. Balfour welcomed Philip Kerr's assistance. There is no office upon which it is more necessary that the Prime Minister of the day should keep a constant oversight than the Foreign Office. With the multifarious duties which fell upon me in clearing up the inevitable chaos of transferring the activities of government and the nation from war to peace, I could not have kept fully in touch with events abroad without Mr. Kerr's intelligent and informed vigilance. Some friction arose when Mr. Balfour resigned and Lord Curzon became his successor. He resented Kerr's interventions. That is what one might expect from one who never got over the autocratic experiences of his Viceregal days.

4. NORTHCLIFFE

WHEN the election was impending I had the luck—bad or good— to have an unmendable break in my relations with Lord Northcliffe. They were always precarious. He wielded great power as the proprietor of the most widely read daily paper and also as the owner of the most influential journal in the kingdom. He was inclined to exercise and to demonstrate that power. When he did so most politicians bowed their heads. He was one of the outstanding figures of his generation. He was far and away the most redoubtable of all the Press Barons of my time. He created the popular daily, and the more other journals scoffed at it and the populace derided it at every political gathering of all parties, the more popular it became. But apart from his success with the half-penny paper he also made *The Times*, which was then a rather discredited and down-at-heel pundit of the Press, once more a power in the land. He was an unrivalled window dresser, but in spite of all that was said to the contrary by rivals and by snobs who worshipped the conventional, the goods on the shelves were none the less excellent because they were attractive and cheap. I remember his telling me at one of the few political dinner parties he ever attended—and how uneasy and unhappy he was in unfamiliar surroundings—that he had a far better organisation for obtaining foreign news that mattered than the cumbrous, costly and ineffective machinery of the Foreign Office. There was too much truth in his observation. His quest of sensational news landed him once or twice—not oftener—in disastrous exposures. He was just as biased in his opinions as any other partisan paper, but the bias was his own and not that of any party or party leader. He influenced opinion by selection of news, choice of its page, spacing, and headlines. In effect, this method was often unfair and suggestive of something which was contrary to the truth. He owed no allegiance to any party, so that every genuine party man deplored his paper. Most of them bought it and read what was in it and then damned it.

During the War no one could doubt his patriotism. It was sincere and fearless. In the disclosure of shell shortage he defied censorship and ran grave risks. He was burnt in effigy in the City of London—but he helped to get the shells. He rendered conspicuous service in administrative capacities, in America, and in directing propaganda behind the enemy lines. But he could not understand comradeship in any enterprise. He only appreciated the value of team work when he was the captain of the team. He resented that co-operation which implied equality and give and take. He had no confidence in any show which he did not run himself. He was too indifferent to anybody else's views to be a good conversationalist. When he visited me on a few occasions at Downing Street he would initiate a topic, sometimes by a question. But you could easily see that he was not interested in the least in the answer. He had called to tell you and not to listen to your reply. The preliminary query was only a matter of form. By this time he had acquired the telephone manner which had degenerated into the telephone mind—the ejaculating of short and sharp orders into a tube which could not question the command. He gave the impression of being bored by the talk of his fellow men. He preferred talking to telephones. He had cultivated the worst mannerisms of a dictator. His impatience grew with power.

I fell in and out with him several times both before and during the War. After the War we drifted finally apart. When I took up the manufacture of munitions he and Lord French were jointly responsible for the agitation that made it possible for me to circumnavigate the War Office and work independently of its crippling interference. But when I subsequently disagreed with the senseless and sanguinary offensives in France and urged a reconsideration of the strategy of the War, he came to the War Office when I was Minister for War and told my Private Secretary that unless I ceased harassing Sir William Robertson and Haig he would expose me in his papers. I took no notice of his warning and he withheld his support from me for several months. When I became Prime Minister without his help he made up the quarrel, but he was always an unreliable helper. He asked for support from no man; he gave it to no one. He was accustomed to subordinates who did what they were told and not to associates who worked on agreed lines.

As soon as the War was over he conceived the idea that he must be one of the official delegates of the Empire at the Peace Conference. For many reasons that was obviously impossible. Apart from the offence that would be given to other powerful papers by according this special distinction to the proprietor—the unpopular, perhaps also the envied proprietor—of a successful rival group, he never did or could work with others on terms of equality. If he did not get his way he would threaten resignation. Had he been made a member of the Peace Delegation he might be depended upon not to face temporary unpopularity to see his fellow delegates through a difficult situation, but to take full advantage of their difficulties to display his power and if possible to seize supreme control for himself. He would have taken this course suddenly, without hesitation, and what would have been still worse, without notice. Resignation would certainly have come and come at a most inconvenient moment in the negotiations. The deference paid to him by politicians and by Generals—home and foreign—had by this time completely turned a head which at this period was beginning to be affected by the nervous disease that soon disabled and finally killed him. Haig received him always at his Headquarters with the deference due to a foreign potentate whose help was indispensable and whose opposition or disparagement would be fatal. I had to refuse Northcliffe's request. I had also to consider that, in order to place

Northcliffe on the panel of five, I should have had to exclude another. Whose name should I leave out:—Bonar Law, Balfour, the Labour representative, or the Dominion Premiers? I knew what this refusal meant as far as his powerful support at the coming election went, and afterwards in my conduct of the peace negotiations. He was visibly astonished and upset by my declining to accede to his request. He sent to me an emissary who was a mutual friend, to ask me to reconsider my decision. This peace maker made it clear what consequences would ensue if I persisted. I must expect the implacable hostility of the Northcliffe papers at the impending electoral contest and afterwards. Nevertheless, I resolved not to give in. Had I done so I should have been his man in possession at Downing Street, and he would want to make it clear to his readers that I was his nominee. That position was incompatible with the independence and dignity of the high office I held. I elected to break with him.

He called on me personally once more. This time he had a new proposition. He wanted to take the Hotel Majestic at Paris and there organise the whole of our official propaganda for the home and foreign Press during the Peace Conference. I thought the suggestion dangerous in the extreme. Indirectly it would have given him great power in the direction and control of our policy. So once more I rejected his offer. He became angry and threatening. I curtly told him to go to Hades. And as poor Bonar Law said afterwards: "He came straight to me at the Treasury." Bonar Law was no more receptive than I was, and that was the last either he or I ever saw of Northcliffe. He became the inveterate and implacable enemy of the Administration up to the very hour of his death. At the elections he supported anti-Government candidates, generally Labour. He distributed freely amongst the soldiers abroad large consignments of the *Daily Mail* appealing to the troops to vote against the Government. He criticised our conduct at the Peace Conference, generally for its excessive leniency towards Germany; and for four years he pursued us with fierce hostility from conference to conference and between and after conferences in all we did or said, or neglected to do or say. At the various international conferences held during and after the Peace his principal representative conspicuously absented himself from all the gatherings of British journalists which I addressed. All relations—even courteous relations—were broken off. Information as to what happened at the Conference was sought from French Ministers and the news was inspired by them and the bias was invariably French.

When he supported me I always expected to hear the arrow that flies in the noon-day sun hiss past my ear from behind, an arrow always dipped in poison. With men of that kind it is safer to have them confronting you than behind you. That has been my observation and my experience.

CHAPTER VI

PROGRESS AT THE CONFERENCE

1. FRAMEWORK OF THE TREATY

AFTER we had provisionally disposed of the preliminary arrangements and dealt with situations which demanded immediate attention, we attacked the task of building up the framework of the Treaty. Here we found President Wilson rather vague in his plans. He was definite and clear as to the objectives he desired to reach and he was a master of ideological phraseology, but although he had worked hard at his phrases and the expression of the truths they contained, the artistic perfection of the words seemed to have satisfied his conscience, and he had never developed for himself the practical outlines of any of the ideas which inspired his speeches. He had not for instance taken any serious trouble with the formulation of a detailed and workable scheme for a League of Nations. His Secretary of State, Mr. Lansing, thus describes his utter unpreparedness for the realities of a Peace Congress:

The trouble was that the President was not prepared to seize the opportunity and to capitalise this general popular support. He came to Paris without, so far as I know, a definite outline of a treaty with Germany. He did have a draft of a covenant of a league of nations, but it was a crude and undigested plan, as is evident by a comparison of it with the document finally reported to the Conference on the Preliminaries of Peace. He, of course, had his famous Fourteen Points, and the declarations appearing in his subsequent addresses as bases of the peace, but they were little more than a series of principles and policies to guide in the drafting of actual terms. As to a complete *projet*, or even an outline of terms which could be laid before the delegates for consideration, he apparently had none; in fact when this lack was felt by members of the American Commission they undertook to have their legal advisers prepare a skeleton treaty, but had to abandon the work after it was well under way because the President resented the idea, asserting emphatically that he did not intend to allow lawyers to draw the treaty, a declaration that discouraged those of the profession from volunteering suggestions as to the covenant and other articles of the treaty. The President, not having done the preliminary work himself, and unwilling to have others do it, was wholly unprepared to submit anything in concrete form to the European statesmen, unless it was his imperfect plan for a league of nations. The consequence was that the general scheme of the treaty and many of the important articles were prepared and worked out by the British and French delegations. Thus the exceptional opportunity which the President had to impress his ideas on the Conference, and to lead in the negotiations, was lost, and he failed to maintain his controlling position among the statesmen who were, as it turned out, to dictate the terms of peace; while his utterances, which had been the foundation of his popularity, suffered in a measure the same fate.

If the President had adopted the customary method of negotiation through commissioners instead of pursuing the unusual and in fact untried method of personal participation, the situation would have been very different. Without the President present in Paris, detailed instructions would have been prepared, which could have been modified during the negotiations only by reference to him at Washington. Instructions of that sort would of necessity have been definite. There would have been no uncertainty as to the objects sought. But with the President on the ground, written instructions seemed to him, and possibly were, superfluous. He was there to decide the attitude of the United States and to give oral directions concerning the minutest detail of the negotiations as the questions arose; and since diplomatic commissioners are in any event only agents of the President and subject always to his instructions, the American commissioners at Paris possessed no right to act independently or to do other than follow the directions which they received, which in this case were given by word of mouth. As these directions were meagre and indefinite, and as they did not include a general plan, the situation was unsatisfactory and embarrassing for the President's American colleagues.

I doubt if Mr. Wilson had worked out, even tentatively, the application of the principles and precepts which he had declared while the war was in progress, and which had been generally accepted at the time of the armistice as the bases of peace. The consequence was that he must have had a very vague and nebulous scheme for their introduction into the treaty, because many of his declarations required accurate definition before they could be practically applied to the problems which awaited solution by the Conference. Naturally there was an atmosphere of uncertainty which prevented the American commissioners from pressing for definite objects. The whole delegation, the President included, lost prestige and influence with the foreign delegates by this lack of a programme.

Here is shown one of the inherent weaknesses of Mr. Wilson which impaired his capacity as the head of a diplomatic commission to negotiate so intricate a settlement as the treaty with Germany. He was inclined to let matters drift, relying apparently on his own quickness of perception and his own sagacity to defeat or amend terms proposed by members of other delegations. From first to last there was no team work, no common counsel, and no concerted action. It was discouraging to witness this utter lack of system, when system was so essential. The reason was manifest. There was no directing head to the American Commission to formulate a plan, to organise the work and to issue definite instructions.*

An unworthy attempt has been made by the President's apologists in America (*vide* Baker and House) and in Britain to enumerate amongst his personal triumphs over reluctant and resisting colleagues the incorporation in the Treaty of idealistic sections like the Covenant of the League. This section was the fruit of careful preparation undertaken at the instance of these condemned European colleagues, before the Congress ever met and even before the War came to an end. Two or three extracts from the official *procès-verbaux* of the proceedings will illustrate the gross unfairness of these suggestions. This is what occurred. As soon as M. Clemenceau invited us to commence the task of drafting the Treaty:

MR. LLOYD GEORGE said that he agreed that these questions should be studied forthwith. He would suggest that, in the first place, the League of Nations should be considered, and that, after the framing of the principles, an international committee of experts be set to work out its constitution in detail. The same remark applied also to the question of indemnities and reparation. He thought that a committee should also be appointed as soon as possible to consider International Labour Legislation.

PRESIDENT WILSON observed that he had himself drawn up a constitution of a League of Nations. He could not claim that it was wholly his own creation. Its generation was as follows: He had received the Phillimore Report, which had been amended by Colonel House and re-written by himself. He had again revised it after having received General Smuts' and Lord Robert Cecil's reports. It was therefore a

* Robert Lansing: "The Big Four," pp. 40–44.

compound of these various suggestions. During the week he had seen M. Bourgeois, with whom he found himself to be in substantial accord on principles. A few days ago he had discussed his draft with Lord Robert Cecil and General Smuts, and they had found themselves very near together.

MR. BALFOUR suggested that President Wilson's draft should be submitted to the Committee as a basis for discussion.

Mr. Balfour's intervention meant that up to that date we had not been privileged to see the President's draft. We never saw it even after Mr. Balfour's request. According to Mr. Lansing, at best it was "crude and undigested." The British and French drafts were both carefully worked out to the last imaginable contingency. In these circumstances the insinuation so often repeated by American apologists of the President that European statesmen were dragged into the League against their convictions and inclinations is thoroughly discreditable to those who make it. In the case of men who knew what was going on from day to day it is thoroughly dishonest. I feel certain the President was quite incapable of so completely misleading his friends as to what had actually occurred. It is refuted by the facts I have narrated as to the steps taken by the British and French Governments before the end of the War to appoint powerful committees of experts to draft a constitution for the League. The President in the speech I have quoted admitted that part of these schemes were embodied in his plan. As the Conference proceeded, I had the honour of moving in the Conference on behalf of the British Empire the resolution in favour of establishing the League as an integral part of the Treaty.

MR. LLOYD GEORGE read a draft of preliminary resolutions for a League of Nations. This document was intended primarily for the guidance of a special Committee to be appointed to draw up the constitution of the League of Nations.

After a discussion, the following text was adopted:

The Conference, having considered the proposals for the creation of a League of Nations, resolves that:

(a) It is essential to the maintenance of the world settlement, which the associated nations are now met to establish, that a League of Nations be created to promote international co-operation, to ensure the fulfilment of accepted international obligations, and to provide safe-guards against war.

(b) This League should be created as an integral part of the general treaty of peace, and should be open to every civilised nation which can be relied on to promote its objects.

(c) The members of the League should periodically meet in inter-national Conference, and should have a permanent organisation and secretariat to carry on the business of the League in the intervals between the Conferences.

The Conference therefore appoints a Committee representative of the associated Governments to work out the details of the constitution and functions of the League.

In the course of the discussion M. Clemenceau, who is sup-posed to have been the most inveterate of the passive resisters to the idea of a League of Nations, made a very remarkable speech in support of the League:

. . . He would at once take up the question of a League for the preservation of Peace. He greatly favoured such a League, and he was prepared to make all sacrifices to attain that object. If it was in-sisted upon, he would assent to a League with full powers to initiate laws, but he would ask that his objections be recorded, as he had no confidence in such a scheme. He might be too conservative—that being a fault of age. In a speech which he had made to the Chamber of Deputies a few days ago he had stated that if, before the war, the Great Powers had made an alliance pledging themselves to take up arms in defence of any one of them who might be attacked, there would have been no war. To-day they had not only five nations in agreement, but practically the whole world. If the nations pledged themselves not to attack anyone without the consent of the members of the League, and to defend any one of them who might be attacked, the peace of the world would be assured. Such an alliance might well be termed a League of Nations. Such procedures and tribunals as might be thought necessary could be added. He would accept all these. If Mr. Lloyd George were to promise that he would accept these two conditions, the League of Nations would be created in less than three days.

Every delegate at the Conference assisted with conviction and goodwill in the promotion of the Covenant of the League. Had America not been a member of the Conference at all, the consti-tution of the League of Nations would not only have been an essential part of the Treaty, but it is fair to add that its provisions would not have been weakened in a single particular.

I also proposed at the Congress the resolution upon the foundation of which the International Labour Office was built. In consultation with Mr. Barnes I had given a great deal of thought to this idea and felt convinced that a peace conference at which all the great industrial nations of the world were represented afforded an unprecedented opportunity for setting up a body which would organise international co-operation ameliorating the condition of industry throughout the world. My resolution was:

That a Commission, composed of two representatives apiece from the five Great Powers, and five representatives to be elected by the other Powers represented at the Peace Conference, be appointed to enquire into the question of the international adjustment of conditions of employment, and to consider what forms of permanent international machinery should be established to enable the several countries to secure joint action on matters affecting conditions of employment, and to recommend what steps should be taken to set up an appropriate organisation for the above purposes in connection with the League of Nations.

The resolution I proposed in reference to Reparations is significant in so far as it indicates clearly the doubt that the British Government felt as to the capacity of Germany to pay for all the damage she had inflicted.

That a Commission be appointed with three representatives apiece from each of the five Great Powers and two representatives apiece from Belgium, Greece, Roumania, and Serbia, to examine and report on the question of the amount of the sum for reparation which the enemy countries should pay, and are capable of paying, as well as the form in which payment should be made.

Another resolution I proposed, and to which I attached great importance, had reference to a general reduction in armaments:

That a Commission be appointed with two representatives apiece from each of the five Great Powers, and five representatives to be elected by the other Powers represented at the Conference:

(1) To advise on an immediate and drastic reduction in the armed forces of the enemy.

(2) To prepare a plan in connection with the League of Nations for a permanent reduction in the burden of military, naval, and aerial forces, and armaments.

The Commission of the League was immediately set up. I nominated General Smuts and Lord Robert Cecil as the British representatives with the full approval of the British Empire Delegation. These two men were convinced advocates of the idea and had devoted a great deal of careful thought to the details of a scheme. They were both eminent jurists experienced in government. Clemenceau, Orlando and I decided not to go on any committee ourselves. We considered that we could render better service by applying ourselves to settling the principles upon which the general framework of the Treaty should be drafted, and to exercising general supervision over the work of all committees alike, and to being available for consultation when difficulties arose in any direction. Whether it was the League of Nations or Reparations, I knew that for some weeks committee work on either would be almost a whole-time job. It would not be so much the attendance and discussions at full meetings of the committees as the numerous conversations and communications between leading members with a view to removing difficulties and solving problems.

M. Clemenceau took the same view, and so did Signor Orlando. President Wilson, on the other hand, decided to join the League Commission and preside over it himself. Had there been any doubt as to the whole-heartedness of the members nominated by the various governments, his sacrifice would have been justifiable. But every member of the Commission was a League zealot. This was particularly true of the ablest and most influential members—Cecil, Smuts, Léon Bourgeois, House, and Veniselos: as formidable a combination in intellect and experience as ever sat on a drafting committee. Wilson might have safely entrusted the fortunes of the League to such capable enthusiasts. It was then that one realised more than ever the blunder into which the President's partisanship had led him when he refused to bring with him men like ex-President Taft and Elihu Root. Had they been on this Commission they could have been trusted to make a good job of it. They were constitutional lawyers of the highest standing and genuine League men withal. A Covenant which either of them had helped to fashion would have withstood all the attacks of Cabot Lodge.

But for President Wilson the League of Nations meant, if not the whole Treaty, at least the only part of the Treaty in which he was interested. He intended that it should conform to his ideas, and that it should be recognised that they were his ideas and not those of anyone else, be he associate or subordinate. His abnormal confidence in himself and limited confidence in others were largely responsible for his reluctance to delegate his duties. Thus it was that what he could not attend to himself he often neglected altogether.

From his own point of view it was a fatal decision. It helped to break him down physically. At the time he insisted on attending every meeting of the League Commission; he also insisted on receiving personally the agents of all States and would-be States that crowded the Paris hotels, and listening to all their tales of woe and their hopes of loot. Here again he would not depute any of his staff to have preliminary interviews with the innumerable races that thronged his anteroom, and to inform him fully beforehand of the points to be raised and confine them to the issues that mattered. No nervous system could stand for months the constant strain of the work which the President unnecessarily took upon himself. About half way through the Congress there were distressing symptoms in his face of this wear and tear on his system, which ultimately ravaged and undermined his health, and in doing so wrecked all his cherished schemes and ambitions. Long before the Congress came to an end he emerged out of the ordeal a shaken man. His labours on the League Commission helped to produce a scheme which in some vital particulars did not go as far as the plans elaborated by General Smuts and M. Léon Bourgeois. That could have been achieved without involving the President in prolonged discussion over questions of detail which exhausted the reserves of vitality needed for the wide issues of the Congress.

It turned out to be not only a personal disaster affecting

President Wilson alone; it destroyed his poise, so that when he came to handle a refractory Italy and an inimical American Senate he did it with a brusqueness which provoked resistance. The result was that America never signed the Treaty. The undelegable duties cast upon the head of a great international conference are heavy enough without adding to them any works of supererogation. I never worked harder or more continuously even during the most anxious days of the War than during the Paris Conference. I started on my papers for the day's Agenda at seven in the morning (and often much earlier). My breakfast, luncheon and dinner were generally interviews with colleagues, officials, or Ministers representing foreign States. When the Conference adjourned there were interviews with the Foreign Secretary, Sir Maurice Hankey, Dominion Premiers or Allied delegates. As to M. Clemenceau, one of his Ministers complained to me that he got up at four in the morning and sometimes sent for one or other of them at six. He generally went to bed at 9 P.M. He must have had a marvellous physique, for he was then seventy-eight. He recovered with surprising rapidity from the bullet wound in his shoulder, though the shock to his system took away some of his resilience for a few weeks. But at his vital best he could not have gone through the perpetual grind to which the American President subjected his nervous system. To add committee work and other deputable tasks to those with which the principals alone could deal was to court a nervous breakdown for the strongest man.

I cannot give a better idea of the variety and scope of the conversations which took place outside the Council Chamber than by publishing the following "Notes of an interview between M. Clemenceau, Colonel House and myself which was held at the Ministry of War, rue Dominicq, at 10.30 A.M., 7th March, 1919." I appear to have taken the very unusual course of dictating this Memorandum as soon as I returned from the interview.

I first of all introduced the question of the German Navy, suggested that so far as the Germans were concerned all that concerned them was the ships of which they were to be deprived and that the disposition of these ships was entirely a matter for ourselves. I indicated that as the French Navy even at the commencement of the war was deficient in certain classes of modern ships, the attempt should be made to supply that deficiency out of the German surrendered ships, and that as to the rest America and ourselves might agree to destroy, upon the understanding that we should not in the future enter into a building competition against each other. A competition of this kind would endanger the peace of the world and as Great Britain could not, whatever the cost, permit any other Power to get ahead and be in a position to starve her out in the event of war, the burden might ultimately become intolerable. I then asked M. Clemenceau to supply us with a list of the ships they were deficient in. Both he and Colonel House cordially agreed to the general proposition, and M. Clemenceau indicated that the French would sink some of the battleships they possessed at the present moment as they did not want so much to increase their navy as to improve its quality. He promised to give instruction to Admiral Le Bon; Colonel House promised to instruct Admiral Benson in the same sense, and I promised that instructions should be given to Admiral Wemyss and that these three should work out the details. Yesterday, in making this proposal to Colonel House at the rue Nitot I said that if an agreement could be arrived at between the United States and ourselves on the question of building, we might make a demonstration for the sinking of the German ships by taking them out to the Mid-Atlantic under an escort of British and American warships, and then destroying them. This he thoroughly approved of.

I submitted to M. Clemenceau and Colonel House a rough draft of the proposal which I intend putting up this afternoon, as an alternative to Marshal Foch's scheme of Disarmament.

DRAFT RESOLUTION

"The Military terms of peace with Germany should be based on the following principles:

"(1) That the German Army shall be raised entirely by voluntary service.

"(2) That the minimum period of service for all ranks shall be twelve years with the colours.

"(3) That the strength of the German Army shall not exceed 250,000 men of all ranks, organised in not more than 15 divisions and 5 cavalry divisions."

M. Clemenceau and Colonel House approved, except that Clemenceau objected to the number of cavalry divisions proposing that they should be reduced to three and that the number 250,000 should be reduced to 200,000. Colonel House and I accepted this amendment.

I placed before M. Clemenceau and Colonel House the position in respect of indemnity; that we could not agree to any proposal that postponed payment in respect of indemnity until the reparation claims had been completely discharged; that it was more than possible that Germany might not be able to do more than pay the reparation claims, in which case Britain would be left out altogether. I further suggested that the instalments should be divided in the proportion of three to two—three being allocated to reparation, and two to indemnity, in proportion to the claims allowed for each country under each head. M. Clemenceau said that of course he could not be expected to answer without further consideration, but that he would let me know soon. He then asked Colonel House what he thought of the plan, and Colonel House replied that he thought that it was a very fair plan and he afterwards repeated this observation. This seemed to make an impression on Clemenceau.

Here M. Clemenceau spoke strongly in favour of Tardieu's plan. Colonel House said he thought we might come to an agreement on these proposals provided the principle of self-determination was postponed until the whole of the terms of peace had been fulfilled. M. Clemenceau objected very strongly to this. He said that he did not believe in the principle of self-determination, which allowed a man to clutch at your throat the first time it was convenient to him, and he would not consent to any limitation of time being placed upon the enforced separation of the Rhenish Republic from the rest of Germany. I informed him that the British Government were really more alarmed about Foch's proposal for an Army of Occupation to hold the Rhine from the Dutch to the Swiss frontier for an indefinite period. When I said it would mean an army of at least 300,000 Clemenceau said he did not think it would take more than 100,000, and that they would only hold two or three bridgeheads. I then informed him that I did not believe Great Britain could make a permanent contribution to this army. Clemenceau replied that France might undertake that two-thirds of the army might be hers. I asked Colonel House whether America would contribute to a permanent Army of Occupation. He expressed great doubts but said he would put it to the President. I then said that Marshal Foch had not explained what his plan really meant. Clemenceau said there was a good reason why he had not explained it; it was because he did not understand it himself. He did not think he had thought it out and that as a matter of fact he was always changing his mind from day to day and that he never knew where he was. He promised to get Marshal Foch to submit the details of his proposal for our consideration.

I informed him that the British Government did not like Marshal

Foch's proposal for placing the Polish frontier on a line drawn from Danzig to Thorn; that this would mean incorporating the whole of Eastern Prussia, which was overwhelmingly German, in the Republic of Poland, and that we did not want any more Alsace-Lorraines in Europe, whether in the East or the West. Clemenceau answered neither did he, he had had enough of them. Colonel House said that the American delegates had come to the conclusion that Danzig ought to be incorporated in Poland and he expected that ultimately the British delegates would also agree. We then went to look at the map and found that if Danzig were included in Poland Eastern Prussia presented a very serious geographical difficulty. Colonel House then said that Eastern Prussia might either be internationalised or converted into a separate republic. Clemenceau said that the more separate and independent republics were established in Germany the better he would be pleased. It was decided to await the Report of the Commission on this subject before continuing the discussion.

I asked Colonel House whether America would be prepared to accept a mandatory in respect of the Turkish Empire, and I pressed him specially as to their view for taking a mandate for Armenia and Constantinople. He replied that America was not in the least anxious to take these mandates, but that she felt she could not shirk her share of the burden and he thought America would be prepared to take mandates for Armenia and Constantinople. He talked of a plan he had for raising money for the improvement of Constantinople at a low rate of interest. He also said in reply to a question that America would be prepared to exercise some sort of general supervision over Anatolia. I then said to M. Clemenceau: "France, I suppose, will undertake Syria." He answered: "And Cilicia." I said: "That is a question between America and yourselves." He said: "No, it is a question between you and ourselves." I replied: "No, we have no interest in Cilicia in the least; we make no claim except to Mosul, which you agreed to give us." He assented to this and said: "Any agreement which you make with the Americans we shall certainly assent to." And I suggested that in order to save time somebody of a conciliatory mind should discuss this matter with both sides. I said: "Have you anybody of that kind?" He replied, putting his finger on his own chest: "Only myself." I said: "Colonel House and I were discussing this yesterday and said exactly the same thing—that you are the only man it is possible to come to an agreement with in France." I then urged him to come to an agreement with Feisal. He said that was a question for us. I said: "No, if we try to get at Feisal your newspapers say that we are stuffing him up. So, therefore you had better deal with him." He said that he had failed and could not do this. "I am afraid we shall have to fight him." I said that that would be a disaster and we did not want another Ab-del-Kader. "We have had some experience in fighting these Arabs in the Sudan, and Feisal is a very formidable fighter. You would beat him in the end, but it would be a very expensive operation, so I strongly urge that you should arrange things with him." M. Clemenceau said that he would do his best. I told him we might send for Allenby. M. Clemenceau spoke of him in the highest possible terms. He said he had a great opinion of him and he would be very pleased if I would wire for him. I then said that America would accept a mandate for Constantinople, Armenia, and supervision for Anatolia; France would be mandatory for Syria and such part of Cilicia as would be agreed upon between the Americans and the French; we would take Palestine and Mesopotamia, which includes Mosul. Then something was said about the Italians. I then remarked that if we decided not to remain in the Caucasus the Italians had shown some indication of a desire to occupy that territory. Neither the French nor the Americans greeted this announcement with any enthusiasm. Colonel House suggested the Georgians could be asked whether they would like to have the Italians there. Clemenceau answered: "That is an excellent proposal." We then came to Adalia, and M. Clemenceau asked whether the Italians still stood by the Treaty of London. If they did not they had no right to claim Adalia. I said that I understood that they still adhered to the Treaty where it suited them. Clemenceau said that under the Treaty of London they could not get Fiume, and that they dared not go back to Rome if Fiume were handed over to the Jugo-Slavs, so that they were therefore bound to repudiate the Treaty of London. We had some discussion here about the Italian claims generally. I found M. Clemenceau very hostile. He said public opinion in France had been antagonised a good deal by d'Annunzio's claim that Italy had won the war, and he was by no means disposed to discuss favourably Italian claims anywhere. He was very sanguine, however, that a settlement would be arrived at in the Adriatic and informed me that the Italians were prepared to give up Dalmatia, provided Fiume was internationalised. That he was disposed to agree to. I told him something of the Italian claims in Somaliland, and he promised to look into it.

We then discussed the feeding of Germany. I communicated to him the information we had received from a military officer who had just returned from Germany as to the deplorable condition of the German population and the danger of spreading Bolshevism unless Germany were fed. He treated that as purely a German story, circulated with a view to intimidating the Allies into giving favourable terms to Germany. He was rather scornful of the idea. He was not disposed to accept any proposal from the Germans which looked like the acceptance of dictation from them, but I proposed that wheat should be released to them in proportion to the number of ships they surrendered. He thought it was a fair proposal, but it was clear that if the Spa delegates this afternoon revealed that the Germans had proposed something of this kind M. Clemenceau would be hostile. He is not prepared to take the proposal on its merits. He is anxious to preserve the demeanour of a conqueror towards Germany. There will therefore be some difficulty, I fear, in inducing the French to assent to any reasonable plan for feeding Germany.

I then introduced the subject of Russia, and I told M. Clemenceau of the experience we have had in getting estimates of cost out of military and naval authorities; that Marshal Foch had great plans for invading Russia with Czecho-Slovaks, Finns, Poles, and released Russian prisoners, but that he never submitted any estimates of costs. I revealed to him the estimates we had just received after considerable delay and pressure from our Military advisers, as to the cost of present operations. The figures staggered him, and I informed him that these did not include the expenses of Franchet d'Esperey's expedition. I intimated to him that it was our intention to evacuate Murmansk and Archangel and clear our troops out of Omsk and Vladivostok, but that we were prepared to join the Allies in supplying Denikin and Koltchak with any guns, ammunition and equipment we could spare which would enable them to defend their own territories against Bolshevik attack. Both M. Clemenceau and Colonel House agreed to this plan and they were both hostile to any plan for the invasion of Russia.

We had some discussion as to the debts incurred during the war by one Allied country to another and Colonel House suggested that the leading financiers of the various countries should meet together and discuss this question on broad lines. I said that it was very undesirable that we should have debtor and creditor relations to each other after the war; that there was no relationship that was more fatal to the continuance of affection between two individuals or two nations. The Turkish pre-war debt was also mentioned and the question of its distribution between various mandatory provinces of the Turkish Empire, but no practical conclusion was come to under this heading, as it was understood that there was a Committee appointed to consider this question.

Talks of this kind did not represent final agreements between the principal delegates of France, the U.S.A. and Great Britain, or even definite conclusions at which any one of them had individually arrived. We were hewing our way through the jungle and seeking the best direction in which to work. We had almost daily interchanges of this informal kind with each other. They occupied a good deal of time, but they were often more helpful in enabling us to arrive at an understanding than the more elaborate proceedings at the official conclaves.

2. FOOD SUPPLIES FOR ENEMY COUNTRIES

NOTWITHSTANDING the decisions arrived at by the Allies in December as to the victualling of enemy countries that were short of food, there was delay and difficulty in carrying out the plans. We found, on the question being brought up at the Conference in Paris, that somehow or other obstacles were being constantly interposed, and difficulties presented to prevent supplies from reaching the necessitous populations. In January the question had been raised, and expedition urged in supplying food to Germany.

I was receiving constant messages from our representatives in Germany as to the urgency of supplies reaching the hungry civilians if disaster were to be averted, and Mr. Hoover, who was in charge of food supplies, had reported difficulties and delays. In March I felt bound to call the attention of the Allied representatives once more to what was going on.

MR. LLOYD GEORGE said that he had been rather staggered by Marshal Foch's suggestion that we were parting with a very great effective power of exerting pressure on Germany. The difficulty was, however, more apparent than real, for the Allies were not in reality parting with the considerable power which food gave them. As a matter of fact there were only two contingencies which might call for the exercise of that power. The Germans might refuse to carry out the terms of the Armistice, but in that case the Armistice would at once come to an end, and therefore the provisions of Clause 8 would apply. Again, the Preliminary Terms of Peace would shortly be presented to Germany, and if Germany refused to accept those terms, that would put an end to the Armistice. But, when that happened, the Allies would be quite entitled to decide not to advance into Germany, but to exert the necessary pressure by the stoppage of food supplies. Consequently, due provision was made for the only two contingencies in which food pressure might be required. The Conference was therefore not parting with any potent weapon. On the other hand, he wished to urge with all his might that steps should at once be taken to revictual Germany. The honour of the Allies was involved. Under the terms of the Armistice the Allies did imply that they meant to let food into Germany. The Germans had accepted our Armistice conditions, which were sufficiently severe, and they had complied with the majority of those conditions. But so far, not a single ton of food had been sent into Germany. The fishing fleet had even been prevented from going out to catch a few herrings. The Allies were now on top, but the memory of starvation might one day turn against them. The Germans were being allowed to starve whilst at the same time hundreds of thousands of tons of food were lying at Rotterdam, waiting to be taken up the waterways into Germany. These incidents constituted far more formidable weapons for use against the Allies than any of the armaments which it was sought to limit. The Allies were sowing hatred for the future: they were piling up agony, not for the Germans, but for themselves. The British troops were indignant about our refusal to revictual Germany. General Plumer had said that he could not be responsible for his troops if children were allowed to wander about the streets half starved. The British soldiers would not stand that, they were beginning to make complaints, and the most urgent demands were being received from them. Furthermore, British officers who had been in Germany said that Bolshevism was being created, and the determining factor was going to be food. As long as the people were starving they would listen to the arguments of the Spartacists, and the Allies by their action were simply encouraging elements of disruption and anarchy. It was like stirring up an influenza puddle next door. The condition of Russia was well known, and it might be possible to look on at a muddle which had there been created. But now, if Germany went, and perhaps Spain, who would feel safe? As long as order was maintained in Germany, a breakwater would exist between the countries of the Allies and the waters of revolution beyond. But once that breakwater was swept away, he could not speak for France, and he trembled for his own country. The situation was particularly serious in Munich. Bavaria, which once had been thought to represent the most solid and conservative part of Germany, had already gone Bolshevik. He was there that afternoon to reinforce the appeal which had come to him from the men who had helped the Allies to conquer the Germans, the soldiers, who said that they refused to continue to occupy a territory in order to maintain the population in a state of starvation. Meanwhile the Conference continued to haggle. Six weeks ago the same arguments about gold and foreign securities had been used, and it had then been decided that Germany should be given food. He begged the Conference to re-affirm that decision in the most unequivocal terms for, unless this people were fed and if, as a result of a process of starvation enforced by the Allies, the people of Germany were allowed to run riot, a state of revolution among the working classes of all countries would ensue with which it would be impossible to cope.

M. CLEMENCEAU expressed his desire to make a few observations in reply to Mr. Lloyd George's statement; and would preface his remarks with the affirmation that he quite agreed with Mr. Lloyd George's conclusions, namely, that Germany must be fed as soon as possible. That, however, was not the question now under discussion. Mr. Lloyd George had said that the honour of the Allies was involved, since they had given the Germans to understand that food would be sent into Germany. That was not altogether a correct statement of facts. In the Armistice no promise had ever been made to feed Germany.

MR. BALFOUR, intervening, remarked that almost a promise had been made.

M. CLEMENCEAU, continuing, said he would not argue the point because, as he had already said, he was ready to give the food, whether promised or not. On the other hand, his information tended to show that the Germans were using Bolshevism as a bogey with which to frighten the Allies. If the Germans were starving, as General Plumer and others said they were, why did they continue to refuse to surrender their merchant fleet? The Germans certainly did not act as if they were in a hurry, and it was curious that a people which was said to be so hard up for food should appear to be in no hurry to assist in obtaining it by giving up their ships. No doubt very pitiful reports were being received from certain parts of Germany in regard to food conditions; but those reports did not apparently apply to all parts of Germany. For instance, General Mangin had told him that morning that there was more food in Mayence than in Paris. In his opinion, the food hardship was probably due to bad distribution. Mr. Lloyd George had said that the Germans must be made to observe the conditions of the Armistice. But the Germans had promised to surrender their merchant fleet, and so far they had not done so. In his opinion, the Germans were trying to see how far they could go; they were simply attempting to blackmail the Allies. To yield to-day would simply mean constant yielding in the future.

MR. LLOYD GEORGE: . . . before proceeding further, asked permission to read the following telegram which he had just received from General Plumer at Cologne, dated the 8th March, 1919, 2.45 P.M.:

"Please inform the Prime Minister that, in my opinion, food must be sent into this area by the Allies without delay. Even now the present rations are insufficient to maintain life, and, owing to the failure of supplies from Germany, they must very soon be still further reduced. The mortality amongst women, children, and sick is most grave, and sickness due to hunger is spreading. The attitude of the population is becoming one of despair, and the people feel that an end by bullets is preferable to death by starvation. All this naturally results in great activity by subversive and disorderly elements. Apart from the imminence of danger from the situation, the continuance of those conditions is unjustifiable. I request therefore that a definite date be fixed for the arrival of the first supplies. This date should not be later than the 16th March, even if from that date regular supplies cannot be maintained."

He thought that General Plumer's telegram disclosed a very serious state of affairs, and he felt certain that the Conference did not wish to create sympathy with Germany by a continuance of a system of starvation. To bring the discussion to a head, he desired to make the following definite suggestion, namely, that the terms of the ultimatum to be presented to the Germans prior to the discussion of the conditions for the supply of food should be made to read as follows:

"On condition that Germany formally acknowledges her obligations under Clause 8 of the Armistice of the 16th January, that is to say (Here insert the text of Article 8 of the agreement for the prolongation of the Armistice, dated the 16th January, 1919), the Delegates of the Associated Governments are authorised and directed to proceed upon their instructions as to revictualling."

MARSHAL FOCH thought that the mere recognition of Germany's obligations under Clause 8 of the Armistice would hardly be sufficient, as the Germans had already recognised their obligations by accepting the clause. He suggested that the clause should be made to read: "On condition that Germany formally acknowledges and undertakes to execute her obligations."

M. CLEMENCEAU said that that proposal having been agreed to, the conditions to govern the supply of food should next be settled. Clause 1 of the original draft now disappeared and would constitute a separate document to be presented to the German Peace Delegate by a British Admiral, as a preliminary to the discussion of the remaining clauses of the original draft.

Clauses 2 and 3 of the original draft had been unanimously accepted. In regard to Clause 4, sub-heads (a), (b) and (c) had been accepted, but he would call on M. Klotz to make a statement in regard to sub-heads (d), (e) and (f).

M. KLOTZ expressed the view that sub-heads (*a*), (*b*) and (*c*) by themselves would be sufficient to meet all requirements, and M. Clemenceau's statement that the Germans should be made to work in order to earn their food had merely confirmed that view. If the Allies put on the table all the German gold and foreign securities which the Allies held in trust, there would be no incentive for the Germans to work. In order to reach an agreement he would, however, suggest the addition of the following paragraph at the end of Clause 3, namely: "The methods of payment provided in (*d*), (*e*), and (*f*) shall not be resorted to until, in the judgment of the Supreme Economic Council, the possibility of payment under (*a*), (*b*) and (*c*) shall have proved inadequate."

M. LOUCHEUR thought that some misunderstanding existed in regard to the text. The United States Delegates had stated to him that two or three months would have to elapse before it could be known whether methods (*a*), (*b*), and (*c*) would provide sufficient funds. That was not the intention of the Council. The wherewithal for the necessary payments would at once be made available by releasing the necessary quantities of gold and other securities. On the other hand, the Germans should be required to work in order to produce the raw material which would pay for the food supplies. Consequently, if at the end of a month or two it were found that the Germans were not producing any greater quantities of coal and other raw materials, the question as to whether the Allies should continue to feed people who refused to work would have to be reconsidered. It was essential that the Germans should not live at ease on the gold which was required for the payment of reparation for the damages deliberately committed by them.

MR. LLOYD GEORGE said that on the 13th January exactly the same speeches had been made by M. Klotz, and he had then been overruled by the Supreme War Council. M. Klotz should, therefore, submit to the decisions then taken by the Supreme War Council. In support of his statement, he would read to the Conference extracts from the *procès-verbal* of the meeting of the Supreme War Council held on Monday, January 13, 1919:

"President Wilson expressed the view that any further delay in this matter might be fatal, as it meant the dissolution of order and government. They were discussing an absolute and immediate necessity. So long as hunger continued to gnaw, the foundations of government would continue to crumble. Therefore food should be supplied immediately not only to our friends, but also to those parts of the world where it was to our interest to maintain a stable government. He thought they were bound to accept the concerted counsel of a number of men who had been devoting the whole of their time and thought to this question.

He trusted the French Finance Department would withdraw their objection, as they were faced with the great problems of Bolshevism and the forces of dissolution which now threatened society.

"M. Klotz said he would gladly meet President Wilson's wishes. But it was not altogether a question of food supplies. They were all fully agreed as to the necessity of feeding the Germans, but he would appeal to President Wilson to consider also the question of justice. He was quite willing to admit that German foreign securities should be earmarked for this purpose. But they were creating a new German debt. There were other German debts which were just as honourable and noble. Therefore he would ask as a matter of justice why Germany should pay for food in preference to paying off debts incurred for the restoration and for the reparation of damage committed elsewhere. Why should exclusive priority be given to such a debt? As a solution of the difficulty he would agree that payment for this food should be made in foreign securities and values. But he would add that 'those assets shall be pooled and distribution shall be made by the Allies taking into account such privileged claims as the Peace Conference would admit.'

"He would merely point out that it was not a question of food supply; it was purely a financial question, and no delay need therefore occur in the supply of food.

"President Wilson urged that, unless a solution for the immediate situation could be found, none of these debts would be paid. The want of food would lead to a crash in Germany. The great point, however, was this, that the Associated Governments have no money to pay for these supplies. Therefore Germany must pay for them, but if they were not paid for and supplied immediately there would be no Germany to pay anything.

"Mr. Bonar Law pointed out that in calculating the sums they had been going on the assumption that the supply of food would last for one year. He did not think that it would need to last more than a few months, or, say, up to the harvesting of the next crop. The suggestion had also been made that the German merchant ships to be requisitioned would yield funds for the payment of a portion of the sum in question.

"M. Klotz proposed that they should accept for a period of two months the text as it stood. At the end of that period the Peace Conference would be able to come to a decision on the whole question of policy.

"Mr. Bonar Law considered that if sanction for two months' payment only were obtained, the food supplies could only last for two months.

"M. Klotz thought that this showed some confusion of ideas. It was not a question of supplying food for two months. Food supplies could continue. The question to be settled during the course of the two months was merely as to the priority to be given to the payments to be made by Germany. It would be admitted that foreign securities must be considered as gilt-edged securities.

"Mr. Bonar Law thought they were arguing in a circle. The first question to be settled was whether a new debt which they had no necessity to incur should be added to previous debts.

"M. Klotz agreed, but suggested that at the end of the two months a priority list could be prepared.

"M. Pichon said he thought that an agreement had now been reached. Everyone was agreed that payment had to be made. The proposal could therefore be accepted. But the Conference could reconsider the question later on, should they wish to do so. (This was agreed to.)"

It was true that M. Klotz had then suggested that the question should be reconsidered at the end of two months, but in the interval nothing had been done, and as long as people were starving they could not be expected to work, as M. Klotz proposed.

M. KLOTZ asked permission to point out that his contention in reality was in complete agreement with what had originally been settled on the 13th January. It had then been agreed that two months later the whole clause would be reconsidered. In other words, he had then agreed to the sum of 450 million francs being expended during a period of two months, an expenditure which could, in his opinion, be incurred without endangering the finances of his country. Now, however, the proposal involved an expenditure of 2 milliards of francs up to the 1st September next, and for that purpose it was proposed to use up all the funds which might eventually become available for the payment of reparations. That was what he objected to. He had been willing and he was still willing to agree to an expenditure of 450 million francs, but he hesitated to go beyond that sum without a full and careful reconsideration of the whole question. Consequently, he had already shown a very conciliatory spirit and had made great sacrifices in agreeing to accept clauses (d), (e) and (f), with certain reservations, but it would be impossible for him to go further without compromising his country's interests, which had been placed in his charge.

MR. LLOYD GEORGE appealed to M. Clemenceau to intervene in the matter. It was true that on the 13th January it had been suggested that the question might be reconsidered at the end of two months. Nothing had, however, been done during those two months, and now the question had been brought up for discussion with all the old arguments. He would not have raised the matter but for the fact that during the past two months, in spite of the decision reached by the Supreme War Council in January last, obstacles had continually been put in the way, with the result that nothing had been done. He appealed to M. Clemenceau to put a stop to these obstructive tactics, otherwise M. Klotz would rank with Lenin and Trotsky among those who had spread Bolshevism in Europe.

MR. HOUSE said that it always made him unhappy to take sides against France. But the United States Delegates had told him that they had gone to the utmost limits to meet the wishes of the French, and unless Clause 4 were accepted practically as it stood, it would have no value.

M. CLEMENCEAU exclaimed that his country had been ruined and ravaged; towns had been destroyed; over two million men had lost their lives; mines had been rendered unworkable; and yet what guarantees had France that anything would be received in payment for all this destruction? She merely possessed a few pieces of gold, a few securities, which it was now proposed to take away in order to pay those who would supply food to Germany; and that food would certainly not come from France. In a word, he was being asked to betray his country, and that he refused to do.

However, after a little more persuasion, it was agreed to take the necessary measures to send supplies of food to both Germany and Austria. Mr. Hoover, who organised the distribution, seemed to have ruffled French susceptibilities by his manner of extracting money from them. He had a surliness of mien and a peremptoriness of speech which provoked a negative answer to any request he made. He did not mean it. But how were foreigners to know that? The French are a humane people with generous instincts, but they were in a mood of natural exasperation when they saw the ruin which had been wrought in their finest provinces and when they contemplated the sorrow brought to myriads of their homes. It needed tact to handle any appeal for help to those who had been the perpetrators of all this misery. Mr. Hoover has many great qualities, but tact is not one of them.

3. ANARCHY IN MIDDLE EUROPE

WHILST the delegates of the Great Powers were occupied with deciding the outlines of the Peace Treaty with Germany, their deliberations were constantly interrupted by reports of armed conflict in every corner of the vast battle area of the War, from the Pacific shores to the Black Sea and the Baltic, and from the frozen rivers of Siberia to the sunny shores of the Adriatic. There were scores of little wars going on—some conducted with a savagery which looked as if man had reverted to the type of barbarian he was in the ferocious days of Tamerlane and Attila. What happened in the ruthless struggle between Red and White in Siberia, in Southern Russia and in the Ukraine, is too ghastly to perpetuate in the memory of man. It is an agony to dwell upon the details of horror enacted in these orgies of hate. Hell was let loose and made the most of its time.

But these little wars came nearer to us than Russia. The emancipated races of Southern Europe were at each other's throats in their avidity to secure choice bits of the carcases of dead empires. Pole and Czech were fighting over Teschen. The Poles and the Ukrainians had both pounced on Galicia, whilst Roumanians and Serbs were tearing up Hungary and Austria. Poles and Lithuanians had their fangs on the same cities and forests. Where races were mixed near frontiers, the snarling and clawing were deafening. The Congress could not get on with its work for the uproar. These areas were the mangrove swamps where the racial roots were so tangled and intermingled that no peacemakers could move inside them without stumbling. The resurrected nations rose from their graves hungry and ravening from their long fast in the vaults of oppression. They were like Athelstane, in "Ivanhoe," who rose from his bier with the insatiable cravings of famine raging in his whole body. Like him they clutched at anything that lay within reach of their hands—not even waiting to throw off the cerements of the grave and array themselves in the apparel of living nations. The Supreme Council did its best to persuade and pacify. At the meeting of the Congress on the 24th of January:

PRESIDENT WILSON read the following communication, which he suggested should be published and transmitted by wireless telegraphy to all parts of the world:

"The Governments now associated in conference to effect a lasting peace among the nations are deeply disturbed by the news which comes to them of the many instances in which armed force is being made use of, in many parts of Europe and the East, to gain possession of territory, the rightful claim to which the Peace Conference is to be asked to determine. They deem it their duty to utter a solemn warning that possession gained by force will seriously prejudice the claims of those who use such means. It will create the presumption that those who employ force doubt the justice and validity of their claim, and purpose to substitute possession for proof of right and set up sovereignty by coercion rather than by racial or national preference and natural historical association. They thus put a cloud upon every evidence of title they may afterwards allege and indicate their distrust of the Conference itself. Nothing but the most unfortunate results can ensue. If they expect justice they must refrain from force, and place their claims in unclouded good faith in the hands of the Conference of Peace."

(This was agreed to.)

It was all in vain. Some nations had contributed their best to the victory and meant to be recompensed for their sacrifices. Some, who had contributed little, or had fought almost to the end on the other side, were just as clamorous for a share of the spoil of a victory which they had not helped to achieve.

No one gave more trouble than the Poles. Having once upon a time been the most formidable military Power in Central Europe —when Prussia was a starveling Duchy—there were few provinces in a vast area inhabited by a variety of races that Poland could not claim as being historically her inheritance of which she had been reft. Drunk with the new wine of liberty supplied to her by the Allies, she fancied herself once more the resistless mistress of Central Europe. Self-determination did not suit her ambitions. She coveted Galicia, the Ukraine, Lithuania and parts of White Russia. A vote of the inhabitants would have emphatically repudiated her dominion. So the right of all peoples to select their nationhood was promptly thrown over by her leaders. They claimed that these various races belonged to the Poles through the conquering arm of their ancestors. Like the old Norman baron who, when he was asked for the title to his lands, unsheathed his sword, Poland flourished the sword of her warrior kings which had rusted in their tombs for centuries.

They found a leader well fitted for the task of enforcing a claim which did not rest on justice but upon force, and with whom patriotism was the only judge of right. Pilsudski was a Pole born in Russian territory, but out of hatred for Russian oppression of his country he recruited a contingent of Poles for the Austrian Army and at its head fought against the Russians in the War. When subsequently he discovered that the Central Powers had no intention of conceding independence to Poland, he gave trouble and the Germans threw him into prison. He had thus a double appeal to Polish sentiment—he had fought both against the Russians and the Germans. He was a member of the Socialist party and therefore not qualified to lead a patriotic movement which depended at first almost entirely upon the support and leadership of the old Polish landed aristocracy. But the Pole, who is the Irishman of Continental Europe, is like him a good politician. Both are highly gifted races—both temperamentally highly geared. Germany had still a powerful army in her Eastern provinces. The Allies had entrusted to her the task of maintaining order in that disturbed area. The Poles, who had no arms or ammunition to defend themselves against the Bolsheviks, were therefore entirely at the mercy of the Germans. They were terrified of their Russian neighbours and none more than those who had something to lose. Had the German Government been hostile, the Poles thought it would go hard with them. At that time there was a Socialist Government in Germany. It was therefore deemed prudent at Warsaw to choose a Government of a political complexion that would be regarded in a friendly spirit in Berlin. Pilsudski was immensely popular with the Poles of Posnania, and from that time onward until the day of his death, this forceful personality, whether in or out of office, dominated the government of his country. John Morley once said to me that "there is no worse Jingo than a Jacobin turned Jingo." This doctrine was applicable to Pilsudski. From the moment he attained supreme power he devoted the whole of his mind and character to a policy of territorial expansion by force of arms. Protests of inhabitants went unheard and unheeded. The opposition of the Supreme Council and the admonitions of President Wilson were equally disregarded by this fierce and ruthless patriot.

There were two circumstances which encouraged Pilsudski's aggressions. The first was that a greater Poland suited French policy—and the greater the better. French foreign policy has always been swayed by one paramount aim—the weakening of Germany and the strengthening of its potential opponents. This victory was the supreme opportunity for achieving that purpose. French statesmen had always in their minds the fact that Germany had a warlike population more than half again as numerous as that of France. Their first object was to reduce the disparity by carving as many provinces out of Germany as they could find a decent pretext for taking away. It accounts for their anxiety to sever from the dominion of the Reich the whole of Silesia and the territories on the left bank of the Rhine without regard to ethnological or democratic considerations. But even if the whole of that mutilation had been accomplished, there would still have remained a preponderance of 50 per cent. of Germans. To meet this sinister contingency France encouraged the creation of powerful States on the Eastern and Southern frontiers of the Reich, which would owe their origin and their permanent security to the friendship of France. Therefore a great Poland was one of the principal desiderata of French military strategy. A few million men—Ukrainians, Lithuanians and White Russians—incorporated into Poland meant so much more strength added to the Eastern frontiers of France.

The second circumstance which favoured Pilsudski's grasping raids was the hold which the Poles had on the American Delegation, owing to the existence of a powerful Polish vote in the United States. This had been thoroughly roused to activity during the War by the efforts of another notable Pole—Paderewski. This great artist had thrown up his musical career and devoted himself to the task of stirring up the Poles of America to a sense of the opportunity offered to them by the War to recover their national independence. He developed oratorical powers of a high order and his seductive personality made a great impression on the President and his entourage. The President came to Europe an enthusiastic pro-Pole. He did not like the reckless way in which the Poles trampled on his principles and he remonstrated mildly with them, but Pilsudski, encouraged by the French, turned a deaf ear to these expostulations, and his defiance was triumphant. Both the French and Pilsudski understood the President's predilection and took full advantage of it. The cynicism of French diplomacy was never more apparent than in its dealings with Polish delinquencies. On the plea—which was not altogether a pretext—that the Poles were afraid of a Bolshevik invasion with German connivance, the French military urged the Allies to send arms and ammunition to Poland through Danzig. They also recommended that the divisions of the Polish legion formed out of the Polish prisoners captured in the War should be sent to Poland immediately to enable helpless Poland to resist the double menace to her young life.

The Supreme Council assented to these expedients. The Poles were armed and the Polish divisions, equipped with the necessary artillery, were despatched to Warsaw under a General Haller. The division was henceforth known as Haller's Army. Pilsudski out of these supplies of men and material created a formidable force. Haller's Army, which was ready for war when it arrived, was immediately marched into Galicia, ostensibly to drive off the Bolsheviks, but in reality to conquer the country and annex it to Poland. The Supreme Council sent a message to General Haller ordering his withdrawal. Of this command he did not take the slightest notice. Subsequently he pretended that he had never received the telegram in time to act upon the instructions it conveyed. Whether it was intercepted and held up by Pilsudski's orders—whether it had never been despatched from France —or whether they were all in a conspiracy to ignore it—we never discovered. President Wilson was not over-anxious to offend his Polish friends by pressing the enquiry too insistently. The result was that despite the appeals of the Galicians themselves to the Council of the Powers, their country was overrun and annexed to Poland.

The Polish case was presented to the Peace Congress by an exceedingly able and cultured Pole of the name of Dmowski. He addressed us first in fluent French and afterwards in perfect English. He made no secret of the rejection by the Poles of the

application to some of their claims of the principle of self-determination: "In settling the boundaries of Poland, the principle of
including within those boundaries only those territories where
the Poles were in a large majority must not be accepted altogether." He suggested that in reaching a settlement of the territory to belong to Poland they should start from the date 1772,
which was before the first partition. This would not mean that
she must be reconstituted with the same boundaries as then
existed; that must be only the point of departure and the boundaries should be rectified according to present conditions. That
basis would include in Poland races that were not Poles, and as
for the present conditions which had to be taken into account in
the rectification of the 1772 boundary, Pilsudski was engaged at
that moment in creating those conditions without reference to
majorities. The Poles in Galicia did not number more than one-
fourth of the inhabitants. The rest were Ukrainian and as hostile
to the idea of Polish rule as the Poles themselves were to Russian
rule.

The difficulties created by the unrestrained rapacity of nations
that owed their freedom to a victory won by the tremendous
efforts and sacrifices of the Great Powers, whose leaders were now
engaged in trying to effect a just world settlement, were not a
good omen for the success of a League of Nations. Boundaries
that involved the annexation of territories which by every principle of justice belonged to other nations were an accomplished
fact before the Powers ever adjudicated upon their fairness.
Decisions given by the Council that for the time being represented the federated nations of the world were flouted whenever
they interfered with the ambitions of the nation against whom
judgment was given. Most ominous of all was the fact that one
of the Great Powers connived at the defiance of decisions in
which it had taken part whenever it suited her policy that these
decisions should not be carried out. It was premonitory of what
would ensue when the Treaty was signed. Vilna taken from the
Lithuanians in contempt of a League order by an active League
Power with the connivance of another—pledges of disarmament
treated with scorn by the nations whose representatives drafted

the pledge—territories invaded and annexed in Asia and Africa by leading League Powers in open derision of the solemn judgment delivered by the League: we had a foretaste of it at Paris. The nations responsible then are likely to be the victims now of the cynicism, selfishness and lack of good faith displayed by their rulers in the years following the great victory.

CHAPTER VII

RUSSIA

DIFFERENCES which arose from day to day in the actual working of the Armistice conditions engaged a good deal of our attention. The only discussion, however, at this preliminary stage which has a permanent interest was that which occurred over the Allied attitude towards Russia. I was becoming more and more convinced that world peace was unattainable as long as that immense country was left outside the Covenant of Nations. I acted upon that conviction up to the end of my Premiership. My last efforts to persuade the Allies to act upon that policy were at the Cannes and Genoa Conferences early in 1922. These endeavours encountered the united opposition of the Continental Powers led by Poincaré and Barthou, and were thus not realised until after the revival of the German military power and the Confederacy of the Dictators warned France of her real peril. It is significant that it was M. Barthou who after many fateful years negotiated the Franco-Soviet Pact because of the imminent dangers to the security of France which could have been easily averted at Genoa.

It was clear in the winter of 1918-19 that peace could not be established on solid foundations as long as Russia was rent by civil war and the Allies were taking sides in the sanguinary conflicts which were devastating that vast country. I was desirous that we should withdraw our forces from this internecine struggle, but that before doing so we should exert our influence to make peace between the warring sections. In order to give an idea as to how matters stood at that date, I had a map prepared showing the territories in European and Asiatic Russia which were occupied by the Bolsheviks and their adversaries respectively, and laid it before the Conference in order to demonstrate the impossibility of bringing this strife to an end by any military effort the Allies were prepared to make. We could prolong the civil war perhaps for years until Russia had become a continent of desolation stretching from Central Europe to the eastern shores of Asia, but we could not achieve any solution by force and certainly not a final or satisfactory solution.

The situation of the Allies in reference to Russia was eminently unsatisfactory. Our honourable obligations to the remnants of the Russian Army which, disregarding the Treaty of Brest-Litovsk, remained in the field to fight the Germans, put us in the embarrassing position of being under an obligation to help one of the parties in the Russian Civil War. We were thus drifting without any definite aim or purpose into a war against the rulers of at least two-thirds of that vast and unconquerable country. When the Germans were pushing forward with the intention of raiding the fertile grainfields and the overflowing oil wells of Russia, we felt it was imperative to consolidate and strengthen the scattered elements of anti-German resistance that still remained in some of the Russian provinces. We did so without reference to their political, social or economic views. We were not organising and subsidising an anti-Bolshevik campaign, but an anti-German front. If the Germans had penetrated to Baku and secured control of the inexhaustible oil supplies of that region and the rich granaries of the intervening areas, the War might have gone on indefinitely. But as soon as the Armistice was signed and Germany had surrendered the bulk of her war material and the Allies had occupied the bridgeheads of the Rhine, and the Austrian Army had dispersed into imperceptible atoms, or had been re-formed in the Slavonic areas as pro-Ally contingents, then every practical reason for continuing our costly military efforts in Russia disappeared. The forces that stood by the Allies in resisting the German advance, and in the process had held on the Russian front a considerable number of enemy troops that might otherwise have gone to France or the Balkans, were without exception anti-Bolshevik. To withdraw support from them the moment they had ceased to be useful to us and to leave them to the mercy of their relentless foes without giving them a chance to save themselves or to make terms, would have been an act of dishonour. We felt bound to see that they were sufficiently

well equipped to enable them to hold their own and to try conclusions with the Bolsheviks on their claim to represent the
people of Russia. If they were right in their estimate of the position in their own country, the Bolsheviks were a small minority
of resolute, but desperate men who had seized authority in a
country whose population was overwhelmingly opposed to them.
As the Bolsheviks were badly equipped and badly organised and
most of the trained officers were with their opponents, they could
not long maintain their position amongst a people who were
antagonistic to their rule. On the other hand, if the workmen and
peasants who constituted between them nine-tenths of the Russian people on the whole preferred Bolshevik rule to that of their
White opponents, then it would have been an impertinence and
an outrage for the Allies to attempt to impose an objectionable
Government upon them by force of arms. We claimed that we
had fought to establish the right of every nation to control its
own destiny without dictation from outside.

The evidence that came home from our own most trusted and
best informed agents in Russia convinced me that although the
vast majority of the people were not Communists, they preferred
Bolshevik rule to that of the supporters of the old régime, and
that they certainly were not prepared to join in any military
enterprises designed to restore the old conditions. The peasants
distrusted the Whites for two reasons. The first was that they
had had enough of war. They were not prepared to do any more
fighting alongside or against any foreigners so long as they did
not invade Russia. The Bolsheviks to them seemed to represent
that attitude of mind. They placed peace in the forefront of
their aims, and the Brest-Litovsk Treaty demonstrated that they
were prepared to pay any price for it short of their own extinc-
tion. The second reason was equally—perhaps more—potent in
its influence on peasant impassivity. They did not want the landowners back. The Revolution had given them the control if not
the ownership of the land they imperfectly cultivated, and they
did not like the idea of foreigners coming with arms into their
country to restore the old order of landlord domination and
exaction. The Germans had gone. That fact gave them much

satisfaction, for they had no affection for the interfering Teuton who regulated their actions and reactions and requisitioned the fruits of their labour. But they did not like the French or the British much better. These strangers were all alike—seeking their own advantage and not that of the Russian peasant. That is how the commons of Russia reasoned and nothing could move them. About Bolshevik theories they were indifferent. Towards the Allies they were suspicious and unhelpful neutrals.

There was throughout the Allied countries, especially amongst the propertied classes, an implacable hatred, born of real fear, of Bolshevism with its predatory doctrines. But only a few—very few—in any land were prepared to start another war, even to suppress a creed which to them was obnoxious. Organised labour viewed the rule of the proletariat in Russia with a certain measure of sympathy, and some hankering after a change everywhere in the particular class that exercised dominion. This sentiment, coupled with the genuine distaste for another war, was strong enough to ensure that if demobilisation had been stopped in order to divert the troops from France to Odessa or Archangel, there would have been a mutiny. The attempt to raise a force of volunteers for the purpose of waging war against the Bolsheviks was a miserable failure.

There can be no doubt that the great majority of the inhabitants of Western Europe and of America would have liked to see Bolshevism crushed, but no one was prepared to undertake the task. My view had been consistently that it was a question for Russia herself to fight out and that foreign interference was unjustifiable. I was also certain that such an intervention would enure to the advantage of the Bolsheviks. The patriotic sentiment of the country would be roused to a pitch of resentment by foreign invasion of Russian soil. Patriotism would therefore come to the aid of Bolshevism.

The first discussion between the Allies on the subject of Russia took place at the Interallied Conference early in December. It arose on the question of whether Russia should be represented at the Peace Conference. Mr. Balfour urged that Finland, Esthonia and Latvia should be given an opportunity to present their case

to the Conference, and he assigned reasons for his advice, but he
said that he had come to the conclusion that the same considerations did not apply to Soviet Russia. Lord Curzon was disposed
to take the same line. M. Clemenceau supported them strongly:

M. Clemenceau said that the art of politics was to solve problems
as they arose. He did not expect to settle anything for eternity at the
present meeting. In general, he agreed with Mr. Balfour. He would
resist with the greatest energy any representation of Russia, which
had betrayed the Allied cause during the war. The peace which was
to be settled did not concern her. As to our attitude to the small
nations, and their attitude towards us, our peace policy would be the
determining factor. If we made a just peace they would be attracted
to us. If we re-established a world of rival coalitions, we should produce
among them the same troubles that had brought about this war. We
were not bound to recognise the small nations at once; to use a col-
loquial phrase: "let them cook," and when they appeared ready we
should recognise them.

I urged the case for bringing Russia into conference at this stage:

Mr. Lloyd George said that, as America was not represented at
the meeting, he felt that it was in any case premature to make any
decision on the subject of Russia. It was not premature, however, to
discuss the matter in order to ascertain the feeling on the subject.
He himself felt that we could not proceed as if there were no Russia.
He admitted that if any of the Allies were answerable for bringing
about the war, Russia was the one. The first declaration of war was
against Russia. But it must be recognised that, great as had been the
sufferings of the other Allies, Russia had probably lost more lives than
any. Their troops had fought without arms or munitions; they had
been outrageously betrayed by their Government, and it was little
to be wondered at if, in their bitterness, the Russian people had re-
belled against the Alliance. He doubted whether any other country
would have borne as much as Russia and remained in the war so
long. Russia, after all, represented something like two-thirds of Europe
and a large part of Asia. It was a problem that must be faced. Could
it be faced without giving the Russian people a right to present their
case? The affairs of nearly two hundred million people could not be
settled without hearing them. It was not possible to say that the
Tartars, the Finns, the Letts, should come to the Peace Conference
and not the Bolsheviks, who stood for two-thirds of the whole population. The Bolsheviks, whatever might be thought of them, appeared to

have a hold over the majority of the population. This was a fact, a sinister one no doubt, but facts could not be neglected because they were unpalatable. He reminded the meeting that 120 years ago similar feelings had been experienced, and similar views had been expressed in that very room, with Mr. Pitt, whose portrait was hanging on the walls, in the Chair, in regard to the French revolutionaries, and the dissidents in Vendée and in the south of France. He therefore strongly deprecated the adoption of any fixed attitude towards Central Russia.

Sir Robert Borden supported my appeal. He "drew attention to Conclusion 4, in which the term 'embryo nations' was used. If this term applied to Esthonia and the Jugo-Slavs, did it not equally apply to the various Governments in Russia, for instance Siberia and the Bolsheviks themselves?" Baron Sonnino was also doubtful as to the wisdom of ruling out Soviet Russia at this stage:

BARON SONNINO asked whether it was not premature to rule out Russia. A month would elapse before the Conference met, and Russia was in revolution. It was in the common interest that Russia should exist. He did not necessarily mean by this a unitary Russia, but possibly a Federation of autonomous States. A collection of very small and mutually hostile States would give Germany a chance of creating the same kind of trouble that had disturbed Europe in the Balkans. If it were decided that the larger Russia was not to appear at the Peace Conference, but that small fractions of it should be admitted, the meeting would be promoting the centrifugal contagion that was spreading through Europe. Not only would small States, but possibly even towns, ask for autonomy. He thought that assistance should be given to the various Governments forming in Russia, and that sympathy should be shown in order to promote the creation of a future Federation of Russian States. The feeling in the country in question was rather against the systems of Government prevalent in Russia to-day and in the past than against Russia as such. His conclusion, therefore, was that it was premature to decide this matter finally at once.

This was support from an unexpected quarter, for Baron Sonnino's views about the government of the world were as far removed from those of Lenin as the Arctic is from the Equator. It was generally agreed that no conclusion could be arrived at on the subject of Russian representation at the Peace Conference without first ascertaining the views of the United States Government. But enough was said to show that the Russian Bolsheviks had excited animosities and apprehensions in Western Europe which would make it impracticable to bring them into conference on equal terms with the Allies. It was not merely their atrocities that excited resentment, but their abandonment of the Allied cause at a critical stage in the struggle. This betrayal very nearly precipitated an irreparable disaster in the spring of 1918. As France had gone into the War to back up Russia when she was attacked, French statesmen regarded the Treaty of Brest-Litovsk as an unpardonable act of perfidy.

Mr. Bonar Law shared my views on the Russian problem. Mr. Balfour, as usual, saw very clearly the arguments on both sides, and felt that whichever way we decided there would be a strong case. He was therefore on the whole indifferent and prepared to support either course, but with a natural disinclination for energetic action on either side. Mr. Hughes was in full agreement with Mr. Bonar Law and myself. In the course of a short discussion on the subject, referring to certain decisions which were being asked for from the Cabinet by Mr. Winston Churchill, in reference to sending troops to Russia, he said

that great principles were involved in these decisions. Was the new world to be one in which each nation should live? In his opinion newly-enfranchised people should be allowed to choose their own way. We should withdraw from Russia and allow the Russians to adopt what Government they liked. He quoted the opinion of one of his colleagues in the Australian Parliament, an opinion reflecting the feelings of half Australia. This opinion was that the Allied professions of fighting for justice and liberty would be entirely stultified by a continuance of intervention in Russia.

But there were two powerful men in the Government who were zealous and untiring advocates of the policy of intervention. One was Lord Curzon. He was mostly concerned about rescuing Georgia from the contamination of Bolshevism. He had a special affection for the Caucasus. He had paid a visit to that region some years before and had acquired great admiration for its gallant mountaineers. The thought of abandoning them to the despotism of Lenin and Trotsky filled him with horror, and he fought to the end for the retention of British forces in Georgia. But the most formidable and irrepressible protagonist of an anti-Bolshevik war was Mr. Winston Churchill. He had no doubt a genuine distaste for Communism. He was horrified, as we all were, at the savage murder of the Czar, the Czarina and their helpless children. His ducal blood revolted against the wholesale elimination of Grand Dukes in Russia.

Feeling that under the impulse of these two brilliant Ministers we were gradually being drawn into war with Russia, I thought the time had come to bring the matter to a point, and at the meeting of the Imperial War Cabinet on the 31st of December, 1918, when Mr. Churchill sought a decision in favour of his particular policy, I intervened with a statement of the conclusions I had come to. The discussion was raised by Mr. Barnes, who spoke with his usual shrewdness and common sense.

MR. BARNES expressed his agreement with the view previously put forward by Sir Robert Borden, that we could not leave the Peace Conference with Russia still a scene of warfare. It was equally clear that we could not fight Bolshevism in Russia except on a large scale. It was no use merely poking with sticks into the kennel to infuriate the dog. He would be in favour of getting all sections of Russians, including the Bolsheviks, to meet, at the instance of the Peace Conference, with a view to adjusting their own differences. If this failed, then intervention might be justified, though he considered that it should be limited to economic pressure. He did not consider that we could suppress Bolshevism forcibly without American help.

MR. CHURCHILL expressed the conviction that the more the Allies attempted to get away from this problem the more it would stick to them. He was in favour of joint action by the five great Powers, or, if America refused to act, by the rest. The intervention should be collective, and not by one Power only, and with joint contingents. He was all for negotiation, with the object of securing a satisfactory settlement without fighting. But he considered that there was no chance of securing such a settlement unless it was known that we had the power and the will to enforce our views. What we should say to the Russians was that if they were ready to come together we would help them: and that if they refused, we would use force to restore the situation and set up a democratic Government. In his view, Bolshevism in Russia represented a mere fraction of the population, and would be exposed and swept away by a General Election held under Allied auspices. A decision on this question was urgent. It was the only part of the war which was still going on, and if we ignored it we should come away from the Peace Conference rejoicing in a victory which was no victory, and a peace which was no peace: and in a few months we should find ourselves compelled to gather our armies again, and summon the Conference anew in order to deal with the situation.

MR. LLOYD GEORGE agreed that the question was one upon which we should come to a decision before anything else. Even a few weeks' delay might easily drift us into disaster. He felt that we had never yet arrived at any satisfactory decision. He himself had found himself frequently leaning first in one direction, and then in another, owing to the absolute contradiction between the information supplied from Russia by men of equally good authority. We were, in fact, never dealing with ascertained, or, perhaps, even ascertainable, facts. Russia was a jungle in which no one could say what was within a few yards of him. In any case nothing could be worse than having no policy, and it was better to proceed resolutely on a wrong hypothesis than to go on hesitating as the Allies had been doing. He wished to lay before the Imperial War Cabinet the views which he was in favour of putting forward to President Wilson and M. Clemenceau in Paris, if his colleagues concurred.

He was definitely opposed to military intervention in any shape. In the first place, it appeared to him a tremendously serious undertaking. The Germans, who had occupied only a relatively small part of Russia, within striking distance of Petrograd and with practically nothing in front of them, had found themselves unable, either to go to Petrograd or to save the situation in the west, while all the time they and the Austrians had something like a million men stuck in that morass, the greater part of whom they had not even yet succeeded in disentangling. In our case the Allies were on the mere fringe of Russia, with less than 100,000 troops. The Bolsheviks had raised their forces to 300,000, which might exceed 1,000,000 by March, and had greatly improved their organisation. Where were we to find the troops with which to march into the heart of Russia and occupy the country? We already had to find troops for Germany, Palestine, Mesopotamia, and the Caucasus. He asked what contribution Australia, Canada, or South Africa were prepared to furnish to the task of conquering and keeping down Russia? No British troops could be found for the purpose without conscription, and if Parliament endorsed conscription for that purpose he doubted whether the troops would go. Our citizen army were prepared to go anywhere for liberty, but they could not be convinced that the suppression of Bolshevism was a war for liberty.

A further reason which weighed with him was the danger that military intervention would only strengthen the very force which we set out to destroy. It was impossible to ignore the parallel of the French Revolution. There, too, there had been horrors as bad as, or worse than, those of the Bolsheviks, perpetrated by a small fraction, which had secured the control of France. There, too, we were invited to help. Toulon and La Vendée corresponded to Riga and the Ukraine. But the very fact that we intervened enabled Danton to rally French patriotism and make the terror a military instrument. When the Revolution was followed by a military dictatorship we were worse off. France became organised as a great military machine imbued with a passionate hatred against us.

Were we prepared to face a revolutionary war against a population of over 100,000,000, associating ourselves in this intervention with allies like the Japanese, against whom feeling in Russia was so passionately strong? He knew of no authority on the strength of which we could be justified in hypothecating our resources and our manhood in the belief that the Russians would regard us as deliverers. For Russia to emancipate herself from Bolshevism would be a redemption, but the attempt to emancipate her by foreign armies might prove a disaster to Europe as well as to Russia. The one sure method of establishing the power of Bolshevism in Russia was to attempt to suppress it by foreign troops. To send our soldiers to shoot down the Bolsheviks would be to create more Bolsheviks there. The best thing was to let Bolshevism fail of itself, as it might and probably would if it did not represent Russian sentiment. That would serve as a deterrent for similar experiments elsewhere, just as the failure of similar movements to establish Communism in 1848 had had a salutary effect in Europe.

In conclusion, he hoped that the Cabinet would agree to support him in refusing to countenance any military intervention, and in inviting the representatives of all sections of Russia to appear before the Peace Conference, as Sir Robert Borden had suggested, with a view to their composing their differences.

LORD ROBERT CECIL, while generally agreeing with Mr. Lloyd George that any invasion of Russia would be fantastic, said there were difficulties arising out of our existing obligations to the Czechs and other parties, whom we had been helping and whom we could not suddenly leave in the lurch. He presumed that assistance in the shape of money and equipment would still be furnished to them. It was also necessary to take into account the possibility that the Bolsheviks were organising those great forces with a definitely aggressive purpose, largely for economic reasons. Colonel Boyle, a Canadian officer who had just returned from Russia, was of the opinion that the Bolsheviks were determined, as a next step, to invade Roumania and other adjoining countries, such as Poland. The Imperial War Cabinet would have to face the possibility of such an aggression, and would have to take measures to assist these countries in defending themselves.

LORD CURZON, who was opposed to sending British troops to any part of Russia except Georgia, pointed out, as an additional argument against military intervention, that neither France, nor America, nor Japan, meant to furnish soldiers for the purpose, and that the whole burden would have to fall upon ourselves.

It was generally agreed that, in cases where there was an external aggression by the Bolsheviks against an existing Government with which we had been co-operating, we should be entitled to support that Government in any manner which did not involve military intervention, and that our general policy should be that, as Sir J. Cook expressed it, of "walling off a fire in a mine."

Subject to the above considerations, the Imperial War Cabinet endorsed the general policy with regard to Russia outlined by Mr. Lloyd George.

On the 16th of January I brought the whole situation in Russia before the Peace Congress. As a revelation of the attitude then adopted by the leading statesmen of the democratic countries of the West and of the British Dominions and dependencies, West, East and South, towards the uprising of the Russian proletariat at that date, the whole debate will always have a historical value. The newer progressivism, which was concerned more with conditions than with forms, viewed the upheaval, in spite of its crudities and barbarities, with tolerance and a few regarded it with a considerable measure of sympathy. That did not mean any degree of acceptance of Communism as a creed. But there was a strong feeling amongst political thinkers of this class that the old order had engendered its own ruin; that it had been guilty of exactions and oppressions which were accountable for the ferocity displayed by Revolutionaries; that it had been inept, profligate and tyrannical. Its ineptitude and corruption had been entirely responsible for the Russian defeat and the huge losses entailed. There was also a strong sentiment in favour of allowing the Russian people to work out their own salvation in their own way. All popular revolutions against age-long tyranny which has crushed the workers down in a hopeless slough of poverty, squalor and superstition, have begun with excesses and extravagances, but they have gradually settled down to a new, a better and a higher order adapted to the genius of the people who had passed through these experiences.

This view was also taken by President Wilson. Our attitude was that of the Fox Whigs towards the French Revolution. Men like Clemenceau, however, who forgave all the terrors of the French Revolution because they thought them unavoidable in an insurrection of the masses against their oppressors and despoilers, judged harshly the violence and horrors perpetrated in the Russian Revolution, although the provocation was if anything greater. In the former case the French Radicals considered that the achievement of liberty and the call of patriotism offended by foreign intervention condoned every excess and outrage perpetrated by the Revolutionaries.

Personally I would have dealt with the Soviets as the *de facto* Government of Russia. So would President Wilson. But we both agreed that we could not carry to that extent our colleagues at the Congress, nor the public opinion of our own countries which was frightened by Bolshevik violence and feared its spread. I therefore accepted as a compromise a proposal that we should proceed along the line of inviting delegates from all the contending sections to meet the Allies at some convenient time and place in the immediate future to effect a settlement which would bring peace to Russia and a good understanding between Russia and the rest of the world. At the Conference I gave my support to this effort and I assigned the following reasons for doing so:

(*a*) We did not know the facts about Russia. Differing reports were received from our representatives in Russia, and often reports from the same representative varied from day to day. It was clear that, unless we knew the facts, we should not be in a position to form a correct judgment.

(*b*) On one subject there could certainly be complete agreement, to wit, that the condition of Russia was extremely bad. There was anarchy and starvation, and all the suffering resulting from both. It was impossible to know which party was gaining the upper hand, but hopes that the Bolshevik Government would collapse had certainly been disappointed. Bolshevism appeared to be stronger than ever. Mr. Lloyd George quoted a report from the British Military Authorities in Russia, who could not be suspected of leanings towards Bolshevism, to the effect that the Bolshevik Government was stronger now than it had been some months previously. The peasants feared that all other parties would, if successful, restore the ancient régime and deprive them of the land which the Revolution had put into their hands.

(c) As to the Ukraine, where we had supposed a firm Government had been established, our information was that an adventurer with a few thousand men had overturned it with the greatest ease. This insurrection had a Bolshevik character, and its success made it clear that the Ukraine was not the stronghold against Bolshevism that we had imagined. The same movement was therefore beginning in the Ukraine which had been completed in Great Russia. The former Government of the Ukraine had been a Government of big landlords only maintained in power by German help. Now that the Germans had withdrawn, the peasants had seized their opportunity. Were we going to spend our resources in order to back a minority of big landlords against an immense majority of peasants? There were three policies from which to choose.

(i) We could say that Bolshevism was a movement as dangerous to civilisation as German militarism had been, and that we must therefore destroy it. Did anyone seriously put forward this policy? Was anyone prepared to carry it out? He believed that no one could be found to do so. The Germans, at the time when they needed every available man to reinforce their attack on the Western Front, had been forced to keep about a million men to garrison a few provinces of Russia which were a mere fringe of the whole country; and, moreover, at that moment Bolshevism was weak and disorganised. Now it was strong and had a formidable army. Was anyone of the Western Allies prepared to send a million men into Russia? He doubted whether a thousand would be willing to go. All reports tended to show that the Allied troops in Siberia and in Northern Russia were most unwilling to continue the campaign and were determined to return to their homes. To set Russia in order by force was a task which he for one would not invite Britain to undertake, and he questioned whether any other Power would undertake it.

(ii) The second policy was a policy of insulation, the policy known as the "cordon sanitaire." This policy meant the siege of Bolshevik Russia, that is to say, the Russia that had no corn, but a large famished population. These people were dying by thousands, if not by hundreds of thousands, of famine. Petrograd had been reduced from the proportions of a great city to those of a moderate town. Our blockade of

Russia would lead to the killing, not of the Chinese ruffians alleged to be enlisted by the Bolsheviks, but of the ordinary population, with whom we wish to be friends. This was a policy which, if only on grounds of humanity, we could not support. It might be suggested that the continuance of this policy in Russia would lead to the overthrow of the Bolsheviks; but who in Russia was able to overthrow them? General Knox reported that the Czecho-Slovak forces inside Russia were tainted with Bolshevism and could not be trusted. Neither were the Russian troops of Kolchak equal to the task. He had just seen a map revealing the area held by Denikin. He occupied with an effective force of perhaps 40,000 men what might be described as a little back-yard near the Black Sea. Denikin was said to have recognised Kolchak, but he was quite unable to get into touch with him, as an immense Bolshevik area intervened between them. Kolchak, moreover, appeared to contemplate the revival of the old régime in Russia; hence the lukewarmness of the Czecho-Slovaks in his cause. They were unwilling to fight in order to set up another Tzarist régime. So also were the British. That would not be helping to create a new world.

(iii) The only other way he could think of was the plan he had proposed—that of asking representatives of the various Russian Governments to meet in Paris after a truce among themselves. The name of M. Sazonoff had been mentioned as representing the Government at Omsk. M. Sazonoff had been long out of Great Russia. It was questionable whether he knew anything of the conditions at Omsk. He was a strong partisan, and might as well be consulted on the present temper of Russia as the *New York Tribune* on the opinions of President Wilson. We could not leave Paris at the conclusion of the Peace Conference congratulating ourselves on having made a better world, if at that moment half of Europe and half of Asia were in flames. It had been alleged that if Bolshevik emissaries came to France and England they would proselytise the French and British peoples. It was possible that Bolshevism might gain ground in these countries, but it would not be as a consequence of the visit of a few Russian emissaries. He himself had no fears on this score. Moreover, conditions could be imposed on the delegates, and if they failed to observe them they could be sent back to Russia. With this threat over them it was most likely that they would avoid giving offence, as they would be anxious to explain their case.

M. PICHON asked whether the meeting would care to hear M. Noulens, the French Ambassador in Russia, who had just returned from Archangel. If so, M. Noulens could attend the meeting on the following day, and would be able to give very interesting information concerning Bolshevism.

PRESIDENT WILSON said that in his mind there was no possible answer to the view expressed by Mr. Lloyd George. This view corresponded exactly with the information received from Russia by the United States Government. There was certainly a latent force behind Bolshevism which attracted as much sympathy as its more brutal aspects caused general disgust. There was throughout the world a feeling of revolt against the large vested interests which influenced the world both in the economic and in the political sphere. The way to cure this domination was, in his opinion, constant discussion and a slow process of reform; but the world at large had grown impatient of delay. There were men in the United States of the finest temper, if not of the finest judgment, who were in sympathy with Bolshevism, because it appeared to them to offer that régime of opportunity to the individual which they desired to bring about. In America considerable progress had been made in checking the control of capital over the lives of men and over Government; yet, even there, labour and capital were not friends. The vast majority who worked and produced were convinced that the privileged minority would never yield them their rights. Unless some sort of partnership between these two interests could be obtained society would crumble. Bolshevism was therefore vital because of these genuine grievances. The seeds of Bolshevism could not flourish without a soil ready to receive them. If this soil did not exist, Bolshevism could be neglected. British and American troops were unwilling to fight in Russia because they feared their efforts might lead to the restoration of the old order, which was even more disastrous than the present one. He recollected making a casual reference of sympathy to the distressed people of Russia, in a speech mainly dealing with other topics, to a wealthy audience in America. The enthusiasm evinced by this remark had surprised him, especially as coming from such an audience, and this incident remained in his mind as an index of the world's sympathies. These sympathies were against any restoration of the old régime. We should be fighting against the current of the times if we tried to prevent Russia from finding her own path to freedom. Part of the strength of the Bolshevik leaders was doubtless the threat of foreign intervention. With the help of this threat they gathered the people round them. The reports of the American representatives in Russia were to this effect. He thought, therefore, that the British proposal contained the only suggestion that led anywhere. If the Bolsheviks refrained from invading Lithuania, Poland, Finland, etc., he thought we should be well advised to allow as many groups as desired to do so to send representatives to Paris. We should then try to reconcile them, both mutually and with the rest of the world.

M. PICHON again suggested that before coming to a decision the meeting should hear M. Noulens, whose news from Russia was fresh.

BARON SONNINO suggested that M. de Scavenius, who had been Danish Minister in Petrograd and was now in Paris, could also give very valuable information.

It was decided that M. Noulens and M. de Scavenius should be invited to attend the meeting on the following day at 10.30 A.M.

On the 21st of January M. Noulens came to give us his views as to what was happening in Russia. He was not a good witness. He was inclined to be pompous, sententious and not informative. He was a shallow and unintelligent partisan rather than a witness. He repeated the gossip and hearsay of the Parisian journals of the Extreme Right about the horrors of Bolshevism. His observations on Russia were certainly not fresh and they were not the fruit of any experience he had himself acquired. We found he had left Petrograd for Archangel in February, 1918, and had left Archangel in July. He quoted with histrionic emphasis one illustration of Bolshevik atrocity which he thought especially sinister. He had received a telegram from Ekaterinberg stating that "on triumphal arches erected to celebrate the anniversary of the accession of the Bolsheviks to power were inscriptions reading 'He who does not work, neither shall he eat.'"

This Pauline dictum he evidently thought to be one of those nefarious doctrines propounded by Lenin, and designed to undermine the very foundations of respectable society!

He was certain the Red Army would dissolve if faced by regular troops. They were not soldiers, but men driven by famine to take service.

He did not make a good impression. The French Ministers were themselves disappointed with their witness.

M. de Scavenius, the Danish Minister in Russia, who came next was a much better type. He was distinctly hostile to the Bolsheviks but on the whole he gave us much more reliable and valuable information:

M. DE SCAVENIUS said that in Russia there were two classes—one Bolshevik, and one opposed to Bolshevism. He would begin by describing the former. When the Bolsheviks overthrew Kerensky they had behind them the soldiers and most of the peasants and workmen; the soldiers backed them because they wanted peace at any price, the peasants because they wanted land, the workmen because they desired privileges for themselves. At the present time the original soldiers had been demobilised and had become peasants. The peasants were neither Bolshevik, Socialist, nor Monarchist. All they desired was land. They now had it. Their present requirement was order, which would enable them to cultivate their holdings.

As to the workmen: there was among workmen a considerable amount of discontent. Though they had become the privileged class, they were in straits for food, and felt that Bolshevism had not kept its promises. Consequently, it might safely be said that the Bolsheviks could only depend on about half the workmen of Russia, whose total numbers might be put at 2,000,000.

The nucleus of the Red Army was composed of foreigners—Letts, Hungarians, Germans and Chinese. Some Russians, no doubt, had been collected by Trotsky around this nucleus, but the best fighting elements in the force were foreigners, especially the Hungarians and the Chinese.

His statistics did not bear out his estimate of the non-Russian character of the Red Army. When asked for the number of the Mongolian contingent, he estimated the Bolshevik Army at 300,000, of whom 20,000 only were Chinese. He said that Denikin's Army consisted of Cossacks who were not prepared to advance beyond the confines of their own country. This applied also to the Krasnoff Cossacks. He admitted the weakness of Czarism. The Monarchists were recruited from "the upper classes, the landed proprietors and the officers."

When I asked him whether he advocated immediate Allied intervention, he replied in the affirmative. But he was emphatically of the opinion that "it would be a great mistake to intervene by means of small forces as had hitherto been attempted, *because, as in the case of the Germans, the troops sent would become contaminated with Bolshevism in a few months.*" This was not consistent with the theory that the triumph of Bolshevism was entirely due to terror, and that it had no other hold on the bulk of the population.

Here is another very revealing passage in his testimony. He was advocating a converging movement on Moscow of allied

Finnish and Polish troops, with Denikin's Army marching from the south:

MR. LLOYD GEORGE asked whether M. de Scavenius meant to convey that Russian troops could not be depended upon without the support of foreign armies.

M. DE SCAVENIUS replied that that was his opinion. He thought a stiffening of 100,000 to 150,000 volunteers from the Allied countries would be sufficient to reinforce the Russian armies he had already enumerated, and to ensure success.

M. CLEMENCEAU said that he had understood from M. de Scavenius' remarks that Denikin's forces were unwilling to go to Moscow.

M. DE SCAVENIUS said that this would be the case if they felt that they had to do all the fighting.

MR. BALFOUR asked whether M. de Scavenius assumed that if the Allies appeared in Moscow they would be able to gather round them an effective Russian force. As a matter of fact, a similar experiment had already been tried, for instance, in Siberia and at Archangel, which were areas of considerable extent. In both instances, the moment when foreign support had been withdrawn the native forces had dissolved. The Russians appeared incapable of forming an independent force, and could only lean on foreign troops.

M. DE SCAVENIUS said that the mistake hitherto committed had been that of employing too small forces.

MR. LLOYD GEORGE said that the British Government had recently received a report that the Mensheviks and Revolutionary Socialists had been driven by Allied intervention to act with the Bolsheviks.

M. DE SCAVENIUS said that, as he had before remarked, the Bolsheviks were appealing to the patriotism of the lower middle class, and persuading them that the Allies were Imperialists who intended to exploit Russia as the Germans had done. Such propaganda as this would have the effect to which Mr. Lloyd George had alluded.

At this stage there was an interruption which illustrated the difficulties which confronted the Allies in their efforts to make peace on frontiers where the racial and national affinities were undefined or intermingled. As soon as M. de Scavenius had left the Chair:

PRESIDENT WILSON read a letter addressed to him by M. Paderewski. The letter concluded by suggesting that the Allies should send a collective Note to the Ukrainian Directorate at Kieff ordering them to withdraw from Galicia and to cease interference in Polish territory.

He further suggested that an Allied Commission be sent to Warsaw to gauge the situation, and that the Polish Government be supplied with artillery and German rifle ammunition.

MR. LLOYD GEORGE questioned whether it was safe to admit that Galicia was Polish territory. Any summons to Kieff should be accompanied by a similar summons to the Poles to abstain from entering disputed territory such as Eastern Galicia.

The Galician problem gave us no end of trouble. The trouble, however, did not come from Bolsheviks but from Polish aggression.

The President then read a very remarkable message he had just received from his agent at Stockholm as to confidential conversations with Litvinoff:

Litvinoff stated that the Soviet Government are anxious for a permanent peace, and fully endorse the telegram which he sent to President Wilson the 24th December. They detest the military preparations and costly campaigns which are now forced upon Russia after four years of exhausting war, and wish to ascertain whether the United States and the Allies have a desire for peace.

If such is the case, peace can easily be negotiated, for, according to Litvinoff, the Soviet Government are prepared to compromise on all points, including protection to existing foreign enterprises, the granting of new concessions in Russia, and the Russian foreign debt. It is impossible now to give the details as to possible compromises, because Litvinoff has no idea of the claims which will be presented by the Allies, nor of the resources which will be available to Russia for the satisfaction of those claims. The particulars in all phases can be worked out by experts when the data mentioned above are available. The Soviet Government's conciliatory attitude is unquestionable.

Litvinoff showed me an open wireless message which he had just received from Tchitcherine, the Soviet Foreign Minister, affirming the willingness of the Government to be conciliatory with reference to the question of the foreign debt. Litvinoff and his associates realise fully that Russia will need, for a long time, expert assistance and advice, particularly in financial and technical matters, and that she cannot get on without manufactured imports, including, especially, foreign machinery.

In view of the important rôle M. Litvinoff has played in the diplomatic developments of the last few years, this memorandum has a special significance. At that date, unfortunately, he had no official position which would give his offer the status of an official pronouncement by the Bolshevik Government.

Knowing that there were considerable differences of opinion, even amongst supporters of the Government, as to the attitude which we should take in reference to the civil war in Russia, and especially as to the recognition or otherwise of the Bolshevik Government, I decided to bring the matter before the British Empire Delegation that evening, so as to ensure unanimity as far as the Empire was concerned in any policy that I presented to the Peace Conference. The discussions which took place at this meeting are a fair representation of the doubts and hesitations which filled men's minds when they contemplated this terrible portent in Eastern Europe.

MR. LLOYD GEORGE said that that morning they had seen the late French Ambassador at Petrograd, M. Noulens, who had been brought to give them information on the situation in Russia. It appeared that he had not been in Petrograd since February, since when he had practically been a fugitive. He had no information of any value as to the existing state of affairs, and only gave them an elementary description of Bolshevism and a rhetorical attack upon it. His figures were inaccurate. The French were taking a strong line as to the need for crushing Bolshevism, whilst President Wilson was supporting the British proposals. M. Noulens was brought in merely to support the French view. After hearing M. Noulens they had adjourned the meeting, and they had been unable to meet again that afternoon. On the whole, the British representatives had a feeling that they were not getting on with their work. All last week had been spent on procedure, altering and re-altering regulations, passing resolutions and rescinding them. A whole week had gone by and no real business had been done. He thought they must insist on getting on with the business of the Conference. He gathered that President Wilson was of the same opinion. There was a general feeling in England that they wanted to get done with the German part of the business with as little delay as possible.

· · · · ·

MR. LLOYD GEORGE said that he had had a long talk that afternoon with General Franchet d'Esperey, who was in command of the troops going to the Ukraine, in the presence of the Foreign Secretary. General Franchet d'Esperey had explained the French attitude very clearly. He had fully admitted the facts contained in the British War Office

Paper, circulated yesterday. He had admitted that the Bolshevists had 800,000 or 900,000 troops, that their army was very formidable, and that discipline had been restored. Should these troops attack the Ukraine, nothing could stand against them. Questioned as to his policy, he said that it was a united Russia. When asked how this was to be achieved and who was to represent Russia, he said that MM. Lvoff and Sazonoff were the best representatives of authority, and their plan would be to form a *cordon sanitaire* around the Bolshevist area, and then destroy Bolshevism by starvation. He was asked what would happen should the Bolshevists conquer the Ukraine. He said he would occupy three bases, Sebastopol, Odessa, and Nikolaieff; he would organise Russia, equip the forces with aeroplanes, guns, &c., and raise volunteer armies under Allied command. The Allies would have to pay. They would have to guarantee the rouble, and would have all the assets of the country as their security.

That, Mr. Lloyd George observed, practically meant war organised by the Allies. He thought that was the French idea.

MR. BALFOUR said that President Wilson would certainly not allow an American Army to go to Russia, and would regard a volunteer army with suspicion.

MR. LLOYD GEORGE said that America would certainly not send an army. Would Canada?

SIR ROBERT BORDEN replied in the negative.

MR. LLOYD GEORGE said that M. Clemenceau would decidedly not allow any Bolshevists to come to France. The other proposal was that a Commission should go to Russia to confer with representatives of all parties.

MR. BALFOUR agreed that M. Clemenceau would not have the Bolshevists here. He (Mr. Balfour) thought that that decision had at least this merit, that publicly to announce that they were treating with the Bolshevists would strengthen the Bolshevists' hand. That need not be discussed. Nothing would induce the French Government to alter their decision. Ministers and members of the Chamber were unanimously opposed to the Bolshevists coming here, and M. Clemenceau had said that if the Conference forced that course upon him he would have to resign. M. Clemenceau had then thrown out, on the spur of the moment, a half-baked scheme of a kind which he thought might satisfy President Wilson. The scheme, if thoroughly worked out, would, he thought, amount to something like this. The main object was to prevent the Bolshevists from attacking adjoining countries. We should tell them: "You must not attack your neighbours. If you want food, show us that you will distribute it fairly and we will supply it." It was well known that the Bolshevists were using the food scarcity for propaganda purposes; were feeding those who joined the Red Guards, and allowing the rest of the population to starve. Mr. Balfour said that he did not know whether the Bolshevists would accept such a proposal, but it would give them a chance to make out a case if they had one, and it would put us right with the world. If the Bolshevists declined, it would put them wrong with their own people, as they had had a chance to obtain food and had gone on fighting instead. He thought that was a far sounder scheme than General Franchet d'Esperey's, which meant making war on Russia, and that it was at least worthy of consideration in the present difficult situation.

SIR ROBERT BORDEN asked how the Allies would get into touch with the Bolshevists.

MR. BALFOUR suggested by a wireless message sent out publicly.

LORD READING asked how it would be possible to control distribution, without intervention.

MR. HUGHES said that the scheme would break down in two ways. First, food could not be sent without causing prices to rise in Allied countries, which would light the fires of Bolshevism there. Food prices were already high and profiteering rampant. People would say: "We should have had cheap food here if you had not sent it to Russia." Second, the Bolshevists would not distribute the food fairly, and we would be powerless to intervene. On the other hand, the Bolshevists might refuse to accept the conditions upon which we offered them food. The Bolshevists would say that this scheme was only an effort to undermine the authority of the Proletariat. The granaries of Europe were open to them, they would pay tribute to the Bolshevists, who would snap their fingers at our demands that they should distribute the food equitably.

. . . . .

MR. LLOYD GEORGE asked whether the Bolshevists would not say: "We do not want your food; we want the Ukraine, where there is all the food we need"; and it looked as if they would be there in a few weeks.

MR. BALFOUR agreed that the food was there, and the Ukraine could make no resistance. But could the Bolshevists get it out of the peasants?

. . . . .

SIR ROBERT BORDEN suggested that the right thing was to get in touch with the Bolshevist Government. We clearly could not organise control over the distribution of food. The main point was to get some understanding which would prevent hostilities, and if they declined to agree, then to bring such economic pressure to bear as was possible. The only alternative was to go in and fight, which was impossible.

LORD READING said that he had heard on good authority that Lenin's policy would be to expand beyond Russia. Bolshevism, confined to Russia, would be killed, and it must spread West in order to live. In other words, it was a form of internationalism.

SIR JOSEPH COOK suggested that we were distributing our forces too far. He thought the fear of Bolshevism was exaggerated. It was a movement caused by high prices. The only cure was to try to bring prices down in our own countries.

MR. HUGHES agreed with Lord Reading that Bolshevism knew no country. There was plenty of Bolshevist material in Australia and elsewhere, though it had not had the same opportunity to develop. Mr. Lockhart's memorandum, he thought, explained the whole position, which was previously inexplicable. Bolshevism had power because it had large armed forces. He referred to the statement on page 4 of Mr. Lockhart's report, that they had 213,000 troops in November, 1918, and now they had 820,000. He thought that the Anti-Bolshevist representatives ought not to be received. They did not represent Russia, and he thought it would be a great mistake to receive the Bolshevist representatives. The great body of Russia, the peasants, could not make themselves heard: their wants were known. They wanted the land. As we could not intervene effectually, we ought to keep Bolshevism inside Russia and apply economic pressure. Bolshevism must inevitably die if confined within the borders of Russia.

SIR ROBERT BORDEN said that that would mean fighting them. Force would be necessary if the Bolshevists were to be confined.

MR. HUGHES replied that it would not unless they came out of Russia, in which case we must fight them.

MR. LLOYD GEORGE asked what would happen if they advanced into the Ukraine.

MR. HUGHES asked whether there was a *de facto* Government there.

MR. LLOYD GEORGE replied that there were two, at least.

MR. HUGHES admitted that that increased the difficulty. If any Ukrainian Government which was sufficiently in control to be called *de facto* asked for help, he would propose to help them.

MR. LLOYD GEORGE enquired where he would get his troops from. Sir Robert Borden had said that he would not keep Canadian troops there. Would Mr. Hughes send Australian troops?

MR. HUGHES replied in the negative.

MR. LLOYD GEORGE said that they were not meeting the difficulty. Non-interference did not mean keeping 20,000 European troops there, and supplying them with munitions and money. The question was whether we should withdraw. The decision of the War Cabinet had been (1) non-intervention; (2) to summon Bolshevist delegates to Paris.

MR. BALFOUR said that the first proposal stood; the second had become impossible.

MR. LLOYD GEORGE insisted that they must come to a practical solution. Were we to keep troops in Russia, or to subsidise troops there, and would the Dominions join?

SIR ROBERT BORDEN said that public opinion in Canada would not support his doing so. That might be considered final.

MR. LLOYD GEORGE said that he thought the same was the case in England. They could not send troops, but could they send arms and equipment?

GENERAL RADCLIFFE said that the equipment would amount to enormous sums. He could not give exact figures, but they represented many millions. Denikin had asked equipment for 250,000 men. Equipment for 200,000 had already been promised to Kolchak.

SIR ROBERT BORDEN enquired whether there was not a large amount of Allied or enemy material which, now that Germany had ceased to fight, could be utilised.

MR. LLOYD GEORGE agreed that that might be possible. But they were also asking for money. General Franchet d'Esperey had said that they were also asking us to guarantee the rouble.

SIR ROBERT BORDEN said that the Bolshevist forces were rapidly increasing in numbers. They were in control of affairs, and we were bound to negotiate with them, whatever their opinions might be. They could not go back from the Peace Conference leaving five or six governments fighting amongst themselves in Russia.

MR. BALFOUR said that the Conference could not be blamed for not keeping the peace if the governments would not supply troops or money to suppress the fighting.

GENERAL SMUTS said that force was out of the question, and so was unlimited supply of cash. But they could not leave the matter altogether alone. The French objected to any recognition of the Bolshevists. But there was not the same objection to summoning them before a Court. He suggested that as soon as the League of Nations was created it might appoint a Commission to summon all *de facto* governments before it. Pending the investigation it would insist on an armistice. This would mean a little delay, but it would get over the difficulty of recognition.

MR. LLOYD GEORGE asked whether, meanwhile, the Canadian forces would remain.

SIR ROBERT BORDEN feared not, unless the business of the Conference went a little faster. They might stay until June, perhaps, or even a little longer.

MR. BALFOUR pointed out that it would be a most unfortunate

precedent if the League of Nations concerned itself with an enquiry between factions within a country, especially a country which was not part of the League.

MR. MONTAGU asked whether we were not forced to the conclusion that we could withdraw our troops and leave Russia alone.

LORD READING said there was also the possible alternative of a limited assistance, particularly with equipment and food.

MR. MONTAGU replied that we could logically withdraw now on the ground that we went in during the war with Germany, a state of affairs which had now ceased, but we could not make war by halves. If we left it until later we would be drawn into further intervention.

MR. LLOYD GEORGE said that the position would be like the policy of Gladstone in the Soudan—"military operations, but not war." We must either back them right through, or not at all. Mr. Lloyd George suggested that the decision should be: That unless some effort was made to bring the parties together, we must make it clear that we must immediately cease intervention or subsidies to troops. In the case of any State that we think ought to be independent, we would join in any steps which the Great Powers think necessary to protect it against invasion.

MR. HUGHES suggested that the decision should not be conditional; that we had determined on a policy of non-intervention in any event.

MR. LLOYD GEORGE said that that was what he intended to express. But in the event of steps, which the Conference thought satisfactory, being taken to bring the parties together the withdrawal would not be immediate pending the result.

LORD READING enquired whether the policy was not that whatever happened they would take no further part in intervention.

MR. LLOYD GEORGE said that that was not exactly it. If the French agreed to meet the Bolshevists anywhere—say at Salonica or Lemnos— the withdrawal would be temporarily withheld pending the negotiations.

(It was agreed:

(1) That the Prime Minister and the Secretary of State for Foreign Affairs should make it clear at the conversations that we could not agree to a continuance of intervention in Russia, or of subsidies to the forces of the other Allies engaged in operations with this object. If, however, some effort could be made to bring the contending parties in Russia together, which the British Empire Plenipotentiaries could regard as satisfactory, such as summoning the various parties to meet, for example, at Salonica or Lemnos, the withdrawal of the British Empire forces at present in Russia would not be immediate.

(2) That as regards any steps which the Great Powers might think

it necessary to take in order to protect against invasion any independent State about to be set up, we should be ready to co-operate.)

The discussion on Russia at the Peace Conference was resumed
on the 21st of January. In the interval before the adjourned discussion Clemenceau had made representations to President Wilson and to me as to the impossibility of allowing Bolshevik delegates to come to Paris. When the rumour went round that I had
proposed to invite them to the Conference, the Paris press of the
Right were up in arms and the *couloirs* of the Chamber of Deputies hummed with indignation. The propertied classes were
alarmed by the fact that there was considerable disaffection
amongst the Parisian workmen, especially amongst those who
on demobilisation found they were without a job, and that the
Bolshevik and German revolutionary examples of soldier and
workman committees appealed to the discontented elements in
the French cities. It was therefore suggested that if we must
needs confer with the Russian sections the Conference should be
held elsewhere, preferably at some convenient centre in the
Eastern Mediterranean. It is significant of the universal fear
created by the Bolshevik outbreak that we experienced great
difficulty in finding a suitable location to meet these terrors of
the East. No country could be found willing to receive their envoys. It was as if I had proposed that we should invite a delegation of lepers from the stricken isle of Molokai.

PRESIDENT WILSON said that in order to have something definite
to discuss, he wished to take advantage of a suggestion made by
Mr. Lloyd George and to propose a modification of the British proposal. He wished to suggest that the various organised groups in
Russia should be asked to send representatives, not to Paris, but to
some other place, such as Salonica, convenient of approach, there to
meet such representatives as might be appointed by the Allies, in
order to see whether they could draw up a programme upon which
agreement could be reached.

MR. LLOYD GEORGE pointed out that the advantage of this would
be that they could be brought straight there from Russia through the
Black Sea without passing through other countries.

M. SONNINO said that some of the representatives of the various

Governments were already here in Paris, for example M. Sazonoff. Why should these not be heard?

PRESIDENT WILSON expressed the view that the various parties should not be heard separately. It would be very desirable to get all these representatives in one place, and still better, all in one room, in order to obtain a close comparison of views.

MR. BALFOUR said that a further objection to M. Sonnino's plan was that if M. Sazonoff was heard in Paris, it would be difficult to refuse to hear the others in Paris also, and M. Clemenceau objected strongly to having some of these representatives in Paris.

M. SONNINO explained that all the Russian parties had some representatives here, except the Soviets, whom they did not wish to hear.

MR. LLOYD GEORGE remarked that the Bolsheviks were the very people some of them wished to hear.

M. SONNINO, continuing, said that they had heard M. Litvinoff's statements that morning. The Allies were now fighting against the Bolsheviks, who were their enemies, and therefore they were not obliged to hear them with the others.

MR. BALFOUR remarked that the essence of President Wilson's proposal was that the parties must all be heard at one and the same time.

MR. LLOYD GEORGE expressed the view that the acceptance of M. Sonnino's proposals would amount to their hearing a string of people, all of whom held the same opinion, and all of whom would strike the same note. But they would not hear the people who at the present moment were actually controlling European Russia. In deference to M. Clemenceau's views, they had put forward this new proposal. He thought it would be quite safe to bring the Bolshevik representatives to Salonica, or perhaps to Lemnos. It was absolutely necessary to endeavour to make peace.

PRESIDENT WILSON asked to be permitted to urge one aspect of the case. As M. Sonnino had implied, they were all repelled by Bolshevism, and for that reason they had placed armed men in opposition to them. One of the things that was clear in the Russian situation was that by opposing Bolshevism with arms they were in reality serving the cause of Bolshevism. The Allies were making it possible for the Bolsheviks to argue that Imperialistic and Capitalistic Governments were endeavouring to exploit the country and to give the land back to the landlords, and so bring about a reaction. If it could be shown that this was not true and that the Allies were prepared to deal with the rulers of Russia, much of the moral force of this argument would disappear. The allegation that the Allies were against the people and wanted to control their affairs provided the argument which enabled them to raise armies. If, on the other hand, the Allies could swallow their pride and the natural repulsion which they felt for the Bolsheviks, and see the representatives of all organised groups in one place, he thought it would bring about a marked reaction against Bolshevism.

M. CLEMENCEAU said that, in principle, he did not favour conversation with the Bolsheviks; not because they were criminals, but because we would be raising them to our level by saying that they were worthy of entering into conversation with us. The Bolshevik danger was very great at the present moment. Bolshevism was spreading. It had invaded the Baltic Provinces and Poland, and that very morning they had received very bad news regarding its spread to Budapest and Vienna. Italy, also, was in danger. The danger was probably greater there than in France. If Bolshevism, after spreading in Germany, were to traverse Austria and Hungary and so reach Italy, Europe would be faced with a very great danger. Therefore, something must be done against Bolshevism. When listening to the document presented by President Wilson that morning, he had been struck by the cleverness with which the Bolsheviks were attempting to lay a trap for the Allies. When the Bolsheviks first came into power, a breach was made with the Capitalist Governments on questions of principle, but now they offered funds and concessions, as a basis for treating with them. He need not say how valueless their promises were, but if they were listened to, the Bolsheviks would go back to their people and say: "We offered them great principles of justice, and the Allies would have nothing to do with us. Now we offer money, and they are ready to make peace."

He admitted his remarks did not offer a solution. The great misfortune was that the Allies were in need of a speedy solution. After four years of war, and the losses and sufferings they had incurred, their populations could stand no more. Russia also was in need of immediate peace. But its necessary evolution must take time. The signing of the world peace could not await Russia's final avatar. Had time been available, he would suggest waiting, for eventually sound men representing common sense would come to the top. But when would that be? He could make no forecast. Therefore they must press for an early solution.

To sum up, had he been acting by himself, he would temporise and erect barriers to prevent Bolshevism from spreading. But he was not alone, and in the presence of his colleagues he felt compelled to make some concession, as it was essential that there should not be even the appearance of disagreement amongst them. The concession came easier after having heard President Wilson's suggestion. He thought that they should make a very clear and convincing appeal to all reasonable peoples, emphatically stating that they did not wish in any way to interfere in the internal affairs of Russia, and especially that they had no intention of restoring Czardom. The object of the Allies being to hasten the creation of a strong Government, they proposed to call together representatives of all parties to a Conference. He would beg President Wilson to draft a paper, fully explaining the position of the Allies to the whole world, including the Russians and the Germans.

Mr. Lloyd George agreed, and gave notice that he wished to withdraw his own motion in favour of President Wilson's.

Mr. Balfour said that he understood that all these people were to be asked on an equality. On these terms he thought the Bolsheviks would refuse, and by their refusal they would put themselves in a very bad position.

M. Sonnino said that he did not agree that the Bolsheviks would not come. He thought they would be the first to come, because they would be eager to put themselves on an equality with the others. He would remind his colleagues that, before the Peace of Brest-Litovsk was signed, the Bolsheviks promised all sorts of things, such as to refrain from propaganda, but since that peace had been concluded they had broken all their promises, their one idea being to spread revolution in all other countries. His idea was to collect together all the anti-Bolshevik parties and help them to make a strong Government, provided they pledged themselves not to serve the forces of reaction and especially not to touch the land question, thereby depriving the Bolsheviks of their strongest argument. Should they take these pledges, he would be prepared to help them.

Mr. Lloyd George enquired how this help would be given.

M. Sonnino replied that help would be given with soldiers to a reasonable degree or by supplying arms, food, and money. For instance, Poland asked for weapons and munitions; the Ukraine asked for weapons. All the Allies wanted was to establish a strong Government. The reason that no strong Government at present existed was that no party could risk taking the offensive against Bolshevism without the assistance of the Allies. He would enquire how the parties of order could possibly succeed without the help of the Allies. President Wilson had said that they should put aside all pride in the matter. He would point out that, for Italy, and probably for France also, as M. Clemenceau had stated, it was in reality a question of self-defence. He thought that even a partial recognition of the Bolsheviks would strengthen their position, and, speaking for himself, he thought that Bolshevism was already a serious danger in his country.

Mr. Lloyd George said he wished to put one or two practical questions to M. Sonnino. The British Empire now had some 15,000 to 20,000 men in Russia. M. de Scavenius had estimated that some

150,000 additional men would be required, in order to keep the anti-Bolshevik Governments from dissolution. And General Franchet d'Esperey also insisted on the necessity of Allied assistance. Now Canada had decided to withdraw her troops, because the Canadian soldiers would not agree to stay and fight against the Russians. Similar trouble had also occurred amongst the other Allied troops. And he felt certain that, if the British tried to send any more troops there, there would be mutiny.

M. SONNINO suggested that volunteers might be called for.

MR. LLOYD GEORGE, continuing, said that it would be impossible to raise 150,000 men in that way. He asked, however, what contributions America, Italy and France would make towards the raising of this army.

PRESIDENT WILSON and M. CLEMENCEAU each said none.

M. ORLANDO agreed that Italy could make no further contributions.

MR. LLOYD GEORGE said that the Bolsheviks had an army of 300,000 men who would, before long, be good soldiers, and to fight them at least 400,000 Russian soldiers would be required. Who would feed, equip and pay them? Would Italy, or America, or France, do so? If they were unable to do that, what would be the good of fighting Bolshevism? It could not be crushed by speeches. He sincerely trusted that they would accept President Wilson's proposal as it now stood.

M. ORLANDO agreed that the question was a very difficult one for the reasons that had been fully given. He agreed that Bolshevism constituted a grave danger to all Europe. To prevent a contagious epidemic from spreading the sanitarians set up a *cordon sanitaire*. If similar measures could be taken against Bolshevism, in order to prevent its spreading, it might be overcome, since to isolate it meant vanquishing it. Italy was now passing through a period of depression, due to war weariness. But Bolsheviks could never triumph there, unless they found a favourable medium, such as might be produced either by profound patriotic disappointment in their expectations as to the rewards of the war, or by an economic crisis. Either might lead to revolution, which was equivalent to Bolshevism. Therefore, he would insist that all possible measures should be taken to set up this cordon. Next, he suggested the consideration of repressive measures. He thought two methods were possible—either the use of physical force or the use of moral force. He thought Mr. Lloyd George's objection to the use of physical force unanswerable. The occupation of Russia meant the employment of large numbers of troops for an indefinite period of time. This meant an apparent prolongation of the war. There remained the use of moral force. He agreed with M. Clemenceau that no country could continue in anarchy, and that an end must eventually come; but they could not wait; they could not proceed to make peace and ignore Russia. Therefore, Mr. Lloyd George's proposal, with the modifications introduced after careful consideration by President Wilson and M. Clemenceau, gave a possible solution. It did not involve entering into negotiations with the Bolsheviks; the proposal was merely an attempt to bring together all the parties in Russia with a view to finding a way out of the present difficulty. He was prepared, therefore, to support it.

PRESIDENT WILSON asked the views of his Japanese colleagues.

BARON MAKINO said that, after carefully considering the various points of view put forward, he had no objections to make regarding the conclusion reached. He thought that was the best solution under the circumstances. He wished, however, to enquire what attitude would be taken by the representatives of the Allied Powers if the Bolsheviks accepted the invitation to the meeting and there insisted upon their principles. He thought they should under no circumstances countenance Bolshevik ideas. The conditions in Siberia east of the Baikal had greatly improved. The objects which had necessitated the despatch of troops to that region had been attained. Bolshevism was no longer aggressive though it might still persist in a latent form. In conclusion, he wished to support the proposal before the meeting.

PRESIDENT WILSON expressed the view that the emissaries of the Allied Powers should not be authorised to adopt any definite attitude towards Bolshevism. They should merely report back to their Governments the conditions found.

MR. LLOYD GEORGE asked that that question be further considered. He thought the emissaries of the Allied Powers should be able to establish an agreement if they were able to find a solution. For instance, if they succeeded in reaching an agreement on the subject of the organisation of a Constituent Assembly, they should be authorised to accept such a compromise without the delay of a reference to the Government.

PRESIDENT WILSON suggested that the emissaries might be furnished with a body of instructions.

MR. BALFOUR expressed the view that abstention from hostile action against their neighbours should be made a condition of their sending representatives to this meeting.

PRESIDENT WILSON agreed.

M. CLEMENCEAU suggested that the manifesto to the Russian parties should be based solely on humanitarian grounds. They should say to the Russians: "You are threatened by famine. We are prompted by humanitarian feelings; we are making peace; we do not want people to die. We are prepared to see what can be done to remove the menace of starvation." He thought the Russians would at once prick up their ears and be prepared to hear what the Allies had to say. They would add that food cannot be sent unless peace and order were re-established. It should, in fact, be made quite clear that the representatives of all parties would merely be brought together for purely humane reasons.

It was agreed that President Wilson should draft a proclamation for consideration at the next meeting, inviting all organised parties in Russia to attend a meeting to be held at some selected place, such as Salonica or Lemnos, in order to discuss with the representatives of the Allied and Associated Great Powers the means of restoring order and peace in Russia. Participation in the meeting should be conditional on a cessation of hostilities.

On the 22nd of January President Wilson presented his draft to the leaders of the Russian section:

President Wilson read a draft proclamation which he had prepared for the consideration of his colleagues, in accordance with the decision reached at yesterday's meeting.

After a discussion the following text was adopted, to be publicly transmitted to the parties invited:

"The single object the representatives of the associated Powers have had in mind in their discussions of the course they should pursue with regard to Russia has been to help the Russian people, not to hinder them, or to interfere in any manner with their right to settle their own affairs in their own way. They regard the Russian people as their friends, not their enemies, and are willing to help them in any way they are willing to be helped. It is clear to them that the troubles and distresses of the Russian people will steadily increase, hunger and privation of every kind become more and more acute, more and more widespread, and more and more impossible to relieve, unless order is restored and normal conditions of labour, trade and transportation once more created, and they are seeking some way in which to assist the Russian people to establish order.

"They recognise the absolute right of the Russian people to direct their own affairs without dictation or direction of any kind from outside. They do not wish to exploit or make use of Russia in any way. They recognise the revolution without reservation, and will in no way, and in no circumstances, aid or give countenance to any attempt at a counter-revolution. It is not their wish or purpose to favour or assist any one of those organised groups now contending for the leadership and guidance of Russia as against the others. Their sole and sincere purpose is to do what they can to bring Russia peace and an opportunity to find her way out of her present troubles.

"The associated Powers are now engaged in the solemn and responsible work of establishing the peace of Europe and of the world, and they are keenly alive to the fact that Europe and the world cannot be at peace if Russia is not. They recognise and accept it as their duty, therefore, to serve Russia in this matter as generously, as unselfishly, as thoughtfully, as ungrudgingly as they would serve every other friend and ally. And they are ready to render this service in the way that is most acceptable to the Russian people.

"In this spirit and with this purpose, they have taken the following action: They invite every organised group that is now exercising, or attempting to exercise, political authority or military control anywhere in Siberia, or within the boundaries of European Russia as they stood before the war just concluded (except in Finland) to send representatives, not exceeding three representatives for each group, to the Princes Islands, Sea of Marmora, where they will be met by representatives of the associated Powers, provided, in the meantime, there is a truce of arms amongst the parties invited, and that all armed forces anywhere sent or directed against any people or territory outside the boundaries of European Russia as they stood before the war, or against Finland, or against any people or territory whose autonomous action is in contemplation in the fourteen articles upon which the present negotiations are based, shall be meanwhile withdrawn, and aggressive military action cease. These representatives are invited to confer with the representatives of the associated Powers in the freest and frankest way, with a view to ascertaining the wishes of all sections of the Russian people, and bringing about, if possible, some understanding and agreement by which Russia may work out her own purposes and happy cooperative relations be established between her people and the other peoples of the world.

"A prompt reply to this invitation is requested. Every facility for the journey of the representatives, including transport across the Black Sea, will be given by the Allies, and all the parties concerned are expected to give the same facilities. The representatives will be expected at the place appointed by the 15th February, 1919."

This well-meant effort at the pacification of Russia and her restoration to the comradeship of nations was not successful. Neither of the parties concerned was willing to meet the other in conference. The Bolsheviks were not prepared to recognise that their opponents had any status. They were rebels against the Government and they could not consent to negotiate with them on equal terms under the auspices of foreign Governments. Moreover, they were convinced that the military superiority was on their side and that an armistice would enure to the advantage of the Whites. If, at the time of the French Revolution the Royalist Governments of Europe had proposed to the French Revolutionaries a meeting at Geneva at which not only Britain, Russia, Prussia and Austria, but the Emigrés, the Vendeans and the Royalists of the Midi should also be represented, the proposal would have met with the same disdainful refusal as that which was accorded to our Prinkipo invitation. On the other hand, the anti-Bolsheviks would not treat with persons whom they regarded as a junta of anarchists, pillagers and assassins. They would not discuss concord with rapine and murder. And so the quarrel between the rival factions had to be fought out at the expense of incalculable suffering to the Russian people.

The failure of our endeavours to end chaos by conciliatory methods made me more determined than ever that confusion should not be worse confounded by British intervention. I devoted myself to effecting a withdrawal of our soldiers and a cessation of our supplies and subsidies except in those areas which were definitely anti-Bolshevik and where the population had taken up arms at the request of the Allies in order to arrest the German advance into the corn and oil regions. There were powerful and exceedingly pertinacious influences in the Cabinet working for military intervention in Russia, and as I was not on the spot in London to exercise direct influence and control over the situation, for a while I was out-manœuvred, and Mr. Bonar Law, who presided over the Ministers in my absence, was overridden. Mr. Winston Churchill in particular threw the whole of his dynamic energy and genius into organising an armed intervention against the Russian Bolshevik power. Early in February President Wilson returned to the United States to cope with the internal political difficulties that had been created by the fact that the control of Congress had passed from the Democrats to the Republicans. Republican opinion in the main was out of sympathy with his peace policy, both on the question of the League of Nations and the settlement with Russia. The opposition was becoming more vocal and gaining ground, largely through the absence of his personal influence and leadership, just as in my case the press communications from Paris which appeared in Opposition papers tended to poison public opinion. Wilson therefore deemed it necessary to make a special voyage to America in order to deal with the situation. Shortly after his departure I found a complication of labour difficulties in Britain which called for my presence in London. I left Mr. Balfour in sole charge of the negotiations in Paris. Mr. Churchill very adroitly seized the opportunity created by the absence of President Wilson and myself to go over to Paris and urge his plans with regard to Russia upon the consideration of the French, the American and the British delegations.

There can be no doubt that the French military authorities, with the full propagandist support of the press of the Right in France, were anxious to organise active military intervention in Russia. They found in our Secretary of State for War a man who was in entire sympathy with these projects. They were operating on the intense and profound anxiety in the minds of the great majority of the population as to the possible spread of the Bolshevik movement. The dread was genuine. The presence in Paris of a number of distinguished Russian leaders had also its effect in stimulating action on the lines of a military offensive against Bolshevism. Amongst these were M. Sazonoff, the famous Czarist Foreign Minister, M. Miliukoff, the eloquent Duma leader and M. Savinkoff, the notorious Russian revolutionary who had organised some sensational outrages in the days of the Czarist régime. I have never been able to explain why he objected to the Bolsheviks. However, no one can say that the anti-Bolshevik junta in Paris lacked variety of experience and of opinion. On the whole, the ablest of them all was Savinkoff. His assassinations were always skilfully arranged and had been a complete success. He was a man of great intelligence, resource and infinite daring. When I met him I was surprised to find that so frail a body and so modest a demeanour should have been compatible with such a deadly spring. He was essentially feline in his movements, his appearance and his leap. He was definitely in favour of Allied intervention, but he was wise enough not to ask for men, either conscript or volunteers, because, as he put it, it was unreasonable to expect the Allies to go on fighting after four years of war. I think he was also shrewd enough to perceive that the presence of foreign troops on Russian soil would rather antagonise than assist.

What he did ask for was the active support of the Allies in money and supplies. He computed that the Bolshevik Army consisted of 400,000 men, which would rise to 600,000 by the spring; but of these he thought only 50,000 or 60,000 were any good. On the other side, the anti-Bolshevik forces he estimated at 200,000 men. His plan was to organise in Czechoslovakia and Poland an army of 200,000 men, composed of ex-Russian prisoners, Czech, Yugoslav and Polish volunteers and so forth, paid and equipped by the Allies. He proposed that with the aid of this force there should be a concerted offensive on all fronts, which in his opinion would indubitably smash up the Bolshevik armies. His view was that they could not resist modern technical equipment, and that owing to shortage of railway transport, they were incapable of moving their reserves about from place to place with sufficient rapidity to prevent a break through. How reluctant are the most intelligent of men to read the lessons of experience! Even a really great soldier like Foch was persuaded by this seductive Nihilist. It was reported to me that this scheme was being actively encouraged by Foch and all his retinue of Generals, and that at a meeting of the Council of Four held when I was absent in England Marshal Foch "outlined a scheme for a vast attack on Soviet Russia by Finns, Esthonians, Letts, Lithuanians, Poles, Czechs, Russians—in fact, all the peoples that lie along the fringe of Russia—all under Allied direction. The base of this force was to be Poland. He is now doing everything he can to keep back Haller's Army in France, because he wants to train it to act as the spearhead of the Russian invasion, and he fears that if it goes to Poland it will become demoralised if not scattered." Pilsudski defeated this last project by insisting on the immediate transport of Haller's Army to Poland in order to enable it to conquer Galicia and annex it to the new Poland. Thus one selfishness often neutralises another, to the common advantage of mankind.

Nevertheless the French military authorities persisted in their intrigues for armed intervention in Russia and there was a real danger that we might be committed to measures from which we could not easily recede. The wounding of the French Prime Minister by a would-be assassin temporarily removed the one figure in France who was strong enough to stand up against the military, the Elysée and the Right in the French Press and Parliament. Mr. Philip Kerr, whom I left in Paris to report to me everything that was taking place in connexion with either Russia or the general negotiations, telegraphed to me some alarming news as to the progress made under Mr. Churchill's powerful impulse towards organising an armed anti-Bolshevik intervention in Russia.

I immediately sent the following telegram:

Am very alarmed at your second telegram about planning war against the Bolsheviks. The Cabinet have never authorised such a proposal, they have never contemplated anything beyond supplying Armies in anti-Bolshevik areas in Russia with necessary equipment to enable them to hold their own and that only in the event of every effort at peaceable solution failing. A military enquiry as to the best method of giving material assistance to these Russian armies is all to the good, but do not forget that it is an essential part of the enquiry to ascertain the cost; and I also want you to bear in mind that the War Office reported to the Cabinet that according to their information intervention was driving the anti-Bolshevik parties in Russia into the ranks of the Bolshevists. I had already drafted a reply to be sent to Philip Kerr about your first telegram. I am sending that reply along with this. I adhere to it in its entirety. If Russia is really anti-Bolshevik then a supply of equipment would enable it to redeem itself. If Russia is pro-Bolshevik not merely is it none of our business to interfere with its internal affairs, it would be positively mischievous, it would strengthen and consolidate Bolshevik opinion. I beg you not to commit this country to what would be a purely mad enterprise out of hatred of Bolshevik principles. An expensive war of aggression against Russia is a way to strengthen Bolshevism in Russia and create it at home. We cannot afford the burden. Chamberlain tells me we can hardly make both ends meet on a peace basis even at the present crushing rate of taxation and if we are committed to a war against a continent like Russia it is the direct road to bankruptcy and Bolshevism in these islands.

The French are not safe guides in this matter. Their opinion is largely biased by the enormous number of small investors who put their money into Russian loans and who now see no prospect of ever recovering it.

I urge you therefore not to pay too much heed to their incitement. There is nothing they would like better than to see us pull the chestnuts out of the fire for them.

I also want you to bear in mind the very grave labour position in this country. Were it known that you had gone over to Paris to prepare a plan of war against the Bolsheviks it would do more to incense organised labour than anything I can think of; and what is still worse it would throw into the arms of the extremists a very large number of thinking people who now abhor their methods.

I sincerely hope you will stand by your first proposals subject to the comments which I have passed upon them. Please show these telegrams to the Foreign Secretary.

Mr. Philip Kerr sent me the following memorandum in reply on the 17th:

Your various telegrams and messages about the importance of not drifting into the war against the Bolsheviks have been received and have I think had their effect. There was a meeting of the B.E.D.* on the Russian situation this morning at which Mr. Balfour set forth very much your view. The discussion showed pretty clearly that everybody was agreed that effective war against the Bolsheviks was probably impracticable because of public opinion at home, and that it was probably undesirable on its merits because it would strengthen Bolshevism at home. On the other hand there was a consensus of opinion, I think, that it would be very undesirable to allow the Bolsheviks to over-run Siberia and the small communities along its borders, and so gain a great access of strength and a huge territory. There was also a general agreement that it was desirable to have a careful investigation made of what it would cost in men, money and equipment, to maintain the anti-Bolshevik forces more or less in their present positions.

In accordance with your instructions I showed copies of your telegrams to Colonel House. Colonel House said that he entirely agreed with your view, except that he was opposed even to the appointment of a Commission of Enquiry because it would certainly be boomed by the French as the beginning of an anti-Bolshevik war which in turn would produce anxiety among the working classes in England and America, which would force both the British and American Govern-

* British Empire Delegation.

ments immediately to declare their Russian policy. He also asked me
to say that the principal object of his policy was to prevent the Germans and the Russians being driven together for that would inevitably
mean a great aggressive combination stretching from Yokohama to
the Rhine. He thought the French anti-Bolshevik policy would drive
straight to this result and he could not imagine what possessed them
in advocating it. He was in favour of keeping in touch with the Bolsheviks with the object of gradually bringing them to terms, restoring
Allied influence in Russia and so composing the peace.

I told both Mr. Balfour and Mr. Churchill that I was showing your
telegrams to Colonel House because you wished him to know what
your views were. Mr. Churchill was very indignant at this on the
ground that it revealed to the Americans the internal disagreement of
the British Government and made it seem as if you had not confidence
that he would represent your views. I told him that I was certain
that there was no such idea in your mind, that you regarded Colonel House as a friendly member of a body which was responsible
for working out the peace of the world and that you habitually communicated documents to the other members of the Conference. I said
that I was certain that you had no idea of showing the slightest want
of confidence in him, but that your sole object was that Colonel House
should understand your personal attitude towards the whole question
of intervention. The question is before the Conference this afternoon
and Mr. Churchill will probably return to London to-night. I have no
doubt that the Conference will declare against an active Bolshevik
policy. Mr. Balfour is against it, so are the Americans and so is Clemenceau. The latter's idea is to maintain a barrage against the Bolsheviks
on their existing line, because we have not the strength to do anything
else!

P.S. I have just heard that the Conference has decided *against*
setting up an inter-allied Commission of Enquiry, but will await an
informal investigation by their military advisers, before deciding on
what answer to send to the Bolsheviks.

A report sent in at that time from General Du Cane confirmed
the information as to the importance which Foch attached to
helping the anti-Bolshevik forces actively. After outlining Foch's
views on the German settlement, Du Cane quotes Foch as having
said that:

If the conditions of a preliminary peace treaty can thus be imposed
on Germany, the Allies can then turn their attention to the Russian
Problem, which must take time to solve. The Marshal thinks the

Allies may lose the War if they fail to arrive at a satisfactory solution of the Russian question, either by Germany settling it in her own interests, or by the spread of anarchy. He favours the solution of helping all the anti-Bolshevik elements in Russia, and all the neighbours of Russia who are resisting Bolshevik encroachment. He would go so far as to accept Germany's co-operation after the signing of the preliminary treaty of peace, and thinks it might be very valuable.

Immediately after the news of the attempt on M. Clemenceau's life, I wrote to Mr. Philip Kerr:

19th February, 1919.

My dear Kerr,

I was very shocked to hear the news of the attempt on Clemenceau, but I am delighted to find that nothing serious has happened. He is a gallant old boy—one of the bravest men I ever met.

If the attempt is a Bolshevist one it shows what lunatics these anarchists are for nothing would do them as much harm as a successful attempt on Clemenceau's life and even a failure will exasperate opinion in France and make it quite impossible to have any dealings with them. Public opinion would be irritated and angry and not particularly reasonable. They will assume that the attack was organised by Lenin and Trotsky, though probably they had nothing to do with it for they are not fools.

It rather alters the character of the reply which I give to your letters. If it is true that the attempted assassins were Russians you may take it that Prinkipo is off. France would regard it as an insult to their stricken hero. I am afraid, therefore, that we can for the moment only consider alternative policies. My view with regard to that was set forth in the messages I sent to you and Winston on Sunday. No foreign intervention in Soviet Russia. No foreign troops to be sent to the aid of non-Bolshevik Russia unless volunteers choose to go of their own accord; but material assistance to be supplied to these Governments to enable them to hold their own in the territories which are not anxious to submit to Bolshevik rule. If these territories are sincerely opposed to Bolshevism then with Allied aid they can maintain their position. If, on the other hand, they are either indifferent or very divided, or lean towards Bolshevism though they must collapse, I see no reason why, if this represents their attitude towards Bolshevism, the Powers should impose upon them a government they are not particularly interested in or attempt to save them from a government they are not particularly opposed to. Our principle ought to be "Russia must save herself." Nothing else would be of the slightest use to her. If she is saved by outside intervention she is not really saved. That kind of parasitic liberty is a sham and in this case it would be a very costly one for the Powers.

When you come to Poland, Finland and the other states which are to be carved out of Russia and are to be placed under the protection of the League of Nations, there I think we are bound not merely to give moral but material, and, if* necessary, full military support to protect these newly established states against any Bolshevik invasion from Soviet Russia. But I see no evidence at the present moment that the Soviet Government have any intention or desire to invade these territories.

We have not yet decided the fate of Esthonia, Lithuania, and Livonia. If these are to be placed in the same category as Poland, then they will have to be supported on the same terms.

The military in France, as well as here, frankly like intervention. They would like to make war on the Bolshevists and I hear of fantastic French schemes to organise an army of Russian prisoners in Germany, supported by Czecho-Slovaks and other odds and ends, to invade Russia. The French military staff have gone so far as to suggest even using German units that have been left in Esthonia. I would suggest to Colonel House that before anything of this kind is sanctioned the military should be asked the cost. Hitherto they have declined absolutely to commit themselves to the expense. Who is to pay these mercenary armies? How much will France give? I am sure she cannot afford to pay; I am sure we cannot. Will America bear the expense? Pin them down to the cost of any scheme before sanctioning it.

I have just received your message about going over. I might get there Saturday—strikes permitting.

Ultimately the Allied attitude towards Russian Bolshevism was settled substantially on the lines which I indicated in my communications. I insisted that we should not ourselves undertake, or join in undertaking with others, any military enterprise which would resolve itself into a war against Bolshevism in Russia. The situation was complicated by the fact that the anti-Bolshevik armies of Kolchak and Denikin had been called into existence by an Allied appeal and endeavour to organise an effective front against the Germans in Russia. We were in honour bound not to throw them over as soon as they had served their purpose. The policy to which the Allies finally gave their assent was set forth in detail in a memorandum prepared by Mr. Churchill:

Our policy in Russia has been repeatedly explained to Parliament. Russia must work out her own salvation. It is only by Russian manhood that it can be achieved. We have no intention and we never had any intention of sending British or Allied Armies into Russia to enforce any particular solution of their internal affairs. We are, however, bound in honour to assist those Russian forces which were called into the field largely at our instigation and in the Allied interests during the period of the war with Germany. We are doing so by munitions, supplies and practical assistance attached to military missions. At Omsk, the centre of Admiral Kolchak's government we have two British Battalions under Colonel John Ward, M.P., and some small detachments of French and Italian troops. These men are not fighting but their presence gives moral support to the Omsk Government. The Czechs, the Japanese and the Americans are keeping the Siberian Railway in working order and are preventing it from being destroyed by roving bands. This they will continue to do. We British have an army of about 30,000 in the Caucasus, which it has been decided to withdraw at the earliest possible moment.

The process of evacuation has already begun and in three or four months should be complete. In North Russia we are engaged in extricating our troops from the position in which they have been placed during the war with Germany and where they were cut off by the ice in the winter. For this purpose a relief force of volunteers has been despatched and is now landing. This relief force will cover the withdrawal of the conscript troops which are now there. They are themselves only recruited on a twelve months' engagement, and it is intended to withdraw them at an early date when there is good reason to believe that the local Russian forces which are rapidly increasing in strength will be able to look after themselves. The evacuation of the tired conscript troops has already begun.

It does not seem necessary to explain what is happening on the Western Front of Russia from the Balkans to the Black Sea. There can be no dispute about our duty to help those little or new states, Esthonia, Latvia, Lithuania, Poland, Roumania, to make some headway against the invasion of the Bolshevik armies by which they have been threatened. No British troops, however, are engaged on the whole of this front and assistance which is being given to these small new states to protect themselves from being over-run is part of the definite policy undertaken in concert by the Allied Powers.

Finally, there is no use in concealing the fact that we are helping the anti-Bolshevik forces of Russia against the Bolsheviks and that with our help their position is rapidly improving. This makes it all the more necessary at the present time to secure from these anti-

Bolshevik governments which have themselves all accepted the
Ukraine authority of Admiral Kolchak's government, definite guarantees that their victory will not be used to re-establish a reactionary
Czarist régime. We do not intend a Red Terror to be succeeded by a
White one. We are therefore seeking guarantees from Admiral Kolchak's government which will secure the summoning of a Constituent
Assembly based on a wide democratic franchise, which Assembly will
decide the future government of Russia and secondly will secure an
agrarian policy of a genuinely democratic kind. Failing these guarantees, we are holding ourselves free to consider the whole position.

In justifying in the course of debate in the House of Commons
our supplying the anti-Bolsheviks with the necessary equipment
for their forces I used these words:

. . . I should not be doing my duty as head of the Government
unless I stated quite frankly to the House my earnest conviction—
that to attempt military intervention in Russia would be the greatest
act of stupidity that any Government could possibly commit. But
then I am asked if that be the case, why do you support Kolchak and
Denikin? I will tell the House with the same frankness as I put the
other case. When the Brest-Litovsk treaty was signed, there were
large territories and populations in Russia that had neither hand nor
part in that shameful pact, and they revolted against the Government
which signed it.

Let me say this. They raised armies at our instigation and largely,
no doubt, at our expense. That was an absolutely sound military
policy. For what happened? Had it not been for those organisations
that we improvised, the Germans would have secured all the resources
which would have enabled them to break the blockade. They would
have got through to the grain of the Don, to the minerals of the Urals,
and to the oils of the Caucasus. They could have supplied themselves
with almost every commodity of which four or five years of rigid
blockade had deprived them, and which was essential to their conducting the War. In fact, the Eastern front was reconstructed—not on the
Vistula. It was reconstructed at a point that hurled the German Armies
to their own destruction, and, when they got there, deprived them of
all the things they had set out to seek. What happened? Bolshevism
threatened to impose, by force of arms, its domination on those populations that had revolted against it, and that were organised at our
request. If we, as soon as they had served our purpose, and as soon
as they had taken all the risks, had said, "Thank you; we are exceedingly obliged to you. You have served our purpose. We need you no
longer. Now let the Bolshevists cut your throats," we should have

been mean—we should have been thoroughly unworthy indeed of any great land. As long as they stand there, with the evident support of the populations—because wherever the populations are not behind them every organised effort to resist Bolshevism has failed—in the Ukraine, where the population is either indifferent or, perhaps, friendly, we have there populations like those in Siberia, the Don, and elsewhere, who are opposed to Bolshevism—they are offering a real resistance. It is our business, since we asked them to take this step, since we promised support to them if they took this step, and since by taking this stand they contributed largely to the triumph of the Allies, it is our business to stand by our friends. Therefore, we are not sending troops, but we are supplying goods. Everyone who knows Russia knows that, if she is to be redeemed, she must be redeemed by her own sons. All that they ask is—seeing that the Bolsheviks secured the arsenals of Russia—that they should be supplied with the necessary arms to enable them to fight for their own protection and freedom in the land where the Bolshevists are antipathetic to the feeling of the population. Therefore I do not in the least regard it as a departure from the fundamental policy of Great Britain not to interfere in the internal affairs of any land that we should support General Denikin and Admiral Kolchak. . . ."

But I placed three definite limitations on our support:

(1) There must be no attempt to conquer Bolshevik Russia by force of arms.

(2) Support would only be continued as long as it was clear that in the areas controlled by Kolchak and Denikin the population was anti-Bolshevik in sentiment.

(3) The anti-Bolshevik armies must not be used to restore the old Czarist régime. I emphasised especially the importance of not reimposing on the peasants the old feudal conditions under which they held their land.

Mr. Churchill accepted these conditions.

What finally defeated the intervention plans was the failure or refusal of the anti-Bolshevik leaders to honour their pledges as to the land. Their officers were all the product of Czarism and in their hearts they meant restoration and not emancipation—the restoring of the old order and not the setting up of a new and a better one. They repeated the blunders of the Royalists in the French Revolution and encountered the same fate. The Russian peasant was not a Communist—far from it. It was therefore assumed that he would eagerly join an anti-Bolshevik movement. This easy inference overlooked the greater hostility of the mujik to the old order, that kept him and his family toiling in squalid wretchedness throughout their lives to uphold the extravagant, profligate and corrupt aristocracy and bureaucracy which had brought disaster upon Holy Russia. Choosing between two evils, the peasant preferred the one that put an end to this misery and bondage of centuries. The French peasants were not Jacobins, but the Jacobins guaranteed the freedom of the soil from the servitude, the exactions and the humiliations of the ancient régime. That is why they supported the Revolution and sent their sons to fight under the Tricolour.

CHAPTER VIII

THE RHINE

THE decision to make it one of the conditions of peace that the Rhine should thenceforth be the Western boundary of Germany was taken by the French Government as far back as January, 1917, but their intention was not communicated to the British Government. M. Briand, in a note sent by him to M. Paul Cambon on the 12th of January, 1917, intimated that "Alsace-Lorraine was not, so to speak, in the reckoning; we are merely resuming possession of what was torn from us against the wishes of the population." Alsace-Lorraine must be restored not in the "mutilated condition" of 1815, but with the frontiers as they existed before 1790. The geographic and mineral basin of the Saar was to be given to France. Moreover the Rhine must "serve as a rampart for France."

M. Cambon, with his sapient understanding of the British mind, did not communicate the purport of this message to the British Government at once. Six months later, however, he seems to have informed Mr. Balfour that the French "do, however, desire to see the territory to the West of the Rhine separated from the German Empire and erected into something in the nature of a buffer State." Mr. Balfour does not appear to have attached any particular importance to this communication, for he never imparted the information to me or to the War Cabinet. At no subsequent discussion on peace terms at the War Cabinet or the Imperial Cabinet was it ever alluded to. The French Ambassador probably never pressed it on the Foreign Minister, but in the true Cambon manner he threw the idea out lightly, as a possible suggestion, and Mr. Balfour probably thought it was just a "try on." The British Government were not aware that M. Briand had given instructions in March to M. Doumergue, the French delegate to the St. Petersburg Conference, to secure a definite pledge from the Czar personally that at the Peace

Conference he would support the French claim to the Saar coal-
fields and to the entire separation of the territories on the left
bank of the Rhine from Germany. This pledge was wrung from
the poor monarch a few weeks before his deposition. M. Doumergue did not inform his British colleague at the Conference of
these negotiations. I heard of this clandestine transaction for the
first time when the Bolsheviks, after their accession to power,
published the despatches sent by Sazonoff, the Czarist Foreign
Minister, to the Russian Ambassador in Paris. It was my first
experience of the underhanded diplomacy which sent M. Frank-
lin Bouillon to Angora to negotiate a pact with Mustapha Kemal
behind our backs, and which in recent years tangled M. Laval
in a surreptitious understanding with Signor Mussolini that frustrated straightforward and effective co-operation in the League
of Nations over Abyssinia.

I have already referred to the first occasion when the question
of the Rhine frontier was officially brought to the attention of
the British Government by Marshal Foch on his visit to London
after the Armistice. It is significant that, although Clemenceau
was also in London and had come there purposely to discuss the
preliminaries of the Peace Conference, he was absent from the
meeting at which Foch raised the Rhine issue. And it is still more
significant that he never raised it at any of the subsequent official
meetings of the Peace Conference. He was anxious to avoid a
rebuff which would be recorded in the minutes of the Conference.
He therefore confined his activities on the question to sounding
members of the British and American Delegations. In personal
interviews with President Wilson and myself, not together but
separately, he urged the insistence of the great mass of French
people on the establishment of a Rhine frontier as an essential
part of the Peace Settlement. There can be no doubt that Foch
and subsequently Tardieu pressed the French view on the Council, not only with Clemenceau's full consent and approval, but
with all his powerful urge. Mr. Philip Kerr, in his report on the
Rhineland discussions, states that the Tardieu proposition "is
being pushed for all it is worth by Clemenceau himself." Tardieu,
who was one of Clemenceau's most trusted Ministers—or, to be

more accurate, one of his least mistrusted Ministers—states categorically that his memorandum on the Rhine frontier was presented to the Council with M. Clemenceau's sanction.

It will be recollected that at the end of the discussion on the Rhine question in London in December, Foch promised to submit a memorandum setting forth his views on the subject. This document was laid by him before the plenipotentiaries on January 10th, 1919. It is said in the preliminary note that the memorandum states "from the point of view of the military security of the Allied and Associated Powers, the problem of the German Western Frontiers. The question of the frontiers, special to France and Belgium, is not examined, but only the European collective and international guarantees necessary for the whole mass of States, which, after having fought for right, freedom and justice, intend to prepare, on new bases, inspired by these three ideas, the relations between Nations."

It begins with a warning not to trust too implicitly to the moral sense of a society of nations organised into a League: "It is necessary that this rising society should receive at once a sufficiently secure basis and an especial strength that will ensure its development."

Marshal Foch then traces the history of the Prussianisation of Germany, by which "all classes, all resources of action or production, all associations as well as all individuals were drilled, centralised and militarised."

Here he again utters a warning as to the future, which has its bearing upon the problems of to-day:

Now that the Hohenzollerns have left, under conditions which are of especially disqualifying character for this dynasty, and for all military monarchies, the reinstalment of the Imperial system appears to be improbable at least for some time. But a Republic, built on the same principles of centralised authority and militarism, taking in hand the whole of Germany, will be as dangerous and remain as threatening for European peace. . . . Moreover, a German Republic, freed from the hindrance due without any doubt to the existing small principalities, has a chance of finding a surplus of forces in her unity thus completely achieved, and also in the vitality and activity, especially on economic grounds, of a country now more in touch with its government.

With a remarkable flash of prevision he talks of the possibility of control by an executive power in Germany, that may be "in appearance Republican, which should have otherwise all the strength of a despotic authority."

He then dwells on the comparative populations of France and Germany, emphasising the inferior numbers of the French population of 64 millions, in comparison with 75 millions of Germans. His remedy is not to make friends with a new republic across the Rhine, but to make the Rhine a military barrier against any hostile action that may come from the people who dwell on the right bank of this historic river:

Henceforward the Rhine ought to be the Western military frontier of the German countries. Henceforward Germany ought to be deprived of all entrance and assembling ground, that is, of all territorial sovereignty on the left bank of the river, that is, of all facilities for invading quickly, as in 1914, Belgium, Luxemburg, for reaching the coast of the North Sea and threatening the United Kingdom, for outflanking the natural defences of France, the Rhine, Meuse, conquering the Northern provinces and entering upon the Parisian area.

He regards this as *"an indispensable guarantee of peace"* on account of: "(1) the material and moral situation of Germany; (2) her numerical superiority over the democratic countries of Western Europe." He makes it quite clear that unless these territorial securities for France are established by the Peace Treaty, the League of Nations will be of no avail.

The spirit of this document interpreted by M. Poincaré, M. Barthou and others, in the years immediately following the Treaty, was largely responsible for the failure of the League of Nations. The success of the Covenant of Peace enshrined in the Treaty was, according to this, to be sought not in the restoration of goodwill between warring nations, but in guaranteeing conditions which would establish beyond challenge the strategical superiority of the victors in the last war in any future war which might break out between Germany and any of her neighbours.

The next move from the French side to bring pressure to bear on the Council to accept their scheme about the settlement of the Rhine provinces took the form of a couple of memoranda, one written by Marshal Foch on the 18th of February, the other by M. Tardieu on the 20th of February. These two proposals, taken in conjunction, represented the considered proposals of the French Government—including the President of the Republic and the President of the Council (M. Poincaré and M. Clemenceau).

The Foch memorandum begins with a statement that there was no German army in existence capable of resisting the Coalition and that the German Government could not therefore refuse any categorical demand made to it.

. . . What the people of Germany fear the most is a renewal of hostilities since, this time, Germany would be the field of battle and the scene of the consequent devastation. This makes it impossible for the yet unstable German Government to reject any demand on our part if it is clearly formulated. The Entente, in its present favourable military situation, can obtain acceptance of any peace *conditions* it may put forward, provided that they are presented without much delay. All it has to do is to decide what they shall be.

It is a characteristic soldier's argument, based primarily on force. In the same spirit Foch developed his argument on strategical grounds, disdaining all arguments based on race, language, tradition and patriotic sentiment. The frontier was to be fixed without regard to the sentiment or the wishes of the population severed from their fellow-countrymen across the Rhine. The territorial arrangements which he proposed were based exclusively on his conclusions as to what was necessary from a military point of view for securing France against the possibility of future invasions. The argument with which Moltke overruled Bismarck in 1870 and forced the annexation of Alsace-Lorraine was identical with that used by Marshal Foch after his victory in 1919.

As to the Western frontier of Germany his claim was:

(1) Germany to relinquish all sovereign and proprietary rights over the Rhine territories now occupied by the Allied and Associated Armies (territories on the left bank and bridgeheads).

(2) Any union of Germany with countries South of the German-Austrian frontier of 1914 to be forbidden.

As to the status of the Rhine territories which were to be excluded from Germany, he added that "the status of these territories shall be settled by the Allied and Associated Powers at the Peace Congress."

He proposed that an immediate demand should be presented to Germany on the subject of the Rhineland and Reparations, leaving further details to be hammered out at the Peace Conference before the final Treaty was settled.

As to Reparations to be imposed on Germany, he thought "it would be proper and opportune for the same Convention [of the Allies] to determine the payment of at least *a first instalment* by Germany—say 100 milliards to be spread over a term of years, with guarantees of a satisfactory nature." He was insistent that all these conditions should be imposed upon Germany whilst

we would be faced with an enemy who is at present disarmed, and not only obliged to surrender but desirous of doing so.

But there is no time to be lost. Victory has been ours in the West since 1918; we must now establish it by settling the principal Peace conditions, and more especially by finally disarming Germany and fixing the limit of her power, i.e. her frontiers.

The distinguished French soldier claimed that the strategical considerations ought to dominate the decision of the Peace Conference in fixing the boundaries of Germany in both the East and the West.

The whole of Silesia and the town of Danzig were to be handed over to the Poles without any reference at all to the wishes of the inhabitants.

He then turned to Russia and proposed that those nations which bordered on Russia should be organised into a combination for suppressing Bolshevism in that country. The nations whom he indicated as instruments for this repressive enterprise were Finland, Poland, Czechoslovakia, Roumania and Greece.

He ended up in characteristically peremptory phrases: "To

sum up, we propose to bring about an immediate and summary settlement with Germany. It will allow us to consider how we shall deal with Eastern Europe, which we propose to do at once." That is a typical military view by the greatest soldier of his day as to the surest way to establish permanent peace.

The explanation of Marshal Foch's sudden move to press the Peace Council to negotiate and force through a preliminary peace promptly and peremptorily was given in a note I received from General Du Cane, who was our Liaison Officer on the Staff of the Allied Commanders-in-Chief. In an interview he had with the Marshal on the day of writing his memorandum Foch explained that as a result of the recent discussions with the German representatives at Trèves, he had come to the conclusion that they would accept any terms for an immediate settlement. He therefore strongly advocated "the settling at once of the three principal conditions of the peace that the Allies intended to impose upon Germany." These are set forth in his memorandum. General Du Cane adds that Marshal Foch considered "that if these matters could be settled by the Peace Conference during the next few days, and if he could be entrusted with the mission of proceeding again to Trèves *with the allied terms, say this day week* [those words are underlined in General Du Cane's note], the Marshal would guarantee that the Germans would accept the terms on the following day . . . and there would be universal rejoicing." He was very insistent on making it clear to the Germans that "under no circumstances will the German Empire extend beyond the Rhine."

The Tardieu Report of February 20th gives no indication that the French Government took the view of their Commander-in-Chief about the imposition of an immediate and interim treaty upon Germany confined to provisions dealing with the two questions of the Rhine and Reparations. But as far as the former question was concerned, it adopted in substance both the argument and the plan proposed by Marshal Foch in so far as it affected the left bank of the Rhine. Tardieu follows pretty closely the military argument advanced by Marshal Foch as to the peril to French security involved in the occupation by Germany of ter-

ritories on the left bank of the Rhine. He quotes an interesting
letter written by Castlereagh to Wellington on October 1st, 1815:
"Mr. Pitt was quite right when, as long ago as 1805, he wished
to give Prussia more territory on the left bank of the Rhine, and
thus place her in closer military contact with France." (The
object of the allies then being to weaken the strategic position of
France in relation to Germany.)

M. Tardieu argued that the limitation of the military forces of
Germany did not constitute a sufficient guarantee, as the experience of Napoleon had proved that she was quite capable of
eluding any plan which had for its purpose the number of men
trained to the use of arms in Germany. He also contended that
the League of Nations could not at present furnish sufficient
guarantees to France, and he came to the same conclusion as
Marshal Foch that:

Failing these two guarantees (i.e. limitation and the League of Nations), we demand, at least temporarily, a guarantee of another kind,
against a Germany with twice the population of France, a Germany
whose word it will not be possible to trust for a long time—we demand
a physical guarantee. . . .
The Rhine on the one hand by its breadth and on the other by the
straightness of its course affords to the people on both its banks a
natural and equal guarantee against attack.

He disclaims any idea of annexing the Germanic territory on the
left bank of the Rhine to France:

In this question France asks nothing for herself; *neither an inch of
territory nor any sovereign rights.* . . .
France does not demand the left bank of the Rhine for herself.
She has no use for it and her interests, like her ideals, dissuade her
from claiming it.
France demands only one thing:—that the measures, and the only
ones calculated surely to prevent the left bank of the Rhine from becoming once more the base of a German attack, should be taken by
the Powers now assembled at the Peace Conference.
In other words, without any territorial ambition, but convinced of
the necessity of establishing protection at once international and national, France expects from an Inter-Allied occupation of the Rhine

that which Great Britain and the United States expect from the maintenance of their naval forces—nothing more and nothing less.

This principle, having regard to Europe and the present state of the world, can be stated as follows:—

(a) *The western frontier of Germany should be fixed at the Rhine.*

(b) *The bridges of the Rhine should be occupied by an Inter-Allied force.*

(c) *The above measures should not involve any annexation of territory to the advantage of any Power.*

The formal demand set forth in the Foch and Tardieu documents created a grave situation in the Peace Conference. At one time a serious rupture between France and her Allies was threatened. The most powerful leaders in France—Poincaré, Clemenceau, Tardieu, Briand and Barthou—were in full sympathy with the claim and the sentiment expressed in these memoranda. The heads of the Army were unanimously behind the proposal. As far as they were concerned it represented the only fruit worth snatching from the tree of victory. President Wilson had left for a short visit to America. But I had talked the matter over with him repeatedly and we were both resolutely opposed to the plan. We regarded it as a definite and dishonourable betrayal of one of the fundamental principles for which the Allies had professed to fight, and which they blazoned forth to their own people in the hour of sacrifice. We were also convinced that any attempt to divide Germany into two separate communities would ultimately fail, and that meanwhile it would cause endless friction and might provoke another war. We therefore unhesitatingly declined to entertain the proposition. Thus a serious deadlock appeared inevitable and imminent.

On February 18th an attempt was made to assassinate M. Clemenceau. He was shot in the shoulder as his car was leaving his residence. This dastardly outrage was fortunately not fatal, but it incapacitated the French Premier for some days. For that reason the actual terms of the Tardieu memorandum were probably not submitted to the stricken statesman. Nevertheless, he had given instructions for its preparation and the policy had his zealous approval. The events of 1870 when, as Mayor of Montmartre, he saw the German Army enmesh and starve Paris to surrender, had rankled in his implacable mind and he wanted to keep these redoubtable Goths on the other side of the Rhine.

M. Clemenceau's temporary disablement may have been the reason why the question of the Rhenish frontier was not raised at the Peace Council. On his recovery, however, he approached me on the subject. We were both anxious to avoid a head-on collision on a highly controversial topic, and as President Wilson had not returned from America, it was arranged that the Foch and Tardieu memoranda should be relegated for examination to a committee consisting of M. Tardieu, Mr. Philip Kerr, representing Great Britain, and Dr. Mezes representing President Wilson. This Committee had prolonged discussions, but came to no conclusion. M. Tardieu laid on the table a series of resolutions which provided (1) that the frontier of Germany should be the Rhine, (2) that the Rhenish provinces should be constituted an independent State, and (3) that there should be Allied occupation of the Rhine bridges. His arguments were wholly strategic. They consisted of a repetition of the arguments which had already been set forth in the Foch memorandum.

On the question of the occupation of the Rhine bridges M. Tardieu made it quite clear that the French contemplated a permanent occupation of the line of the Rhine frontier by an Inter-allied force on which the Americans and ourselves would be represented. He stated that he did not want large forces; it was the moral effect that mattered and he wanted to know whether the British public would object to maintaining a brigade or a division on the Rhine. Mr. Kerr left no doubt in his mind that "there would be a large party in England which would object to being mixed up in any way whatever with the Continent on these lines; that the experience of the Hanoverian connection with its consequence of wars in Europe and the separation from America was still very strong, and that these natural feelings would unquestionably be aggravated by propaganda not only from within England itself but from residents in the occupied territories in Germany, who would probably provoke continual incidents with the object of making the position intolerable." He said there was

a real danger of an estrangement between France and Great
Britain, because the settlement imposed too great burdens on
Great Britain or committed it to obligations such as the permanent separation of the Rhenish provinces from the rest of Germany against their will, which might offend its sense of justice or
fairplay.

The American representative, Dr. Mezes, took no conspicuous
part in the proceedings. He preserved a strange silence during most of these lengthy discussions. He did however say
"that he had talked the matter over with Colonel House,
who wished him to say that President Wilson was very sympathetic to France and was very interested in the proposal, but in
view of the fact that he was due to arrive in the course of the next
forty-eight hours, Colonel House thought that it would be better
to await his arrival before any conclusions were reached." It was
a surprise to me to find that the American Delegation was even
prepared to entertain the French proposals; but it was clear from
M. Tardieu's attitude that the French Government were under
the impression that President Wilson was not altogether opposed
to the idea of a severance of the German population on the left
bank of the Rhine from their fellow-countrymen on the right.
Colonel House seemed to have conveyed that impression to
M. Clemenceau, but the President had clearly not imparted to
Colonel House his views on the question. House himself appeared
to have been talked over by Clemenceau and Tardieu. M. Tardieu
must have been aware of the critical attitude I had adopted
towards the proposal when it was first mentioned to me by
Marshal Foch. But he evidently thought that I stood alone
amongst British Ministers in my opposition. French Ministers
had built up their hopes of a final acceptance by Britain of their
Rhineland scheme on the fact that the British Government did
not protest when M. Cambon first mentioned the project to
Mr. Balfour.

I instructed Mr. Kerr, however, to leave no doubt in M. Tardieu's mind that the British Government was resolutely opposed
to the proposition. After some discussion, M. Tardieu agreed that
it might be possible to arrange that Allied troops should not be

quartered on the soil of Germany proper, which meant, according to him, Germany on the right bank of the Rhine; "they would, however, have to be stretched along the Rhine within immediate contact with the bridges." Mr. Kerr asked for a short adjournment in order to consult me on this variation of the original proposal. I informed Mr. Kerr that I had just as strong objections to "maintaining Allied troops in the Rhenish provinces as in Germany proper."

Whilst the French Government were pressing for this severance of the Germanic populations on the left bank of the Rhine from the Reich, they were urging a demand of a different character in so far as the Saar Valley was concerned. The French claim in respect of the Saar Basin was practically tantamount to an annexation to France. It was a coal-mining and industrial area to the north-west of Alsace-Lorraine. The coal produced in these mines was essential to the industries of Alsace-Lorraine. A portion of the Saar had been French territory at the date of the Revolution and at the Peace of 1814 the Allies recognised that this part of the Saar Valley ought to be restored to France. In 1815, however, it was taken away from France and given to Prussia. The French claim at the Peace Conference was not satisfied with demanding the restoration of the 1814 frontier. This would only give them a comparatively insignificant section of the Saar Basin in population, and especially in resources. The richest coal-mines were outside this boundary. The historical justification for the French claim was therefore inadequate. The French Government supplemented their arguments by bringing in the question of reparation for the damage done by the German armies to the coal industries of France, and also the fact that France would now be practically the sole customer for Saar coal.

The argument was an ingenious one. The population of the Saar Basin was a community by itself. Its miners were also peasants. They and their families tilled the land adjoining the mines. Industries entirely dependent on Saar coal had sprung up in the vicinity. France claimed that the ownership of the Saar coal, which belonged to the Prussian and Bavarian State, should be transferred to France by way of compensation for the destruction of the French coal-fields. They then argued that it was unreasonable and impracticable to sever the surface of the soil from the coal measures underneath it, and that it was essential that there should be the same governmental control for both. The agriculture and the industries of the Saar were inseparable from its mines. To quote the words of the French memorandum:

In other words, the Saar Basin forms an entity, the three elements of which are: a mining zone (very incompletely developed); an industrial zone, which is the outgrowth of the former; and finally a workers' zone, which extends beyond the other two and is connected with them by railroads of which Homburg is the most important centre.

In this basin, the component parts of which are so interdependent, any artificial separation would be ruinous. . . . To separate it into several sections would be ruinous and a source of innumerable vexations for the inhabitants.

This separation moreover would render the operation of the mines impossible, or in any event exceedingly difficult. It should therefore not be considered.

For these reasons a plan was put forward which was indistinguishable in effect from annexation to France.

Inasmuch as the population was preponderatingly German, ethnical considerations and the wishes of the inhabitants were entirely overruled by this plan. There was more than a suggestion that the inhabitants, in spite of their racial origin and their language, had as genuine a preference for French nationality as the German-speaking population of Alsace. Both the American and British Delegations opposed this project on the ground that another Alsace-Lorraine problem would be created which would cause trouble in future.

These various projects for severing territory occupied by Teutonic populations from the German Reich were not due to greed of possession. They were prompted by the obsession of France with the fact that in spite of the victory Germany would have a population nearly twice as large as that of France. The French military and French statesmen therefore suggested every kind of scheme for reducing that menacing disparity for the future. That accounts for the French eagerness to chip off from the German bulk towns and territories on the Eastern and Western frontiers containing in the aggregate a preponderant German population numbering several millions. On her Western boundaries Germany was to be deprived of the Rhineland and the Saar Valley; on her Eastern boundaries of the whole of Upper Silesia, the City of Danzig and two or three almost purely Germanic areas in East Prussia. These were the demands with which we were confronted as far as the settlement of the new frontiers of Germany was concerned.

When we came to discuss with the French Delegation the problem of reparations, here also we encountered demands of a most extravagant character. The demand put forward in respect of damages to French property in the aggregate exceeded the total capital value of all French property of every kind before the War. In this respect the Belgians were equally greedy.

It looked as if we had arrived at a point where it was impossible to reach any agreement with our French colleagues unless we were prepared to throw over all the declarations which we had made during the War with regard to the Peace Settlement.

M. Clemenceau did not at any stage of the discussions take any active interest in the subject of reparations. He left that entirely to M. Loucheur. But he was deeply concerned about the failure of the negotiations over the Rhineland, and perhaps to a less degree about the Saar. He told me that his country could not face the prospect of France with a population of only 40,000,000 against a hostile Germany with a population of 65,000,000 and a footing on both sides of the Rhine. He made it clear that it was this situation that prompted all his proposals to divide Germany in such a way as substantially to reduce the disparity and to give France the barrier of the Rhine. He asked me if I could suggest any counter-proposals to meet the situation. I then conceived the idea of a joint military guarantee by America and Britain to France against any aggression by Germany in the future. President Wilson agreed to this proposal. On the 14th of March, 1919, President Wilson and I informed M. Clemenceau that we could not consent to any occupation of the left bank of the Rhine, except a short occupation as provisional guarantee for payment of the German debt. On the other hand, we formally offered our immediate military guarantee against any unprovoked aggression on the part of Germany against France. In the course of further conversations we agreed to the demilitarisation of a zone on the right bank of the Rhine. But Tardieu and Foch, backed by the French President, were not satisfied with these undertakings, and there was a temporary deadlock.

I therefore decided that it was desirable that the British Delegation should make quite clear in writing the limits to which they were prepared to go. I retired with some of my advisers— General Smuts, Sir Henry Wilson, Sir Maurice Hankey and Mr. Philip Kerr—for two or three days to the seclusion of the Forest of Fontainebleau, to work out definite proposals for the kind of treaty of peace to which alone we were prepared to append our signature. The result of our deliberations was put in the form of a memorandum, the main points of which I shall now summarise.

March 25th, 1919.

SOME CONSIDERATIONS FOR THE PEACE CONFERENCE BEFORE THEY FINALLY DRAFT THEIR TERMS

I

WHEN nations are exhausted by wars in which they have put forth all their strength and which leave them tired, bleeding and broken, it is not difficult to patch up a peace that may last until the generation which experienced the horrors of the war has passed away. Pictures of heroism and triumph only tempt those who know nothing of the sufferings and terrors of war. It is therefore comparatively easy to patch up a peace which will last for thirty years.

What is difficult, however, is to draw up a peace which will not provoke a fresh struggle when those who have had practical experience of what war means have passed away. History has proved that a peace, which has been hailed by a victorious nation as a triumph of diplomatic skill and statesmanship, even of moderation in the long run, has proved itself to be shortsighted and charged with danger to the victor. The peace of 1871 was believed by Germany to ensure not only her security but her permanent supremacy. The facts have shown exactly the contrary. France itself has demonstrated that those who say you

can make Germany so feeble that she will never be able to hit back
are utterly wrong. Year by year France became numerically weaker
in comparison with her victorious neighbour, but in reality she became
ever more powerful. She kept watch on Europe; she made alliances
with those whom Germany had wronged or menaced; she never ceased
to warn the world of its danger and ultimately she was able to secure
the overthrow of the far mightier power which had trampled so brutally
upon her. You may strip Germany of her colonies, reduce her armaments to a mere police force and her navy to that of a fifth-rate power;
all the same in the end if she feels that she has been unjustly treated
in the peace of 1919 she will find means of exacting retribution from
her conquerors. The impression, the deep impression, made upon the
human heart by four years of unexampled slaughter will disappear
with the hearts upon which it has been marked by the terrible sword
of the great war. The maintenance of peace will then depend upon
there being no causes of exasperation constantly stirring up the spirit
of patriotism, of justice or of fairplay. To achieve redress our terms
may be severe, they may be stern and even ruthless, but at the same
time they can be so just that the country on which they are imposed
will feel in its heart that it has no right to complain. But injustice,
arrogance, displayed in the hour of triumph, will never be forgotten
or forgiven.

For these reasons I am, therefore, strongly averse to transferring
more Germans from German rule to the rule of some other nation
than can possibly be helped. I cannot conceive any greater cause of
future war than that the German people, who have certainly proved
themselves one of the most vigorous and powerful races in the world,
should be surrounded by a number of small States, many of them consisting of people who have never previously set up a stable government
for themselves, but each of them containing large masses of Germans
clamouring for reunion with their native land. The proposal of the
Polish Commission that we should place 2,100,000 Germans under
the control of a people which is of a different religion and which has
never proved its capacity for stable self-government throughout its
history must, in my judgment, lead sooner or later to a new war in
the East of Europe. What I have said about the Germans is equally
true of the Magyars. There will never be peace in South-Eastern
Europe if every little state now coming into being is to have a large
Magyar Irredenta within its borders. I would therefore take as a
guiding principle of the peace that as far as is humanly possible the
different races should be allocated to their motherlands, and that this
human criterion should have precedence over considerations of strategy or economics or communications, which can usually be adjusted by

other means. Secondly, I would say that the duration for the payments of reparation ought to disappear if possible with the generation which made the war.

But there is a consideration in favour of a long-sighted peace which influences me even more than the desire to leave no causes justifying a fresh outbreak thirty years hence. There is one element in the present condition of nations which differentiates it from the situation as it was in 1815. In the Napoleonic war the countries were equally exhausted, but the revolutionary spirit had spent its force in the country of its birth, and Germany had satisfied legitimate popular demands for the time being by a series of economic changes which were inspired by courage, foresight and high statesmanship. Even in Russia the Czar had effected great reforms which were probably at that time even too advanced for the half savage population. The situation is very different now. The revolution is still in its infancy. The supreme figures of the Terror are still in command in Russia. The whole of Russia is filled with the spirit of revolution. There is everywhere a deep sense not only of discontent, but of anger and revolt amongst the workmen against pre-war conditions. The whole existing order in its political, social and economic aspects is questioned by the masses of the population from one end of Europe to the other. In some countries, like Germany and Russia, the unrest takes the form of open rebellion; in others, like France, Great Britain and Italy, it takes the shape of strikes and of general disinclination to settle down to work—symptoms which are just as much concerned with the desire for political and social change as with wage demands.

Much of this unrest is healthy. We shall never make a lasting peace by attempting to restore the conditions of 1914. . . .

The greatest danger that I see in the present situation is that Germany may throw in her lot with Bolshevism and place her resources, her brains, her vast organising power at the disposal of the revolutionary fanatics whose dream it is to conquer the world for Bolshevism by force of arms. This danger is no mere chimera.* The present Government in Germany is weak; it has no prestige; its authority is chal-

---

* In its essential features there is nothing to distinguish Nazism from Bolshevism—the iron rule of a centralised dictatorship, the ruthless suppression of all criticism, freedom of thought and expression, the treatment of criticism of the Government as treason to the State (in neither Russia nor Germany is the existence of a constitutional opposition to the Government tolerated), the overriding interference and control of the State in every branch of industrial and intellectual activity. In both countries an autocracy has been established more complete and pervasive than that of Czar or Kaiser. In Germany the advent of Nazism to power is referred to as the Nazi Revolution.

lenged; it lingers merely because there is no alternative but the spartacists, and Germany is not ready for spartacism as yet. . . .

. . . If we are wise, we shall offer to Germany a peace, which, while
just, will be preferable for all sensible men to the alternative of Bolshevism. I would, therefore, put it in the forefront of the peace that
once she accepts our terms, especially reparation, we will open to her
the raw materials and markets of the world on equal terms with ourselves, and will do everything possible to enable the German people
to get upon their legs again. We cannot both cripple her and expect
her to pay.

Finally, we must offer terms which a responsible Government in
Germany can expect to be able to carry out. If we present terms to
Germany which are unjust, or excessively onerous, no responsible
Government will sign them. . . .

*From every point of view, therefore, it seems to me that we ought to en-
deavour to draw up a peace settlement as if we were impartial arbiters,
forgetful of the passions of the war. This settlement ought to have three
ends in view. First of all it must do justice to the Allies by taking into
account Germany's responsibility for the origin of the war and for the way
in which it was fought. Secondly, it must be a settlement which a responsible
German Government can sign in the belief that it can fulfil the obligations
it incurs. Thirdly, it must be a settlement which will contain in itself no
provocations for future wars, and which will constitute an alternative to
Bolshevism, because it will commend itself to all reasonable opinion as a
fair settlement of the European problem.*

II

IT is not, however, enough to draw up a just and far-sighted peace
with Germany. If we are to offer Europe an alternative to Bolshevism
we must make the League of Nations into something which will be
both a safeguard to those nations who are prepared for fair dealing
with their neighbours, and a menace to those who would trespass on
the rights of their neighbours, whether they are imperialist empires
or imperialist Bolshevists. An essential element, therefore, in the peace
settlement is the constitution of the League of Nations as the effective
guardian of international right and international liberty throughout
the world. If this is to happen the first thing to do is that the leading
members of the League of Nations should arrive at an understanding
between themselves in regard to armaments. *To my mind it is idle to
endeavour to impose a permanent limitation of armaments upon Germany
unless we are prepared similarly to impose a limitation upon ourselves.*
I recognise that until Germany has settled down and given practical
proof that she has abandoned her imperialist ambitions, and until

Russia has also given proof that she does not intend to embark upon a military crusade against her neighbours, *it is essential that the leading members of the League of Nations should maintain considerable forces both by land and sea in order to preserve liberty in the world. But if they are to present an united front to the forces both of reaction and revolution, they must arrive at such an agreement in regard to armaments among themselves as would make it impossible for suspicion to arise between the members of the League of Nations in regard to their intentions towards one another. If the League is to do its work for the world it will only be because the members of the League trust it themselves and because there are no apprehensions, rivalries and jealousies in the matter of armaments between them.* The first condition of success for the League of Nations is, therefore, a firm understanding between the British Empire and the United States of America and France and Italy that there will be no competitive building up of fleets or armies between them. Unless this is arrived at before the Covenant is signed the League of Nations will be a sham and a mockery. It will be regarded, and rightly regarded, as a proof that its principal promoters and patrons repose no confidence in its efficacy. But once the leading members of the League have made it clear that they have reached an understanding which will both secure to the League of Nations the strength which is necessary to enable it to protect its members and which at the same time will make misunderstanding and suspicion with regard to competitive armaments impossible between them its future and its authority will be ensured. It will then be able to ensure as an essential condition of peace that not only Germany, but all the smaller States of Europe undertake to limit their armaments and abolish conscription. If the small nations are permitted to organize and maintain conscript armies running each to hundreds of thousands, boundary wars will be inevitable and all Europe will be drawn in. *Unless we secure this universal limitation we shall achieve neither lasting peace, nor the permanent observance of the limitation of German armaments which we now seek to impose.*

I should like to ask why Germany, if she accepts the terms we consider just and fair, should not be admitted to the League of Nations, at any rate as soon as she has established a stable and democratic Government. Would it not be an inducement to her both to sign the terms and to resist Bolshevism? Might it not be safer that she should be inside the League than that she should be outside it?

Finally, I believe that until the authority and effectiveness of the League of Nations has been demonstrated, the British Empire and the United States ought to give to France a guarantee against the possibility of a new German aggression. France has special reason for asking for such a guarantee. She has twice been attacked and twice invaded by Germany in half a century. She has been so attacked because she has been the principal guardian of liberal and democratic civilization against Central European autocracy on the Continent of Europe. It is right that the other great Western democracies should enter into an undertaking which will ensure that they stand by her side in time to protect her against invasion, should Germany ever threaten her again or until the League of Nations has proved its capacity to preserve the peace and liberty of the world.

III

IF, however, the Peace Conference is really to secure peace and prove to the world a complete plan of settlement which all reasonable men will recognize as an alternative preferable to anarchy, it must deal with the Russian situation. Bolshevik imperialism does not merely menace the States on Russia's borders. It threatens the whole of Asia and is as near to America as it is to France. It is idle to think that the Peace Conference can separate, however sound a peace it may have arranged with Germany, if it leaves Russia as it is to-day. I do not propose, however, to complicate the question of the peace with Germany by introducing a discussion of the Russian problem. I mention it simply in order to remind ourselves of the importance of dealing with it as soon as possible.

OUTLINE OF PEACE TERMS

Part I

.   .   .   .   .

Part II

THE LEAGUE OF NATIONS

(1) All high contracting parties, as part of the Treaty of Peace, to become members of the League of Nations, the Covenant of which will be signed as a separate Treaty by those Powers that are admitted, subject to acceptance of the following conditions:

(i) An agreement between the principal members of the League of Nations in regard to armaments which will put an end to competition between them.

(ii) The lesser members of the League of Nations to accept the limitation of armaments and the abolition of conscription.

(iii) An agreement to be made between all members of the League of Nations for the purpose of securing equal and improved conditions of labour in their respective countries.

Part III

POLITICAL

A. *Cession of territory by Germany and the consequential arrangements*

EASTERN BOUNDARY OF GERMANY

(1) Poland to be given a corridor to Danzig, but this to be drawn irrespective of strategic or transportation considerations so as to embrace the smallest possible number of Germans.

(2) Rectification of Bohemian frontier. . . .

WESTERN BOUNDARIES OF GERMANY

(3) No attempt is made to separate the Rhenish Provinces from the rest of Germany. These Provinces to be demilitarised; that is to say, the inhabitants of this territory will not be permitted to bear arms or receive any military training, or to be incorporated in any military organization. . . . As France is naturally anxious about a neighbour who has twice within living memory invaded and devastated her land with surprising rapidity, the British Empire and the United States of America undertake to come to the assistance of France with their whole strength in the event of Germany moving her troops across the Rhine without the consent of the Council of the League of Nations. This guarantee to last until the League of Nations has proved itself to be an adequate security.

(4) Germany to cede Alsace-Lorraine to France.

(5) Germany to cede to France the 1814 frontier, or, in the alternative, in order to compensate France for the destruction of her coal-fields, the present Alsace-Lorraine frontier with the use of the coal-mines in the Saar Valley for a period of 10 years. Germany to undertake, after the expiration of 10 years, to put no obstacle on the export of the produce of these coal-mines to France.

·   ·   ·   ·   ·

NORTHERN BOUNDARIES OF GERMANY

(9) Germany to cede certain portions of Schleswig to Denmark as provided by Danish Commission.

GERMAN OVERSEA POSSESSIONS AND RIGHTS

(10) Germany to cede all rights in the ex-German colonies and in the leased territory of Kiauchow.

·   ·   ·   ·   ·

Part IV

REDUCTION OF ARMAMENTS

Preamble explaining that the disarmament of Germany is the first step in the limitation of the armaments of all nations.

(*a*) Military terms ⎫
(*b*) Naval terms ⎬ as already agreed on.
(*c*) Air terms ⎭

(*d*) Questions as to restoration of prisoners of war and interned persons.

(*e*) Waiver by Germany of all claims on behalf of prisoners of war and interned persons.

Part V

REPARATION

(1) Germany to undertake to pay full reparation to the Allies. It is difficult to assess the amount chargeable against Germany under this head. It certainly greatly exceeds what, on any calculation, Germany is capable of paying. It is therefore suggested that Germany should pay an annual sum for a stated number of years. This sum to be agreed among the Allied and Associated Powers. Germany to be allowed a number of years within which to work up to payment of the full annual amount.

It has been suggested that a Permanent Commission should be set up to which Germany should be able to appeal for permission to postpone some portion of the annual payment for adequate reasons shown. This Commission would be entitled to cancel the payment of interest on postponed payments during the first few years. The amount received from Germany to be distributed in the following proportions:

50 per cent. to France;
30 per cent. to the British Empire;
20 per cent. to other nations.

Part of the German payments to be used to liquidate debts owed by the Allies to one another. . . .

This document was sent to both M. Clemenceau and President Wilson. The first impression in French circles was one of extreme resentment and indignation. M. Tardieu drafted a reply which was irreconcilable in its tone and indicated a determination to abide by the demands put forward by him on behalf of the French Government. M. Clemenceau, who had a store of prudence and practical sagacity underneath all his truculence of demeanour and speech, threw over this document, and drafted a reply which although contentious in temper did not indicate a decision on his part to refuse altogether to meet the British view.

GENERAL OBSERVATIONS ON MR. LLOYD GEORGE'S NOTE OF MARCH 26TH

(1) The French Government is in complete accord with the general purpose of Mr. Lloyd George's note: that is to say, to make a durable and consequently a just peace.

It does not believe, on the other hand, that the principle which it shares, really leads to the conclusions drawn by the note in question.

(2) The note suggests that moderate territorial conditions should be imposed upon Germany in Europe in order not to leave a profound feeling of resentment after peace.

This method might have value, if the late war had been for Germany a European war. This, however, was not the case. Before the war Germany was a great naval power whose future lay upon the water. This world power was Germany's pride; she will not console herself for having lost it.

But, without being deterred by the fear of such resentment, all of her colonies, her entire navy, a great part of her commercial fleet (as a form of reparation), and her foreign markets over which she held sway, have been taken from her, or will be taken from her. Thus the blow which she will feel the most is dealt her and people think that she can be appeased by a certain amelioration of territorial conditions. This is a pure illusion, and the remedy is not proportionate to the evil.

If a means of satisfying Germany is sought, it should not be sought in Germany. This kind of conciliation will be idle, in case Germany is severed from her world policy. If it is necessary to appease her she should be offered colonial satisfaction, naval satisfaction, or satisfaction with regard to her commercial expansion. The note of the 26th of March, however, only takes into account European territorial satisfaction.

(3) The note of Mr. Lloyd George fears that too severe territorial conditions will be playing the game of Bolshevism in Germany. Is it not to be feared that the method suggested will have precisely this result?

The Conference has decided to call to life a certain number of new States. Can the Conference, without committing an injustice, sacrifice

them, out of consideration for Germany, by imposing upon them in-
acceptable frontiers?

If these peoples, especially Poland and Bohemia, have been able to
resist Bolshevism up to now, it is because of a sense of nationality.
If violence is done to this sentiment, Bolshevism will find these two
peoples an easy prey, and the only barrier which at the present moment
exists between Russian Bolshevism and German Bolshevism will be
shattered.

The result will be either a confederation of Eastern and Central
Europe under the domination of a Bolshevist Germany, or the enslavement of the same countries by a reactionary Germany, thanks to the
general anarchy. In both cases, the Allies will have lost the war. On
the contrary, the policy of the French Government is resolutely to
aid these young peoples with the support of the liberal elements in
Europe, and not to seek, at their expense, ineffectual attenuations of
the colonial, naval, and commercial disaster inflicted upon Germany
by the Peace. If one is obliged, in giving to these young peoples
frontiers without which they cannot live, to transfer to the sovereignty
the sons of the very Germans who have enslaved them, it is to be regretted and it must be done with moderation, but it cannot be avoided.

Moreover, while one deprives Germany totally and definitely of her
colonies, because she maltreated the indigenous population, by what
right can one refuse to give Poland and Bohemia normal frontiers
because the Germans have installed themselves upon Polish and Bohemian soil as guarantors of oppressive pan-Germanism?

(4) Mr. Lloyd George's note insists—and the French Government
is in agreement—upon the necessity of making a peace which shall
seem to Germany to be a just peace. But, in view of German mentality,
it is not sure that justice is conceived by the Germans as it is conceived
by the Allies.

Furthermore, it should not be forgotten that this impression of
justice must be obvious not only to the enemy, but also and principally
to the Allies. The Allies who have fought side by side must terminate
the war with an equitable peace. But what would be the results of
following the method suggested by the note of March 26? A certain
number of total and definitive guarantees will be acquired by maritime
nations which have not known an invasion. The surrender of the
German colonies would be total and definitive. The surrender of the
German navy would be total and definitive. The surrender of a large
portion of the German merchant fleet would be total and definitive.
The exclusion of Germany from foreign markets would be total and
would last for some time. On the other hand, partial and temporary
solutions would be reserved for the continental countries; that is to

say, those which have suffered most from the war. The reduced frontiers suggested for Poland and Bohemia would be partial solutions. The defensive agreement offered to France for the protection of her territory would be a temporary solution. The proposed régime for the coal-fields of the Saar would be temporary. Here we have a condition of inequality which might risk leaving a bad impression upon the after-war relations between the Allies, more important than the after-war relations between Germany and the Allies.

In Paragraph 1 it has been demonstrated that it is vain to hope by territorial concessions to find sufficient compensation for Germany for the world disaster which she has undergone. It may be permitted to add that it would be an injustice to impose the burden of these compensations upon those of the Allies who have felt the weight of the war most heavily.

These countries, after the expenses of war, cannot incur the expenses of peace. It is essential that they also should have the sensation of a just and equitable peace. In default of this, it is not alone in Central Europe that Bolshevism is to be feared, for no field can be more favourable to its propagation, it has been well noted, than the field of national disappointment.

(5) For the moment, the French Government desires to limit itself to observations of a general nature.

It renders full credit to the intentions which have inspired Mr. Lloyd George's memorandum. But it believes that the deductions made in the present note are in harmony with justice and with general interest of all.

The French Government will be inspired by these considerations in the forthcoming meetings when the terms suggested by the British Prime Minister are discussed.

To this document I sent in the following reply:

If the document put in by M. Clemenceau in reply to my statement really represents the attitude of France towards the various questions which come up for settlement, there ought to be no difficulty in making a peace with Germany which will satisfy everybody, especially the Germans.

Judging by the memorandum, France seems to attach no importance to the rich German African colonies which she is in possession of. She attaches no importance to Syria, she attaches no importance to indemnity and compensation, not even although an overwhelming priority in the matter of compensation is given her, as I proposed in my memorandum. She attaches no importance to the fact that she has Alsace-Lorraine, with most of the iron-mines and a large proportion of the potash of Germany. She attaches no importance to receiving a share of the German ships for the French ships sunk by submarines or to receiving any part of the German battle-fleet. She attaches no importance to the disarmament of Germany on land and sea. She attaches no importance to a British and American guarantee of the inviolability of her soil. All these are treated as matters which only concern "maritime people who have not known invasion." What France really cares for is that the Danzig Germans should be handed over to the Poles. Several months of insistent controversy on Syria and compensation and the disarmament of Germany and the guarantees of the inviolability of French soil, etc. etc., had led me to the conclusion that France attached an overwhelming importance to these vital matters. But M. Clemenceau knows France best, and as he does not think all these things worth mentioning, I am perforce driven to reverse my views on this subject. Especially would it be welcome to a large section of opinion in England who dislike entangling alliances to know that M. Clemenceau attaches no importance to the pledge I offer on the behalf of Britain to come to the support of France if the invader threatens. M. Clemenceau suggests that the peace we propose is one which is entirely in the interests of Britain. I claim nothing for Britain which France would not equally get. In compensation, although including the expenses of the war it has cost as much to Britain as to France, I propose that France should get twice as much of the indemnity, and, if my proposals seem to M. Clemenceau to favour Britain, it is because I was, until I read his document, under the delusion that France also attached importance to colonies, to ships, to compensation, to disarmament, to Syria, and to a British guarantee to stand by France with all her strength if she were attacked. I regret my error, and shall be careful not to repeat it.

I may be permitted to correct one out of many misrepresentations of my document. It is true I suggested temporary ownership of the whole of the Saar coal-field, with guarantees for permanent access to the coal, but this proposal was made as an alternative to another which I placed first—namely, the restoration of the 1814 frontier. Inasmuch, however, as M. Clemenceau treats this suggestion as a further proof of British selfishness, I promptly withdraw it.

D. LLOYD GEORGE.

President Wilson in the main favoured the proposals which I had put forward. Considerable pressure was brought to bear upon him through Colonel House to modify his attitude, but he remained firm in his determination to resist the French proposals as to the Rhineland and the Saar Basin.

The French had set their hearts on the Rhine frontier and used all their arts to persuade President Wilson to withdraw from the position he had taken up. Clemenceau backed up Tardieu, always avoiding an open rupture by never raising the issue formally at the Council. Foch sent us on the 31st March another written appeal entreating us to change our minds. It ended with passionate words of protest and supplication:

> To give up the barrier of the RHINE is to admit the following unthinkable monstrosity: that, although she be beaten, GERMANY, all covered with blood and crime, GERMANY, who is responsible for the death of millions of human beings, GERMANY, who wanted to destroy our country and turn it into a heap of ruins, GERMANY, who has undertaken to dominate the world by sheer force, would be, by our voluntary withdrawal from the RHINE, maintained in such a position that she could renew her undertakings just as if she had been victorious.
>
> I instantly beg the Allied and Associated Governments, who, in the most critical hours of the War entrusted me with the leadership of their Armies and the welfare of the common cause, to consider that, to-morrow just as to-day, that welfare can only be ensured in any lasting manner, by making the RHINE our military frontier, and by holding it with Allied forces. We must, therefore, maintain our present indispensable position.

To quote from M. Tardieu's "Truth about the Treaty":

> Every day, often twice a day, M. Clemenceau renewed his efforts. . . . Mr. Lloyd George kept to his invariable formula: "You must fully understand the state of mind of the British public. It is afraid to do anything whatsoever which might repeat the mistake Germany committed in annexing Alsace-Lorraine."

On March 31st M. Clemenceau summoned Marshal Foch and the Commanders-in-Chief of the Allied Armies before the Council of Four. Marshal Foch repeated with his usual vigour and emphasis the arguments he had already presented in his notes. He read to us the report which I have already quoted. He received no support from the Allied Commanders-in-Chief. On April 4th that wise monarch King Albert of Belgium was invited to join the Conference of the Heads of the Governments to give his views. Despite all the pressure which had been put upon him by French statesmen and soldiers, he gave no support to the French proposals.

Inasmuch as it was an essential part of the Foch-Tardieu plan that the severed provinces should be garrisoned by an Inter-allied force, M. Clemenceau ultimately realised that it was quite impossible to carry through the Foch and Tardieu schemes in the face of the combined resistance of both the U.S.A. and Great Britain, and the reluctance of Belgium to countenance the French plan. The French Government abandoned their proposal for the setting up of an independent State on the Rhine and accepted the scheme, which I put forward in my Fontainebleau document, for a joint guarantee by Britain and America, provided we agreed to a temporary occupation of the Rhine bridgeheads for a defined period.

This last proposal involved the occupation by foreign troops of a considerable and important section of German territory for a number of years, sufficient to provide security for the carrying out of the conditions of the Treaty on disarmament and on reparations. This territory included towns of considerable importance, like Cologne, Aix-la-Chapelle, Coblenz, Wiesbaden, Mannheim, Karlsruhe, and the occupation was near enough to Frankfurt to dominate that great and historic city. I regarded the proposal with grave misgivings. Nothing was more likely to create a feeling of bitterness and of exasperation than the presence of a foreign soldiery under conditions of martial law in land inhabited by a proud people. The memories of such an occupation by a foreign invader in France and Belgium for a period of over four years, was responsible for a great deal of the hatreds which impeded the task of peace-making. I stubbornly refused to agree to the plan. President Wilson adopted the same attitude and appeared to me to be equally irreconcilable. However, when I left for England at the beginning of April to deal with a difficult Parliamentary situation, to which I shall allude later on, Clemenceau had a series of conversations with Colonel House. In the course of these he was able to persuade the latter to use his influence with President Wilson to withdraw his opposition, and to agree to an occupation of the right bank of the Rhine by French, British and Belgian troops for periods ranging from five to fifteen years. The Saar was to be also occupied by Allied troops for fifteen years.

At that time the attacks on the President in the Parisian press had assumed proportions which were an outrage on international decencies. He felt the sting and shame of these spiteful gibes and calumnies so acutely that they impaired his health, and he had a week of severe illness. As soon as he recovered, Colonel House approached him with a view to inducing him to agree to a compromise. It was an essential part of that compromise that these attacks in the French Press should cease. Ultimately, the harried President withdrew his opposition and thereupon Clemenceau, to use the words of Colonel House, immediately "summoned his Secretary and told him in French, with much emphasis, that all attacks of every description on President Wilson and the U.S.A. must cease; that our relations were of the very best and that there was no disagreement between our countries upon the questions before the Peace Conference."

Colonel House comments in his "Intimate Papers" that "the effect was magical. All the Parisian papers appeared on the morning of the 16th with the most enthusiastic praise of President Wilson."

There is a very dramatic account given by Colonel House of his visit to Clemenceau to impart the news of the President's surrender:

"I went to the Ministry of War to see Clemenceau immediately after the President left. I said to him, 'I am the bearer of good news. The President has consented to all that you asked of me yesterday.' He grasped both my hands and then embraced me. . . ."

This is the "new world" which I found on my return from London. The outlook had entirely changed. I did my best to convince President Wilson of the mischievous possibilities of the occupation, but in vain. To quote Colonel House further:

"The agreement on the Rhine occupation was not formally approved by Lloyd George before April 22nd, but from the 15th

on [the 15th being the date of the compromise], it was clear that
the crisis had passed, and that the Treaty would be ready for the
German delegates who had been summoned to appear at Versailles."

This compromise I considered to be one of the mistakes of the
Treaty and it added a great deal to the difficulties of appeasement. Provocative incidents are the inevitable consequence of
any occupation of territory by foreign troops. The irritating and
occasionally odious accompaniments of such an occupation of
German towns by troops, some of whom were coloured, had
much to do with the fierce outbreak of patriotic sentiment in
Germany which finds its expression in Nazism.

The compromise, however, did not in the least satisfy the ideas
of that formidable section of French opinion which looked forward to this crushing victory as the best opportunity ever offered
to France of satisfying her age-long ambition for the establishment of French control, not only on the left but on both sides of
the Rhine. The President of the Republic constituted himself the
official exponent of this sentiment and on the 28th April sent
the following memorandum to M. Clemenceau as President of
the Peace Congress:

Paris, April 28th, 1919.

My dear President,
Before any definite decisions are taken, I think it might be useful
to sum up certain observations which the proposals put forward suggest to me, and which I have acquainted you with from time to time.
You will thus be able to communicate my opinion, if you think fit,
to the Allied and Associated Governments.

The amount of the claim which the Allied and Associated Powers
will have to bring against Germany cannot be definitely assessed until
after the Commission set up during the peace preliminaries has made
its valuations. But it would already appear from the work of the Delegations that the annual payment will very likely spread over some
thirty years at least. It would therefore be fair and logical for the
military occupation of the left bank of the Rhine and the bridgeheads
to last for the same length of time.

In the first place, in favour of this occupation, the serious considerations can be quoted which were set out in the two memoranda submitted by Marshal Foch to the Allied and Associated Governments.

The Marshal thinks, as do the military authorities, that the Rhine is the only barrier which really guarantees, in the event of another German attack, the common defence of England, Belgium and France. It is therefore to our interest not to abandon this barrier before Germany has fulfilled all the terms of the Peace Treaty.

There is, moreover, something quite unusual in the idea of renouncing a security before the amount secured has been completely paid.

Seeing that the occupation is to terminate in the event of payment in advance, the logical counterpart of this clause is for the occupation to continue in any case until the total liquidation of the debt.

After the war of 1870, the Germans occupied various French provinces until they received the last centime of the indemnity imposed on France, and M. Thiers only succeeded in obtaining the evacuation of the territory by discharging in advance the milliards which the conquerors exacted.

Occupation as security for a debt which represents reparation for war losses is in no way contrary to the principles proclaimed by President Wilson and accepted by the Allies. It has not, of course, any connection with annexation. It does not interfere with the national sovereignty of the defeated nation; it does not involve the inhabitants in a change of their native land; by its very definition it is temporary and dependent upon the duration of the debt which it guarantees; it merely constitutes a safeguard, a means by which the creditor assures payment without resorting to force.

One is at a loss to understand how this occupation could be shorter than the period fixed for annual payments. The figure of fifteen years is purely arbitrary, and it is equally arbitrary to make provision for three successive stages of evacuation during these fifteen years, when, on the expiry of this time-limit, France and her Allies may still be Germany's creditors.

It is argued that even when the occupation ceased, it could be resumed in the event of nonpayment. This option to renew occupation may look tempting to-day on paper. But it is bristling with drawbacks and risks.

Let us imagine ourselves sixteen or seventeen years ahead. Germany has paid regularly for fifteen years. We have evacuated the whole of the left bank of the Rhine. We have returned to our side of the political frontiers which afford no military security. Imagine Germany again a prey to Imperialism or imagine that she simply breaks faith. She suspends payment and we are obliged to reoccupy. We give the necessary orders, but who will vouch for our being able to carry them out without difficulty?

In the first place, Germany by her customary methods of propaganda will be sure to misrepresent facts and to assert that it is we who are the aggressors, and as it will actually be our troops who are returning to German soil, we shall easily figure as the invaders.

And, further, shall we be sure of finding the left bank free from German troops? Germany is supposedly going to undertake to have neither troops nor fortresses on the left bank and within a zone extending 50 km. east of the Rhine. But the Treaty does not provide for any permanent supervision of troops and armaments, on the left bank any more than elsewhere in Germany. In the absence of this permanent supervision, the clause stipulating that the League of Nations may order enquiries to be undertaken is in danger of being purely illusory. We can thus have no guarantee that after the expiry of the fifteen years and the evacuation of the left bank, the Germans will not filter troops by degrees into this district. Even supposing they have not previously done so, how can we prevent them doing it at the moment when we intend to reoccupy on account of their default?

It will then be simple for them to leap to the Rhine in a night and to seize this natural military frontier well ahead of us.

The option to renew the occupation should not therefore from any point of view be substituted for occupation.

It is objected that prolonged occupation will constitute a heavy military drain. Marshal Foch thinks, on the other hand, that the defence of the Rhine will require fewer troops than the defence of our political frontier, and assuredly he is best qualified to speak on this matter. Besides, for the present, it is not a question of our being compelled to occupy; but of compelling Germany to accept this occupation. The Allies will always be free to abandon it if they think fit.

It is also objected that a prolonged occupation may embitter relations between the troops and the inhabitants and cause trouble. If the objection held good, it would apply equally well to an occupation lasting for fifteen years as to an occupation guaranteeing a debt. It would be even more valid in the former case, since this occupation, which fixes an arbitrary time-limit, does not appear to have any clearly defined object, whilst the second, which constitutes a security for payment, is easily grasped by everyone and particularly by the inhabitants of the locality occupied. It should be added that on the one hand those inhabitants are amongst the most friendly in Germany and have never cherished the same feelings of hostility against the Allies as the Prussians; and on the other hand, the French troops will have enough tact, once the Peace is signed, not to treat these people as enemies. If there were a risk of friction, it would be more likely to occur early because of war memories; but as time goes on, the relations between the armies of occupation and the civil population are bound to improve.

In brief, everything calls for the type of occupation which represents the natural consequence and the security for the debt. The one should cease when the other is liquidated. Neither sooner nor later.

No one esteems more highly than I the offers of alliance which have been generously extended to France by the President of the United States and the Prime Minister of Great Britain. The permanent alliance of our Three Nations in defence of justice and liberty will be a fine and splendid thing. But the valuable assistance which our friends are in a position to render us in the event of German aggression cannot unfortunately ever be instantaneous. Besides it will not directly affect the security for the debt. It will thus be no substitute for occupation.

I am fully confident that the Allied and Associated Governments will take this situation into consideration and that they will be willing to confer on France, who has suffered so heavily, the one safeguard which in my opinion can guarantee effectively the payment of our debt.

Believe me, my dear President

Yours very sincerely,

(*Sd.*) POINCARÉ.

It will be observed that M. Poincaré very adroitly put his case not on the ground of the desirability of annexing this territory to France, but on the more plausible basis of the importance of occupying it as a security for the payment of Germany's claims in respect of reparation. He evidently thought this line of reasoning might appeal to the practical experience of two great business and banking communities like the British and American. But the whole of his argument, especially towards the end of his letter, makes it clear that he was not thinking of a possession redeemable by the payment of debt, but that he contemplated a permanent occupation with the goodwill of the inhabitants of the Rhineland. He was fully convinced—as all Frenchmen were—that the friendly feelings which the Rhinelanders had from time to time displayed towards France would in the course of a prolonged occupation develop into a real desire to remain under the French flag. The letter was considered by the Council of Four, but M. Clemenceau had already accepted our proposals and he never went back on an arrangement to which he had assented—however reluctantly.

The French military and the parties of the Right never forgave M. Clemenceau for what they regarded as his failure to take full advantage of the opportunity afforded by the victory to realise traditional French ambitions on the Rhine. They stigmatised it as a betrayal of France, and when the chance came they recorded their verdict on his conduct by intriguing a humiliating defeat of his candidature for the Presidency.

Clemenceau's defence against those who criticised him in the French Chamber is a characteristic sample of his oratory:

The state of mind of our Allies is not necessarily the same as our own, and when we are not in agreement with them, it is unjust to blame those who do not succeed in convincing them or to blame them for evil intentions which are not in their hearts.

What are you going to do about it? Each of us lives encased in his own past. Auguste Comte said that we live dead men's lives and it is true.

We are encased by the past which holds us in its grip, and spurs us forward to new efforts. Neither an Englishman, nor I, nor anyone will cast off his historical way of seeing things and of thinking because he has contracted a temporary alliance with a foreign country.

. . . . .

How can a man be expected to renounce his past, when he is sacrificing the blood of his countrymen to uphold it?

Men retain their virtues and their faults together. You must take them as they are. They are what they are. They have a past as we have a past. As far as I am concerned, merely because they differ from me even on very serious questions, I do not feel called upon to break with them as has been suggested. . . . There should be no surprise at the resistance we have encountered. The one said or thought: "I am English"; the other thought: "I am American." Each had as much right to say so as we had to say we are French. Sometimes it is true, they made me suffer cruelly. . . .

It is worthy of note that all vocal criticism of the peace delegations in France, as well as in England, came from powerful political groups who were anxious to make the terms harsher and more stern than those which the Peace Council ultimately presented to Germany. During the progress of the Peace Conference there was not a voice raised in favour of moderation except from the men who were conducting the negotiations, and who for that reason were assailed with suspicion, a misrepresentation and abuse. I cannot recall a word uttered in the French Assembly or a sentence printed in the French Press pleading for clemency to the vanquished. In Britain even, when I had to face hundreds of my own supporters in Parliament who were disaffected by Press reports about the leniency of my attitude towards Germany, not a voice was heard from any section of the Parliamentary Opposition which expressed any sympathy with the fight I was putting up against redoubtable critics for moderation on reparations, frontiers or disarmament, nor did I receive any tender of support in my struggle on any of these vital issues.

CHAPTER IX

REPARATIONS

A S soon as the Armistice was signed on the 11th of November, the Governments of the principal victorious countries entered into communication with each other with a view to settling the preliminaries of the Peace Conference. Before that Conference could meet with any prospect of getting on successfully and speedily with business, there was a vast amount of preparation required to enable the general principles of the settlement which had been laid down by the Allies to be developed into workable and practical propositions. Take, for instance, the doctrine of self-determination on the basis of race, language, tradition and predilection. A careful study by experts was necessary in order to ascertain and define boundaries drawn in accordance with the conditions prescribed by the Allied ideal of national freedom and independence. Reparation called for an examination by financial experts, economists and jurists into the amount to be exacted and the methods and possibilities of payment. There were many other important questions demanding a close survey of the relevant facts and considerations. The War had come to an end with unexpected suddenness; few anticipated so complete a collapse of enemy resistance before 1919. To the end of the struggle the various Government Departments were all absorbed in the tasks of the War and there had not been time for them to transfer their machinery to the details connected with the problems of peace. Nevertheless a considerable amount of preliminary investigation had been undertaken into many of these essential questions.

As we knew that reparations would be one of the most perplexing and difficult of all the subjects with which we should have to deal, the Government had already ordered enquiries to be instituted into the possibilities of recovering from Germany some proportion of the damage done by the German forces on land and

sea and from the air. The Germans on their part had been conducting a similar enquiry as to the methods by which, in the
event of victory, they could extract an indemnity from their defeated foes.

So much slovenly vituperation has been let loose on the question of reparations that the truth about its origin, its justification,
the views of the Government about it and, what is still more
reprehensible, the truth about the actual proposals of the Treaty
on this subject, has been completely overlaid by a muddy sedi-
ment of denunciation. The consequence is that there are multitudes of simple people who in all innocence and honesty seem to
have come to the conclusion that the idea of exacting reparations
from Germany was projected for the first time in December, 1918,
from the brain of an astute electioneer, as a device for winning
the votes of heavily taxed—and therefore highly incensed—
British voters, and that a promise was conveyed that the whole
cost of the War could and would be levied from the vanquished.
All this is a grotesque and wilful travesty of the real facts.

That the Central Powers were the aggressors has been established beyond a doubt. That question is fundamental. If the
Central Powers were not primarily responsible for the War, the
basis of reparations disappears. But the liability to pay compensation for damage done by a wrong-doer, and the payment by a
defeated suitor of the costs incurred in a vindication of justice are
among the integral principles of law in every civilised community. States are not immune from the application of that elementary doctrine of jurisprudence. A critical attitude towards
the exacting of reparations after a war has been dictated by an
undefined and unacknowledged feeling that war is part of the
legitimate business of States and that it cannot be treated as a
tort in respect of which the trespasser can in honour be held responsible for repairing the devastation wrought by him, or for
paying the costs incurred by the wronged in securing justice.
This frame of mind has, largely because of the capricious exigencies of party manœuvres, been adopted by sections which
make a special profession of inculcating the criminality of all
wars. This is one of the perplexing human paradoxes that con-

front one in walking through life. In ordinary transactions, if a civilian brings a vexatious suit against another, relying on his superior resources to win his case, and if the verdict goes against him, then it is an accepted rule that he should pay the costs of the winner. If he has inflicted personal injury upon his adversary or victim, or destroyed any of his property, he is liable to pay full damages, and if the damage done is malicious and intentional, he may in addition be prosecuted under the criminal law. This principle applies equally to corporations and, as far as criminal jurisdiction is concerned, to the heads of those corporations. Why should States and their responsible directors be the only corporations to escape responsibility for their injurious acts? Why should rulers be more immune than their subjects from the consequences of criminal acts which they have committed upon their neighbours? The axiom that the King can do no wrong received a rude shock in the days of Charles the First. In practice it has never applied to damages for torts committed by his agents. And if these transgressions are perpetrated by a foreigner against British subjects, why should the liability therefore be blotted out? If an aggressor confronted by a heavy verdict pleads bankruptcy, his assets are forfeit to the limit of the claim. But in a civil case the fact that payment of costs or damages will impoverish the offender is not a plea which is accepted as a ground for exemption. If the assets of the debtor are insufficient without continued service on his part, in order to fructify them adequate allowance is made in respect of his maintenance in estimating the amount that can be exacted. These are in substance the principles applied by established law in every civilised country where damages are imposed for a wrong committed by one citizen against another.

It is an entirely new doctrine that nations who make war upon other nations should not be held responsible for the consequences because of any inconvenience or deprivation to them involved in liquidating the liabilities they have deliberately incurred. As far as the principles of right are concerned, States must abide by the rules of justice which they impose upon their own citizens. To what extent it is desirable to enforce these rules in any particular case is a question of ordinary prudence or expediency. It may well be that penalties exacted from a nation may be so difficult of collection, may inflict such hardships upon a people, may disturb the course of business to such a degree, and may perpetuate feuds and hatreds to such an extent that wisdom indicates the advisability of relaxing the stern rules of law. But prudence demands that an aggressor should bear at least some part of the burden he has cast upon others.

Indemnities were not invented by the Treaty of Versailles. It is true that in the old days the methods of collecting the indemnity were ruder and more summary than those embodied in the Versailles Treaty. In olden days compensation was sought in pillage, loot and in annexation of territory. Napoleon exacted levies from the territories he invaded and the towns he occupied. His armies lived on the countries they overran and garrisoned.

At the beginning of the nineteenth century money indemnities paid as a condition of peace were substituted for these crude and barbarous methods. To quote from a document prepared by Lord Sumner for one of the committees of the Peace Congress:

In 1815, the Allies imposed upon France the payment of seven hundred million francs in order to cover the costs of the war; in 1849, Sardinia had to pay Austria seventy-five million francs in order to cover the costs of the war; in 1866, after a very short war, Prussia imposed upon Austria an indemnity of forty million thalers and considerable sums upon several German states, in order to cover her war expenses. Finally, in 1871, Prussia imposed upon France an infamous indemnity which exceeded considerably the cost of the war.

In those days wars did not cost the colossal sums which are incurred in modern warfare, and the damage wrought was a trifle compared with the devastation inflicted in the Great War. If custom is a source of law for nations, as well as for individuals, the practice was thus established by the Central Powers that the victor might impose upon the vanquished the payment of the costs incurred by him in the war and something beyond in the nature of exemplary damages.

The idea of reparation was in the minds of the Allied Governments from the commencement of this reckless and wanton war.

The first assertion by British statesmen of a claim to reparations may be said to have been implicit in Mr. Asquith's historical deliverance of the 9th of November, 1914: "We shall never sheathe the sword . . . until Belgium recovers in full measure *all and more* than all that she has sacrificed." The kind of indemnity indicated in this statement, it will be noticed, contained a punitive element the application of which would have involved more than a mere restoration. At that date the damage was mostly inflicted on Belgian towns and Belgian individuals, and as the Germans marched rapidly through Belgium and the fighting was not heavy, the destruction was not comparable with that which ensued as the struggle developed and the great cannon scattered ruin over the land unceasingly night and day. The wholesale havoc wrought in the North-West provinces of France had barely commenced, nor had there been any serious shipping losses at sea through enemy action, nor any bombing raids on our cities. No one at that time contemplated the enormous cost of the War, or the ruin to which it would reduce cities, villages and industries over hundreds of kilometres in whole provinces. The Treaty of London, which brought Italy into the War in the spring of 1915, provided for the levying of an indemnity on the Central Powers and stipulated that Italy should have her share. By 1916 the character of the devastation had developed, and the categories multiplied beyond the limits of any previous apprehension. The vast destruction of property which took place was partly incidental to the operations of modern warfare, with its millions of enormous shells and bombs charged with high explosive fired or dropped where they could effect the greatest destruction. But a great deal of the damage was deliberate. Machinery was dismantled in France and set up in Germany; much of it was systematically destroyed in order to cripple French industry for the future. The German military boasted that the effect of this process of systematic destruction would be that, after the War, French industry would be eliminated from competition with Germany in the brisk world markets that must, it was then supposed, necessarily follow the termination of hostilities owing to arrears which had to be made up.

Lest it be suggested that this is one of the accusations made in the moment of uncontrolled anger in every war by one belligerent against another, I will quote one or two passages from a document issued by the Quarter-Master General of the German Imperial Armies early in 1916 to all the Chambers of Commerce and the financial, industrial and commercial associations of the German Empire. It was compiled and published officially at a time when the armies of Germany and her allies seemed to be victorious in every battle area: on the Western Front, in Russia, in the Balkans, in the Dardanelles, in Mesopotamia and Palestine. The document was discovered after the War, and was communicated to the Supreme Council in Paris. It was prepared by 200 Reserve Officers who had technical qualifications and who had investigated in great detail the destruction inflicted upon French industries at that time. It was obviously intended to excite the cupidity of German industrialists and to enlist them on the side of the War Lords by a demonstration of concern for the future benefit of German industry and of the forethought by which methods of warfare were adapted to the attainment of that purpose. Here are a few samples:

Textile Mills. As all metals lacking in Germany, such as copper, brass, bronze, etc., have been seized and taken away from French factories . . . resumption of work will encounter great difficulties. An enormous market, especially for German manufacturers of textile machinery, will be found in the north of France.

Foundries. Production will fall off heavily in these foundries, owing to the removal of the machinery.

This loss, which will be considerably increased by the cost of reconstruction, will so prejudice numerous enterprises, from the financial point of view, that it will be difficult for them to resume operation, or to restore this to its former level.

Woollen Mills. In the region of Avesnes and of Sedan, several factories have been so gutted that a certain number of their looms, abandoned to the weather, may be looked upon as scrap iron. . . .

Germany should be in a position to resume her full productive capacity in the manufacture of yarn at least one or two years sooner than France. This result will be all the more satisfactory in that the sister industries of weaving and dyeing, as well as the export trade, will benefit equally thereby, and that this last, especially, will be in a position, not only to recapture the markets it has lost, but even to acquire new ones where France so far has been the only furnisher.

There are similar quotations applicable to the wrecking of other rival industries. The report on the coal industry has a significance of its own because of a doubt which seems to have been in the mind of the German military at that date as to whether the coal-mines in the North-West of France at the end of the War should be left in the possession of France.

Coal Mines. The districts will be unproductive for years to come, owing to the removal of the machinery and the flooding of the shafts.

France will have to buy her machinery in Germany and, *even if the rich beds in the French territory occupied by German troops were to continue in the possession of France*, it might be foreseen that Germany would have to deliver a higher percentage than in the past, owing to the deficit in French production.

As far as the coal-mines were concerned, the destruction was not due to bombardment nor even to the removal of the machinery to Germany. The Germans systematically destroyed the pits and the whole apparatus, blowing up by dynamite the props, cylinders, boilers and galleries, and crashing them all into one inextricable ruin. This organised and directed sabotage was in the minds of the Allied representatives at the Paris Conference in June, 1916, when they passed the following resolution dealing with it:

The Allies declare their common determination to ensure the re-establishment of the countries suffering from acts of destruction, spoliation and unjust requisition, and decide to join in devising means to secure the restoration to those countries, as a prior claim, of their raw materials, industrial and agricultural plant, stock, and mercantile fleet, or to assist them to re-equip themselves in these respects.

This statement covers the specific wrecking methods to which I have alluded, but it goes far beyond that, for it sets out in summary form the general principle of reparation for all damage on land and sea as the result of enemy action. By the end of 1916 the havoc was so vast that it was clear that no country could command the necessary currency or foreign securities to pay so immense a bill across its own frontiers, and even the raw materials which could be drawn from Germany would not substantially reduce the amount. The export trade of Germany therefore had to be brought into requisition in order to contribute towards the deficiency, and the question arose whether this could be done over a period of years without injury to the trade of the recipients. At that date there was no experience to guide Governments as to the limit beyond which payments from one country to another could be extracted without harm to both. The Board of Trade was therefore asked at the end of 1916 to investigate and report "concerning the probable economic effect on our trade of an indemnity (whether in money or in kind) paid by the enemy at the conclusion of the War, or within a reasonable time afterwards, to make good damages in the territory overrun." The appointment of the Committee by the Asquith Government showed that the exaction of an indemnity was then contemplated as one of the conditions of peace. The Report, which was issued early in 1917, deprecates imposing on the Central Powers terms of peace inspired by motives of commercial revenge. But on the question of indemnity it reports that "assuming a complete victory, the Board of Trade see no reason to doubt the expediency of exacting an indemnity, though the proceeds of any indemnity which the Central Powers could pay will necessarily go but a short way towards meeting the cost of the War. The indemnity imposed on France after the Franco-German War, large as it was then considered to be, would not nearly pay for a month's cost of the present war." The Report indicates the directions in which compensation could be found. It attempts no estimate of what amount could be recovered by these expedients; it contents itself with the statement that there is no prospect of receiving any indemnity which would approach the gigantic expenditure of the War.

This Report is accompanied by a memorandum which the Board of Trade had procured from Professor Ashley and Mr. J. M. Keynes "on the probable effects of an indemnity on our trade," and which is significant as being the first declaration made on either side which suggests an indemnity spread over a

long term of years. Dealing with the pernicious effect produced
in Germany by the payment of the French indemnity of 1871 in
stimulating speculation, etc., it quotes an eminent German economist to prove that the mischief could, to a large extent, have
been avoided by spreading the payment over a longer period and
by enforcing payment to a large extent in things other than
money. The Ashley-Keynes conclusions are thus summarised by
the Board of Trade in their Report: "Briefly, the result is to
show that, from an economic point of view, indemnity in kind is
to be preferred, so far as practicable, to indemnity in money, and
that any cash payments should be spread over a considerable
period." Professor Ashley and Mr. Keynes are thus the joint
authors of the long-term indemnity which was incorporated in
the Treaty. Their estimate of the possibilities and practicabilities
of an indemnity are condensed in two paragraphs which subsequently formed the basis of the inflated estimates of Lord Cunliffe and Lord Sumner:

It will be seen from the foregoing paragraphs that the popular conception of an indemnity as consisting in a number of periodical payments of cash (mainly through bills of exchange) as the result of a
voluntary loan, mainly internal—on the analogy of the Franco-German
indemnity described above—*by no means exhausts the possibilities of
the situation.* The actual payment of the loan may take place, as we
have seen, to a greater or less extent by means of the immediate transference of various forms of property other than bills; and although
it will be necessary for the German Government to raise a loan in
order to compensate the owners of private property transferred to the
Allies, that loan may be a compulsory one, i.e., the compensation may
consist in an equivalent, determined by the State, in Government
bonds.

But when the fullest use has been made of the methods already
mentioned, *it will remain to be considered whether a part, even a considerable part, of the indemnity should not consist of a number of payments
spread over a period of years.* A demand of this latter kind would differ
from those already suggested in two respects. In the first place, it
would leave it to the indemnity-paying country to find the means
of payment, instead of prescribing the transference of certain defined
forms of wealth. *In the second place, it would involve a charge not so
much on wealth already accumulated as on future accumulations.* The
two methods are, therefore, in a sense, alternatives; and the method

of prescribed forms of immediate payment has the advantage of enabling the indemnity-receiving country to guard against the danger inherent in the other method. On the other hand, the indemnity demand may be too large to be covered by the transference of immediately available wealth; and, if so, the methods will naturally be regarded as complementary.

The future accumulations on which an indemnity would draw would come from two sources: from the income from external investments, *and from the savings from internal economic activity.*

This is the first time that a proposal was put forward for hypothecating Germany's future earnings over a long period of years to liquidate the Allied claim for reparations. At this date the Germans also had set their experts on to enquire into the most practicable methods of collecting a war indemnity from the Allied countries when they were beaten. Coal-mines, railways, investments and colonies were to be seized, but they had not hit upon the idea of levying a tribute for 30 or 40 years on the profits and earnings of the Allied peoples. Mr. Keynes is the sole patentee and promoter of that method of extraction. All the extravagant estimates formulated after the War as to Germany's capacity to pay were based on this plan submitted to the British Government in February, 1917. It was impossible to set any limit to the possible profits of the trade and industry of a great productive country. Science had multiplied the income and wealth of all industrial countries so rapidly that it was impossible to make any reliable estimate of what the German national income might be in 1940 or 1950. To the minds of City financiers and of all burdened taxpayers, the Keynes-Ashley plan of payment by instalments, growing with the growth of Germany's wealth, opened a vista of an expanding annual tribute which would ultimately cover the war taxes. The prospect of keeping the German workers of all ranks in a condition of servitude for 40 years did not dim the prophetic vision or abate the extortionate zeal of these twin economists. They shared the natural feelings of the ordinary Briton that as Germany made the War, she must pay for it to the limit of her capacity. If she did not, then the crushing burden would fall on the British and French taxpayers who were guiltless. The burden had to be carried by someone. Why should a

part of it not be thrown on the shoulders of those who were responsible for the calamity? On the question of capacity they for
the first time suggested to the Government methods by which
the German ability to liquidate this debt could be profitably
extended.

The question of the practicability of levying a large indemnity
on Germany was not considered further until October, 1918,
when the end of the War was in sight. The War Cabinet were too
much absorbed in the interminable questions connected with the
conduct of this tremendous struggle to devote much time to the
details of a final settlement when victory had not yet crowned
the Allied efforts and the issue or the completeness of the victory
was still in doubt. But when a speedy and overwhelming triumph
was assured they directed the Board of Trade on the 17th of
October, 1918, to prepare a Memorandum on the Economic Considerations affecting the Terms of Peace. This was issued on the
26th of November, 1918—fifteen days after the Armistice.

In regard to indemnities and reparation, the memorandum
advised that

the total claims under the head of reparation will certainly be very
great, and as the satisfaction of these claims must take precedence
over an indemnity proper, it is suggested that no useful purpose would
be served by putting forward a claim for an indemnity proper unless
it be thought expedient to do so for bargaining purposes.

·   ·   ·   ·   ·

As regards the total sum to be demanded for purposes of reparation,
it may be said at once that the probable claims may conceivably
amount to so colossal a figure that *the limit of the sum to be demanded
will be fixed rather by the capacity of the Central Powers to pay than by
the sum necessary to make good all the damage caused to the Allies.*

·   ·   ·   ·   ·

On the whole, it would not be safe, on our present information, to
put the total claims for reparation (direct and indirect) at less than
£2,000 million, and it is a question whether it is practically possible
to exact so great a sum from the Central Powers, whether in kind,
cash or securities, unless payment is spread over so long a time that
a long period of occupation of German territory would be necessary
to enforce it.

The memorandum examined Germany's available resources for payment of a reparation bill, and came to the conclusion that the value of the ships, reconstruction materials, potash, coal, dye-stuffs and other miscellaneous commodities, and gold which she could hand over within a short period, would be not more than £400,000,000. Her external investments which could be acquired and handed over might make another £400,000,000. (So much of Germany's pre-war external investment had been in Austria-Hungary, and of Austria-Hungary's in Germany, that if these countries were joined as debtor nations for reparations their mutual investments could not be reckoned as external invest-ments, capable of being realised for reparations.) Thus £800,000,000 was estimated as the total sum which Germany could pay over in transferable goods or external securities. If £1,000,000,000 was fixed as the sum to be charged her, £200,000,000 of this would have to be procured by Germany for payment by mortgaging her future credit. And any increase above £1,000,000,000 would have to be made in this way. The memorandum said that any very large sums falling under this head—i.e. paid in bonds against which Germany had no external assets or transferable property—"could only be raised with very great difficulty, and their exaction would involve very severe economic pressure on the Central Powers maintained for a long period of time."

On the other hand, the memorandum recognises that a sum of £2,000,000,000 would barely pay for the damage done, and would contain no margin for ordinary war expenses. The actual fixing of the sum to be demanded thus became a matter of a calculation of possibilities and not of the surest methods of attaining it.

Accordingly, the Board of Trade recommended:

(1) That a sum be demanded for reparation for destruction and damage and to meet all other pecuniary claims arising out of the war, the total amount to be exacted being fixed by the Allies in accordance with their views as to the economic capacity of the Central Powers to pay, and all other relevant considerations of policy.

(2) Of the total sum payable, about £400,000,000 should be paid in material commodities, including ships, barges, railway material,

rolling stock, other raw or semi-manufactured materials necessary for reconstruction, coal, potash and gold, and the remainder in interest-bearing securities acquired by the Governments of the Central Powers and handed over to the Allies, including *inter alia* the whole of the securities external to the Central Powers and held within their territories which it is possible for their Governments to acquire.

(3) That as an essential part of Reparation, the whole of the shipping belonging to the Central Powers above 1,600 tons gross, wherever the ships may be situated (i.e. all except those captured and condemned) should be handed over to the Allied Maritime Transport Council, to be employed by them to the best advantage during the reconstruction period, and thereafter allotted to the various Allied States in proportion to their losses through illegitimate action by the enemy.

(4) That machinery removed from Allied factories by the enemy and still existing in good condition be immediately restored, and that the enemy Powers be required also to place at the disposal of the Allies any other machinery of non-enemy manufacture that exists in enemy territories and that the Allies consider suitable to replace machinery destroyed or otherwise lost through enemy action. That in placing orders at the expense of the Reparation Fund for new machinery to fill gaps that still remain, care should be taken to avoid the danger of tying the devastated territories to enemy sources of supply for renewals and maintenance in future.

(5) That the materials, coal, rolling stock etc., included in the payment for reparations be applied for the purpose of reconstruction of the devastated areas as and where required to repair losses.

(6) That the potash and gold be allocated by Inter-Allied Committees among the Allied States in equitable proportion to their requirements, the value of these commodities being credited to the Reparation Fund.

(7) That in the same way the value of the ships, materials, rolling stock, coal, etc., allocated to the various Allied countries be credited to the Reparation Fund.

(8) That the general Reparation Fund, consisting of the securities handed over and the value of the commodities credited as above, be applied to repair the losses of the Allies according to a scale of priority to be agreed among them, the claims having first priority to be those recognised by Resolution B 1 of the Paris Economic Conference, i.e. the material reconstitution of the devastated districts and the rebuilding of merchant ships.

I had given some thought to the question of the indemnity which it was possible to exact from the enemy countries, and I was entirely sceptical as to their capacity to contribute any sum which would be a substantial aid to the Allies in liquidating their war burdens. Mr. Bonar Law took the same view of the possibilities. The Board of Trade confirmed us in the opinion we had formed on that subject. During a discussion which took place on reparations at the Imperial War Cabinet on the day when the Board of Trade issued its Report, the Australian Prime Minister strongly urged the exaction of a full war indemnity. Mr. Hughes pointed out that Australia alone had spent £300,000,000 on the War, and that she could ill afford it with her population of only five millions and her enormous undeveloped territory. In reply I said (I am quoting from an official note taken at the time)

. . . that the question of a war indemnity was a very difficult matter. . . . I then gave, as an example, the instance of a possible claim by Australia for £300,000,000, and pointed out that it was not an easy matter to say how such a claim would be paid. I asked if it was Mr. Hughes' intention that Australia should be paid in gold, or by Germany selling goods, and to this question Mr. Hughes replied "By credit." I then pointed out that, in order to pay the debt in this manner, it would be necessary for Germany to sell goods, and asked who was going to buy them. The total liability of Germany would probably amount to some £20,000,000,000, and it would be very easy for the Allied Powers to say to Germany that she had got to pay this amount, but I suggested that it would mean that for two generations we would make German workmen our slaves. I further pointed out that someone must buy the goods manufactured in Germany, and, for the moment, I did not see which nation would provide the dumping ground for such goods. Further, we would have to allow Germany to import raw material for the manufacture of the goods. I thought the only way in which Germany could pay a large indemnity would be by manufacturing cheaper than other nations and by selling to them.

This statement was made by me the day after the dissolution of Parliament and before I had opened my electoral campaign. I was anxious that the members of the Government should not be responsible during the election for arousing or encouraging any false hopes in the minds of the electorate by anything said by them in the course of that contest.

Mr. Bonar Law was equally desirous of discouraging extravagant anticipations. He had as Chancellor of the Exchequer appointed a Treasury Committee to work on the problem. Their Report, which was issued in December, was largely inspired by Mr. Keynes. It took a more sanguine view than that of the Board of Trade experts. The Treasury Committee placed the maximum figure of possible indemnity at £3,000,000,000. Mr. Bonar Law thought the figure of £2,000,000,000 was too low, and was more inclined to accept the Treasury estimate.

As to the methods of securing payment, the Treasury Report suggested two alternative policies:

(1) To obtain *all* the property which can be transferred immediately or over a period of three years, levying this contribution ruthlessly and completely, so as to ruin entirely for many years to come Germany's overseas development and her international credit; but, having done this (which would yield more than £1,000,000,000, but less than £2,000,000,000), to ask only a small tribute over a term of years, and to leave Germany to do the best she can for the future with the internal resources remaining to her.

(2) To levy less ruthlessly in the immediate future, and to supply Germany with considerable quantities of raw material, with a view to her developing for the benefit of the Allies an export trade on a far greater scale than hitherto; and having thus nursed her back into a condition of high productivity, to compel her to exploit this productivity under conditions of servitude for a long period of years.

The former of these two courses was the one strongly recommended in the Treasury memorandum. The second course would be difficult to carry out, and in all probability it would not, after all, be very productive. The main difference between the Board of Trade and the Treasury Report was the emphasis placed by the latter on the levy of a tribute on Germany's internal resources extending over a period of years. According to whether this tribute were small or great would be the total sum to be expected by way of reparation from Germany. The Report leaned towards the small tribute but did not rule out the other as impracticable. The Board of Trade were shy of this proposition. The Treasury experts naturally had their minds primarily set on securing some source of revenue which would reduce the crushing burden of taxation involved in the payment of interest in our gigantic war debt for the next two generations. The Board of Trade experts attached more importance to trade and industry. They were of opinion that any obligation which would have the effect of increasing the export trade of Germany must necessarily be detrimental to the interests of Britain as the greatest international trader in the world.

The recommendations of these two Reports—that of the Board of Trade, supplemented by the Treasury Report—formed in substance the proposals with regard to reparations which were embodied in the Treaty of Versailles. The only difference was that the Treaty did not commit itself to figures but left them to be ascertained and fixed by a special body appointed for the purpose. These figures were to be determined from time to time, after an examination of the actual cost of the damage done and after hearing what the Germans had to say on that subject and also on the question of the capacity of Germany to pay.

The charge is often made that politicians in Britain and France, ignorant of the rudiments of international finance, were foolish enough to think Germany could pay tens of thousands of millions of pounds on account of her reparations debts, and that for their own ambitious purposes they encouraged the electors to cherish the same delusion. From these charitable suppositions the inference is drawn that these same politicians, having committed themselves from base motives of political advantage to this extravagance, found it necessary to enshrine their electioneering expedients in the Treaty they negotiated.

As a matter of fact, however, in this country it was politicians, relying on the advice of their departmental advisers, who were persistently doubtful as to the possibilities of extracting payment on a huge scale, and it was financial and business experts who were exultantly confident. In France both politicians and business men professed confidence that Germany could pay to the full. No protest was raised here from the City, or from any of the organisations who are supposed to represent the views of the commercial and industrial leaders of the country, as to the fantastic amount of the reparations which it was suggested by their foremost authorities could be recovered from Germany. Indeed, the highest estimates of Germany's capacity to pay came from men of high repute in the world of finance and business.

There was one Dominion Premier and perhaps one British Minister who held the opinion that Germany ought to and could bear the cost of the War into which her rulers, with the enthusiastic support of her people, had plunged the Allied nations. I am not aware that any other leading politician in the Empire shared their wild optimism. But the majority of financiers and business men were convinced that Germany could pay colossal sums. As to the first proposition—that Germany ought to pay— it was difficult to controvert its justice. As to the second—her capacity to pay what was expected of her—I was more than doubtful. But I was equally doubtful as to the actual sum that she was able to pay. When pundits disagreed, who was to decide? I had some hopes that a careful examination by responsible experts of the practical difficulties of securing the payment of a large indemnity would become evident the moment the issue was transferred from the realm of declamation to the more mathematical sphere of investigation. Germany must pay to the limit of her capacity. The question was to ascertain that limit. I therefore decided to appoint an influential committee which, with the assistance of Treasury and Board of Trade officials, would examine the possibilities. It was appointed not merely in order to guide the Government as to the demands which could reasonably be put forward at the coming Conference, but also with a view to obtaining an authoritative report that would damp down the too fierce anticipations of an expectant public.

I was so confident that, when men of real practical ability came into contact with the actualities of the problem, they would acknowledge the futility of exaggerated anticipation, that I decided to place on the Committee Mr. W. M. Hughes, a believer in high figures, and Mr. Walter Long. Walter Long was that kind of politician who gains the confidence of a party with a reputation for caution, sound common sense and moderation, because his utterances never transgress the commonplaces and clichés of that party, and he never startles the public by any originality of thought or suggestion, or by any audacity or brilliancy of phrase. In their day such men wield great influence and authority in the councils of every party. Future generations either forget them or only remember them to be puzzled at the position they attained amongst their contemporaries. And the fact that each generation in its turn admires and trusts the same type does not prevent them from wondering why their ancestors did the same thing.

To counter-balance further the optimism of Mr. Hughes and keep the Committee in touch with realities, I added the name of Sir G. E. Foster, the Canadian Finance Minister, a statesman of recognised sanity and moderation, and with great experience in public finance; Mr. W. A. S. Hewins, the economist; Lord Cunliffe, the Governor of the Bank of England—a cautious, shrewd, and level-headed financier; and the Hon. Herbert Gibbs, one of the great City bankers. These last two were specially nominated to serve on the Committee as business men of high repute who were in close touch with the soundest City opinion. There was another reason why the Governor and Mr. Gibbs were placed on the Committee. The general public had not yet realised the difference between paying interest and sinking fund on an internal debt, and finding the necessary currency to make large payments on account of an external debt. If Germany could in four years raise loans aggregating £10,000,000,000 to pay for her own expenditure, why could she not find a similar or a larger sum in twenty years to pay an indemnity to neighbours she had wronged? That one country could only pay another even interest on borrowed money by a sale of its produce, had not been grasped by the country as a whole. The two City representatives had a long and extensive experience in this kind of business, and I was convinced that their special knowledge would act as a check on the more general acquaintance of the politicians with these financial questions. It will thus be seen that this Committee was very far from being dominated by the irresponsible politicians or speculative financiers. I entertained no doubt that such a combination would ensure a cautious report that would discourage excited estimates. I have never seen trustfulness so completely befooled by the sequel. In its findings the Committee proposed that the

Central Powers should be required to make an annual reparation payment for a long period of years of £1,200,000,000—which figure would, they calculated, represent the interest charges on the whole cost of the War to the Allies. It will be seen that on this basis the Germans would have been required to pay within a generation a sum of nearly £40,000,000,000.

In the light of subsequent events the findings of this Committee make interesting reading and lead to useful reflexions on the opinions of the big business class on large issues which necessitate long views, a wide perspective and a grasp of fundamental realities. They are summarised as follows:

(1) The total cost of the War to the Allies is the measure of the indemnity which the Enemy Powers should in justice pay.

(2) Although it is not yet possible to estimate what the total cost of the War will be, the figures available indicate that so far the direct cost of the war to the Allies had been £24,000,000,000; and the Committee have certainly no reason to suppose that the Enemy Powers could not provide £1,200,000,000 per annum as interest on the above amount when normal conditions are restored.

(3) The Indemnity should be payable in cash, kind, securities, and by means of a funding loan.

(4) The fear of economic ill-effects to Allied countries from the repayment of the costs of the War is not well founded; whilst without repayment the Allied countries—with their man-power seriously reduced, their territory laid waste, their industries paralysed and burdened with a huge load of debt—would be unable to compete successfully in the markets of the world.

(5) The enforcement of an Indemnity will operate as a deterrent to future aggression, and be a substantial guarantee of the world's peace.

Mr. Bonar Law and I regarded the conclusions of this Report as a wild and fantastic chimera. It was incredible that men of such position, experience and responsibility should have appended their names to it. What is still more remarkable is that it represented the opinions formed and expressed by the Associated Chambers of Commerce and the Federation of British Industries. So much for the infallibility of business men in business matters which go beyond their day-to-day transactions. It showed that outside his office the great financier or industrial

magnate was just a man in the street. I was repelled and shocked
by the extreme absurdity of this document. In view of the election then proceeding I decided not to publish it. It would be
foolish to excite insane hopes that the enemy would shoulder the
whole or even a substantial proportion of our heavy war burdens.
Mr. Bonar Law was emphatically of the same opinion. As Chancellor of the Exchequer, who had to face the continued imposition of heavy taxes, he did not want to be confronted with the
statement that he had, like the French Finance Minister, misled
the taxpayer into the comfortable belief that Germany would pay.*

The only reference I made to reparations during the election
campaign was a few days before the poll in a speech I delivered
at Bristol and it was intended to depress exalted hopes. The words
I used were carefully considered at a conversation I had with the
Chancellor of the Exchequer before I went down to Bristol. We
both realised that at this stage it would be impossible to suggest
a figure. There was no previous experience or precedent that
would help us. Germany must pay to the utmost of her capacity,
but the payment must not be exacted by methods which would
injure the recipients.

These are the words I used, and I challenge anyone to find a
single sentence in the declaration I then made which committed
the Government to the recovery of vast sums of money from
Germany:

. . . Now I come to the second question I mean to talk about, and
that is the question of indemnity. (Cheers.) Who is to foot the bill?
(A voice—"Germany.") I am again going to talk to you quite frankly
about this. By the jurisprudence of every civilized country in the
world, in any lawsuit, the loser pays. It is not a question of vengeance,
it is a question of justice. It means that the judge and the court have
decided that one party is in the wrong. He has challenged judgment.
By the law of every civilized country in the world the party who is
guilty of the wrong pays the costs. (Cheers.) There is absolutely no
doubt about the principle. What we hope for in future is that in dealings between nations the same principle shall be established as in
dealings between individuals—the same principles of right and wrong.
If you do that, it is inevitable that the nation that does the wrong and

* Klotz: "L'Allemagne paiera."

challenges a lawsuit to determine it must pay the costs. (Cheers.) (A voice—"In full.") I am coming to that. Certainly in full, if they have got it. But if you do not mind, listen to what I have got to say to you right through to the end.

There is another reason why Germany should pay the bill, apart from the general principles of equity. The war has cost them less than it has cost us. We have had to maintain and build up a great Army for it. We have had to maintain a gigantic Navy. We have had practically to police the seas of the world. Our soldiers are very much better paid, and their dependents are very much better provided for, than is the case with Germany, and, therefore, the cost, as far as we are concerned, is very much greater than that of Germany. The cost to us is, I think, eight thousand millions—a gigantic sum. Germany's bill is about six or seven thousand millions. It is absolutely indefensible that a person who is in the wrong and who has lost should pay less than the person who was declared to be in the right and who has won (cheers), and to the extent of the difference there is no doubt that that extra thousand millions, for a population of 45 millions, whereas their population is 70 millions—to that extent it would handicap us in competition for the future. Well, that is unfair. (Cheers.)

I am now coming to the reason why Germany should pay to the utmost limit of her capacity. Why have I always said "up to the limit of capacity"? Well, I will tell you at once. It is not right for the Government to raise any false hopes in the community, and least of all is it right to do so on the eve of an election. You have no right to mislead your public at any time, and I venture to claim that during the whole of this war I have never misled the public (cheers), and I am not going to do so now, whatever the result. (Cheers.) If I were to say to you, "Not merely ought Germany to pay, but we can expect every penny," I should be doing so without giving you the whole of the facts. Let me give you the facts. We consulted our financial advisers—not international financiers, those are not our financial advisers—(cheers)—I mean the financial advisers you get in every Government Department. They were doubtful. I will give you their reasons. Before the war it was estimated that the wealth of Germany was between 15,000 and 20,000 millions. That is the figure that was given as an estimate. The bill is 24,000 millions, so that if that estimate (of the total assets of Germany) was correct—that is, our estimate before the war—it is quite clear that, even if you take the whole of this wealth away—and you cannot do that, because there are 70,000,000 people who have got to work in order to make that wealth available—there would not be enough. . . .

I have not finished all the story yet. We appointed a very strong committee some weeks ago—the Imperial War Cabinet—to investigate further the capacity of Germany and the whole question. We also recommended to the Allies that we should have an Inter-Allied Commission. The British Imperial Committee has met. The Inter-Allied Commission has not yet met, but I received last night the report of the British Imperial Committee, and you will be glad to hear that they take a more favourable view of the capacity of Germany than do the officials of the Government Departments. They think that the assets of Germany, the wealth of Germany, have been underestimated in the past—that she is wealthier, that she has a greater capacity than we have given her credit for. There is no doubt that Germany herself thinks so. If that is so, you may find that the capacity will go a pretty long way. (Laughter.)

There are only two conditions which, if I were responsible, I should make, and here the Committee agree with me. There must not be an army of occupation, a large army of occupation, kept in Germany indefinitely in order to hold the country down. (Hear, hear.) That simply means keeping hundreds of thousands of young men from this country occupying Germany, maybe for a generation, maybe for more, withdrawing them from industry, whilst at the same time you would have to keep an Army in order to maintain your Empire. That would be bad business. Besides, it would simply provoke fresh conflict, fresh wars, and instead of coming to an end of war we should be simply manufacturing fresh wars.

The second condition which the Government would make, and which the Committee agree with, is that the interest on the money must not be paid by dumping sweated goods in this country (cheers), and you must remember, if the 1,200 millions had to be paid in sweated goods it would be something which would be far more than anything we have ever experienced. I should say the balance of trade between Germany and this country before the war was hardly 20 or 30 millions. If you had to take hundreds of millions of goods from Germany, whether it were coal, or ships, or cotton, or what not, well, then greater injury would be inflicted upon the industries of this country than anything you could possibly hope to gain by merely exacting an indemnity. The Committee are of opinion that it will not be necessary to do either. This is what the Committee have reported to the Cabinet. It will not be necessary to have an army of occupation. They believe that the pressure can be brought to bear upon them by economic and international means, and that will be best of all. I agree. In the second place, they believe it to be quite unnecessary in order to exact an indemnity to take a large consignment every year of German goods in order to pay the cost of the indemnity.

The only other point I should like to make about the indemnity is this: Germany has a war debt of six or seven thousand millions. It is quite clear that, when you come to the settlement, the cost of the Allies ought to come before their own war debt—the first charge to be in favour of what is due to the Allies rather than in favour of what is due to them. (Cheers.) That is justice. It is what one would apply in any judgment between man and man. The costs of the winning party must come before the costs of the litigant who has lost the suit. Therefore, whatever our indemnity is, it must come before the six or seven thousand millions which is owing to the Germans themselves in their own country.

That is the position, and I have given it quite frankly to you—the whole of the position. Let me summarize. First, as far as justice is concerned, we have an absolute right to demand the whole cost of the war from Germany. The second point is that we propose to demand the whole cost of the war. (Cheers.) The third point is that when you come to the exacting of it you must exact it in such a way that it does not do more harm to the country that receives it than to the country which is paying it. The fourth point is that the Committee appointed by the British Cabinet believe that it can be done. The fifth point is that the Allies, who are in exactly the same boat as we are, because they have also got a claim to great indemnities, are examining the proposal in conjunction with us. When the report comes it will be presented to the Peace Conference, which will put our demands together, and, whatever they are, they must come in front of the German war debt. (Cheers.) You may depend upon it that the first consideration in the minds of the Allies will be the interests of the people upon whom Germany has made war, and not the interests of the German people who have been guilty of this crime against humanity.

In fact I repeated to the electors on the eve of the poll the precautionary counsel which I had already given to the Cabinet. No other allusion was made by me to this topic in any of my election speeches.

In 1919 public opinion both here and in France was out and out in favour of making Germany pay. Everywhere the people were confronted with unparalleled losses in life and property. In Britain the total cost of the War was £7,000,000,000, and in addition the capital charge in respect of war pensions alone was estimated at £3,000,000,000. Taxation was high beyond the vituperative nightmares of the pre-war period. In those happy days a shilling in the pound on the income tax, with a moderate super-tax, was regarded as profligate. In the early summer of 1914 I had to face a serious split in my own party when I proposed an extra twopence to meet urgent social needs. At the end of the War a rich man contributed two-thirds of his income to the Exchequer, and even moderate incomes paid several shillings in the pound. The prospect of continuing such exactions for a generation appalled all who had comfortable incomes. For the immense material damage and expenditure incurred by the Allies in the War, German reparations provided the sole hope of recoupment, and it is not surprising that in estimating her capacity to pay, the wish became a hope, and the hope sometimes ripened into a confident anticipation. Any suggestion to the contrary was angrily resented. Germany was responsible. Why should not Germany pay? Someone must pay. Why the victim whilst the culprit was let off? That represented the opinion of the ordinary taxpayer.

Nevertheless I stood persistently by these three principles that I laid down in my Bristol speech: (1) that Germany must pay for the damage she had caused, up to the limit of her capacity; (2) that the extent of her capacity to pay could only be ascertained after a careful enquiry and that an investigation into that question would be undertaken; and (3) that we must be prepared to scale down our ultimate demands below the total of what was due, to the level of what could be paid by Germany without inflicting injury on the trade of the recipients by the methods of payment.

The view that Germany must be made to pay was held no less definitely by responsible statesmen of all parties in this country. On the day when I made my Bristol speech, Mr. Asquith, addressing the electors of East Fife, said he was in favour of exacting from the wrongdoer the uttermost farthing. The following day, at Pittenween, in reply to the question: "Will you make the Germans pay for the war?" he replied: "Yes, I am in agreement on that matter with what the Prime Minister said yesterday." And on December 13th, asked at Ladybank: "Are you prepared to see that Germany pays to the last halfpenny?" he answered:

"I have said so at at least twelve meetings." Similar views were expressed on Labour platforms. Mr. Henderson, speaking at Cardiff on December 7th, 1918, said: "Full indemnity he would support, exacting from Germany the fullest possible restitution for devastation and wrong-doing outside legal warfare. . . . How the Germans should be taxed to meet indemnity it was not our business to dictate."

If one thought it worth rummaging amongst the speeches and election addresses of the candidates of all parties at that election, one would find the same sentiments echoed about Germany's liability to pay and the resolve of each particular aspirant for electoral favour to compel payment to the last available penny. In this respect there was no distinction between Government and anti-Government candidates. It can hardly, therefore, be said to have been an issue at the election.

In so far as it was an electoral issue at all it was made so by Lord Northcliffe's attempt to create a suspicion against the Government that its members, and more particularly its Chief, were not in earnest in their insistence on the payment of reparations by Germany. He based his attack on that part of my Bristol speech which indicated grave doubts as to the capacity of Germany to pay the Allies the full amount of the damage inflicted upon them. His papers criticised my policy on these lines. When I was addressing an election meeting at Leeds I received the following telegram from Lord Northcliffe:

The public are expecting you to say definitely amount of cash reparation we are to get from Germany—they are very dissatisfied with the phrase quote limit of her capacity unquote which they say may mean anything or nothing they are aware that France has named her amount—I am apprehensive of serious trouble in the country over this matter.

This telegram was obviously intended for publication if I failed to give a satisfactory answer. I replied promptly:

You are quite wrong about France—stop—No Ally has named figure—stop—Allies in complete agreement as to demand for indemnity—stop—Interallied Commission will investigate on behalf of all on identical principles—Dont be always making mischief.

Neither of these two wires was published. I received no answer to my wire, but Lord Northcliffe pursued his campaign to the end.

I cannot find that any candidate on either side, except Mr. Bonar Law and myself, thought it necessary to utter a cautionary word in restraint of anticipation. No responsible persons committed themselves publicly to any figure. Most of them, like Mr. Asquith, declared that Germany would have to pay "to the last farthing."

The Economist, the most restrained and responsible of the financial journals, in its issue of December 7th, 1918, while pointing out that the Allied claims on Germany must be in accordance with the terms of the Armistice—i.e. for reparation, not for a war indemnity—contended that Germany could be made to pay.

As for collecting the bill without damaging our industries, this should not be a very difficult matter. Germany, it is true, can only meet the bill that the Allies will present by delivering up ships, plant, securities, gold, and any goods that she can produce in excess of what she needs for subsistence, efficiency, and maintenance of productive power. . . . If she is to pay, that productive power has to be maintained, since it is in goods that the bulk of the payment will have to be made. This means that she will be a keen competitor in all the markets of the world with our products and those of our Allies. So she would have been in any case, and the only effect of her having to pay damages will be that a large part of the profits of her competition will go in enabling us and our Allies to meet part of our War debts. Our War debts raised abroad amount to nearly £1,300,000,000 sterling, and we have sold abroad many hundreds of millions worth of securities which we could gladly replace. If by selling goods Germany is able to pay us in bills of other countries, we shall be able to use them to comfortable advantage. . . .

In the following April, during the peace negotiations, Mr. Bonar Law spoke in the House of Commons repeating my warning against cherishing extravagantly high hopes of what could be extracted in payment from Germany. *The Economist* of April 5th, 1919, challenged these doubts. It wrote:

In normal times, when it is allowed to do business on business methods, Lombard Street has little difficulty in transferring any amount of money between nations that are in economic communication. . . . Germany's power to pay is not, as Mr. Bonar Law seemed to think, any the less because before the War she had an adverse balance on visible goods of £70,000,000 a year. We had an adverse balance of about £130,000,000, but we were investing abroad about £200,000,000 a year, according to the usual received estimate. Germany must also have been investing abroad, and any sum that she then had available for investment abroad she can, if her industry is able to grow to its old figures, put into meeting the debt to her creditors on war account. As her industry expands that power will increase.

These quotations sufficiently illustrate and support my claim that City authority of the highest order was far more confident than were the politicians that large sums in respect of reparations should and could be paid by Germany. As to the question whether the claim of the Allies on Germany was to be for an indemnity which would cover the cost of the War, or only for reparations in respect of civil damages suffered by their people, it was obvious that Germany's capacity to pay would be exhausted long before the bill for reparations alone had been fully met, so that the question as to whether what we received from her should be classed as an indemnity or a reparation payment became a matter of purely academic interest.

The French official view as to the prospect of recovering large sums from Germany was much more sanguine than ours. The late M. Klotz was Clemenceau's Finance Minister, and as such attended discussions on the indemnity question. M. Clemenceau once said of him that he was the only Jew he ever met who knew nothing of finance! After this cruel comment, it will surprise no one to read that M. Klotz held always to the view that Germany must and could pay in full. In the Chamber of Deputies, "*L'Allemagne paiera!*" was his answer to every financial claim or complaint. Men of great ability like M. Tardieu, and other French statesmen of high reputation like M. Doumer, afterwards President of the Republic, shared that view. The late M. Loucheur, on the other hand, was more doubtful. He was shrewd, clear-headed and practical, but he lacked the necessary moral courage to express unpopular views. He always shrank from the thankless and risky duty of telling his countrymen what the true facts were. He knew Germany could not pay the immense sums expected from her and frankly admitted that unpleasant but incontrovertible truth in confidential discussions. I think he must have warned M. Clemenceau in private that his Finance Minister was raising hopes that could not be realised. But in the state of French opinion at that time neither of them dared to give expression to his misgivings. Even Clemenceau's tried courage shrank from the unwelcome task of throwing a bucket of cold water on hopes inflamed with victory.

Our own representatives on the Reparation Committee at the Conference were Mr. W. M. Hughes, Lord Cunliffe, and Lord Sumner. I placed Lord Sumner on this Committee because as a judge of great distinction, capacity and experience and a man who possessed one of the clearest, coolest and best-balanced brains on the Bench, he could bring to bear on this difficult question a judicially moderate view. Lord Cunliffe, coming from the Bank of England with a wide experience of business and high finance, made himself responsible for the highest estimate given by anyone of Germany's capacity to pay, which he put at £24,000,000,000. Lord Sumner, so far from exerting any restraining influence upon Lord Cunliffe's strange lapse into megalomania, himself caught the infection and gave logical and literary form to its ravings. It is what happens when men of natural and disciplined sobriety of mind suddenly lose control of their judgment. But what makes it more remarkable is the astonishing fact that the contagion spread far and wide amongst their associates. I am not aware that any leading British, French or American authority in financial or economic circles at that time seriously challenged the proposition that very large sums could be obtained from Germany. The British Civil Service alone kept its head.

M. Tardieu reveals in his book, "The Truth about the Treaty," that the American experts considered the following as the maximum payments possible:

	Gold Marks
Payments before 1921	20,000,000,000
Payments from 1922 to 1931	60,000,000,000
Payments from 1932 to 1941	80,000,000,000
Payments from 1942 to 1951	100,000,000,000
	260,000,000,000

or say £13,000,000,000

The total of these payments, allowing for interest, represented at current rates a present value of 140,000 million gold marks.

M. Tardieu admits that at the Peace Congress I was opposed to these large estimates, and records that I declared in regard to them: "We are going to throw Germany into the arms of the Bolsheviks. Besides, for her to pay the sum which we have in mind, and which it is just she should pay, she would have to occupy a still greater place in the markets than before the War. Is that to our interest?"

I have no recollection of ever having heard M. Clemenceau express any opinion on the amount of German reparations, or the capacity of Germany to pay. He generally listened to all the discussions about reparations without himself expressing any definite conclusions. He was not interested in figures or finance. Statistics bored him.

At the discussion which subsequently occurred at the Imperial Cabinet on the Hughes Report, the Chairman of the Committee, Mr. Long, and Sir George Foster explained how they came to arrive at their conclusions. The whole discussion·throws a light on the attitude of the British Government and the Empire towards the prospect of recovering large sums from Germany. Mr. Hughes first gave his ideas on the subject:

He reminded the Imperial War Cabinet that the Committee which had sat under his chairmanship had been appointed to inquire into firstly the economic effects of any indemnity, with regard to which some doubts had been expressed, secondly the amount of the indemnity and thirdly the mode of payment. The Committee did not consider whether under the terms of the Armistice we were entitled to ask for an indemnity at all. It had suggested, however, that no just distinction could really be drawn between payment by way of indemnity for the cost of the war and payment by way of reparation for damage done by the enemy to property. The only reason why in paragraph 2 the Report said that reparation should have precedence was in order to indicate the urgency of reparation in such cases as that of Belgium, where it meant restoration of property that had been destroyed and of materials that had been taken away.

As regards the question of the economic effects of indemnity, they had had before them the investigations by Professor Ashley and Mr. Keynes on the French indemnity after the war of 1870, which showed that the receipt of an indemnity by Germany had not been harmful to that country, and, broadly speaking, it was more advantageous to be a creditor country and receive an indemnity than to bear the cost of the war.

As regards the question of the amount which Germany could pay, the evidence before the Committee was of the vaguest character. Lord Cunliffe, as the result of his inquiries in the City, came to the conclusion that Germany could pay 1,200 million pounds a year or even more. The 1912 Report of the Dresdner Bank gave some remarkable figures of the rate of German progress. As far as the evidence went, the Committee concluded that it leaned towards the probability of Germany being able to pay a very substantial amount. The Committee looking at the matter as it would be regarded by a tribunal thought it right to state the amount Germany ought to pay, leaving upon the Germans themselves the onus of proving their inability to pay the whole of the sum demanded. It was no use starting out with the assumption that Germany could not pay; he did not think that such a view could be taken up publicly, it could at most be whispered with bated breath. Our business was not to act as advocates for Germany, but as champions for our own country. If Germany stood in our position she would undoubtedly make us pay to the full, and we could do it. He quite realised that the matter would have to be referred to an Allied Commission. The question was, what was to be the attitude of the Empire's delegates on that Commission? He considered that Germany would have a stable Government, and thought there was no country less likely to fall under the sway of Bolshevism.

It will be seen that Mr. Hughes' confidence in the German capacity had been temporarily—but only temporarily—shaken. There is not the same note of assured conviction in this speech as to Germany's ability to pay £24,000,000,000 that was so apparent in the Report.

LORD MILNER suggested that the most certain way of "bolshevising" Germany would be to put an excessive burden on her.

MR. CHURCHILL asked if Mr. Hughes had investigated the effects which would be produced upon the ordinary working-class household in Germany by an indemnity? He had reckoned that the full indemnity proposed in Mr. Hughes' Report would mean that each household would have to manufacture £85 worth of goods for export in a year over and above sustaining itself.

MR. HUGHES replied that the Committee had been more concerned in considering the effects upon the working-class household in Great Britain, or in Australia, if the Germans did not pay an indemnity. Of course the Germans were human beings and had to live in the world, but not at other people's expense. He only wanted to give them a spur to constant industry. A salutary course of industry was the best cure for Bolshevism.

To sum up, all he wanted was that the instructions to the British delegates on the Allied Commission should be to endeavour to secure the greatest possible indemnity which Germany could pay without damage to our own finances and industries and without danger to the peace of the world.

MR. MONTAGU asked Mr. Hughes how the indemnity could be exacted without an army of occupation, a point on which his Report had laid special emphasis?

MR. HUGHES replied that the circumstances were such that the economic and financial pressure which we could apply would compel Germany to pay, providing she had the capacity to do so. If she did not have that capacity even an army of occupation could not get it from her.

THE PRIME MINISTER thought that the instructions should certainly include a proviso that the collection of indemnity should not only not involve economic injury to the Empire or create a menace to the peace of the world, but should also not require an army of occupation for its collection.

MR. LONG reminded the Imperial War Cabinet of the fact that Mr. Hughes' Committee had been required to present its Report in a very few days. His own conclusion as a member of the Committee had been that no one could give any information really worth having as to Germany's capacity to pay. But the fact that men of such standing in the business world as Lord Cunliffe and Mr. Gibbs were emphatic in their belief that a large indemnity could be imposed, *and that similar conclusions had also been arrived at in the Reports of the Federation of British Industries and the Associated Chambers of Commerce,* would create a very awkward situation if the Government did not press its full demands in accordance with the cost of the war to ourselves. This would be without prejudice to fuller information disclosing reasons for modifying that demand.

SIR ROBERT BORDEN concurred in the view expressed by the Committee that Germany, subject to the considerations just mentioned, which in his mind were controlling considerations, should pay a full indemnity. He agreed that it would be for the peace of the world that a Power which had broken that peace should be punished. On the other hand if the Report really was a statement of what Germany was in fact capable of paying, he did not find it convincing and was not prepared to concur in it. If one applied its conclusions to the case of Canada, which had about one-eighth of the population which would be left to Germany after the loss of Alsace-Lorraine and Posen, one would find that Canada would have to pay an indemnity of 150 million pounds a year over and above the cost of maintaining the government of the country and developing its resources. Even with the enormous natural resources which Canada had in proportion to her population, that would be impossible. He doubted if Canada could pay even one-tenth of that amount.

SIR GEORGE FOSTER said that the Committee was appointed to report to the Imperial War Cabinet, and he thought for the purpose of enabling the Imperial War Cabinet the better to reach a decision about the matter afterwards. He was under the impression the Report would not be made public. Such a Committee had not the time nor the sources of information at its disposal to enable it to determine what Germany could pay without injury to her or to us. There were three sources of evidence available to the Committee in regard to the capacity of Germany to pay:—a Report of the Board of Trade; the evidence of Mr. Hirst, who estimated that Germany could pay 125 million pounds annually; and that of Sir Charles Addis, who estimated that Germany could pay from 60 to 65 million pounds annually. Apart from such evidence the Report of the Committee was based on the opinions of its members, framed in each case on such information as each possessed. He had signed the Report subject to certain protests, in order to expedite its consideration by the Imperial War Cabinet. He agreed with the Report so far as it was in favour of presenting a bill for the total cost of the war to the parties which had wrongfully originated and carried on the war. This would be a helpful lesson to mankind. He was in favour of reparation plus indemnity—the one grew out of the other. We should first have reparation and then indemnity. Germany should be made to pay to the last farthing, with the proviso that regard must be had to her capacity to pay and to the effect of the mode of payment of the indemnity on the economic interests of the Allies. But when an attempt was made to fix the precise amount which could be extracted from the enemy Powers, then examination must be made by some commission with more information than was in the possession of the Committee.

MR. BONAR LAW said he did not object to our taking the line that we wanted Germany to pay up to her capacity, but he would have protested if the intention had been to ask for the Cabinet to agree to the suggestion that the obtaining from Germany of any such sum as mentioned in the report was possible. He did not agree with the view that President Wilson might not urge that we were not dealing fairly with his fourteen points in this matter. If on examination it was found that all Germany was able to pay was what would cover reparation, then it was foolish to quarrel about indemnities. On the 2nd December they had agreed with the Allies—apart from the United States—to appoint an Inter-Allied Commission to examine what Germany could pay. Until they knew the result of that enquiry why should they raise the question of principle?

MR. LLOYD GEORGE said that . . . unless President Wilson was prepared to pool the whole cost of the war, and for the United States to take its share of the whole, he was not in a position to reject our claims for indemnity.

As regards the figure claimed for Reparations, he did not believe that that sum could be obtained.

MR. HUGHES said he agreed that it might not be possible to get that sum. But it was not for us to limit our demand, but for Germany to prove to our satisfaction that she could not pay all that she ought to do.

MR. LLOYD GEORGE continuing, said he understood the German debt was between 6,000 and 7,000 million pounds, and the annual charge on it about 300 millions, which she would have to pay to her investors. In his view, Germany's debt to us should be a first charge on her resources, and the payment of interest on her own national debt should come after our claims had been met.

Subject to the above considerations, he was in favour of appointing three delegates as members of the proposed Inter-Allied Commission. They should find out what Germany could pay without damage to us. He suggested that the instructions to the delegates should be:

"To endeavour to secure from Germany the greatest possible indemnity she can pay consistently with the economic well-being of the British Empire and the peace of the world, and without involving an army of occupation in Germany for its collection."

SIR ROBERT BORDEN said that President Wilson in his fourteen points spoke of reparation and nothing else and thus by implication excluded indemnities. We had spoken of compensation for damage done, but even that was confined to invaded and occupied territories. If President Wilson should put this contention forward to the Prime Minister and Mr. Balfour, what answer could they make?

MR. BONAR LAW suggested that they could point to the great deal of feeling which prevailed in this country on the subject. He, however, hoped they would not discuss the matter further, but wait for reply of the Inter-Allied Commission. He knew of no way of obtaining payment except by gold, securities, and exports, nor did he see a way of our getting more than reparation without being damaged ourselves.

MR. LLOYD GEORGE, in reply to a question from Mr. Montagu, said that while they had spoken during the discussion of Germany only, they did not, of course, exclude the other enemy Powers.

The Imperial War Cabinet accepted the instructions to the British delegates at the Inter-Allied Commission on Reparation and Indemnities as proposed by Mr. Lloyd George, namely:

"To endeavour to secure from Germany the greatest possible indemnity she can pay consistently with the economic well-being of the British Empire and the peace of the world, and without involving an army of occupation in Germany for its collection."

At the first Interallied Conference held after the Armistice early in December, the first discussion which took place was on the subject of reparations. In view of misrepresentations as to the attitude of the political leaders at the time, it is worth setting forth the purport of these discussions with some fullness, as it discloses the fact that the Allied Governments were entirely in the dark as to what indemnity could be exacted from Germany for the damage inflicted by her in the War. A genuine doubt existed not as to Germany's legal and moral responsibility to pay full damages but as to the extent of her capacity. It was agreed that this question should be referred to financial and economic experts. Here is a summary of the discussions:

MR. LLOYD GEORGE said that this was a very difficult question. Public opinion in all the Allied countries demanded that we should obtain as much from Germany as we possibly could. The question arose, therefore, as to how much we could get. The general public were commonly under some illusion in this matter as to the sum which it was possible to extract from Germany. Germany had no very large quantity of foreign securities left. She had only about £150,000,000 in gold and not much else. Hence, in order to strengthen the hand of all the Allied Governments in this matter, he suggested the establish-

ment of an Inter-Allied Commission of Experts to examine what
Germany, Austria and Turkey could pay. The British Government
had set up their own Committee and doubtless the other Allied Governments had done the same. An Inter-Allied Committee, however, would
greatly strengthen the Governments. . . .

M. CLEMENCEAU and SIGNOR ORLANDO said that only one Committee was contemplated. [The Italians were anxious that Germany
and Austria should be jointly responsible for all the Allied claims.]

SIGNOR ORLANDO said that he was in complete accord with Mr. Lloyd
George that a commission ought to be constituted and that it should
be Inter-Allied in character, and should study all the problems of compensation and indemnity affecting Germany and Austria. The question
of the juridical responsibility of Austria-Hungary was really a juridical
question. The Austro-Hungarian State had disappeared and the question arose as to who was responsible for the bill. This was a juridical
and not a political question. It was a question of international law for
jurists to advise upon and did not differ very materially from a private
legal action. When this aspect of the question was being discussed,
jurists ought to be associated with financial experts. Another question
which arose was that of the solidarity of enemy Powers for damage,
which was also a question of principle. For example, Italy had been
fighting in the main against Austria, but Germany had also inflicted
damage upon her. German troops had fought with the Austrians, and
Italian ships had been sunk by German submarines. In fact the worst
damage had perhaps been inflicted on the Italians by Germany. It
was most important to consider the question of Germany's collective
responsibility with Austria for damage. When the Commission had
considered these questions and how much the enemy countries could
pay, it would be for the Governments to consider what special re-
mission, if any, should be made to the constituent nation of Austria-
Hungary.

·   ·   ·   ·   ·

M. CLEMENCEAU suggested that the Commission would probably
have to divide up into several sub-Commissions to examine the legal,
financial, and other aspects of the problem. This would need further
detailed investigation of German resources, such as railways, mines,
etc. Another reason why the size of the Commission was not very
important was that there was unlikely to be any great divergence of
opinion in principle.

MR. LLOYD GEORGE agreed with this view, as the great difficulty
was to ascertain whence compensation and reparation could be obtained.

·   ·   ·   ·   ·

BARON SONNINO suggested that some committee ought to examine from the Allied point of view the amount of the damage and the justice of the various claims put forward. It was very important that these claims should be based on some common principle.

M. CLEMENCEAU suggested that each nation ought to prepare its own claims and bring the list before a committee. How, for example, could he say what Italy ought to claim? Or how could Baron Sonnino say what France ought to claim?

MR. BONAR LAW expressed a preference for M. Clemenceau's method.

MR. BALFOUR suggested that there ought to be a committee to consider the order in which the damage claimed should be recompensed. M. CLEMENCEAU agreed in the expediency of this.

MR. LLOYD GEORGE thought that M. Clemenceau's proposal was the right one. Each country ought to make out its own claim, but the first point to establish was how much the enemy could pay.

MR. BALFOUR supported Baron Sonnino's point of view that there should be some common principle established. Otherwise each nation would work out its claims on a different basis.

BARON SONNINO strongly urged that there should be some common denominator on which the calculations should be based; e.g., a bathing place might put in claims on the ground that it had lost all the patrons owing to the action of the enemy. Would that be a just claim? Then there ought to be principles on which trading claims and family claims should be based.

The Conference agreed that each Allied and Associated Government should enumerate its claims for reparation due from the enemy states, and that these claims should subsequently be referred for examination by an Inter-Allied Commission which would be nominated when the claims were ready.

M. CLEMENCEAU urged the importance of consulting the American Government in regard to this.

MR. LLOYD GEORGE agreed.

The Conference agreed that Mr. Balfour should notify the conclusion to Colonel House.

The Plenary Session of the Peace Conference of January 25th, 1919 (the second Plenary Session of the Conference—the first, of 18th January having been almost entirely formal)—set up various commissions, among them being the "Commission on the Reparation of Damage."

The terms of reference of this Commission were:

That a Commission be appointed with not more than three representatives apiece from each of the Five Great Powers and not more than two representatives apiece from Belgium, Greece, Poland, Roumania, and Serbia, to examine and report:

1. On the amount which the enemy countries ought to pay by way of reparation;
2. On what they are capable of paying; and
3. By what method, in what form and within what time payment should be made.

By February 5th, two delegates had been added from Czechoslovakia, and by February 24th, two from Portugal, bringing up the total number of the Commission to 29. The British representatives, as I have already stated, consisted of Mr. W. M. Hughes, Lord Cunliffe and Lord Sumner.

At the second meeting, three sub-committees were appointed:

Sub-Committee 1.—Valuation of damage.
Sub-Committee 2.—Study of the financial capacity of the Enemy States and of their means of payment.
Sub-Committee 3.—Measures of control and guarantees.

Thereafter the Commission proceeded to spend a great deal of time in trying to agree as to the scope to be given to the term: "Reparation of Damage." Memoranda were put in by the French, British, Italian, Polish, Serbian and American delegates to the Commission.

On the general principles of reparation, all the memoranda except the American claimed that reparation should cover the whole of the damage caused by the War. The U.S.A. memorandum held that no reparation could be exacted unless:

(a) it is clearly due in accordance with accepted principles of international law; or
(b) it is stipulated for in the understanding embodied in President Wilson's points regarding restoration of invaded territories, and in the qualification of these clauses by the Allied Governments conveyed to Germany in the note of the Secretary of State of the United States of November 5, 1918.

The Note of November 5th referred to—the Lansing Note—I have already quoted textually in the chapter which gives an account of the negotiations preceding the Armistice. (Page 39.)

The very marked difference of view between the American and the other delegations as to the scope of reparation claims led to prolonged debate. M. Klotz, speaking on behalf of France, insisted that the Allies were perfectly free to claim the whole cost of the War. The British and Italian members of the Reparation Commission took the same view.

Belgium was not concerned so much with the legal argument as with the practical one, that if the other Allies piled up huge claims for war costs, her chances of getting reparation in full for her losses grew small, as the ultimate dividend in the pound which Germany would be able to pay on a huge bill would be scanty. So the Belgian delegate, Van den Heuvel, was opposed to the inclusion of full war costs by any of the Allies except Belgium. Serbia, however, declared in favour of charging full war costs against the enemy.

The debate dragged on for several meetings. Finally, as so much seemed to turn on the interpretation of the Allied reservation in the Note of the 5th of November, 1918, it was decided that this issue should be referred to the Supreme War Council by which the reservation had been framed. The resolution as finally revised at the tenth meeting of the Commission on February 24th, 1919, ran:

The Commission decided to transmit to the President of the Peace Conference for submission to the Supreme War Council as constituted on the 4th of November, 1918, the following question:

"Would an affirmation of Mr. Klotz' motion, viz., 'That the rights of the Allied and Associated Powers are all-inclusive,' be contrary to the intentions of the members of the Supreme War Council (as then constituted) as expressed in the American Note of November 5th, 1918?"

With this resolution, the further discussion on the issue of whether the Allies' claim for reparation should be confined to the limits proposed by the American Delegation, or should be given a wider connotation, passed out of the hands of the Commission, and came under the direct examination of the Heads of the Peace Conference.

At the time when this resolution was adopted, the "Council of

Ten" was temporarily suspended, since M. Clemenceau had been wounded on the 19th of February by a would-be assassin; I had been compelled, by urgent and occasionally disturbing problems arising out of demobilisation of men and workshops, to visit England, and was away until March 5th; and President Wilson had similarly been obliged to visit America, and was absent until March 14th.

At this stage the British delegates to the First Sub-Committee of the Reparation Commission issued their statement setting out a preliminary valuation of the damage for which the British delegates proposed to submit a claim. This covered (a) shipping losses—ships sunk or damaged, loss of user, loss of cargoes, loss of life; (b) loss of British property in Allied countries through operations of war; (c) losses through bombardments and air raids; (d) cost of war pensions; (e) subventions to food costs and increases of old-age pensions; (f) separation allowances; (g) external war debts; (h) advances to Allies and Dominions; (i) additional budgetary cost of the War. Various other possible claims were held in reserve. I was definitely of the opinion that we were committed by the Armistice terms not to demand an indemnity which would include the cost of prosecuting the War. The Cabinet, to whose notice I brought this detailed statement of claim, accepted my view on the limitations imposed upon us by the terms of the Armistice. I communicated this decision to our representative on the Reparation Commission. The only question therefore left was what was covered by the words "injury to civilians" which were comprised in the conditions under which Germany agreed to surrender.

After a good deal of reflection and discussion with my colleagues, I decided that the British claim for compensation for personal injuries to civilians should be confined to those injuries which had been officially recognised by the Government in the form of pensions either to the injured civilians themselves or, in case of death, to their relatives and dependants. I had two reasons for putting forward this claim. The first is very powerfully stated in memoranda by General Smuts and Lord Sumner, from which I quote later on. The second was that Germany could be expected to pay the full claims of France and Belgium alone for material damage. Unless, therefore, Britain could include pensionable injuries, her share of the total compensation received from Germany would be insignificant in comparison with that received by other Allies, whose real financial burdens through the War were no greater, and some of which were considerably less per head of their population, than those sustained by the British Empire. In the aggregate the expenses incurred by us and the losses directly and indirectly inflicted upon us were heavier than those of any Allied or Associated country.

I had always realised that the total amount which Germany was capable of paying was but a small percentage of the total for which she was morally responsible or liable under the terms of the Armistice; and that, therefore, as far as Britain was concerned, the categories included were a matter of considerable financial importance to us. It made no difference to Germany, but for us it was a question of hundreds of millions of pounds. Our total damages to property would not reach £1,000,000,000, but our expenditure in the War, our loss in international trade and transport and our burden in pensions exceeded that of any other belligerent. In any civil action for damages all these items for damages could have been legitimately claimed. We were precluded by the Armistice terms from claiming in respect of war costs and trade losses, but the Lansing Note enabled us to demand reparation in respect of personal injuries for which we had provided compensation to the sufferers.

This decision is the principal ground on which the Versailles reparations clauses, if not the Versailles Treaty, has been assailed by those anxious to find fault. They have been denounced as a breach of faith having regard to the terms of the Armistice upon the basis of which Germany surrendered. Although the addition of that claim made no practical difference to the position of Germany, as she could not pay two shillings in the pound on the rest, still the bankruptcy of the debtor is no justification for a fraudulent claim by the creditors. The fairness of our claim depends upon whether it was an evasion of the terms of the Armistice. There can be no doubt that the claim was on its merits a

legitimate one, for it represented a real financial obligation incurred by the Allies to individual sufferers from enemy action,
and which they were then actually meeting as it fell due. The
point is whether it was covered by the terms of the Lansing Note,
which was an interpretation of the Fourteen Points insisted upon
by the Allies and conveyed by the American Government to the
Germans before the Armistice was signed. Did the pension claim
go beyond the Lansing clause? The American document confined claims to those for the physical restoration of Belgium and
the occupied areas of France, Roumania, Serbia and Montenegro;
to compensation for physical damage to property of civilians,
and to compensation for all damages directly caused by injuries
to civilians directly due to German military operations. As a
good deal turned upon the interpretation to be placed upon this
particular category, it is advisable to quote the explanation given
by the American experts themselves of the meaning and limits
of these words in the Lansing Note sent to the German Government before they signed the Armistice:

It is not, however, as easy to determine what is injury to a person
as it is to determine what is damage to property. It is possible of course
to limit damage to person to a physical injury occasioned directly as a
rifle wound. Damage to person should be given a more liberal construction than this. In view of the rather adequate provision made for
damage to property, particularly in the invaded areas, it is both wise
and just to construe damage to person in a liberal sense which will
not invite the charge of according a special sanctity to property as
distinguished from life and labour. We construe, therefore, damage
to the civilian population to include damage resulting through injury
to civilians in the way of death, personal injury, enforced labour and
loss of opportunity to labour or to secure a just reward for labour.

On March 30th, 1919, Lord Sumner prepared a long memorandum discussing the question of whether these words would cover
pensionable injuries incurred in actual fighting. His statement
began by examining the legal point as to whether victorious
Powers had a legal right to claim any or all costs of war as reparation—in connection with which he ran over President Wilson's
various pronouncements and the Allied reservation, concluding

that the door was left open for a wide interpretation of reparation claims. The French fought stoutly for this point of view. On this point I felt bound to overrule Lord Sumner and to resist the French contention.

He passed on to argue that "Reparations" and "Costs of the War" were not two diverse and exclusive categories, but overlapping if not identical conceptions:

There is no conflict or opposition between these ideas, and I think no clear guidance is to be found by trying to make one category of "reparation" damage, and another of "cost of the war." The truth is that much "reparation damage" might be described as part of the "cost of the war" to the country concerned.

As to the inclusion of pensions or allowances, he was on more solid ground. His argument here was irresistible:

He [the soldier defending his country] is simply a civilian, called to arms in the cause of justice; his uniform makes no difference; his true position is that he quits civil life only to defend the Commonwealth, and, if he survives, to civil life he will return. I think that History will not find in his case anything to deprive him of civilian rights.

Will it really be contended that the authors of this document (the Allied Reservation) actually intended and had in mind to stipulate for benefits for unenlisted men from which they consciously designed to exclude the uniformed soldier?

He pointed out that of the men called up and enlisted,

great numbers continued to do civil work through unhappily exposing themselves to the risks of war: Labour battalions, stretcher bearers, chaplains, doctors, drivers among the land forces; and at sea the vast naval service which was occupied day in and day out in the perilous duty of mine-sweeping for the protection of the commerce of all nations. . . .

Lord Sumner argued that while in strict logic one might go further on such lines and claim every kind of cost of war, yet without pressing logic to those extremes, the case of the pensions and allowances was so clearly an expense involved for the civilian population that it fell within the scope of the actual terms of the

Allied reservation of 5th November, and must not be ruled out
by the fiat of President Wilson without appeal to legal argument
or common sense.

The most important of all the documents sent to the Council
on this issue was a memorandum submitted by General Smuts
on the 31st of March, 1919. This memorandum argued that by
the reservation known as the Lansing Note, the Allies had made
it clear to the Germans that in their interpretation of President
Wilson's words about "restoration" they included "a general
principle implied of far-reaching scope" which covered "compensation for all damage to the civilian population of the Allies in
their persons or property, which resulted from the German aggression, and whether done on land or sea or from the air. . . ."
The President's limitation to restoration of the invaded territories damaged by the operations of war was clearly abandoned.

General Smuts proceeded to argue with great clarity that the
compensation to which a civilian shopkeeper was entitled for
suffering from a German bombardment was really on all fours
with that to which he was further entitled when, having been
called up to defend his village, he suffered wounds and disablement, or his wife during the absence of her breadwinner was paid
an allowance.

The plain, commonsense construction of the reservation, therefore,
leads to the conclusion that, while direct war expenditure (such as
the pay and equipment of soldiers, the cost of rifles, guns, and ordnance
and all similar expenditure) could perhaps not be recovered from the
Germans, yet disablement pensions to discharged soldiers, or pensions
to widows and orphans or separation allowances paid to their wives
and children during the period of their military service are all items
representing compensation to members of the civilian population for
damage sustained by them, for which the German Government are
liable. . . .

The particular importance of this Smuts memorandum was
that it finally convinced President Wilson that he ought to agree
to the inclusion in the scope of reparations of these charges for
pensions and separation allowances. General Smuts was recognised to be a man of tolerant views, detached from the intensities

of European feeling about the Germans, and in consequence his conclusion on this matter carried great weight. Temperley remarks:

It is of interest to observe that the most generally assailed provision in the treaty, that making Germany responsible for pensions and allowances, was proposed by General Smuts, whom no one can accuse of vindictiveness towards Germany. While there were many who condemned the policy of including pensions in reparation, and it is unquestionably the largest financial item in Germany's indebtedness, it is also well not to forget that there were some high-minded men who supported it.*

After all, there was no substantial difference between the exposition of the Lansing clause by the United States jurists, which I have already quoted, and that which is given by Lord Sumner and General Smuts.

With the production of the Smuts memorandum, and President Wilson's decision to concur in the inclusion of pensions and other allowances in respect of personal injuries in the reparation claim, the main dispute arising under this head was settled. Thereafter the chief business was the drafting of the reparation clauses for the Peace Treaty, and in conjunction therewith the decision as to what deliveries in kind should be demanded, notably of coal. All questions as to what items should be included in the bill to be presented were now agreed amongst the Allies. War costs were dropped by France and pensions incorporated with the willing assent of America. The remaining matters for consideration were, first, how much of her bill Germany could be expected to pay, secondly in what manner she could meet the bill, and thirdly the proportions in which the sum received should be distributed amongst the Allies. On the issue of the total sum which could be recovered from Germany there was just as much difference of opinion between the Allies as had already been exhibited between British experts. The French professed to be confident that Germany was quite capable, given time, of paying the whole bill. Klotz, the French Finance Minister, evinced no doubts on the subject. He was of that hard, merciless type that

* "History of the Peace Conference," Vol. II, p. 14.

gave no thought where money was concerned to anything except cash considerations. The prospect of the suffering inflicted, the hatreds engendered, the old feuds kept alive, the new quarrels provoked, the unrest which would be fomented in Europe, in exacting the last penny, did not move him in the least. His mind and heart were so stuffed with bonds that he had no room left for the humanities. But there were distinguished Frenchmen of a much finer type who agreed with him on the question of what Germany could and must pay. The amiable Doumer, an experienced Minister and future President of the Republic, highly respected by all for his integrity and patriotism—and rightly so— agreed with Klotz. To prove his case he was prepared with a valuation of Germany's opulent assets—land, State forests, railways, docks, coal-mines, factories. How they were to be liquefied for the benefit of the Reparation Fund he could not explain. President Poincaré had no doubt that Germany could pay the whole of the bill, and would do so at the sight of the fixed bayonet pointed at her breast. He had the logical mind which, starting from false or incomplete premises, always arrives unerringly at the wrong conclusion. He harried Clemenceau daily with exhortations not to give in. He only found how thoroughly he had miscalculated four years later when he failed to find his Tom Tiddler's ground in the Ruhr and resigned his office in order to enable another Minister to bear the humiliation of a retirement from an impossible quest. Another equally able man, M. Tardieu, professed and genuinely believed the same comforting doctrines. M. Clemenceau never in my hearing expressed any opinion on financial questions. He delegated all questions relating to figures to those of his colleagues who claimed a closer acquaintance with monetary problems. The view of the British Government I have already given. We were of opinion that no figure could be fixed until (1) we had ascertained the amount of the damage and the cost of restoration; (2) we had enquired more thoroughly into Germany's assets and her ability to pay in negotiable paper or raw material across her own frontiers.

The American estimate fluctuated. An undated memorandum by Mr. Norman Davis, President Wilson's principal financial adviser, gives the view of the U.S.A. delegates on this issue. They were in agreement unanimously after examination of the matter by experts, that Germany could pay within a short period such as two years, a sum of 4,000 to 5,000 million dollars (say £800,000,000 to £1,000,000,000). "Probably all agreed that an additional amount of from $5,000,000,000 to $10,000,000,000 can be paid over a period of years, making a total amount of from $10,000,000,000 to $15,000,000,000 (£3,000,000,000)." So far this corresponds with the opinion expressed by the British Treasury. But they were prepared to go still further.

In addition, the American experts thought there was a strong probability that Germany could pay a further 15,000 million dollars, making a total of £6,000,000,000 in all, if she were allowed to pay half of this in German paper currency. This final figure they subsequently proposed should be inserted in the Treaty. The memorandum used guarded language as to whether it was politically desirable to demand so large a sum, because

(*a*) Germany might refuse to sign;

(*b*) its payment would involve her becoming a competitor with Allied commerce on a scale probably injurious to them;

(*c*) the upshot might well be eventual repudiation, and consequent further disturbance of the peace of the world.

The French urged that Germany was capable of paying a sum of £30,000,000,000. Lord Cunliffe and Lord Sumner proposed £12,000,000,000. The French and the Americans compromised ultimately on a figure of £8,000,000,000.

On March 29th, 1919, I submitted a memorandum to the "Big Four," setting forth the British attitude to the Reparation issue. This memorandum began by stating that while the Allied and Associated Governments had an indisputable claim to full compensation, the enemy would not be able to provide it, and that, therefore, the claim should be limited to full recompense by the enemy, at whatever cost to himself, for "the value of the material damage done and of the personal losses and injuries, including those to the civilian dependants of combatants which the enemy states have caused." This last phrase was further expanded as follows:

Each of the Allied and Associated Powers ought to receive from
Germany a just reparation in respect of the death and disablement or
permanent injury to health directly caused to any of its subjects by
hostilities or by operations of war, whether on sea or land or in the air,
or by the acts of enemy forces, populations or authorities in occupied,
invaded or enemy territory.

Further, reparation should be made for all property, except
military works or material, carried off, seized or destroyed by the
enemy or damaged by operations of war—the carried-off property
to be restored if possible, and payment made for all not so re-
placed. As I felt convinced we could agree on no figure for inserting in the Treaty, I then proposed the setting-up of a Reparation
Commission to which the issues which had divided the Allies on
the question of reparation should be referred: "The amounts to
be paid, the time and mode of payments and the securities to be
given therefor shall be determined by an Inter-Ally Commission
after examining into the claims and giving to Germany just
opportunity of being heard." I also proposed that Germany
should be heard from time to time and at any time on the question of her capacity to pay the annuities fixed by the Commission.

The main factors in discussion were not ascertained, but they
were ascertainable, given time and the conditions which would
make a calm enquiry possible. Neither of these conditions was
attainable before the signature of the Treaty. There was no time
to assess the damage done and the cost of repairing it. The cost
of all the materials required for reparation and reconstruction
was at that time abnormally high—in many cases treble the pre-
war prices. But the prices were bound to come down. The public
temper was still too excited to consider rational abatements in
the demand for recoupment to be made on Germany. Even
usually prudent financiers completely lost their heads. Had the
Germans offered at that date to pay £6,000,000,000, there would
have been a howl, for it would not have liquidated 20 per cent. of
the Allied burden.

My memorandum recommended payment in kind as far as
possible, and an apportionment of any payment made according

to the losses of the respective Allies. An initial payment was proposed to be made in 1919–20 of £1,000,000,000 sterling. Up to the date of this memorandum the representatives of all the Allied Powers on the Reparation Commission except the Americans were committed to a demand which would include the whole cost of the War borne by the Allies. This constituted much the heaviest item in the claims formulated against Germany, and amounted to 75 per cent. of the total. The British Delegation decided to strike it out altogether.

Nothing could more clearly emphasise the difficulty we were under of agreeing to any acceptable figure than Mr. Hughes' letter written to me on March 17th, 1919, enclosing a memorandum from himself and Lords Cunliffe and Sumner, the three British delegates to the Commission on Reparation. This memorandum suggested that in all probability Germany would be able to pay a considerable sum in the coming years, and proposed that she should be called on to pay down within the next 1½ or 2 years an initial £1,000,000,000, and thereafter pay interest and sinking fund on the remainder of her debt (the precise amount of which was not stated in the memorandum). The annual payment was, however, apparently to be on a capital sum of £10,000,000,000, since by 1926 it was to rise to £600,000,000 annually, being £500,000,000 interest at 5 per cent., and £100,000,000 sinking fund. Germany was thereafter to pay this £600,000,000 a year for about 35 years.

The £600,000,000 was to be paid, as to £350,000,000, in gold, and as to £250,000,000, in paper marks. The paper marks "we should have to take our chance of selling or borrowing on as best we may." The actual payment of the whole funded debt would be made by means of bearer bonds with coupons attached, and Mr. Hughes suggested that these when deposited with the Allies should be sold by them as widely as possible among neutrals and raw-material countries, so as to make it less easy for Germany to repudiate them.

The postulate that Germany would be able to pay off a debt of this size at this rate was admitted to be based on hope and assumption.

We advisedly do not base our estimate of the annual sum which Germany can pay on statistics, nor do we offer estimates in support of it. Statistics are of use and have been examined with regard to the sum obtainable in the first two years. For a period of years beginning thereafter, and for conditions of which nothing can be declared with certainty, except that they will differ from those of the past, no statistics can really avail.

. . . . .

If Germany makes money, the paper will be worth money in time; the one thing that we find it impossible to believe is that the Germans, as hitherto known, will not manage to make money somehow. If that is accepted, the real problem is to make them make money for us. . . .

It will thus be seen that, as regards the future, our opinion is mere opinion, though we believe it is sound.

They recognised that for Germany to be able to pay across her frontiers, year by year, such sums, she would have to secure the necessary external credits by exporting goods.

Payment of our claims in exports may seem to displace our internal manufactures and payment of very large claims seems to postulate a very large increase of German exports. Still, Germany can make no substantial payment without exporting something which might have been produced in England; the choice lies between giving some manufacturers a grievance, which is inevitable, and leaving all the taxpayers, the commerce, and the finance of the country to bear, unaided, the present load of debt if it can.

I was not in the least satisfied with the Hughes memorandum. I discussed the matter fully with Mr. Keynes, who was one of the leading advisers of the Treasury on financial questions at the Conference. He agreed to prepare a more detailed scheme, based on a more moderate annual payment from Germany. On March 22nd, 1919, he gave me a memorandum in which such a proposal was set out. This specified as Germany's reparation payments:

(a) the value of her cessions of territory (Alsace-Lorraine and colonies, etc.).

(b) an immediate payment of the whole of her shipping, her gold and silver, and all foreign securities, property, businesses and concessions held by her or her nationals.

(c) annual payments, rising from £50,000,000 a year in 1920 by steady increases until for the concluding ten years of the tributory period, 1951–1960, they would be £400,000,000 a year. The net proceeds of the payments under (b), after paying for the Army of Occupation and any goods supplied to Germany should be reckoned as part of these annual payments. The aggregate payments under this scheme would amount to £11,000,000,000, in addition to the territorial cessions. Their present discounted value, at 5 per cent. would be only £3,800,000,000. At 4 per cent. it would be £4,500,000,000, and at 3 per cent., £5,600,000,000.

Mr. Keynes submitted in a footnote as an alternative a somewhat steeper graduation of payments which would give about £1,000,000,000 more of present discounted value, though the aggregate payments would be rather less. He did not include any proposal that a portion of the payments might be made in paper currency of uncertain value. He sent the following covering note with his memorandum:

Prime Minister:
   The scheme in the text of this paper does not work up to a *present value* of £m.5,000 at *five* per cent. interest, as I found it impossible to achieve this with reasonable annual payments. The trouble is that a rate of interest so high as five per cent. makes the present value of distant payments very low, so that any scheme which aims at moderate payments in the next five or ten years suffers severely.
   In a footnote, however, I have given a scheme which works up very nearly to £m.5,000. Brand with whom I have carefully discussed the enclosed agrees with me in thinking the scheme in the text the highest reasonable, and in disliking the scheme in the footnote.

(Sd.) J. M. KEYNES
22.3.19.

In my memorandum of March 25th, 1919, entitled: "Some Considerations for the Peace Conference before they finally draft the Terms," I referred to the reparation issue in these terms:
   "The duration for the payments of reparation ought to disappear if possible with the generation which made the War."
   "The amount chargeable under full Reparation greatly exceeds what, on any calculation, Germany is capable of paying."
   "Germany should pay an annual sum for a stated number of years" and be allowed "a number of years within which to work up to payment of the full annual amount," and

"A permanent Commission should have power to postpone some portion of the annual payment," and to "cancel the payment of interest on postponed payments during the first few years."

I also proposed that the division of the total sum paid in reparation should be: 50 per cent. to France; 30 per cent. to Great Britain; and 20 per cent. to the other claimants, including Belgium.

On March 28th, 1919, Mr. Keynes sent me a memorandum stating that the French had refused a compromise apportionment of the reparation payments proposed by the Americans. What the American proposal was, he did not mention. But the maximum French concession was to be 56 per cent. to France, 25 per cent. to Britain, and 19 per cent. to the other Powers. Keynes proposed a division which is almost the same as this, except for hinting at a possible reduction in Britain's favour of the amount allocated to the other Powers.

M. Clemenceau was pleased with the British plan of shelving the question of the fixation of a definite figure on to the shoulders of a Commission who could examine it at leisure. It seemed to him reasonable in itself having regard to the absence of any reliable data as to Allied damage and German liquefiable assets. President Wilson took the same view, and was prepared to accept it although his experts pressed for a definite sum. The idea was especially gratifying to the French Premier, who frankly admitted he could not form any estimate of his own. His opponents in the French Chamber and Press were watching him like hawks in the hope that he would stumble into some blunder that would alienate support from him and peradventure end in his overthrow. Had he been defeated on the question of reparations, we should have been confronted with a French Government committed by the very conditions under which it came into existence to extreme and impossible demands.

The proviso that Germany should meanwhile restore or substitute certain machinery, plant and cattle taken from France during the War, supply certain material like coal which France needed, and in addition pay in cash £1,000,000,000 to the Reparation Commission, would be an answer to those who might insinuate that to postpone the fixation of the debt was another way of putting off payment indefinitely.

The proposals as finally agreed to by the Four have been so entirely misrepresented that it is necessary to quote them textually in order that they may be understood before they are criticised. The first Article (231) affirms that:

The Allied and Associated Governments affirm and Germany accepts the responsibility of Germany and her allies for causing all the loss and damage to which the Allied and Associated Governments and their nationals have been subjected as a consequence of the war imposed upon them by the aggression of Germany and her allies.

The second Article (232) begins by a recognition that Germany cannot be expected to pay in full for the damage wrought by her in the War:

The Allied and Associated Governments recognize that the resources of Germany are not adequate, after taking into account permanent diminutions of such resources which will result from other provisions of the present Treaty, to make complete reparation for all such loss and damage.

The Allied and Associated Governments, however, require, and Germany undertakes, that she will make compensation for all damage done to the civilian population of the Allied and Associated Powers and to their property during the period of the belligerency of each as an Allied or Associated Power against Germany by such aggression by land, by sea, and from the air, and in general all damage as defined in Annex I hereto.

In accordance with Germany's pledges, already given, as to complete restoration for Belgium, Germany undertakes, in addition to the compensation for damage elsewhere in this Part provided for, as a consequence of the violation of the Treaty of 1839, to make reimbursement of all sums which Belgium has borrowed from the Allied and Associated Governments up to November 11th, 1918, together with interest at the rate of five per cent. (5 per cent.) per annum on such sums.

The next two Articles set up the Reparation Commission (1) to assess the damage by or before the 1st of May, 1921; (2) to adjudge *from time to time* Germany's capacity to pay and to determine the method of payment within thirty years from May 1st, 1921:

The amount of the above damage for which compensation is to be made by Germany shall be determined by an Inter-Allied Commission, to be called the *Reparation Commission* and constituted in the form and with the power set forth hereunder and in Annexes II to VII inclusive hereto.

This Commission shall consider the claims and give to the German Government a just opportunity to be heard.

The findings of the Commission as to the amount of damage defined as above shall be concluded and notified to the German Government on or before May 1, 1921, as representing the extent of that Government's obligations.

The Commission shall concurrently draw up a schedule of payments prescribing the time and manner for securing and discharging the entire obligation within a period of thirty years from May 1, 1921. If, however, within the period mentioned, Germany fails to discharge her obligations, any balance remaining unpaid may, within the discretion of the Commission, be postponed for settlement in subsequent years, or may be handled otherwise in such manner as the Allied and Associated Governments, acting in accordance with the procedure laid down in this Part of the present Treaty, shall determine.

The Reparation Commission shall after May 1, 1921, from time to time, consider the resources and capacity of Germany, and, after giving her representatives a just opportunity to be heard, shall have discretion to extend the date, and to modify the form of payments, such as are to be provided for in accordance with Article 233 (the above Article); but not to cancel any part, except with the specific authority of the several Governments represented upon the Commission.

The next Article (235) deals with the payment of £1,000 million before the 1st of May, 1921:

In order to enable the Allied and Associated Powers to proceed at once to the restoration of their industrial and economic life, pending the full determination of their claims, Germany shall pay in such instalments and in such manner (whether in gold, commodities, ships, securities or otherwise) as the Reparation Commission may fix, during 1919, 1920, and the first four months of 1921, the equivalent of 20,000,000,000 gold marks. Out of this sum the expenses of the armies of occupation subsequent to the Armistice of November 11, 1918, shall first be met, and such supplies of food and raw materials as may be judged by the Governments of the Principal Allied and Associated Powers to be essential to enable Germany to meet her obligations for reparation may also, with the approval of the said Governments, be paid for out of the above sum. The balance shall be reckoned towards liquidation of the amounts due for reparation. Germany shall further deposit bonds as prescribed in paragraph 12 (c) of Annex II hereto.

To sum up, the damages were not to be assessed for two years. This gave time for passions to cool down. It also reduced the bases of valuation by giving time for a reduction of the inflated prices of the War to something in the direction of normal.

A still more important provision is that contained in Article 234. Germany was not to be compelled to pay in full the damages assessed, or the instalments fixed under Article 233, if she could demonstrate that it was beyond her capacity to meet the obligations. This she was entitled to do "from time to time," which means at any time, and her representatives were to be given "a just opportunity to be heard." She could be let off any portion of her payments with the consent of the Governments represented on the Commission. It is under this provision that after paying a sum which has been variously estimated at anything between £1,000 million and £3,000 million—that is, about one-third of the assessed claims—the balance has by common consent been allowed to lapse. This is the justification of the British plan of not inserting a fixed sum in the Treaty but of leaving the amount to be determined in more tranquil days, when there had been a few years' experience of the possibility of levying huge tributes from another country. Had the figure of £2,500 million been inserted in the Treaty no Allied Ministry would have survived to sign it, for no Allied Parliament at that time nor for several years afterwards would have sanctioned so low a figure. But when the account was finally closed at something less than that figure, not a protest came from any party in any assembly of the Allied Nations.

A word about the Reparation Commission which was to play such an important part in assessment, adjudication and administration of the reparation clauses. It was to represent France, Britain, the U.S.A., Italy and one other Power concerned in the administration of the Fund, which it was practically indicated would be Belgium. Had America signed the Treaty, her presence on the Commission would have ensured the inclusion of one disinterested party. The American representative would, I have no doubt, for that reason have been chosen as Chairman. What a difference that would have made in the whole history of reparations! With America out, France, whose Governments for years adopted a severe and stern attitude as to the exaction of the fullest payment and of the measures to be adopted for enforcing it, claimed and was given the Chair. This, with the vote of Belgium, who was entirely in France's pocket, gave France control of all the decisions taken. The choice of Poincaré as the first Chairman was fatal to judgment and moderation. He took the most ruthless, unreasonable and impracticable view of his duties. His hatred of Germany was an obsession. He performed his task as a bailiff who had a grudge against the debtor and who thought more of quenching his hatred than of collecting the debt.

The whole reparation scheme was thus wrecked by the defection of America. I fought for years to reduce the amount of the annuities claimed, but I never succeeded in securing the assent of France and Belgium to the fixation of a reasonable figure. Even the tolerant Briand when in office had always before his eyes the dread of being denounced by the irreconcilable little Lorrainer as a traitor if he listened to any suggestion of reducing the annuities. It was only by bringing America in informally and outside the Treaty years after its signature, to consider the further payments that Germany was capable of making, that her instalments were first of all reduced and that afterwards the whole of the reparation obligations were brought to an end. Had America signed the Treaty, all this could have been accomplished in good time, and one element in the precipitation of the great financial crisis that affected the whole world would have been eliminated.

Throughout the active lifetime of the Commission the British representative, backed by his Government, took a tolerant and indulgent view of his duties. On the whole Italy was disinclined to take harsh measures. But with France in the Chair, Britain and Italy were in a minority, for the Belgian Commissioner always said ditto to the French Chairman.

CHAPTER X

THE GERMAN COLONIES

NOT a voice was raised in favour of restoring to Germany her colonies. As President Wilson said at the outset of the discussions on this subject: "All were agreed to oppose the restoration of the German Colonies." The revelations as to the military, naval and aerial use which the Germans intended to make of their colonies in the future were responsible for that unanimity.

When that first question as to restoration was decided summarily in the negative by general agreement, I opened the discussion on their disposal. Before coming to the first debate at the Conference, I should say a word about the position of the British Delegation on the colonial question at this date. The conversations we had had at the Imperial Cabinet before Christmas had not removed our difficulties or produced agreement on the trusteeship of the League.

The mandate project encountered serious and, up to a point, growing resistance. When it was first propounded by General Smuts in his December memorandum on the League, there had been no time to examine it in all its practical ramifications. The Imperial Cabinet therefore seemed to acquiesce in it rather than to approve of it. The nimble intelligence of Mr. W. M. Hughes alone perceived its incompatibility with the Australian idea of incorporation in the Commonwealth. Mr. Balfour then wrote a highly characteristic memorandum in which, for two or three pages, he pointed out with ruthless logic all the objections to the proposal, but ended up by stating in a couple of sentences that he did not mind it being tried as an experiment. (Appendix I.)

As the time approached for deciding whether the mandate principle should be incorporated in the Treaty, and if so in what form, the opposition to the whole idea assumed formidable dimensions. Australia and New Zealand were in revolt against it.

General Smuts, one of the authors of the project, would have none of it in so far as the German Colony adjacent to the territory of the South African Union was concerned. In this attitude he had the whole-hearted support of General Botha. France opposed it root and branch. The Japanese thought it quite inapplicable to their captured islands. Orlando was sceptical. I think it is fair to state that President Wilson and I were alone in supporting the principle of vesting the German Colonies in the League of Nations as a trustee, with mandatories nominated by the League to undertake the duties of administration.

When the question of the German Colonies came up for consideration, I arranged that the Dominion representatives should be present. When they appeared there was an amusing interchange of characteristic amenity between M. Clemenceau and Mr. Hughes. In pressing the claims of Australia to complete control of some of the islands she had conquered, I had dwelt on the savagery of some of the tribes inhabiting those islands. I stated that many of them were still cannibals. Announcing the decision of the Conference that the Dominions should be allowed to present their own case, M. Clemenceau turned to me and said: "Bring your cannibals here this afternoon." When the Dominion Premiers arrived, M. Clemenceau went up to Mr. Hughes and, placing his hands on his shoulders, said: "I hear, Mr. Hughes, that you are a cannibal." Hughes merely retorted: "M. Clemenceau, I can assure you the report is grossly exaggerated." From that moment Hughes and Clemenceau were fast friends.

Here is a summary of the discussion:

Mr. LLOYD GEORGE said that the second question, therefore, was to decide in what manner these territories should be dealt with. There were two or three methods proposed. The first was internationalisation or control by the League of Nations. It was generally agreed that these territories could not be directly administered internationally. Therefore, it was suggested that some one nation should undertake the trusteeship on behalf of the League as mandatory. The conditions of the trust would doubtless include a stipulation that the territory should be administered, not in the interests of the mandatory, but in the interests of all. There must be equal economic opportunity for all, and, further, there must be a guarantee that the natives would be treated fairly and would not be exploited, either commercially or militarily, for the benefit of the mandatory. There would also, no doubt, be a right of appeal to the League of Nations if any of the conditions of the trust were broken; for instance, if the missionaries or concessionaires of any nation complained of unfair treatment. He did not suggest that this was an exhaustive account of the conditions, and if his account were in any way inaccurate, it would, no doubt, be set right hereafter.

He would like to state at once that the definition he had just attempted to give did not differ materially from the method in which the British Empire dealt with its Colonies. In all British Colonies there was free trade. He did not think there was such a thing as a preferential tariff in any. Germans or Americans could trade throughout the British Colonies on the same terms as British subjects. In fact, in British East Africa most of the commerce was done by a German firm and Germany subsidised a shipping line which carried the bulk of the trade. No troops, save for police purposes, were raised in the British Colonies. British coaling stations were as free to foreign as to British ships, and German battleships coaled in them as freely as British battleships. As far as Great Britain was concerned, therefore, he saw no objection to the mandatory system.

The next alternative was frank annexation. The German Colonies conquered by Australia, New Zealand and South Africa would be dealt with in detail by the Ministers representing these Dominions.

German South-West Africa was contiguous to the territories of the Union. There was no real natural boundary, and unless the Dutch and British population of South Africa undertook the colonisation of this area it would remain a wilderness. If the Union were given charge of German South-West Africa in the capacity of a mandatory there would be in a territory, geographically one, two forms of administration. It was questionable whether any advantage would be derived from this division capable of outweighing its practical difficulties.

In the case of New Guinea, one-third of the island was already under direct Australian administration, another third had now been conquered from Germany. It was manifest that to draw a customs barrier between one portion of the island and the other presented disadvantages. Yet, if Australia were the mandatory of the League of Nations for the administration of what had been German New Guinea, it might have to administer this portion of the island on lines different from those followed in respect of the territory which she already possessed.

Samoa also would be best administered directly by New Zealand. He pointed out that the task of administering Colonies was an ex-

pensive one. The British Colonial Budget was steadily increasing.
Unless money were to be spent upon them Colonies should be dropped.
The Dominion of New Zealand had a population of a little more than
one million souls. It had put 100,000 men into the field, had incurred
a War Debt of £100,000,000 sterling, had suffered 60,000 casualties
and lost 16,000 killed. New Zealand had taken Samoa, and fully
realised that money would have to be spent upon it if the island
was to be retained.

It might not think it worth while to undertake the task of administration only as a mandatory.

To sum up, he would like the Conference to treat the territories
enumerated as part of the Dominions which had captured them rather
than as areas to be administered under the control of an organisation
established in Europe, which might find it difficult to contribute even
the smallest financial assistance to their administration.

I invited each of the Dominion representatives in his turn to
state his case, more particularly in reference to the territories
which they had respectively conquered and of which they were
now in occupation. Mr. Hughes spoke first and it was quite obvious from his remarks that Australia was determined to retain the
colonies she had captured and that he was definitely opposed to
any mandatory arrangement in respect of them.

MR. HUGHES said . . . as to internationalisation, he would endeavour to show why this principle should not be applied in this particular case. As Mr. Lloyd George had pointed out, part of the country
was under Australian administration, and Australian laws were current there. Control by the League of Nations would lead to confusion
of authority, which could only be harmful. If the mandatory were to
exercise real authority, its policy would have to be directed, presumably, by the League of Nations. In this case the mandatory would
be so overwhelmingly superior in power to Australia that Australian
authority would be completely overshadowed. The mandatory, as it
were, would be living in a mansion and Australia in a cottage. Any
strong Power controlling New Guinea controlled Australia. He questioned whether any country represented at the meeting would consent
to be overshadowed in such a way, even by an international authority.
The policies of nations were liable to change, and history showed
that friends in one war were not always friends in the next. From
this point of view he was prepared to say that in the mandatory Power
established in New Guinea under international control Australia
would see a potential enemy. It was reasonable and fair that the rights

of the natives should be insisted upon. Australia was ready to agree to such requirements, but Australia also had a right to claim freedom from the menace of any enemy such as had weighed upon her before this war. The security of Australia would threaten no one. No State would suffer if Australia were safe, Australia alone would suffer if she were not. Australia had suffered 90,000 casualties in this war and lost 60,000 killed. Her troops everywhere had fought well. Her war debt alone amounted to £300,000,000 sterling, exclusive of another £100,000,000 for the repatriation and pensioning of her troops. Australia did not wish to be left to stagger under this load and not to feel safe.

General Smuts followed with a similar demand on behalf of the Union of South Africa in respect of the German Colony in South-West Africa. He said that the Germans in this territory had fomented a formidable rebellion inside the Union: a rebellion which it would have taken 40,000 troops to suppress. It was only after this that the Union had been able to conquer German South-West Africa.

GENERAL SMUTS said . . . the question to be decided was whether the Union of South Africa should absorb this country, or should be appointed mandatory for its administration. He would point out that this territory was not in the same category as other German possessions in Africa. The Cameroons, Togoland and East Africa were all tropical and valuable possessions; South-West Africa was a desert country without any product of great value and only suitable for pastoralists. It could, therefore, only be developed from within the Union itself. He thought, therefore, that, although there might be a good case for the administration of the other German possessions in Africa by a mandatory, there was not, in this instance, a strong case. It was on this ground that South Africa claimed the country. A white community in South Africa had been established there for two or three centuries. It had done its best to give a form of self-government to three million natives, and its policy had been tested and found good. It was suited as much to the whites as to the natives, and this policy should be applied to the natives in South-West Africa. The fiscal system, he also thought, should be the same. It would be impossible to set up police posts along many hundred miles of desert frontier.

Then came Mr. Massey with the New Zealand claim to Samoa. He said he had received most pathetic letters from people of the native races, begging that never again should they be placed under German rule. They had volunteered very freely for service in the War on the Allied side. He was just as firmly opposed to any idea of international control as either Mr. Hughes or General Smuts (in respect of South-West Africa).

. . . With regard to the League of Nations, which had not yet been established, he hoped that it would be established and that it would be very successful. He would like to remind those present that we had had experiences in the past, which had sometimes been sad experiences, of joint control of native races. Mr. Massey mentioned the case of the New Hebrides. We were the best of friends to-day with the citizens of France and the Government of France, and he hoped and believed that that very satisfactory state of things would continue for all time. But he thought it would be admitted, not only by the people of France, but by others, that our joint control of the New Hebrides had been an ignominious failure. Egypt, too, had not been a success under joint control, neither had Samoa. He was very sceptical in regard to the success of any joint arrangement in regard to the German Colonies.

New Zealand had sent over 100,000 men to the war, 16,456 had been killed, and 41,404 had been wounded. That was a big record for a small country with a small population. They did not regret it, because they believed it was their duty. The men went out to fight for the great cause of civilisation. He believed they would do the same thing again under similar circumstances.

In conclusion, on behalf of his fellow citizens, and on behalf of the people in the Islands of the South Pacific, for the sake of the native races, and for the sake of humanity, he most strongly urged that the claim he was making in regard to Samoa should be granted by the Congress, and that the island should be allowed to remain under British control.

There was one argument used by Mr. Massey which perceptibly nettled President Wilson:

. . . He appealed to the President of the United States to look at the whole question from the New Zealand point of view. He would ask him to recall the period immediately after the American War of Independence. What would Washington and Hamilton and the others associated with them have done or said had it been suggested that a mandatory Power, or even the Colonists themselves as mandatories of a League of Nations, should be given charge of the vast territories in North America not at that time occupied?

Sir Robert Borden supported the claim put forward by his fellow-Premiers. He said

that the Dominion he represented had no territorial claims to advance. There was one thought, however, that he would like to present to the Council on behalf of the claims put forward by the other Dominions. Those Dominions were autonomous nations within an Empire which might more properly be called itself a League of Nations. He realised that the British Empire occupied a large part of the world, but the prejudice raised by the word Empire might be dispelled by considering the matter from the angle he had just suggested. All the cases advanced rested upon the plea of security, and he considered that the arguments put forward deserved the closest attention of the Council.

After these statements the discussion was adjourned in order to give the Congress full opportunity for considering the claims of the Dominion Premiers and the arguments advanced by them in support of them.

The following day, on the nomination of a commission to deal with economic questions, a discussion arose which had a considerable bearing upon the question of mandates and which anticipated the growing difficulties in the way of providing for countries deprived of their colonies the raw materials which are essential to their industries.

MR. BALFOUR observed that the question of preferential dealing in the matter of raw material appeared to involve both kinds of interest. The reconstitution of Belgian and French manufacturing industries was hard to separate from the reconstruction of German industries. Germany could not pay for the rebuilding of the former unless she were herself assisted to restart manufacturing. Priority of supplies, therefore, had a direct bearing on the peace treaty as well as on the arrangements to be made between the Allies.

PRESIDENT WILSON pointed out that it was quite true that Germany could not make reparation unless she had the means therefor. Unless German industries were reconstituted it was clear that Germany could not pay. The means of obtaining reparation from Germany was obviously a question to be considered by the Commission on reparation. He could see ahead certain difficulties in connection with this matter. If he were to carry back to America a treaty in which economic arrangements with America's friends were included in the settlement made with her enemies the Senate might raise objections. Congress was jealous of being forestalled in commitments on economic matters. He could see no objection to the proposal under consideration, provided it were not tied up with other matters in which the constraint of making peace was involved.

MR. LLOYD GEORGE said that he also anticipated considerable difficulty in dealing with matters of this sort. Much of the raw material that would be required by Germany could only be found in the British Empire. France also, by the acquisition of Alsace-Lorraine, would dispose of more raw material than she did before. This would still be more the case were she to acquire the Saar Valley. Germany, therefore, could not start her industrial life again save at the good pleasure of the Allies. There would be in England parliamentary difficulties similar to those alluded to by President Wilson in the United States. It was clear that Germany would be entitled to ask what her economic future was going to be. It would be very difficult to obtain her consent to a peace treaty which took from her all her colonies and left the victorious Powers in exclusive possession of a number of raw materials which she required. Unless we were prepared beforehand, we should be met by a series of questions on these subjects to confront our territorial demands, and we might be at a loss to answer them. He felt that we ought to be prepared to meet this situation, and therefore supported the proposal that a Committee be set up to investigate these questions without in any way committing the Allied Powers.

The French point of view, which was hostile to the idea of a mandate under the League of Nations, was very lucidly stated by M. Simon, the French Minister for the Colonies. He said:

It now remained for them to consider the question of the government to be given to these territories, which had become ownerless.

There were three possible solutions:

1. Internationalisation, pure and simple.
2. A mandate given to one of the Powers by the League of Nations.
3. Annexation, pure and simple, by a Sovereign Power.

Mr. Lloyd George had frankly condemned the first system in the course of the conversation of 24th January, when he had said that it could not be adopted in regard to backward countries—that it would lead to disorder, and that the high ideals for which such a system would be established could not be reached.

He would agree with this view for humanitarian reasons. Similar experiments tried in the past had failed ignominiously. He would only mention the dual control over Samoa, against which the American President himself had spoken, and that of the New Hebrides, which, he hoped, would not be allowed to continue, where, under Franco-British control, there was a tribunal composed of a Spanish judge and a Dutch clerk.

What was impossible for small territories was all the less possible for large regions.

The second system consisted in the appointment of a mandatory by the League of Nations. The Dominions had raised very strong objections to this system, and these objections were supported by France. When, in two territories inhabited by the same population, two different systems of government were created, difficulties would ensue, and the very opposite of what was desired would result.

The mandatory system consisted in empowering one nation to act on behalf of another. Every mandate was revocable, and there would therefore be no guarantee for the continuance of any. There would thus be little inducement for the investment of capital and for colonisation in a country whose future was unknown. The mandatory would be content to live quietly without trying to develop the colony or to improve the conditions of life of the natives, and the desired ideal would not be attained by this means.

Another question occurs: Who would be the mandatory? Would it be a little nation, without colonising traditions, capital or men; or would the mandatory be a large nation whose presence would be a danger and compel the adjoining nations to organise for defence, as Mr. Hughes said in regard to New Guinea? This same remark applied to the Cameroons and to the Congo. It would also be necessary to take into account the uncertainty of alliances, which were always liable to be changed.

He (M. Simon) could not, therefore, favour the system of a mandate to be given to one Power by the League of Nations.

The third system still remained to be considered—that of annexation, pure and simple, which he had come to support that day. It was the only one which would accomplish the double object of every colonial government worthy of the name, namely, the development of the country and the effective protection of the natives during the period required for their development towards a higher plane of civilisation.

He would ask his hearers to consider the objections that could be raised against a policy of annexation. Annexation might be said to lead to the exploitation of the country for the benefit of the individual; it might be said to lead to the ill-treatment of the natives; it might permit of the setting up of the economic policy of the "closed door."

All these points were part of a theory which was to-day quite obsolete and condemned by all. France had higher aspirations, and the

Colonies were no longer considered as a kind of close preserve for exploitation and for the benefit of the individual.

Higher moral principles now guided the nations. All the Great Powers worthy of the name considered their colonies as wards entrusted to them by the world. They accepted this guardianship and the duties connected therewith, duly appreciating their duties in regard to the maintenance of peace, their duties in regard to the protection of the people by the limitation of the sale of alcohol, the prevention of gun-running, etc., and in regard to the provision of social education. Only a great nation in possession of trained administrative services and with men and money at its disposal could undertake and carry through such an enterprise. The work of civilisation could only be carried out under the auspices of a country which was sovereign.

If France were to receive the territories under consideration, she would be prepared to give assurances to those who might still harbour fears. The French formally announced that day that their policy in regard to the territories formerly German would entail the application of a liberal system, practically open to everybody—the "open door" system, without differential tariffs. Everybody would be able to enter Togoland and the Cameroons and to trade there without let or hindrance. France henceforth renounced all economic protective measures. She accepted what she had always done for the protection of the natives, the limitation of alcohol, the stoppage of traffic in arms, etc. She would not attempt to enforce any policy which might appear to be directed against the natives, for she had always co-operated with them. The French had always desired that the natives should take part in the management of their own territory. He had enunciated the general principles which guided the French. These principles were such that they were bound to satisfy all those interested in the moral development and liberties of the population.

President Wilson's fifth point in his message of the 8th January read as follows:

"A free, open-minded, and absolutely impartial adjustment of all colonial claims based upon a strict observance of the principle that in determining all such questions of sovereignty, the interests of the populations concerned have equal weight with the equitable claims of the Government whose title is to be determined."

For a long time France had used all her strength for the purpose of exploring and developing the territories of Northern Africa, and the whole world had been able to enjoy the benefits to be derived therefrom.

France had spent 9 milliards of francs on the Mediterranean coast,

626 millions on West Africa, and 272 millions on Equatorial Africa. When the efforts made by France for the civilisation of Northern Africa were considered, full confidence would be felt that she would be able to carry out the same programme in Equatorial Africa. That was his reply to President Wilson's third condition.

France relied on these facts that day, in asking to be allowed to continue her work of civilisation in tropical Africa, and he hoped the delegates would give her the means of doing so by recognising her right to sovereignty in those regions, subject to the assurances he had outlined.

This powerful statement of the anti-mandate case, following as it did the criticisms directed by the Dominions, provoked President Wilson to a statement which threatened a break-up of the Conference:

PRESIDENT WILSON observed that the discussion so far had been, in essence, a negation in detail—one case at a time—of the whole principle of mandatories. The discussion had been brought to a point where it looked as if their roads diverged. He thought it would be wise to discontinue this discussion for a few hours—say until the next day, as he feared that otherwise it might lead to a point where it would appear as though they had reached a serious disagreement, and this he particularly wished to avoid.

I endeavoured to bridge the differences that had arisen:

MR. LLOYD GEORGE said that he had some discussion about mandatories with the representatives of the British Colonial Department, who raised no difficulties. They thought the difficulties were more imaginary than real. He had been greatly struck by the fact that M. Simon, in his speech, had in the beginning appeared to be bitterly opposed to the whole idea, but in the end he had detailed as acceptable to France the whole list of conditions proposed for a mandatory, except the name. As far as the British Empire was concerned, most of the conquests had been accomplished by British troops, and as far as those territories were concerned, Great Britain would be prepared to administer them under such conditions as might be laid down by the League of Nations. He could see no difficulties, except perhaps difficulties of definition. Exceptions might have to be made, but then every rule had an exception. He could see no reason why any difficulties should arise in laying down general principles.

I concluded by saying I could not stay indefinitely in Paris and therefore would ask my colleagues to face the difficulty and come to a decision.

PRESIDENT WILSON agreed with what Mr. Lloyd George said were the views of his Colonial Department, viz., that the difficulties were more imaginary than real. In the first place, the composition of the League of Nations, whenever spoken of heretofore, had left the lead to the Great Powers.

But he said that he did not agree with me that there was no great difference between the mandatory system and M. Simon's plan (which is not quite what I had said):

. . . He wished he could agree with Mr. Lloyd George that there was no great difference between the mandatory system and M. Simon's plan. The former assumed trusteeship on the part of the League of Nations; the latter implied definite sovereignty, exercised in the same spirit and under the same conditions as might be imposed upon a mandatory. The two ideas were radically different, and he was bound to assume that the French Colonial Office could not see its way to accept the idea of the mandatory.

He pointed out that Australia claimed sovereignty over German New Guinea, the Union of South Africa over German South-West Africa, and Japan over the leased territory of Shantung and the Caroline Islands, while France claimed a modified sovereignty over the Cameroons and Togoland under certain terms. They were at the stage where the only acceptance had been on the part of the Imperial British Government with respect to the area taken from Germany by troops under the direct authority of the Government in London. This was an important exception, in which he rejoiced, but it appeared to be the only exception to the rejection of the idea of trusteeship on the part of the League of Nations.

He appealed to the sentiment of the civilised world which would be outraged by a wholesale annexation of the German Colonies by the victorious Powers.

. . . There must be a League of Nations, and they could not return to the *status quo ante*. The League of Nations would be a laughing-stock if it were not invested with this quality of trusteeship. He felt this so intensely that he hoped that those present would not think that he had any personal antagonism.

.   .   .   .   .

He could not postpone the matter any more than Mr. Lloyd George could. The date of his departure was set; he must go, perhaps only for the time necessary to cross the ocean, to settle some pressing business, and to return.

In the meantime the world would be in suspense, swayed by hope, doubt, conjecture and rumour. For his part he was eager to go on with the discussion, but he did not desire to go on to a point of division, but to a point of union. He regarded this as essential, but he did not mean to insist upon the acceptance of the plan of a mandatory as he had outlined it.

He desired the acceptance of the genuine idea of trusteeship. . . . They must agree on the principle and leave its application to the League of Nations.

SIR ROBERT BORDEN enquired from President Wilson, purely for his information, with a view to the removal of the difficulty in case it became acute, whether the nomination of a mandatory need be postponed until the League of Nations was constituted. Under the scheme for the creation of a League of Nations, he understood that the five Great Powers would form a Council controlling the work of the League. Therefore the difference between making the decision now or leaving it to the Council of the League of Nations was not great. He would, therefore, ask whether President Wilson would take that suggestion into consideration.

PRESIDENT WILSON replied that he had himself, informally, made that suggestion.

M. ORLANDO said that as regards Colonial questions, the Italian point of view was extremely simple. Italy would readily accept whatever principles might be adopted, provided they were equitably applied and also provided that she could participate in the work of civilisation. . . . He thought that the Conference should lay down general principles, whilst leaving to the League of Nations the practical application of these principles to special cases. There were a number of questions that might well be considered during a short period of adjournment. For instance, should all the German Colonies, without exception, be confided to the League of Nations? In other words, was the rule to admit of no exceptions? As was well known, exceptions proved the rule. He agreed that no exceptions could be made for purely private reasons, but if exceptions were made, based on concrete reasons, then such exceptions would not weaken the rule but strengthen it. . . .

Then followed M. Clemenceau, who said that he

wished, in the first place, to say that Mr. Lloyd George had interpreted M. Simon's speech better than President Wilson. The French

Colonial Office had expressed its views, but that did not mean that he himself was not ready to make concessions if reasonable proposals were put forward. All his sentiments were in agreement with those of President Wilson. He agreed with him as to the gravity of the decision to be taken, and the seriousness of the situation that would result therefrom. There was danger in refusing a means of salvation, but there was greater danger in adopting the wrong means of salvation. The League of Nations, he thought, was to be a League of Defence to ensure the peace of the world. But it appeared they had now gone beyond that limit when they proposed to create a League of Nations with governmental functions to interfere in internal affairs, with trustees in various places sending reports to—he did not know whom. Throughout the world, even in Europe, and perhaps in the Adriatic, a control would be set up. President Wilson himself had said so, and, as a result, appeals would be heard from all parts of the world. Who would deal with those appeals? It had been said that an International Legislature and some sort of executive, about which he knew nothing, would have to be created, without any power to administer penalties, since this question had never been raised. The idea of an unknown mandatory acting through an undetermined tribunal gave him some anxiety. He did not regret the discussions which had taken place on the subject, since these discussions had impressed him with the justness of the claims of the Dominions. However, since Mr. Lloyd George was prepared to accept the mandate of a League of Nations he would not dissent from the general agreement, merely for the sake of the Cameroons and Togoland. But, when President Wilson asked that every question should be referred to the League of Nations, he felt a little nervous, and feared that the remedy might be worse than the disease. President Wilson had said that the opinion of the world would rise up against them, and that savagery was ready to flow over the world from the East to the West. That might be, but he was not in full agreement with President Wilson when the latter said that they had to choose between a League of Nations with legislative and initiative powers and the burden of armaments. He would not say anything further on the subject of a League of Nations with legislative initiative, as he had already dealt with that question.

Then followed a passage which I have already quoted in which M. Clemenceau eloquently defended the conception of a League of Nations to enforce world peace.

MR. LLOYD GEORGE, continuing, said that he regarded the system merely as a general trusteeship upon defined conditions. Only when those conditions were scandalously abused would the League of Nations have the right to interfere and to call on the mandatory for an explanation. For instance, should a mandatory allow foul liquor to swamp the territories entrusted to it the League of Nations would have the right to insist on a remedy of the abuse. The Powers now exercise this right by diplomatic correspondence, resulting in the giving of assurances, but frequently nothing was done. He would, however, make an appeal to President Wilson to consider the following point of view. He trusted the President would not insist on postponing the selection of mandatories until after the League of Nations had been established. That was a serious matter, for as long as all these questions were unsettled everything would be unsettled. People were unsettled all over the world, not only the labourers and the soldiers, but also the employers. Great Britain now occupied territories where they had no intention of remaining, even if the League of Nations asked her to stay. For instance, British troops were in occupation of Russian Armenia and Syria. They did not wish to be there, but someone had got to be there. Was Great Britain to be compelled to keep her troops there until the League of Nations was a going concern? Again, as regards German East Africa, if Great Britain was not to be the mandatory she would not wish to keep there the big force which she now had there. Therefore, they must know what their position was to be, and they would not settle down to their own business until these questions were decided. During the past week the question of the renewal of the Military Service Act in the United Kingdom had come under consideration. It appeared that Great Britain was now maintaining large forces—over 170,000 white troops alone—in Syria, the Caucasus, East Africa, and other out-of-the-way places. These troops must, sooner or later, be withdrawn, but that could not be done till it was known who would take their place. These troops could not withdraw and leave the people to massacre each other. They would be compelled to hand the country to someone. Therefore, he would leave the settlement to this tribunal, pointing out that an early solution was urgently needed. As Sir Robert Borden had stated, this Council was practically the League of Nations, which was born on Saturday. He asked whether he had correctly interpreted M. Clemenceau's views to the effect that he was prepared to accept trusteeship.

M. CLEMENCEAU replied that, although he did not approve of it, he would be guided by the judgment of his colleagues.

President Wilson was not satisfied with obtaining a favourable answer to my question, and this disturbing conversation terminated without arriving at any decision. Baron Makino enquired whether the principle of a mandatory had been accepted. M. Clemenceau replied in the negative, and added that the question had been adjourned. We seemed to have reached a deadlock on an issue of primary importance to the Peace Settlement, and it ended in an encounter between Mr. Hughes and the President which was significant of the temperature.

I spent a great part of the next two days in consultations with the Dominion Premiers. I urged them not to take the responsibility of wrecking the Conference on a refusal to accept a principle which Great Britain was quite ready to see applied to much more extensive and important territories in East Africa. Sir Robert Borden was as usual very helpful in abating the pugnacity of Mr. Hughes and Mr. Massey. General Botha took, as he generally did, a broad and conciliatory view and at last I obtained general agreement to a series of propositions which I intended to submit to the Congress at their adjourned discussion on the subject. I circulated the document amongst the other members of the Congress. As it represents in substance the settlement of the question which was ultimately incorporated in the Treaty, there is an advantage in giving the full text here, when the discussions on its principles are in the mind of the reader:

DRAFT RESOLUTIONS IN REFERENCE TO MANDATORIES

(1) Having regard to the record of the German administration in the colonies formerly part of the German Empire, and to the menace which the possession by Germany of submarine bases in many parts of the world would necessarily constitute to the freedom and security of all nations, the Allied and Associated Powers are agreed that in no circumstances should any of the German Colonies be restored to Germany.

(2) For similar reasons, and more particularly, because of the historical misgovernment by the Turks of subject peoples and the terrible massacres of Armenians and others in recent years, the Allied and Associated Powers are agreed that Armenia, Syria, Mesopotamia, Palestine and Arabia must be completely severed from the Turkish Empire. This is without prejudice to the settlement of other parts of the Turkish Empire.

(3) The Allied and Associated Powers are agreed that advantage should be taken of the opportunity afforded by the necessity of disposing of these colonies and territories formerly belonging to Germany

and Turkey, which are inhabited by peoples not yet able to stand by themselves under the strenuous conditions of the modern world, to apply to those territories the principle that the well-being and development of such peoples form a sacred trust of civilisation, and that securities for the performance of this trust should be embodied in the constitution of the League of Nations.

(4) After careful study they are satisfied that the best method of giving practical effect to this principle is that the tutelage of such peoples should be entrusted to advanced nations who, by reason of their resources, their experience, or their geographical position, can best undertake this responsibility, and that this tutelage should be exercised by them as mandatories on behalf of the League of Nations.

(5) The Allied and Associated Powers are of opinion that the character of the mandate must differ according to the stage of development of the people, the geographical situation of the territory, its economic conditions, and other similar circumstances.

(6) They consider that certain communities formerly belonging to the Turkish Empire have reached a stage of development where their existence as independent nations can be provisionally recognised, subject to the rendering of administrative advice and assistance by a mandatory Power until such time as they are able to stand alone. The wishes of these communities must be a principal consideration in the selection of the mandatory Power.

(7) They further consider that other peoples, especially those of Central Africa, are at such a stage that the mandatory must be responsible for the administration of the territory subject to conditions which will guarantee the prohibition of abuses such as the slave trade, the arms traffic, and the liquor traffic, and the prevention of the military training of the natives for other than police purposes, and the establishment of fortifications or military and naval bases, and will also secure equal opportunities for the trade and commerce of other members of the League of Nations.

(8) Finally, they consider that there are territories, such as South-West Africa and certain of the islands in the South Pacific, which, owing to the sparseness of their population, or their small size, or their remoteness from the centres of civilisation, or their geographical contiguity to the mandatory State, and other circumstances, can be best administered under the laws of the mandatory State as integral portions thereof, subject to the safeguards above-mentioned in the interests of the indigenous population.

In every case of mandate the mandatory State shall render to the League of Nations an annual report in reference to the territory committed to its charge.

On the 30th of January I submitted to the Congress the document constituting the charter which to-day safeguards, and for many a generation to come will continue to protect, scores of millions of human beings against cruelties and atrocities such as those once upon a time committed under Belgian rule in the Congo and under German rule in South-West Africa. It also guarantees the open door for all nations to territories which in the aggregate measure 1,350,000 square miles of the richest soil on the earth's surface, and that at a period when doors are slammed and barricaded against the trade and commerce which brings nations together in a beneficial interchange that enriches them all.

In moving it, I said that Britain had deliberately decided to accept the principle of a mandatory. That decision had not been wholly accepted by the Dominions, but they had agreed to this compromise rather than face the catastrophe of a break-up.

The discussion that followed occupied two sittings and was the only unpleasant episode of the whole Congress. Feeling was at moments tense. President Wilson had his own idea of mandates. It was hardly a plan, for he had clearly not worked it out and he had therefore not submitted to the Congress any detailed project. But he vaguely indicated that what he had in mind was an administration of the German Colonies by mandatories under the direct orders of the League. When asked who was to defray the cost of carrying out these orders, he replied that the League would bear the financial burden. He could not explain how the money was to be raised. That essential detail had somehow escaped his consideration. Nevertheless he stuck to his original notion, and as my proposal contemplated placing the financial responsibility on the mandatory, he regarded my plan as an incomplete concession to his ideas. He therefore delivered a long, rambling—and for him, a somewhat muddled—criticism of the British proposal. As a rule, his manner was calm and courteous. But on this occasion he was ruffled and irritable. His demeanour towards the Dominion Premiers was hectoring and occasionally in addressing Mr. Hughes he was inclined to be dictatorial and somewhat arrogant. Mr. Hughes was the last man I would have chosen to handle in that way. Mr. Hughes having stated his case against subjecting to a mandate the islands conquered by Australia, President Wilson pulled him up sharply and proceeded to address him personally in what I would describe as a heated allocution rather than an appeal. He dwelt on the seriousness of defying world opinion on this subject. Mr. Hughes, who listened intently, with his hand cupped around his ear so as not to miss a word, indicated at the end that he was still of the same opinion. Whereupon the President asked him slowly and solemnly: "Mr. Hughes, am I to understand that if the whole civilised world asks Australia to agree to a mandate in respect of these islands, Australia is prepared still to defy the appeal of the whole civilised world?" Mr. Hughes answered: "That's about the size of it, President Wilson." Mr. Massey grunted his assent of this abrupt defiance.

The President accused Mr. Hughes and Mr. Massey of using threats. At last a friendly and most impressive appeal from General Botha to the angry President soothed him down. It was about the most striking intervention in our debates.

The President had some excuse, if not justification, for his exasperation in the appearance that morning in an English newspaper (unfriendly to the Government) of a one-sided account of previous debates on this subject. General Botha very skilfully opened his speech by alluding to this perverted disclosure of our proceedings:

GENERAL BOTHA asked that he might be allowed to address a few words to the Conference. As everybody knew, he was not a British subject of very long standing, and therefore his English was not so good as it might be. He would like to say that he heartily supported President Wilson with regard to what was in the papers that morning. When he saw the paper he had thrown it away. What had appeared in those papers was being sent by cable all over the world. It would upset the people of South Africa, as they did not understand the position. That afternoon he had hoped to have a peaceful lunch, but in the middle of it he received a cable to return at once. They were there as gentlemen and they must keep those things out of the newspapers or it would be impossible for other people to remain there. He was of opinion that such an article ought to be investigated to see whence it came and have a stop put to it. It would create a great deal of mischief.

He would like to tell President Wilson that he had understood that in the speeches which had been delivered that morning there was no threat. He observed that the Prime Minister of Great Britain had met the Dominion representatives and had discussed the question with them and he (General Botha) could assure President Wilson that it was only after very serious discussion, worry and trouble and through the influence of Mr. Lloyd George, that the resolution had been handed in that morning. He was one of those who would give up everything to reach the highest ideal. Therefore he supported Mr. Lloyd George, but he sincerely trusted that President Wilson would also agree. Do not let them stop at small things. If they could gain that bigger and higher ideal, then smaller considerations ought not to stand in the way. He remembered that after the war in his own country, which was on a smaller scale than the present, but which was just as bloody and miserable, they got self-government, but he saw at once that four different self-governing bodies in that country must lead to war. He was one of the original promoters of the Union of South Africa. He had his ideals and they were very high indeed. When he assembled all the leading statesmen he found then that the other people held views which it would be impossible to persuade them to abandon. He had then personally investigated these, and had come to the conclusion that they were smaller things. On that occasion he had asked his colleagues to stick to one thing, to aspire to the higher ideal, and that was the Union of South Africa. They must give way on the smaller things. He would like to say the same on this occasion. They must give way now and get their higher ideal, get a better understanding and bring the people together, and through that they would gain eventually all the things that they wanted to get. It was a small thing on which he had given way after the war in his own country, but unless it had been done that country would be in a very miserable condition that day.

He appreciated the ideals of President Wilson. They were the ideals of the people of the world, and they would succeed if all appreciated them in the same spirit and supported them in the manner in which they were intended. If all departed in an indifferent spirit those ideals would not have the desired success. Therefore, to his own mind, if they differed it was not a threat, because at the back of everybody's heart there was only one idea—that of attaining a better world understanding. Mankind looked upon them for support to do away with all future wars. He felt that by conceding smaller things they made the higher ideal more acceptable and it would have the hearty support of the whole world. They must remember that their various peoples did not understand everything in the same way. In that light therefore they must be guided to the bigger ideal. Personally he felt very strongly about the question of German South-West Africa. He thought that it differed entirely from any question that they had to decide in this Conference, but he would be prepared to say that he was a supporter of the document handed in that morning, because he knew that, if the idea fructified, the League of Nations would consist mostly of the same people who were present there that day, who understood the position and who would not make it impossible for any mandatory to govern the country. That was why he said he would accept it. He hoped that the second document there was entirely unnecessary, because the first document that was handed in that morning was an entirely provisional one. They could not accept anything by resolution now on hard and fast lines; everything depended on the ultimate resolution. That was how he understood the matter, and he hoped that they would try in a spirit of co-operation, and by giving way on smaller things, to meet the difficulties and make the bigger ideal possible.

It is difficult to convey the power of General Botha's deliverance by a mere summary of the words. Behind it was the attractive and compelling personality of this remarkable man. President Wilson was obviously moved. The friendliness and even deference of Botha's tone and manner won him a favourable hearing. The President told me immediately afterwards that it was the most impressive speech to which he had ever listened. The crisis was over and the proposal I had put forward was adopted, subject to the right of reconsideration if the Covenant of the League as finally drafted did not fit in. After the draft had been disposed of, M. Pichon raised a very important question as to the interpretation of the words in my scheme which prohibited the right to levy and train troops inside the mandated territories "for other than police purposes and for the defence of territory." The French Delegation was inclined to resent any restriction upon their desire to "recruit volunteers, not conscripts, from all Colonial territories under French control. This was absolutely necessary for the future security of French territory." M. Clemenceau seemed in his speech to demand an unlimited right of levying black troops to assist in the defence of

French territory in Europe if France were attacked in the future by Germany.

MR. LLOYD GEORGE said that . . . what the document did prevent was the kind of thing the Germans were likely to do, namely, organise great black armies in Africa, which they could use for the purpose of clearing everybody else out of that country. That was their proclaimed policy and if that was encouraged amongst the other nations even though they might not have wars in Europe, they would have the sort of thing that happened in the 17th and 18th centuries in India when France and Great Britain were at war in India, whilst they were ostensibly at peace in Europe. Then they were always raising great native armies against each other. That must now be stopped. There was nothing in this document which prevented France doing what she did before. The defence of territory was provided for.

M. CLEMENCEAU said that if he could raise troops, that was all he wanted.

MR. LLOYD GEORGE replied that he had exactly the same power as previously. It only prevented any country drilling the natives and raising great armies for aggressive purposes against their neighbours.

M. CLEMENCEAU said that he did not want to do that. All that he wished was that the matter should be made quite plain, and he did not want anybody to come and tell him afterwards that he had broken the agreement. If this clause meant that he had a right to raise troops in case of general war, he was satisfied.

MR. LLOYD GEORGE said that so long as M. Clemenceau did not train big Negro armies for the purposes of aggression, which was all the clause was intended to guard against, he was free to raise troops.

M. CLEMENCEAU said that he did not want to do that. He therefore understood that Mr. Lloyd George's interpretation was adopted.

PRESIDENT WILSON said that Mr. Lloyd George's interpretation was consistent with the phraseology.

These arrangements did not dispose of the colonial questions to be settled amongst the Allies, but the following is an outline of the ultimate disposition and classification.

The German Colonies before the War consisted of:

> Togoland
> Cameroons
> German East Africa
> German South-West Africa
> Certain Pacific Islands.

The Treaty of Peace enacts that "Germany renounces in favour of the Principal Allied and Associated Powers all her rights and titles over her overseas possessions."

Article 22 of the Covenant ordains:

To those colonies and territories which as a consequence of the late war have ceased to be under the sovereignty of the States which formerly governed them and which are inhabited by peoples not yet able to stand by themselves under the strenuous conditions of the modern world, there should be applied the principle that the well-being and development of such peoples form a sacred trust of civilization and that securities for the performance of this trust shall be embodied in this Covenant.

The best method of giving practical effect to this principle is that the tutelage of such peoples should be entrusted to advanced nations who by reason of their resources, their experience, or their geographical position can best undertake this responsibility, and who are willing to accept it, and that this tutelage should be exercised by them as Mandatories on behalf of the League.

The character of the mandate must differ according to the stage of the development of the people, the geographical situation of the territory, its economic conditions and other similar circumstances.

(A) Certain communities formerly belonging to the Turkish Empire have reached a stage of development where their existence as independent nations can be provisionally recognized subject to the rendering of administrative advice and assistance by a Mandatory until such time as they are able to stand alone. The wishes of these communities must be a principal consideration in the selection of the Mandatory.

(B) Other peoples, especially those of Central Africa, are at such a stage that the Mandatory must be responsible for the administration of the territory under conditions which will guarantee freedom of conscience and religion, subject only to the maintenance of public order and morals, the prohibition of abuses such as the slave trade, the arms traffic and the liquor traffic, and the prevention of the establishment of fortifications or military and naval bases and of military training of the natives for other than police purposes and the defence of territory, and will also secure equal opportunities for the trade and commerce of other Members of the League.

(C) There are territories, such as South-West Africa and certain of the South Pacific Islands, which, owing to the sparseness of their population, or their small size, or their remoteness from the centres of civilization, or their geographical contiguity to the territory of the

Mandatory, and other circumstances, can be best administered under the laws of the Mandatory as integral portions of its territory, subject to the safeguards above-mentioned in the interests of the indigenous population.

In every case of mandate, the Mandatory shall render to the Council an annual report in reference to the territory committed to its charge.

The degree of authority, control, or administration to be exercised by the Mandatory shall, if not previously agreed upon by the Members of the League, be explicitly defined in each case by the Council.

A permanent Commission shall be constituted to receive and examine the annual reports of the Mandatories and to advise the Council on all matters relating to the observance of the mandates.

There are thus "A," "B," and "C" classes of mandates. On May 7th, 1919, the Supreme Council in Paris decided that:

France and Great Britain should make a joint recommendation to the League of Nations as to the future of Togoland and the Cameroons ("B" Mandate).

The "B" Mandate for German East Africa should be held by Great Britain.

The "B" Mandate for German South-West Africa should be held by the Union of South Africa.

The "B" Mandate for the German Samoan Islands should be held by New Zealand.

Australia should have the "C" Mandate for the other German Pacific possessions south of the Equator (excluding the German Samoan Islands and Nauru).

The "C" Mandate for Nauru should be given to the British Empire.

France and Britain eventually submitted recommendations to the League by which the mandate for Togoland and the Cameroons was divided between them, France in each case receiving the larger portion.

The actual allocation of the German Colonies was not laid down in the Versailles Treaty. The Interallied Committee, which had been set up under Lord Milner's presidency to prepare the draft mandates, had not completed its task when the Treaty was signed in June, and certain difficulties arose subsequently, chiefly concerning the mandates for Palestine and Mesopotamia. America refused to accept a mandate for any of the German Colonies, but although she had not ratified the Covenant or the

Treaty, she still claimed a right to have a say in the disposition of the German Colonies.

The "C" mandates—which enabled the mandatory to govern the mandated territory as an integral part of his domain, subject to native interests being safeguarded by the League—were specially devised to meet such cases as South-West Africa and the Pacific Islands. General Smuts and Mr. Hughes fought hard to obtain sovereign rule over their territories, and to resist the mandatory idea as far as they were concerned. Australia, in fact, was frankly out for the annexation of the German Pacific Islands. But in the end the "C" mandate was awarded to Australia for the German Pacific Islands south of the Equator, with the exception of the islands of Samoa and Nauru. The former was mandated to New Zealand, but the latter island, because of its special position, came in for a good deal of discussion. It contained valuable deposits of phosphates, and on the outbreak of war the German company concerned had been taken over by the British. By decision of the Supreme Council on May 7th, the mandate for Nauru was handed to the British Empire, and an agreement was subsequently arrived at (July, 1919, and ratified August, 1920) by which the responsibility for administering the island (which lies 1,000 miles north-west of Samoa and 1,000 north-east of New Guinea) was passed on to Australia and New Zealand. Under this agreement an administration was to be appointed for five years by the Australian Government, and after that subsequent administrators were to be appointed by the three Governments in question.

Belgium was furious at the allocation to Great Britain of the mandate for the whole of German East Africa, since, as it was agreed, they had played an important part in the conquest of that colony. The fact of the matter had been that the resources of the British Empire were so engaged in reconquering Belgium for the Belgians that they had not enough men to spare for the minor fighting in German East Africa, and had to seek the assistance of the Belgian forces which garrisoned the Congo. But as a result of the Belgian protest an arrangement was arrived at whereby Belgium was given the mandate for the States of Ruandi and Urundi.

This being high ground was more densely inhabited than the malarial jungle which constituted the greater part of German East Africa.

Portugal received as her portion of the German Colonies the district of Kionga.

The draft mandates for Togoland and the Cameroons were only published in May, 1921. It was not until July, 1922, that the mandatory system came into full operation in regard to all the ex-German Colonies, and to Palestine and Syria.

Turkey as a result of the War lost:

Syria, which became a French mandate;

Palestine
Transjordania   which became British
Irak   mandates.

Turkey also lost her suzerainty over Egypt.

The question of mandates for the Turkish possessions will form part of a subsequent chapter.

It will be noted that this is the first occasion on which the Dominions accepted responsibility for the government of territories outside their own frontiers. Three out of the four thereby established little empires of their own within the greater Empire of which they are an integral part. Their readiness to do so was a great relief to all those who, like myself, felt that the British Empire, with its vast distances, its immense territories, its endless problems and its infinite variety of races and languages, was becoming too great a burden for a small island like ours ever to govern efficiently and develop adequately without more definite assistance from the Dominions. It was for that reason that many of us shrank from adding any of even the German Colonies in Africa to our gigantic domain. But America refused to take any African mandates. They probably apprehended that, if they undertook the government of millions of Negroes in tropical Africa, it might create some complications with their own coloured population. Canada was the only Dominion that sought no accession of tropical territory in any quarter of the globe: in fact, she shrank from the idea. Personally, I regretted the disinclination

of her statesmen and her people then to share in the direct
responsibilities of empire. I had many a talk with Sir Robert
Borden on the subject. I had been of the opinion that Canada
might undertake the control and administration of the British
West Indian islands on behalf of the Empire. Those beautiful and
fertile islands were—and still are—suffering from the neglect
which is inevitable in an immense and scattered estate needing
constant care and capital, not only for its full development but
even to prevent its falling into decay. Canada has no tropical or
semi-tropical territory, and I thought the undertaking might
interest the Canadian people. I found that Sir Robert Borden was
deeply imbued with the American prejudice against the government of extraneous possessions and peoples which did not form
an integral part of their own Union. He therefore gave no encouragement to my suggestion, and I dropped it.

APPENDIX

BRITISH DELEGATION,
PARIS.

As I am unable to be present at the meeting this evening, I send
the following notes upon the mandatory power for what they may be
worth.

On the question of expenditure I need say little or nothing: the main
points were made by the Prime Minister this afternoon. If the League
of Nations is to provide money for the development of (what I may
describe as) mandatory States, an almost unworkable fiscal system
will necessarily be created. The mandatory power, as I understand
President Wilson's scheme, will first have to draw up its administrative
budget. If there is a deficit, it will then be its duty to apply for the
necessary funds to the League of Nations. The League of Nations will
have to send out officials for the purpose of satisfying itself, in the
first place that the expenditure is wise; in the *second* place that the
revenues of the mandatory country, as administered, are incapable
of meeting it; in the *third* place, that the money required cannot be
obtained by economies in other branches of expenditure. Having satisfied itself on these points it will then have to apportion the burden
between the various States making up the League of Nations on some
scale which will presumably have been already arrived at.

When this is done, there will still remain the third stage:—that of
inducing the legislators of the various countries belonging to the

League to vote the money; I can hardly conceive a more difficult machine to work, or one whose working will be less conducive to economy.

An observation made I think by President Wilson suggests that, in his view, the cost of protection, and in particular of naval protection, should in like manner be apportioned among the States composing the League. I think the impossibility of such a plan will, on reflexion, appear so obvious that I will not at the present stage waste time on superfluous demonstrations.

There is a second aspect of the mandatory system which seems to me of great importance, to which no reference was made in any of the speeches this afternoon.

Under the President's plan as I understand it, the mandatory power is to have no fixity of tenure but is to be dispossessed by the League of Nations whenever the inhabitants of the mandatory territory make up their minds that they would like a change of *régime*. The President (unless my memory deceives me) went the length of saying in his speech that if the mandatory power wisely fulfilled its functions there would be no chance of the inhabitants of the mandatory State expressing any desire for a change of rulers. Indeed the absence of any such desire seemed to be (in his view) the real test and measure of mandatory success.

This may very often be true, but may very often be quite untrue. I am quite ready to admit that the genuine preferences of a population are a very trustworthy if not an infallible guide to what is best for it; but it is extremely difficult in practice to know what its genuine preferences are. What are commonly called its preferences are not and cannot be based in the least upon any real or direct comparison of the two systems between which it expresses its choice; they are always based on a comparison between a system which it knows and has experienced and some other system, which it neither knows nor has experienced, but which is perhaps represented to it with fantastic optimism by the agitator or the intriguer.

Now what would be the position of a mandatory power carrying out the difficult tasks of its office with no security of tenure? In existing circumstances reasonable men endeavour to make the best of the Government under which they live, if they know that this Government though it may be modified and improved, is going to last. I imagine, for example, that in German East Africa, the Germans in Dar es Salaam if they were certain that they were going to be permanently British or French or American would endeavour to make the best of a system which they might wish to be different. But if by stirring up difficulties among the natives, by constant propaganda, by unceasing efforts to show how much happier everyone would be were they again under German rule, they could hope to induce the League of Nations to turn out the existing mandatory, and to substitute Germany in its place, they would never rest: and German East Africa would never settle down. The evils of German rule might become a faint memory. Contemporary grievances, real or imaginary, would occupy all their thoughts; and without performing any operation which could truly be described as comparing the old with the new, they would clamour for a change. A movable mandatory might thus supply a perpetual incentive to agitation and intrigue.

The only other observation I have to make is that in my judgment the mandatory principle seems necessarily to involve some machinery of inspection—some method of conveying in cases of scandal independent information to the League of Nations. Without this the members of the League would be helpless; but with it, they would be in constant peril of coming in collision with the mandatory power. I admit, however, that the difficulty is of less importance than those to which I previously adverted.

I am, let me add, personally, in favour of attempting the mandatory system, but it is full of difficulties which, so far as my knowledge goes, have not yet been adequately considered. Some of these I have noted above.

(*Initialled*) A. J. B.

27.1.19.

CHAPTER XI

THE PARLIAMENTARY REVOLT

THE TIMES" headed a retinue of papers with a large circulation which kept up a cross fire of criticism and innuendo every day. Everything said and done at the Peace Council was distorted or disproportioned. Lord Northcliffe's attitude towards the Government was at this time that of an extremely angry man, whose decisive contributions to victory had been slighted by unappreciative and envious politicians. The Government had refused to make him a peace delegate, which was a blow to what he regarded as a legitimate recognition of his paramount share in the triumph. The further refusal to hand over to him the propaganda arrangements for the Conference also hurt his pride deeply. He declared war without quarter not only on myself, the chief culprit, but on Bonar Law and Balfour (both of whom he always disliked and despised) and he waged it without scruple. Another set of popular papers did its best to ridicule the Conference, especially the magnificent organisation which had been built up by Lord Hardinge and Sir Maurice Hankey with the help of the Board of Trade, the War Office or the Admiralty, to give expert advice on the vast and varied issues raised by the Treaty. They held it up to the mockery of readers as a costly circus of supernumeraries on pleasure bent. No organisation of any Government represented at the Conference excelled that of the British in efficiency. It was acknowledged that in some respects ours was superior.

The Northcliffe papers at first took up the line that the French and British Governments were antipathetic to President Wilson's great ideals, and that clandestinely we were intriguing to defeat his noble purposes. When it became clear that Wilson and the British representatives were working in zealous harmony to hammer out the Covenant of the League, to delimit frontiers on ethnic and not strategic conditions, resisting demands which were unjust and would ultimately lead to another war, and that we were just as opposed as the President was to a vindictive and annexationist peace, their criticism swung round in the opposite direction. They then adopted the attitude of the Extreme Right in France, that Wilson was bullying Clemenceau and the British Delegation to forego French and British interests on reparations and colonies in order to satisfy a sterile idealism to which he was committed by his speeches. An agitation on the question was assiduously fomented in the lobbies of the House of Commons by Northcliffe's old journalistic partner, Kennedy Jones, who was a Member of the House. He was one of the founders of the half-penny press. With those organising gifts and tenacity of purpose which had made his success, he was able in a short time to work up a formidable discontent amongst supporters of the Government in the House. He showed to his Parliamentary colleagues one by one, in the strictest confidence, communications he had received from "high authority in Paris," which intimated that the British delegates were conspiring with Wilson to "give away" all the pledges made by them at the election and that the French were profoundly alarmed at this sinister development. The names of certain French Ministers and important French officials were sometimes given—more often hinted at—as sources of this disturbing information. Even the French President's name was given in the strictest confidence and passed on with the same solemn injunction that it must not be mentioned.

Loyal supporters of the Government were upset by these representations. The outline of my proposals on the question of reparations had appeared in the critical press, having no doubt been given away by the French, who thought them much too lenient to the Germans. They were severely attacked, and denounced as a betrayal of my election pledges. Mr. Bonar Law had warned me that they "would cause a wild storm" and so they did. He further added: "I have no doubt you realise all this, but perhaps you think opinion in the House has become more sane, and I fear that is not the case."

At the beginning of April a debate was raised in the House of Commons on the subject. Members who had given irrational and

unwarranted assurances to their constituents about making
Germany pay the whole cost of the War felt bound to take part.
I was in Paris and could not attend. The Leader of the House,
Mr. Bonar Law, replied on behalf of the Government and repeated the statements that both he and I had made during the
election. I have already given full extracts from my electoral
speech on the subject of reparation. I will now give the clear and
unambiguous words used by Mr. Bonar Law during the campaign, and repeated by him in the course of this debate:

A good deal has been said about election pledges, and my hon. and
gallant Friend behind me, much to my regret, said he had given a
definite pledge that Germany would pay the whole cost of the War,
and that if she did not he would have to resign. I do not know what
influenced his mind in making that statement, but certainly it was
not anything said by any member of His Majesty's Government.
My hon. and gallant Friend who moved the Motion to-night quoted
a speech of the Prime Minister, and quoted it quite correctly. He did
not quote the whole of it. He quoted the substance of it. The one
part he did not mention was the part which was the basis, I believe,
of all the Prime Minister's speeches, and that was not that he would
make Germany pay the whole cost of the War, but that we should
exact from Germany whatever Germany was able to pay. Every time
this subject has been raised I have had the feeling that I am more
out of sympathy with Members who support the Government on this
subject than on any other which has been raised. If that is due to
any real difference of opinion it cannot be helped because everything
I have said in this House is precisely what I have said during the
election. I have not changed my view. Let me read for example part
of a speech, which happened to be one of the last which I made before
the election at Mile End, where a number of my hon. Friends who
are now Members of the House were present. What I said then was
precisely what I thought then, what I think now, and what I have
said on every occasion the subject has been raised in this House. It
was this:

"The first thing is to find out what she can pay, and we have already proposed to our Allies that an expert scientific committee should
be appointed to examine into the amount which can be paid, not without injury to Germany. The country is responsible for its Government
and for the crimes of its Government, and has a right to suffer for
them.

"What this committee will do, if we have our way"—and we have had our way, for that is what the Allies have done—"is to examine this question with precisely the same amount of scientific skill and energy as an accountant examining the books of a bankrupt to find out how much he could pay his creditors."

I have no doubt there were differences of opinion among members of His Majesty's Government, as among other people, as to what amount could be paid, and some were more sanguine than others. I was not amongst the most sanguine, and in this same speech I said this:

"Whatever amount we get, it would be holding out a hope, the fulfilment of which I cannot conceive, to suggest that Germany could pay our whole war debt. Whatever amount we get, the burden upon this country will only be met, in my opinion, by something in the nature of a different way of living and reduced expenditure."

So far, therefore, as I am concerned the view which I express in this House is precisely the view which I expressed during the election. That view has not changed. There is no change whatever up to this hour in the attitude of His Majesty's Government on this question. The intention still is to obtain, as part of the debt which Germany owes, whatever amount can be got from Germany. That is our case. . . .

This characteristically blunt and straightforward speech, far from beating down the choppy waves, lashed them to perilous breakers. Kennedy Jones gathered the signatures of 233 Coalition members to a Round Robin message which was to be sent to me at Paris. So urgent was the peril these excited members visualised, that it was resolved to wire me without delay. Here is a copy of the telegram signed by these members, some of them men of considerable influence in their party:

The greatest anxiety exists throughout the country at the persistent reports from Paris that the British delegates instead of formulating the complete financial claim of the Empire are merely considering what amount can be exacted from the enemy. This anxiety has been deepened by the statement of the Leader of the House on Wednesday last.

Our constituents have always expected—and still expect—that the first action of the Peace Delegates would be, as you repeatedly stated in your election speeches, to present the Bill in full, to make Germany acknowledge the debt and then to discuss ways and means of obtaining payment.

Although we have the utmost confidence in your intention to fulfil your pledges to the country, may we, as we have to meet innumerable inquiries from our constituents, have your assurance that you have in no way departed from your original intention.

I replied immediately:

My colleagues and I mean to stand faithfully by all the pledges we gave to the constituencies. We are prepared at any moment to submit to the judgment of Parliament and if necessary of the Country our efforts loyally to redeem our promises.

My reply was drafted in conjunction with Mr. Bonar Law, who considered the situation so menacing that he had hurried off to Paris to confer with me as to the Parliamentary action we should take to quell the threatened uprising. In my original draft reply I wished to include our electoral pledges on social problems, so as to make it clear that we meant to stand by those as well. Mr. Bonar Law thought that this would be unnecessarily provocative in the state of his party's mind at that moment, and these words were struck out.

I then decided to cross over to London to face Parliament and demand what would be equivalent to a vote of confidence. I felt that if the uneasiness amongst our supporters represented a real distrust of the Peace Delegation, it would be better to resign my position and hand over the seals to someone who represented more truly the attitude of Parliament. I could not conscientiously become the instrument of forcing upon Germany a peace conceived in the spirit of the Kennedy Jones message. I had a few pressing matters to dispose of in the Council of Four, so I asked Mr. Bonar Law to fix a date the following week for a full Parliamentary debate. The discussion took place on the 16th April. I led off with a lengthy statement of the position and I spoke my mind with complete frankness. I found the unrest was not confined to the question of reparations, but that it had been worked up because of the time occupied by the Conference in making peace, and more particularly because of my attitude towards the Bolshevik Government in Russia.

I dealt first of all with the question of the time occupied in completing the Treaty. I pointed out the immensity and the variety of the problems coming up for decision.

. . . The task with which the Peace Delegates have been confronted has indeed been a gigantic one. No Conference that has ever assembled in the history of the world has been faced with problems of such variety, of such complexity, of such magnitude, and of such gravity. The Congress of Vienna was the nearest approach to it. You had then to settle the affairs of Europe alone. It took eleven months. But the problems at the Congress of Vienna, great as they were, sink into insignificance compared with those which we have had to attempt to settle at the Paris Conference. It is not one continent that is engaged—every continent is affected. With very few exceptions, every country in Europe has been in this War. Every country in Asia is affected by the War, except Tibet and Afghanistan. There is not a square mile of Africa that has not been engaged in the War in one way or another. Almost the whole of the nations of America are in the War, and in the far islands of the Southern Seas there are islands that have been captured, and there are hundreds of thousands of men from those remote regions who have come to fight in this great world struggle. There has never been in the whole history of this globe anything to compare to it. Ten new States have sprung into existence, some of them independent, some of them semi-independent, some of them may be Protectorates, and, at any rate, although you may not define their boundaries, you must give indications of them. The boundaries of fourteen countries have to be re-cast.

That will give some idea of the difficulties, purely of a territorial character, that have engaged our attention. But there are problems, equally great and equally important, not of a territorial character, but all affecting the peace of the world, all affecting the well-being of men, all affecting the destiny of the human race, and every one of them of a character where, if you make blunders, humanity may have to pay. Armaments, economic questions, which are the life of commerce and trade, questions of international waterways and railways, the question of indemnities—not an easy one, and not going to be settled by telegram—and international arrangements for labour practically never attempted before!

At this stage I dwelt upon the powers of revision of the Treaty which would be vested in the League of Nations:

. . . In fact, I do not mind saying that it would have been imperative in some respects that we should have taken more time but for one fact, and that is that we are setting up a machinery which is capable of readjusting and correcting possible mistakes. That is why the League of Nations, instead of wasting time, has saved the time of the Conference.

It is significant that the first announcement of this revisory authority was received by the House without a single adverse comment.

I then referred to the strenuous character of our labours, and explained how they were rendered more difficult by the organised disparagement of all our efforts:

. . . I venture to say that no body of men ever worked harder, and that no body of men have ever worked in better harmony. I am doubtful whether any body of men with a difficult task have worked under greater difficulties—stones clattering on the roof, and crashing through the windows, and sometimes wild men screaming through the keyholes.

Then in effect I asked the House to make it clear whether I had their confidence or not in resuming my task:

I have come back to say a few things and I mean to say them. (An Hon. Member: "Save you from your friends!") I quite agree, and when enormous issues are depending upon it, you require calm deliberation. I ask it for the rest of the journey. The journey is not at an end. It is full of perils, perils for this country, perils for all lands, perils for the people throughout the world. I beg, at any rate, that the men who are doing their best should be left in peace to do it, or that other men should be sent there.

These criticisms are merely artificial difficulties. They are difficulties that are more trying to the temper than to the judgment. But there are intrinsic difficulties of an extraordinary character. You are dealing with a multitude of nations, most of them with a problem of its own, each and every one of them with a different point of view, even where the problems are common, looking from a different angle at questions—sometimes, perhaps, with conflicting interests; and it requires all the tact, all the patience, and all the skill that we can command to prevent different interests from developing into clashing interests. I want the House and the country to bear that in mind. I believe that we have surmounted those difficulties, but it has not been easy. There were questions one never heard of which have almost imperilled the peace of Europe while we were sitting there.

The feeling amongst Conservative members about the overtures which President Wilson and I had made for the pacification of Russia, and which had included the Bolshevik Government in their orbit, was suspicious and resentful. It was an easy task for the nagging section of the Press to stir up a feeling of indignation on this subject. To the majority of British citizens Bolshevism was a hideous and a terrifying monster. The action of the British Government in attempting to deal with it was represented as tendering a friendly hand to murder whilst it was reeking with the blood of its victims. When people take sides in the internal conflicts of another country, they usually overlook the fact that these horrible incidents, which are inseparable from civil war, are never confined to one side—certainly not in a half-civilised country. But Conservative sentiment was so irritated by our efforts to bring the Bolsheviks into a general scheme of appeasement in Russia, that I had to devote a great part of my speech to the handling of this explosive topic. I began by pointing out why we could not recognise either the Bolsheviks or the Whites as the *de facto* Government of Russia:

You have that vast country in a state of complete chaos, confusion, and anarchy. There is no authority that extends over the whole. Boundaries advance and boundaries recede. One day a large territory is governed by one authority, and the next day by another. It is just like a volcano; it is still in fierce eruption, and the best you can do is to provide security for those who are dwelling on its remotest and most accessible slopes, and arrest the devastating flow of lava, so that it shall not scorch other lands.

I dealt with the project for direct intervention by the Allies in the affairs of Russia. The idea had its adherents even amongst Ministers. Mr. Churchill was known to be an ardent advocate of plans for the overthrow of Bolshevism with the aid of Allied arms. I asked:

What is the alternative? Does anyone propose military intervention? I want to examine that carefully and candidly. I will not say before the House, but before any individual commits his conscience to such an enterprise, I want him to realise what it means. First of all there is the fundamental principle of all foreign policy in this country—a very sound principle—that you should never interfere in the internal affairs of another country, however badly governed; and whether Russia is Menshevik or Bolshevik, whether it is reactionary or revolutionary, whether it follows one set of men or another, that is a matter for the Russian people themselves.

I pointed out how costly and how fatuous any attempt to conquer Russia had always been:

Let me speak in all solemnity, and with a great sense of responsibility. Russia is a country which it is very easy to invade, but very difficult to conquer. It has never been conquered by a foreign foe, although it has been successfully invaded many times. It is a country which it is easy to get into, but very difficult to get out of. You have only to look at what has happened in the last few years to the Germans. They rolled up the Russian armies, they captured millions of Russian prisoners, they took Russian guns. The Russians had no ammunition, there was barely anyone to resist them, and at last the Russian Army fled, leaving their guns on the field. There was no Russian Army. Neither M. Kerensky nor any of his successors could get together 10,000 disciplined men to resist the advancing Germans.

I then pointed out how the victorious armies of the Central Powers had only been landed in a morass from which they could not extricate themselves. Even although the Russian Army had ceased to exist, and its equipment had fallen into enemy hands, the Central Powers had to keep a million men in that morass.

Supposing you gathered together an overwhelming army, and you conquered Russia. What manner of government are you going to set up there? You must set up a government which the people want; otherwise it would be an outrage of all the principles for which we have fought in this War. Does anyone know for what government they would ask, and if it is a government we do not like, are we to reconquer Russia in order to get a Government we do like? . . . I should not be doing my duty as head of the Government unless I stated quite frankly to the House my earnest conviction—that to attempt military intervention in Russia would be the greatest act of stupidity that any Government could possibly commit.

I defended our support of certain elements which had been organised during the War after the surrender of the Bolsheviks to prevent the resources of Russia falling into the hands of the Central Powers:

. . . Had it not been for those organisations that we improvised, the Germans would have secured all the resources which would have enabled them to break the blockade. They would have got through to the grain of the Don, to the minerals of the Urals, and to the oils of the Caucasus. They could have supplied themselves with almost every commodity of which four or five years of rigid blockade had deprived them, and which was essential to their conducting the War.

But I qualified our support of the anti-German front in Russia by saying that we could only continue it as long as it was clear that they had the evident goodwill of the population in the areas under their control. I ended by urging the importance of peace in Russia:

But we want peace in Russia. The world will not be pacified so long as Russia is torn and rent by civil war. We made one effort. I make no apology for that. That was an effort to make peace among the warring sections, not by recognising any particular Government, but by inducing them to come together, with a view to setting up some authority in Russia which would be acceptable to the whole of the Russian people, and which the Allies could recognise as the Government of that great people. We insisted that it was necessary they should cease fighting before they started to negotiate. With one accord, I regret to say, they refused to assent to this essential condition, and, therefore, the effort was not crowned with success. . . . Each of them suggested that we were seeking a truce purely because our friends were getting the worst of it. That fact itself shows that the time has not yet arrived for securing the pacification of Russia by means of any outside pressure. I do not, however, despair of a solution being found.

On the general question of standing by our pledges, I said:

. . . Before the War was over, we stated our peace terms. On behalf of the Government, I made a considered statement—which was considered by every member of the Cabinet and by the Trade Union Conference—of what we conceived to be the terms on which we could make peace with the enemy. That was last year. At that time those terms received the adhesion of every section of opinion in this country. There was no protest from any quarter. A few days afterwards President Wilson proposed his famous "Fourteen Points," which practically embodied the same proposals. I am referred to my speeches before the last election. There are some who suggest that at the last election I and my colleagues were rushed into declarations of which now we are rather ashamed, and wish to get out of. I do not wish to get out of them in the least. These declarations were adopted by, I think, every political leader of every section. . . . Those pledges were not the pledges merely of my colleagues and myself, but of every political leader. I tell the House at once that, if on reflection, and if after examination of the problem with the statesmen of other lands—who have not had to fight an election, and therefore could take a calmer and more detached view of these problems—if, after coming in contact with them, I had arrived at the conclusion that I had gone too far, and pledged the Government and the country to something that I could not carry out, I should have come down here and said so, because it would have been folly, even for an electioneering pledge, to imperil the peace of Europe. Then the House of Commons, of course, would have been free to take its own action. But, so far from my coming here to ask for reconsideration—to ask release from any pledge or promise which I have given—I am here to say that all the outlines of peace that we have ever given to the public and asked them to make sacrifices to obtain—every pledge we have given with regard to what we pressed for insertion in the peace terms is incorporated in the demands which have been put forward by the Allies. I observe that some of these pledges are published. I am going to issue an invitation to some enterprising newspaper that when the peace terms, the peace demands put forward by the Allies, come to be published, there should be published in parallel columns the pledges and the promises made by the Government.*

Neither the Coalition protesters, the Independent Liberals nor the Labour members challenged the accuracy of this statement during the debate nor afterwards. On the underlying principle of the peace I added:

We want a peace which will be just, but not vindictive. We want a stern peace, because the occasion demands it. The crime demands it. But its severity must be designed, not to gratify vengeance, but to vindicate justice. Every clause and term in those conditions must be justified on that ground. Above all, we want to protect the future against a repetition of the horrors of this War, by making the wrong-doer repair the wrong and the loss which he has inflicted by his wanton aggression, by punishing any individual who is responsible, by depriving the nations that have menaced the peace of Europe for half a century with a flourishing sword—by depriving them of their weapon—(An Hon. Member: "What about the Kaiser?")—I stand by all my pledges—by avoiding conditions which would create a legitimate sense of wrong, which would excite national pride needlessly to seek opportunities for redress, and by giving the most permanent security to the nations of the earth to federate for a firm purpose of maintaining right.

* This challenge was never accepted.

I want to say one other thing, because I am going back, if the House wants me to—unless it prefers some other choice. (Hon. Members: "No, no!") There are many "eligible offers." But whoever goes there is going to meet the emissaries of the enemy, the enemy with whom we have been confronted for five years, and who has inflicted terrible wounds upon humanity. Whoever goes there must go knowing that he has the fullest confidence of Parliament behind him. I know that Parliament can repudiate the treaty when it is signed. I do not want to contemplate that. It would be difficult to do so once British signatures are attached, but Parliament can do it. So, before anyone goes there, Parliament must feel that, at any rate, it knows that whoever is there will carry out his pledges to the utmost of his power and his gifts. You cannot always be clearing up misconceptions. When you see misstatements you cannot instantly write, and say that they are not true, that they are inaccurate. You cannot always be leaving the Conference to come home to deny or explain this or that. You cannot conduct negotiations under those conditions.

As Lord Northcliffe was the leading spirit in the intrigues that had stirred up trouble for the Government, I felt bound to refer to him as the "reliable source" from which Mr. Kennedy Jones and his friends had derived their information:

. . . At the beginning of the Conference there were appeals to everybody all round to support President Wilson and his great ideals. Where did these come from? From the same "reliable source" that is now hysterically attacking all those great ideals. Just a few weeks ago there was a cartoon in one of these papers representing Bolshevism as a mere bogey, and I as a person trying to frighten the working classes with that mere bogey. Now it is no longer a bogey; it is a monster, and I am doing my best to dress it up as an angel. That is the same "reliable source." Reliable! That is the last adjective I would use. It is here to-day, jumping there to-morrow, and there the next day. I would as soon rely on a grasshopper.

I ended on the note that right and not passion was the foundation of an enduring peace:

Nations with military ambitions have received a cruel lesson, nay, Europe itself has suffered more in the last five years than ever in the whole of its past history. The lesson has been a sharper one than ever. It has been administered to vaster multitudes of human beings than ever. The people have a more intelligent appreciation of what it means than ever. For that reason the opportunity of organising the world on the basis of peace is such a one as has never been presented to the world before, and in this fateful hour it is the supreme duty of statesmen in every land—of the Parliaments upon whose will statesmen depend, of those who guide and direct the public opinion which is the making of all—not to soil this triumph of right by indulging in the angry passions of the moment, but to consecrate the sacrifices of millions to the permanent redemption of the human race from the scourge and agony of war.

It is not a mere boast to state that the Opposition collapsed utterly, without a murmur or a groan. When the leader of the Labour Opposition rose to continue the debate, he expressed the general sentiment when he said:

. . . The House, and the country, have been looking forward with intense interest to the statement from the Prime Minister, to which we have just listened, and I am certain that I will carry general assent when I say that we have not been disappointed.

Neither Mr. Kennedy Jones nor any of his co-signatories made any attempt to justify their misgivings. The Liberal Opposition took no part in the discussion. Apart from the speech of their leader there were two speeches from the Labour benches: one a characteristically generous one from Colonel Josiah Wedgwood:

We are here not only to welcome back the Noble Lord opposite, but also the Prime Minister. He, too, has in a way surprised some of those who did not receive his support at the last election by the admirable way in which he has carried on his work in Paris. The Prime Minister, in spite of all the yapping of the Press and the telegraphing of his followers, has maintained an even course absolutely in accordance with his Liberal past in backing up the Liberal ideas of President Wilson, and doing his best to re-establish the world on the basis of justice and self-determination. Although we have missed him from this House, we have seen that he was doing more useful work for the future of this country in Paris.

The second was from Mr. Clynes, who was critical about the troops we had sent to certain parts of Russia.

The disaffected Press did not entirely cease to grumble and to insinuate, but the knowledge that they had no support in any quarter that counted had a restraining effect upon their chiding and detraction. The discussion was worth while, for it eased off the growing pressure to force us into an entirely irrational and grotesquely impracticable peace.

CHAPTER XII

CLEMENCEAU'S DIFFICULTIES

CLEMENCEAU and Orlando also had their difficulties with the public opinion of their respective countries. The pressure in their case, exactly as in mine, came from the extremists who insisted upon extracting out of the victory before the termination of hostilities, advantages which were in contravention of the fundamental principles of the peace terms formulated by the Allies.

The two issues which created the greatest trouble between France, on the one hand, and Britain and the United States of America on the other, were the fixation of the Western boundaries of Germany (this included the highly controverted questions of the Rhine frontier and the future destiny of the Saar coal-fields); and the extortionate demand put forward by French Ministers for reparations from Germany. It was fortunate for the Conference that France was represented by an exceptionally strong and courageous man, otherwise the Peace Conference would either have been shattered on these passionately controverted topics, or it would have anticipated the process with which we are so familiar in international conferences of to-day, of postponing difficulties to the point of futility and impotence. For his failure to insist upon the extreme French claims on these various issues against all obstacles and opposition, M. Clemenceau was criticised by a formidable junta of Right-Wing and Centre leaders. He met all his critics with the steadiness and the cunning of the best swordsman in France. He exhibited all the qualities of cool and adroit intrepidity which in the course of his stormy career had enabled him to fight so many successful duels with tongue, pen and sword.

The French Press, fearing retaliation from the savage old Tiger, directed its wrath not so much against him as against President Wilson and myself for our resistance to what they

conceived were the legitimate claims of France, with hints that
Clemenceau was not standing up to us as he ought and might.
The bitterness and ferocity of the attacks, when it is considered
that we were special envoys of foreign powers at the French
capital, were quite without precedent, especially when it is remembered that the intervention and sacrifices of the countries
we represented had only just saved France from a more shattering defeat than 1871, which would have left her prostrate under
the heel of German military autocracy without an army to defend her or an empire to enrich her. This conduct could not have
occurred and would not have been permitted in any other capital
in the world. The paragraphs about Wilson and the caricatures of
him were particularly spiteful. Those that were directed against
me were odious enough, but they were of the kind that had been
my daily experience for years in my own country. They did not
therefore cause me any bother. But Wilson was hurt. They cut
every time through his sensitive and unweathered pride and the
smart became visible in his countenance. It had much to do with
his breakdown. The rabble of Parisian lampoonists and slanderers
dragged him from the pedestal on which they had perched him
and around which they had sung their fulsome hymns of praise
to him when he arrived, and rolled him in the gutter of their
malignity and scurrility.

But although the Tiger was not openly attacked, a conspiracy
of detraction was maturing in every corner and cranny where his
numerous adversaries could gather without undue publicity. The
boudoirs and reception rooms of the Élysée and the bureaux of
the General Staff of the Army, the couloirs of the Senate and the
Chamber of Deputies were sibilant with hisses at Clemenceau's
surrender of the rights and opportunities of France. He was never
a favourite son of the Church. He was one of its avowed and un-
relenting enemies. He had therefore no ready defenders in its
cloisters.

The confederates had leaders of distinction and of renown.
Marshal Foch, the greatest living soldier, the man who with
Clemenceau was popularly regarded as joint Saviour of France,
was an open critic of Clemenceau's supposed betrayal of his coun-

try. His frank and straightforward character did not lend itself to clandestine methods of conspiracy, but in the general assembly of the plenipotentiaries of the nations he broke out into an emphatic protest against the terms of peace. In the Chamber of Deputies Barthou was the most powerful public exponent of the extremist attitude. In force and eloquence of speech he was much the ablest of Clemenceau's open adversaries. Briand, with his customary caution, lay low and contented himself with flinging here and there with a casual air occasional jests in the course of conversation, which set his auditors laughing at the Tiger. On the question of severing the territory on the left bank of the Rhine from Germany, he had already committed himself during the War. He favoured the project of constituting an independent German republic out of the Germanic populations dwelling on the left of the Rhine, with Luxemburg thrown in. He was therefore out of sympathy with the arrangements effected by the Peace Treaty. But he was not by nature irreconcilable or implacable. Had he been at the Peace Conference his influence, when he could be stirred to exert it, would have been for appeasement. Unfortunately Clemenceau would have no dealings with Briand and made no effort to win his co-operation or support. He hated him. What was worse, he despised him as a sonorous flapdoodler. Briand was made aware of that contempt, and he returned Clemenceau's detestation in full measure, but with subtler and deadlier methods.

But what gave an almost official sanction to the opposition worked up against Clemenceau's concessions to British and American dictation, as it was called, was the attitude of the President of the French Republic. He and Foch were in complete accord and worked together for the same common end. With a tireless assiduity he interviewed Ministers, politicians and pressmen, urging on all and sundry his views about the importance, in the interests of French security, of pushing the frontiers of Germany for the future well away from the banks of the Rhine. Poincaré favoured all the various attempts made to resurrect the old Rhineland states which were at one time independent of the control of Prussia. The French Generals and administrators who were in control of the Rhine bridgeheads had no difficulty in finding Rhinelanders who were attracted by that prospect and who were quite prepared, if assured of French military support, to make the attempt. The men of the Rhineland had never been reconciled to the iron grip of the Prussian war-lords. Religious prejudices as well as historical traditions combined to create antipathy to the Prussian domination. But they were German to the marrow, and disheartened, disillusioned and prostrate as they were, the masses of the people in the Rhineland believed in preserving that unity of their race which had been won for them by Bismarck and saved them from the feuds and civil strife that had rent, torn and enfeebled Germany for so many centuries.

Both President Wilson and.myself discouraged these hugger-mugger attempts to set up flimsy republics in the area occupied by American and British troops. We protested to Clemenceau against the intrigues of the French Generals in the district under their control, and soon the movement collapsed. But Poincaré and his confederates were sore and resentful. They were genuinely convinced that the French Premier had thrown away the last and the best chance tendered to France for establishing the security of her Eastern frontiers against her oldest and most redoubtable foe. They were equally convinced that Clemenceau could have achieved this secular aim of French patriotism through the centuries had he put up a better fight for it at the Peace Conference.

CHAPTER XIII

DISARMAMENT

THE question of disarmament led to several discussions at the Conference: first of all, the extent to which disarmament should be imposed upon Germany, and secondly, the desirability and method of effecting a general reduction in world armaments.

Early in February the Allied military authorities became alarmed by the prospect of a revival of the military power of Germany before the Peace Treaty could be presented to the German Government for its signature. The demobilisation of the Allied forces was proceeding very rapidly. The American forces were being shipped home in great numbers and so were the British troops. Most of the French divisions were still retained at the front or in readiness behind, but even their numbers had been reduced. It is true that the great German Army had been almost entirely dissolved except for a certain number of divisions on the Eastern front, where there was some trouble with the Poles, and more apprehended. Enormous quantities of German war material had been surrendered immediately after the Armistice, but there was still a formidable equipment of artillery, machine-guns, rifles and ammunition left in German hands. In February, Marshal Foch demanded that as a condition of renewing the Armistice, there should be a further reduction in the German forces and a further surrender of war material. In the course of the discussion I reported that

. . . I had been very much impressed by a conversation I had held with Sir Douglas Haig, who had . . . called attention to the fact that Germany still had the matériel and armament which would enable her within a short period of time to call back three or four million men, fully equipped for war. By that time most of the American and British troops would have gone home and be out of reach and the French would have scattered over the country. If Germany should therefore mean mischief, she could call together millions of well-trained men, with a full complement of officers and non-commissioned officers, thousands of the best guns in the world, and fifty thousand machine-guns.

Ultimately it was decided not to demand any further immediate surrender of German material, but to appoint a commission to draft the military and naval conditions which should be incorporated in the Treaty, and to hurry up the drafting of the Treaty. Both Foch and Pétain were of opinion that the Germans were too demoralised to organise any military resistance in the immediate future and that, provided the preparation of the Treaty was speeded up, the Allies could afford to wait with the forces at their command.

This discussion was interesting as a revelation of the mind of the statesmen around the table, and of their chief military advisers, on the general subject of disarmament. M. Clemenceau was unusually truculent in his animadversions on the Germans. In this debate on disarmament, he exposed more of his deep enmity towards the people who had twice in the course of his lifetime invaded France and sacrificed her cities, than at any time in the course of our prolonged deliberations. He resented every suggestion that emanated from President Wilson or anyone else that seemed to him to be actuated by a desire to placate the Germans or to accord to them better treatment than he thought they deserved.

. . . He wished to repeat what he had already said, namely, that the fortune of war had been such that neither American nor British territories had suffered, whilst the territory of France had been so ravaged that it would seem as though recovery were impossible. The first wish of the French frontier peasants had been to get back the cattle which had been stolen from them by the hundreds of thousands. They could watch them grazing on the German side, and they kept on saying, "We have been victorious, of course, but could not the Germans be asked to give us back our cattle?" Of course that was not a question of world-wide importance. The world would still continue to go round, even if the unhappy peasants were not granted the means of making good (and to how small an extent!) the disasters caused by the war. Nevertheless, Mr. Balfour would not, as a philosopher, contradict him

when he said that there was such a thing as a philosophy of war, when
events accumulated in the human brain and put it out of gear, destroying the balance of entire nations. The Barbarians of whom history
spoke took all that they found in the territories invaded by them, but
destroyed nothing; they settled down to share the common existence.
Now, however, the enemy had systematically destroyed everything
that stood in his way. As M. Klotz had said in his report, nothing
had been left standing. France would be unable to compete with Germany for two years. It had been stated that Germany would be supplied with raw materials, but the industries of France had been scien-
tifically destroyed not for military reasons, but in order to prevent
France from recovering in peace time.

He gave us his ideas as to how to negotiate with Germans:

. . . The Germans must, of course, be spoken to with moderation and
equity, but also with firmness and decision. . . . The degree of pressure to be exerted would be made to fit each case as it arose. But the
Germans must not be told: "Go on, do as you like. Perhaps we shall
some day threaten to break off relations, but just now we will not
be firm."
    . . . If a German thought that the one having the mastery showed
any signs of hesitation, or failed to look him straight in the eyes, he
would concede nothing.

He made one startling statement as to the real opinion of Marshal Foch on the subject of disarming Germany. He said that
"Marshal Foch was not a military Pope; he was sometimes mistaken. He was a great General and all were prepared to do him
honour as such, but as a matter of fact he had always been opposed to the idea of imposing disarmament on Germany."

This statement has an important bearing on the line which
Foch took throughout the consideration of the clauses on German
rearmament. Clemenceau did not explain whether the old soldier's
attitude was due to his conviction that disarmament could not be
enforced, or that it was undesirable. Foch however knew that the
British and American Delegations regarded German disarmament
merely as a prelude to general disarmament. If the German Army
were reduced to a small force, only just adequate to the policy of
a Germany stripped of her empire, then there would be no excuse
for maintaining in France a huge army which, with reserves,

numbered between four and five million men. He could not contemplate with equanimity the prospect of the dismantling of the
French Army, to the building-up of which he had devoted his
life and which was such a source of perpetual pride to him, and
which he regarded as the best security and the supreme glory of
his country. His idea was a German army not numerous or powerful enough to attack France, but large enough to justify the
raising of an army at home to give France unchallengeable preponderance in Europe, with a surplus for the needs of her great
empire abroad.

A committee was appointed to co-operate with the military
authorities in drafting a preliminary report on military and naval
clauses to be inserted in the German Treaty. The British Empire
was represented on this committee by Lord Milner. It reported
in a few days. On the question of personnel it recommended a
limitation to a strength of 25 infantry and 5 cavalry divisions to
be distributed as follows: 5 for the Eastern front; 5 for the Western front; 5 for the Southern front; 10 in reserve in the interior
of Germany; and 5 cavalry divisions.

The only comment made on the size of the army to be permitted to Germany was by Signor Orlando, who expressed his
doubt as to its adequacy for the defence of so great a country:

. . . He, himself, had asked Marshal Foch whether the reduction to
25 divisions corresponded to the maximum force which could safely
be left to Germany as its final establishment. Marshal Foch had replied in the affirmative. Italy, before the war, had 25 divisions on a
peace footing. Germany was a far larger country, and he was therefore inclined to think that 25 divisions must be the minimum required
for internal order.

The question of equipment was left for the consideration of the
Allied Military Committee to be presided over by Marshal Foch.

In those early discussions nothing much was said about general
disarmament. There was an allusion on the 12th February when
President Wilson made the following reference to the subject:

. . . The plan of general disarmament, which had been alluded to,
brought into relief the difficulty of deciding now, as a provisional
measure, what should be the relative strengths of national forces.

Disarmament contained two elements—(1) the maintenance of an adequate force for internal police; (2) the national contribution to the general force of the future League of Nations. At present we did not contemplate that Germany should make any contribution to the latter force. We need, therefore, not take that element into consideration. All we need contemplate was the amount of armed force required by Germany to maintain internal order and to keep down Bolshevism. This limit could be fixed by the Military Advisers. In general, he felt that until we knew what the German Government was going to be, and how the German people were going to behave, the world had a moral right to disarm Germany, and to subject her to a generation of thoughtfulness.

This inference was not followed up, as the Peace Council had not yet come to any final conclusion as to the size and equipment of the German Army.

The scheme submitted by Marshal Foch's committee proposed:

1. *Effectives.*
   (*a*) That the land forces of Germany shall not exceed a strength of 200,000 men (officers not included), and that the number of officers and other persons considered as such of the land forces shall not exceed 9,000.
   (*b*) That the air forces shall not exceed 1,000 men (officers included), and that these forces shall not be maintained after the 1st October, 1919.
2. *Incorporation of large units.*
   All the Delegations agree to fix the maximum number of large units and staffs for these effectives at 15 Infantry divisions and 5 Cavalry divisions and 5 Army Corps and one Army Staff.

As to the method of recruitment, it was compulsory, by drawing lots, or by any other method chosen by Germany, under the reserve that the total length of the men's service should not exceed one year and that the service should be continuous.

The Military Committee made no suggestions as to any general plan of disarmament applicable to all the nations of the world, conquerors and neutrals, as well as to the vanquished. The question was not referred to them, although they undoubtedly had it in their minds when they decided to allow Germany to pile up a large conscript army which in the course of years would number millions. They secured its inferiority as a fighting machine by proposing the restriction of the training of the conscripts to one year, and by limiting the number at any given time to 200,000, so as to dispense with the need for many officers and non-commissioned officers. The creation of a staff was discouraged. The equipment was to be scant and stingy. Still the numbers of trained men, at first prospective, but in the course of years actual, could always be carefully quoted as a good reason for not cutting down the French military establishment. If at any given moment within the next year, those who had passed through a three years' course of training numbered only half a million to a million men, the French War Office could point to the fact that in reserve there were at least three million men who had passed through the fires of war. And the new recruits coming in at the rate of 200,000 a year were ready to fill up inevitable gaps.

I was not present at the meeting at which Marshal Foch presented his Report, and Mr. Balfour had not, in the short time which elapsed between the delivery of the Report and the first meeting called to consider it, been able to give full consideration to its terms and complications. He suggested that the examination of the Report should be postponed until I returned from England.

When I perused it, I had no doubt as to its effect and its purpose. At the meeting of the Council held on my return from England, I presented my criticisms:

MR. LLOYD GEORGE said that before the text came under discussion he wished to ask a few questions. Moreover, he thought that the text itself should not be discussed before so large a meeting.

The British Delegates could not see their way to accept the terms as they appeared at the present moment without large modifications, but these were questions which the Delegates themselves could alone discuss, as they alone would be responsible for the final decisions taken. On the other hand, in the draft regulations certain fundamental questions had been raised regarding which he would like to have explanations and enlightenment. He would, therefore, like to put certain questions to Marshal Foch before the text itself came under discussion.

He would ask Marshal Foch to explain how he proposed that the Germans should raise their army. The maximum number of men which it was proposed to allow to the army was 200,000. How were these men to be raised?

MARSHAL FOCH replied that the 200,000 men could be raised by annual recruitment, either by voluntary enlistment, by calling up recruits, or by any other system of conscription. He would point out, however, that the men so recruited could only serve for a period of one year.

MR. LLOYD GEORGE said that, in accordance with that scheme, the total length of service being restricted to one year, 200,000 men would be recruited and trained annually, so that in ten years 2,000,000 men would have been trained, in fifteen years 3,000,000 men, and in twenty years 4,000,000 men. Was that really Marshal Foch's proposal?

MARSHAL FOCH replied that it was evident that by renewing the *personnel* annually soldiers of a sort would be produced, but in an army it was not the private soldier but the *cadres* that constituted its quality. In accordance with the proposal made by the military advisers a large number of soldiers would undoubtedly come under training, but there would be no corresponding *cadres*—that was the weak point of imposing that system on Germany. On the other hand, even a small standing army represented ready-made *cadres* for the training of a vast force. He would quote the words of Marshal Bugeaud who, early in the nineteenth century, had stated that it would be better to have an army of sheep commanded by a lion than an army of lions commanded by an ass. By that he meant that it was the *cadres* which mattered and not the private soldier, and the system which the military advisers had proposed to impose on Germany prevented the Germans from forming *cadres* which would enable them, after a period of years, to embody and lead the large flocks of sheep which would still be found in Germany.

MR. LLOYD GEORGE said that, with all due respect to Marshal Foch, he did not think the reply given met the real difficulty. Marshal Foch had said that the Germans would have no officers to lead the large army of men available. Trained officers were, however, already plentiful in Germany, and would be for the next twenty-five years. He himself knew many distinguished officers who had fought both in the war of 1870 and again in the present war, and yet an interval of forty-six years had elapsed between those two dates. In Germany at the present moment large numbers of officers and non-commissioned officers existed who had fought in this war and would be ready to come forward, thirsting for revenge, at the first opportunity. He would ask: Why should the Allies present to Germany a scheme which would enable her to raise four or five million men in the next twenty years?

Both England and the United States of America had had some experience of what that meant. Before 1914 Great Britain only had an army of some 200,000 men. Had she had an army of 2,000,000 men, besides the officers and non-commissioned officers whom Germany now had, results would have been very different. Outside the small regular army, Great Britain had merely possessed a few territorial officers, that is to say, civilians who did a little training every Saturday evening. Nevertheless, three months after the declaration of war these men were fighting in the trenches and had given a very good account of themselves. On the other hand, under the proposed scheme, Germany would have an army of three to four million trained men led, not by donkeys, but by officers who had had considerable war experience. Surely that could not be called disarmament. He himself would be very sorry to leave France after the signing of peace with that threat facing her across the Rhine.

MR. LANSING remarked that Mr. Lloyd George's argument was strengthened by the fact that, besides officers and non-commissioned officers, 2,000,000 or 3,000,000 trained soldiers already existed in Germany. Consequently, the whole question was really one of disarmament, that is to say, the Germans must be made to surrender their surplus arms and armaments.

MARSHAL FOCH pointed out that in reality the Allies had to deal both with the present situation and with a future situation in Germany. No doubt to-day Germany had millions of men, besides officers and non-commissioned officers, who had been trained and could be recalled to the colours very rapidly. Consequently, for some time to come Germany would have at her disposal all the elements of a well-organised army. That could not be prevented. Mr. Lloyd George had said that the trained officers and non-commissioned officers would remain available for twenty-five years and more. In his opinion, that would certainly not be the case. The men now demobilised would in three or four years' time be of little value, owing to the interruption of their training. Germany owed her great strength before the war to the large body of 120,000 professional non-commissioned officers, who formed the backbone of the army. Under the proposed scheme that backbone would be broken. If Germany were now to be allowed to raise a permanent standing army consisting of even 40,000 or 50,000 men, that would mean practically 40,000 or 50,000 possible non-commissioned officers available for training large armies. No doubt cadres at present existed, but these would daily lose their value if demobilised as proposed. Mr. Lloyd George had spoken about the organisation of the British army. That army had certainly not been a large one, but it had contained a comparatively large number of professional officers and of non-commissioned officers serving in the colonies and at home, who became available for training new armies. On the other hand, if the German *cadres* were broken up, and if the officers and non-commissioned officers were prevented from training after being demobilised, that would be the best method of rendering the existing army impotent.

MR. LLOYD GEORGE said he would not dare to enter into a military argument with Marshal Foch; but he would point out that what had enabled Great Britain to train the new armies had been the old officers and non-commissioned officers who had returned to the Colours on the outbreak of the war, and that a similar state of affairs would exist in Germany for many years to come. He would enquire, therefore, why a present of this great force should be made to Germany. He thought that history would be repeating itself and that the Allies would be doing exactly the same thing as Napoleon had done after the battle of Iéna. The annual renewal of the whole army as suggested merely meant in the course of years the creation of an enormous army. That was a mistake which should not be repeated.

The British point of view, however, was the following: Germany should not be permitted to maintain a bigger army than Great Britain possessed. Great Britain had no idea of having an army of 4,000,000 men. Consequently, the regulations should lay down that Germany should not maintain a bigger army than Great Britain. It was useless to say that the Germans would not have the *cadres*, for, with millions of trained ex-officers and ex-non-commissioned officers burning with a desire to avenge their defeats, *cadres* would undoubtedly be raised somehow or other. He would therefore ask permission to make a suggestion, namely, that an opportunity should be given to him to put a new proposal before the meeting. He suggested, therefore, that the debate on the military terms should be adjourned to enable him on the morrow or the day after to submit an alternative proposal limiting the German army much more effectively than in the draft regulations now under consideration.

MARSHAL FOCH asked permission to invite the attention of the Conference to the fact that the regulations presented to the Conference had been unanimously accepted after consulting all the Allied Commanders-in-Chief, Marshals Pétain and Haig and Generals Pershing and Diaz, as well as other specially chosen military experts. Those proposals did not therefore reflect merely his own personal views, but represented the agreement reached by all the Allied Military experts.

MR. LLOYD GEORGE said he fully realised that fact. On the other hand, the question was not wholly a military one; it was also political and, therefore, the heads of Governments were entitled to express their views on it.

M. CLEMENCEAU agreed, and said that it would be the duty of the heads of Governments finally to decide the whole question.

After full consultation with Mr. Balfour and Sir Henry Wilson, I drafted my counter-proposals and submitted them to the Council. M. Clemenceau, with whom I had discussed the subject, also preferred a small long-service army of volunteers to a conscript army rapidly expanding into millions. I quote my plan from the proceedings of the Council:

MR. LLOYD GEORGE said that he had the following draft resolution to propose:

"The Military, Naval and Aerial terms of peace with Germany shall be based on the following principles:

(1) The German naval, military and air forces shall be raised entirely by voluntary service.

(2) The minimum period of service for all ranks shall be twelve years with the colours.

(3) The strength of the German army and air force shall not exceed 200,000 men of all ranks, organised in not more than fifteen divisions and three cavalry divisions.

(4) The strength of the German navy shall not exceed 15,000 men of all ranks and ratings."

The object of this proposal was that Germany should not have an annual contingent of recruits, and should not be able to play the same trick on Europe as she did after Iéna. It might be objected that Germany would not have guns and *cadres*. This assumed that she would not be in collusion with any other Power—for instance, Russia. It was absolutely necessary to make this impossible and the method which he proposed offered, he believed, the only means of doing so. A voluntary army was more expensive than a conscript army. If Germany had to maintain a voluntary army in addition to paying compensation to the Allies, there would be no money left for military adventures. The permanent limitation of armaments was an illusion. He had been told that very morning that the jigs and gauges necessary for the manufacture of armaments and munitions for a very large army could be concealed in one small room. Such concealment could not be prevented, and a nation endowed with these standards could gain three months in the race for the production of armaments.

(There being no dissentient, the resolution was adopted.)

M. CLEMENCEAU said that, as there was no objection, the draft read by Mr. Lloyd George would be sent to the Military, Naval and Air Committees for adaptation to the body of their recommendation.

MR. LLOYD GEORGE said that the British Delegation had a complete set of proposals.

MARSHAL FOCH pointed out that in the Commission there were no advocates of Mr. Lloyd George's principles. He would therefore ask that the British Delegation should be instructed to report on the matter. He had received the British project just referred to by Mr. Lloyd George at midday and at first sight he noticed that it dealt with other than military questions. Was the Commission to enter into these matters and in that case would the Governments give them instructions for their guidance? There were, for instance, chapters relating to prisoners of war and to Poland.

M. CLEMENCEAU said that these matters did not concern the military experts. The Commission would be able to judge what part of the proposals concerned them and what part did not.

GENERAL DEGOUTTE said that he, personally, would never agree with the views expressed by the British Delegation in favour of a voluntary long-service army in Germany. He thought this would make Germany far stronger than a short-term conscript service.

M. CLEMENCEAU said that the Governments could not force the Military Authorities to change their opinions. He suggested that a report should be made on the following Monday.

MR. LLOYD GEORGE said that the question of principle must be decided in the Council itself. . . . He would never agree to an army raised in Germany by short conscript service. No General's opinion would shake his decision. This was a matter for Governments to decide. He did not wish to say that he rejected the advice of the Generals. It was to avoid this that he had put forward his resolution. He declared for a long-service army as the only guarantee of a small army. He proposed that this principle should be accepted by the Council and directions given to the military advisers to prepare regulations in accordance with this principle.

M. CLEMENCEAU said that the case had been clearly put by Mr. Lloyd George. He himself was also bound by his acceptance of these principles. The resolution would now be reported on by the Military Committee, who would, of course, remain free to express their own views. The decision would remain with the Governments.

When the French Staff realised that their scheme of a half-trained conscript army for Germany was thrown over, they went to the other extreme and demanded that the figure of 200,000 should be cut down to 100,000. Marshal Foch, at a Council meeting on the 10th March, thus defended the reduction:

MARSHAL FOCH said that if the force left to Germany was to be a police force, 140,000 men represented far more than was required. In support of this, he had a standing army, before the war, of 100,000 men but no *gendarmerie*. Proportionately, therefore, 100,000 men seemed more than enough to police Germany. If Germany were left a permanent army of 140,000 men, together with 15,000 sailors, a *gendarmerie* the number of which was neither known nor limited,— but probably greater than that of the French *gendarmerie* which was 22,000 men,—plus 6,300 forest guards and 23,000 customs officers, she would have a trained force of not less than 206,000. These forces would constitute a shock army able to mobilise at once and make a surprise attack. If all that Germany required was a police force, 206,000 was far too much and 100,000 men would be ample. If the recommendations before the Council were adopted, the Allies would have to maintain 206,000 fully trained men against Germany. Even if this burden were distributed between the four Powers, each would have to keep in readiness over 50,000 *fully trained* men.

It was decided to insert the figure of 100,000 in the Treaty, upon which Mr. Balfour made some pointed observations as to the helplessness of Germany with such a small force unless general disarmament were to be enforced.

MR. BALFOUR said that he had nothing to add to the arguments used, but that the conclusion to which they led was one which the Conference must take into account. The army of Germany was to be reduced to a police force, and that a small one. In that case Germany must be secured against invasion. There was no plan at present before the Conference for general disarmament. If the Germans were told that they were to have only 100,000 armed men, while France, Poland and Bohemia could have as many as they wished, they would say that the Allied Powers were leaving them at the mercy even of their smaller neighbours. What form the guarantee of non-invasion should take he was not prepared to suggest, but some such guarantee would have to be found if the Conference made Germany powerless for attack and weak for defence.

It was clear that the cutting down of the greatest army in Europe to a barely adequate police force of 100,000, imposed the duty upon the Allies as an obligation of honour to set up machinery in the Treaty for reducing the enormous armies then at the disposal of other Powers to a minimum calculated on the same principle.

In the Fontainebleau document therefore, where I sought to sketch an outline of the terms of peace, I put in the forefront of the programme the importance of making provision in the Treaty for the setting up of machinery which would ensure a general reduction of the huge armaments responsible for precipitating the Great War.

I have already quoted that document at some length in Chapter VIII. I shall therefore here only call attention to my insistence upon the importance of an agreement being arrived at between the principal members of the League in regard to armaments which would put an end to competition, I designed such an arrangement as a primary condition of membership of the League of Nations, and I emphasised the futility of imposing a permanent limitation of armaments upon Germany unless we were prepared to impose a similar limitation upon ourselves.

In the Covenant of the League of Nations it is stipulated that the members of the League shall recognise that the maintenance of peace requires the reduction of national armaments to the lowest point consistent with national safety, and it is one of the foremost duties imposed by the Government upon the League to formulate plans for such reduction.

When the German delegates examined the first draft of the Treaty, they called attention to the precariousness of Germany's position with a small army, surrounded by nations each of which had a powerful army considerably outnumbering in personnel and equipment the force permitted by the Treaty to Germany.

The reply given by the Council of Four to the German protest constitutes a fundamental part of the Treaty of Versailles:

The Allied and Associated Powers have already pointed out to the German Delegates that the Covenant of the League of Nations provides for "the reduction of national armaments to the lowest point consistent with national safety and the enforcement by common action of international obligations." They recognise that the acceptance by Germany of the terms laid down for her own disarmament will facilitate and hasten the accomplishment of a general reduction of armaments; and they intend to open negotiations immediately with a view to the eventual adoption of a scheme of such general reduction. It goes without saying that the realisation of this programme will depend in large part on the satisfactory carrying out by Germany of her own engagements.

MILITARY, NAVAL AND AIR CLAUSES

SECTION I

Military Clauses

I

THE Allied and Associated Powers wish to make it clear that their requirements in regard to German armaments were not made solely with the object of rendering it impossible for Germany to resume her policy of military aggression. They are also the first steps towards that general reduction and limitation of armaments which they seek to bring about as one of the most fruitful preventives of war, and which it will be one of the first duties of the League of Nations to promote.

II

THEY must point out, however, that the colossal growth in armaments of the last few decades was forced upon the nations of Europe by Germany. As Germany increased her power, her neighbours had to follow suit unless they were to become impotent to resist German dictation or the German sword. It is therefore right, as it is necessary, that the process of limitation of armaments should begin with the nation which has been responsible for their expansion. It is not until the aggressor has led the way that the attacked can safely afford to follow suit.

These considered and momentous declarations were intended to make it clear that general disarmament on an unprecedented scale was an essential part of the policy and purpose of the Treaty of Peace.

CHAPTER XIV

THE LEAGUE OF NATIONS

AT the first meeting of the Imperial War Cabinet held in London during the spring of 1917, the question of the League of Nations was one of the problems that came up for consideration. It was examined in the first place by one of the committees appointed to report on Peace Terms. Their Report was discussed by the full Cabinet. A detailed account of these deliberations is given in my "War Memoirs." In these post-Armistice discussions on peace the Imperial War Cabinet once more approached the problem. Before I summarise the comments made and the views expressed by Empire Ministers on the subject, I think it desirable to give an authenticated narrative of the steps taken by the various Allied Governments to probe into the difficulties and to work out practical schemes for dealing with them.

Foolish claims have been put forward by partisan boosters that the League of Nations was a project forced on Britain, France and Italy by the insistence of President Wilson, in the face of persistent reluctance and even hostility on the part of these European Powers. Even Colonel House is not free from insinuating the same charge. It is essential in the interest of historical truth and from a sense of bare justice to a much calumniated continent, that has striven as truly and suffered more for liberty and progress than any expanse of territory on the face of the globe, that the real facts as to the origin of the League project should be narrated. It is relevant to this consideration to quote a formal resolution, adopted by the French Chamber on June the 5th, 1917 (more than a year before the end of the War), after a long debate, by a majority of 467 votes to 52:

. . . Foreign to all thought of conquest or enslavement of foreign people, the Chamber trusts that the efforts of the Army of the Republic and her Allies will permit, after Prussian militarism is overthrown, the securing of lasting guarantees of peace and independence from great and small nations alike by association in a League of Nations, already in preparation.

This declaration was by no means the first official step taken by the Allies to place the establishment of a Society of Nations for ensuring world peace amongst the principal aims for which they were striving in the struggle through which they were passing. I always felt that while the establishment of a fraternity of nations to ensure peace was a noble ideal, there were many complications and obstructions to be overcome in its practical application. One of my first acts therefore when I became Prime Minister was to appoint a body of experts to work out a practical scheme for operating a League of Nations to ensure world peace. Lord Robert Cecil (now Lord Cecil of Chelwood), who has been a pioneer in this movement, was Under Secretary for Foreign Affairs and took an active interest in the advancement of this idea. With his advice and assistance the Phillimore Committee was set up in January, 1917. Lord Phillimore was one of the most learned and high-minded of the Judges of the High Court. The French Government followed this precedent by appointing an influential committee for a similar purpose. It had as its Chairman an ex-Premier—M. Léon Bourgeois—a distinguished statesman who was well known to be a life-long advocate of all means for settling international disputes by judicial methods.

Although opinion in favour of setting up some international authority that would prevent a repetition of the terrible calamity under which the world was writhing at that moment was spreading rapidly as the War proceeded, no one had a clear idea as to how the project could be worked out. President Wilson himself had not, even by the end of 1917, conceived any notion of setting up a permanent body to deal with international disputes. In a note sent by the British representative at Washington to the Foreign Secretary on November 15th, 1917, reporting an interview with Colonel House on this subject, he says:

Colonel House told me that the President thought it better that the Government of the United States should not in any way be committed to a cut-and-dried plan for the establishment of a League of Nations. The President hoped that if any nation showed an aggressive disposition, or clearly intended to go to war, Great Britain, the United States, France, and perhaps some other nations should come to an understanding between themselves as to what attitude they should adopt, and that, having come to a decision on that point, they should then determine what steps should be taken to make it effective. Colonel House added that the President and he were discouraging in the United States discussions as to the League of Nations, etc., and that he had succeeded in employing a number of advocates of the League on various work immediately connected with the prosecution of the war.

That was a device to keep them out of untimely and mischievous propaganda about the League which might excite antagonisms in a Senate jealous of its privileges, and thus commit leading statesmen prematurely either to rival schemes or to stubborn opposition to the whole idea. Allied leaders, whilst showing the same resolve that some special machinery should be set up for dealing with international quarrels, were up to 1917 just as indefinite as President Wilson as to the actual methods to be employed for that purpose. That is why both the British and the French Governments had taken the necessary steps during the year 1917 to work out practicable schemes in order to be ready for any peace negotiations that might emerge. They attached great importance to this project and they wished to ensure that there should be no misunderstanding as to what was intended or decided.

The Phillimore Committee was an able and highly experienced body of men. It consisted of Lord Phillimore as Chairman; three historians: A. F. Pollard, Julian Corbett and J. Holland Rose; and three able and experienced officials representing the Foreign Office: Sir Eyre Crowe, Sir Wm. Tyrrell, and Mr. C. J. B. Hurst. The Committee presented its Interim Report to the War Cabinet on March 20th, 1917. The Report states that at their meetings their "attention had been directed mainly to the various proposals for a League of Nations which were formulated in the sixteenth and seventeenth centuries, and to those which had been put forward since the recent revival of the movement." In expressing an opinion upon these proposals, they give an indication of their general view of the immediate possibilities:

The earlier projects which aimed at setting up a kind of European Confederation with a super-national authority we have after consideration rejected, feeling that international opinion is not ripe for so drastic a pooling of sovereignty, and that the only feasible method of securing the object is by way of co-operation, or possibly a treaty of alliance on the lines of the more recent schemes.

They then proceed to submit a draft scheme "on the assumption that a League of Nations may be regarded as a possible solution of the problem." They propose that "no State should go to war without previously submitting the matter to arbitration or to the Conference of the League, nor while the discussion is pending in debate, nor shall seek any further satisfaction than that which the award or the recommendation of the Conference requires."

The Report does not shrink from recommending sanctions to enforce the decisions of the League:

If, which may God avert, one of the Allied States should break the covenant contained in the preceding Article, this State will become *ipso facto* at war with all the other Allied States, and the latter agree to take and to support each other in taking jointly and severally all such measures—military, naval, financial, and economic—as will best avail for restraining the breach of covenant. Such financial and economic measures shall include severance of all relations of trade and finance with the subjects of the covenant-breaking State, prohibition against the subjects of the Allied States entering into any relations with the subjects of the covenant-breaking State, and the prevention, so far as possible, of the subjects of the covenant-breaking State from having any commercial or financial intercourse with the subjects of any other State, whether party to this Convention or not.

For the purpose of this Article, the Allied States shall detain any ship or goods belonging to any of the subjects of the covenant-breaking State or coming from or destined for any person residing in the territory of such State, and shall take any other similar steps which shall be necessary for the same purpose.

Such of the Allied States (if any) as cannot make an effective contribution of military or naval force shall at the least take the other measures indicated in this Article.

For all preliminary work, the vote of the majority was to be sufficient, but it was stipulated that there must be unanimity when the League came to the point of issuing definite recommendations.

A copy of this Report was sent to President Wilson and to the Allied Governments for their observations as soon as it was issued. The only comment President Wilson passed upon it was that he hoped it would not be published, as he thought it would be undesirable at that stage to have a public discussion about the constitution and powers of the League of Nations. He was not sure of his ground in America. He clearly anticipated trouble from the Cabot Lodge faction in the Senate and he was anxious not to stir it up prematurely.

The next authentic draft scheme issued on behalf of one of the Allies, was the Report of the Bourgeois Committee. This is a very remarkable document. It is bolder and more imaginative than the Phillimore Report. They both begin by recalling the fact that "historically the idea is a very old one." The Bourgeois Report dwells on the fact that "actually, during the present War it has been revived under various forms by the Allied Governments in their official declarations, by President Wilson in his Note of December, 1916, and even by our enemies in their replies to the Papal Note, dated August 16th, 1917." It is useful to call attention to this last sentence at a time when one clause after another of the Treaty of Versailles is being repudiated. The establishment of a League of Nations was clearly not one of those harsh and hostile conditions imposed by ruthless conquerors on a prostrate foe. Imperial Germany put forward the same proposition in 1917 as one of her conditions of peace.

The Bourgeois Report was far and away the most detailed, precise, and far-reaching definition of the constitution and powers of the projected League which had yet been presented to any belligerent Government. It is based on the same general principle as had already been enunciated by the Allied leaders in every country: that the Allies meant to insist, as one of the conditions of a peace settlement, "that one of the results of this victory may be to spare the world future recurrence to attempts at violence and hegemony by any people whatsoever, and to establish on a permanent basis the sovereignty of right amongst mankind."

It takes the Phillimore view of the proposal to set up a supernational State:

"It is not the object of the League of Nations to establish an international political State. It intends solely to ensure peace by substituting right for might in the settlement of disputes. It accordingly guarantees to all States alike, both small and great, the exercise of their sovereignty."

It is also in general agreement with the Phillimore draft as to the establishment of an international body for ensuring peace and in its definition of the functions of that body. But when it comes to sanctions it is bolder, more comprehensive, and more definite. At a time when discussions are proceeding about an amendment of the Covenant, the Bourgeois document is worth a re-perusal. Sanctions are divided into diplomatic, legal, economic and military sanctions:

1. DIPLOMATIC SANCTIONS

These sanctions, which result in the banning of the delinquent State by the States Members for a certain length of time, fall into the following categories:

(a) *Suspension or rupture of diplomatic relations* hitherto maintained by this State with the other States Members of the League of Nations;

(b) *Withdrawal of the exequatur granted to its Consuls.*

(c) *Expulsion from the benefit of international agreements of common advantage* to which it is a party.

2. LEGAL SANCTIONS

Certain sanctions moreover, of a legal nature, will enable the League of Nations, as the case may be, to ensure respect for the principles to which it is pledged. . . .

Let us mention, as particularly efficacious from this point of view: *suspension* from the subjects of the *delinquent State of agreements concerning the rights of nationals, of conventions relating to the protection of author's copyrights and industrial property, of conventions of private international law,* which this State has concluded with the other States Members of the League of Nations, *denial of access to tribunals* in the member countries to the nationals of the delinquent State; refusal, in these various countries, of the *exequatur* to the sentences pronounced by its tribunals, in the interest of its nationals; *seizure and sequestration of real estate and other property* belonging to its nationals in the said countries; *prohibition of commercial relations,* and even, if occasion demands, *of every convention of private advantage* with the subjects of States comprising the League of Nations.

.   .   .   .   .

3. ECONOMIC SANCTIONS

Other sanctions, of an economic nature, are potentially at the disposal of the League of Nations. They enable it to exercise an efficacious curb on the State which has repudiated the Covenant, by means of various measures relating to commercial, industrial or financial dealings, even to the extent of a placing under total ban.

These measures are notably:

(*a*) *Blockade*, consisting of forcible opposition to every commercial relation with the territory of this State.

(*b*) *Embargo*, i.e., seizure and temporary sequestration, in the ports and territorial waters of the States Members, of the vessels and cargoes belonging to the delinquent State and its nationals, as well as the seizure of all goods bound for this State.

(*c*) *Prohibition of raw materials* and provisions indispensable to its economic life.

(*d*) *Prohibition to issue public loans* in the territory of the States Members, refusal of *admission to quotation* on the official market of securities issued externally, and even *withdrawal of admission* previously granted.

The sanctions thus provided for will be all the more efficacious and prompt in application because the States Members will have agreed beforehand to secure themselves against any harmful repercussions by economic organisation adapted to facilitate mutual assistance.

This bare list reveals the fact that the League of Nations will not be unarmed when it is a question of making its decisions respected and of imposing, on unruly elements, peace by justice—the maintenance of which constitutes its *raison d'être*.

4. MILITARY SANCTIONS

1. *International Force*

The execution of military sanctions on land and sea will be entrusted either to an international force, or to one or several Powers, Members of the League of Nations, and endowed with a mandate for this purpose.

The international body will have a military force at its disposal supplied by the several States Members and adequate for:

(1) Assuring the execution of its decisions and those of the International Tribunal.

(2) Overcoming, should occasion arise, the forces which might oppose the League of Nations in the event of an armed conflict.

The methods of fixing and raising the contingents for the international force and providing it with a permanent staff and a Commander-in-Chief are entered into fully.

The document proceeds:

It is not a question of making the League of Nations into a super-State, or even a Confederation. Respect for the sovereignty of States, diversity of national traditions, of political and judicial conceptions, discrepancy of administrative systems, clash of economic interests, all rule out the idea of such a creation. But the public opinion of free peoples would suffer disappointment if the present crisis did not give rise to the institution of an international organ capable of contributing by constant vigilance and adequate authority to the maintenance of peace.

.   .   .   .   .

This organ, set up in the form of an International Council, will derive its authority from the reciprocal engagement undertaken by each of the States Members to employ its economic, naval and military power in conjunction with the others against any nation contravening the Covenant.

As to the procedure, either for mediation or arbitration:

It first attempts an amicable settlement and, in the event of its failure, it acts within its own competence and formulates the terms for the settlement of the conflict so as to ensure respect for the rights of each State and the preservation of peace.

This decision shall be communicated to the States concerned. They are informed that, from this date, the conflict no longer exists between the contestant States, but between all the States Members and the State which, in refusing to accept that decision, violates the very principle of the act of association.

If, after a summons, the State concerned refuses to accept the decision taken, the International Council shall notify it of the coercive measures in the diplomatic, legal, economic or military sphere, which, after a specified lapse of time, will be taken against it.

2. *Defence against Attacks issuing from non-Member States*

If a non-Member State of the League of Nations aims at asserting its will by any means whatsoever on one of the States Members, the

International Council, after having exhausted the resources of conciliation, shall decide the steps to be taken and cause the application against this State of the legal, diplomatic and military measures at the disposal of the States Members.

The Report does not stipulate for unanimity as a condition of action. Herein also it differs essentially from the Phillimore plan. M. Léon Bourgeois foresaw the practical difficulty of securing complete unanimity amongst a large number of nations, great and small, on every detail of combined action.

When the Peace Congress set up a commission to draft the Constitution of the League, M. Clemenceau placed M. Léon Bourgeois at the head of the French Delegation. It will be found that in the discussion which took place at the framing of the Covenant of the League, M. Bourgeois put forward this scheme and fought for it in all its integrity with great pertinacity. It is therefore not only unfair, but discreditable, to suggest that France was an unwilling adherent to the idea of the League of Nations, and that the Head of the French Government had to be bullied or bought by President Wilson into acceptance of the Covenant. It is true that Clemenceau was never an enthusiastic believer in the success of the League. He was essentially a man of suspicions and distrusts in his dealings with his fellowmen. He had no more faith in the disinterestedness of nations than he had in the unselfishness of individuals. But he was entirely in favour of trying the experiment, and his Government afforded full support to M. Léon Bourgeois in the very determined fight he put up for his far-reaching and audacious project.

There were a number of other sketchy plans contributed by individuals of more or less influence and position. They were confined to the enunciation of general principles and in no sense did they pretend to constitute worked-out schemes. Lord Robert Cecil took an active and earnest interest in the general idea and did his utmost to promote it, but he was always more of a prophet than a planner. Both the Phillimore and the Bourgeois proposals were available to President Wilson months before the War came to an end. The Phillimore document he seems to have read, but he proffered no comment on its terms. The Bourgeois plan he does not appear to have perused before he came to Europe. If President Wilson had a scheme of his own he certainly never passed it on to the Allied Governments. The nearest he got to the drafting of practical proposals, according to Colonel House, was to examine a paper written by the Colonel himself after the Phillimore plan had been officially sent to the President. This paper sketched a rough outline for the constitution and functions of a League of Nations. President Wilson was not sufficiently convinced as to the merits of the House proposals to think it necessary or worth while to forward them to his European collaborators.

When I met the President at Buckingham Palace in December, 1918, I delivered to him a copy of General Smuts' scheme. He told me he had already read the Phillimore Report. When I asked him if he would give me an opportunity of perusing any draft scheme prepared by or for him so that the British Government and their experts might have a full opportunity of examining it, he informed me that he had worked out no detailed proposals, as he was anxious to have a preliminary discussion with the Allied leaders before committing his thoughts to writing.

In September, 1918, a memorandum on the subject of a League of Nations was addressed by the Scandinavian Government to the Dutch, Spanish and Swiss Governments. A copy was handed to each of the belligerent powers. It treated the question from the point of view of the neutrals in this war:

Experience has shown, moreover, how difficult it is for Neutrals, in a war between several States, to preserve the integrity of their rights against the encroachments of belligerents, and not to let themselves be drawn involuntarily into the fight. It has also shown up, by more than one example, the perils to which the independence and even the existence of small nations are exposed by their participation in those conflicts where the Great Powers are at grips. Finally, experience has made it clearly apparent that the substitution of right for might in the settlement of international disputes would be of supreme importance particularly to those nations whose military resources are reduced.

It assumes that Allied statesmen have been much too absorbed by the pre-occupations and tasks of the War to prepare a better "organisation of international life." In general outline—and its treatment of the problem is more general than detailed—it does not differ from the British and French proposals:

The creation of an international juridical organisation truly worthy of this name constitutes, however, one of the most difficult problems which confront humanity.

Needless to say, it would be vain to claim to solve such a problem in a day and at a single attempt. The complete solution—supposing it exists—will be reached by a series of steps. The problem, moreover, is a complex one, consisting as it does of a whole sequence of peculiarly delicate questions, such as the right of nations to self-determination, the opening of colonies to all without distinction of nationality, international limitation of armaments and international sanctions to be applied to States who violate accepted legal rules.

In particular, it may be stressed that any international organisation which would not have at its disposal some kind of sanctions in the economic or military sphere would plainly reveal a vital defect.

It regards an international limitation of armaments as essential to the success of any scheme:

With regard particularly to the question of international sanctions— whose creation is so important for the whole organisation—it appears inseparable from that of international limitation of armaments and of a nature only to be tackled in conjunction with it. No State anxious to avoid being drawn into world conflicts will willingly undertake the obligation to associate in international coercive measures so long as it would thus be likely to risk finding itself, without immediate and effective support, confronting a more powerful neighbour.

Before the Imperial War Cabinet came to a discussion on the League of Nations, I thought it would be helpful to their deliberations if General Smuts were to prepare a full memorandum which would outline his final views on the Constitution, the functions and the powers of the League of Nations. The Phillimore Report, valuable as it was, did not cover the whole ground. It had also left gaps which would have to be filled in ere the scheme could be regarded as workable. General Smuts undertook the task and fulfilled it with his usual insight and comprehension. The document he turned out is one of the most notable products of this extremely able man. It is pellucid in style, eloquent in diction, penetrating in thought and broad in its outlook. It contains one or two striking phrases which will live in the literature of peace. It is difficult to summarise, for every sentence is full of fruitful suggestion and couched in language of stately impressiveness. This ideal State paper will have its place in history, not only for its intrinsic merit, but as the model upon which the Covenant of the League was built. Unfortunately for my readers, the document is too long to reproduce here in its entirety, and I shall therefore confine my observations to pointing out the respect in which General Smuts' proposal differed from the other plans of which I have given a sketch.

In its general structure the memorandum followed the schemes of M. Léon Bourgeois and Lord Phillimore. It visualised a body representing all nations on earth, whose function would be to take cognizance of all international situations and developments likely to endanger peace. This Association of Nations would be equipped with full powers of investigation, conciliation and recommendation. The scheme also contemplated international action where persuasion and moral pressure failed. The League would be empowered to enforce its recommendations on a recalcitrant by penalties, economic, social and—in the last resort—military. But the project differs from M. Léon Bourgeois' scheme by declining to associate itself with the French proposal for the setting up of an independent military force to be placed at the disposal and under the sole control of the League.

It has two or three outstanding features which distinguish it from all predecessory plans. The first is that it extends and broadens out the functions of the League. It comes to the conclusion that it is not sufficient for the League to be merely a *deus ex machina*, called in when grave emergencies arise, or when the spectre of war has actually appeared. If it is to last as an effective agency for the promotion of peace and goodwill, it must be something more than that. It must become part and parcel of the common international life of States; it must be an ever visible, living, working organ of the policy of civilised communities. It must function so strongly in the ordinary practical intercourse of States as to become inevitable and irresistible in their disputes;

its peace activity must be the foundation and guarantee of its war power. How would it be possible to build the League so closely into the fabric of our international system?

General Smuts illustrates this proposition by reference to the condition of things that will be created by the decomposition of the Russian, Austrian and Turkish Empires, and in the second place by dealing with the situation created in the colonies of the German Empire. With regard to the first he treats the creation of empires as a natural historical development:

Nations in their march to power tend to pass the purely national bounds; hence arise the empires which embrace various nations, sometimes related in blood and institutions, sometimes, again, different in race and hostile in temperament. In a rudimentary way all such composite empires of the past were leagues of nations, keeping the peace amongst the constituent nations, but unfortunately doing so not on the basis of freedom but of repression. Usually one dominant nation in the group overcame, coerced, and kept the rest under.

He then points out how these empires have all broken down and how "to-day the British Empire remains the only embryo league of nations because it is based on the true principles of national freedom and political decentralisation." The others have been swept away,

not to leave an empty house for political individualism or anarchy, but for a larger and better League of Nations. Europe is being liquidated, and the League of Nations must be the heir to this great estate. The peoples left behind by the decomposition of Russia, Austria and Turkey are mostly untrained politically; many of them are either incapable of or deficient in power of self-government; they are mostly destitute, and will require much nursing towards economic and political independence.

In substance he advocates the placing of the League of Nations *in loco parentis* to these emancipated peoples. It will be an essential part of its function to protect all of them against the greed of their powerful neighbours. Some of them it will have to help to walk in the paths of self-government until they can stand on their own feet and walk in their own paths without peril to themselves or their neighbours.

"Surely the only statesmanlike course is to make the League of Nations the reversionary in the broadest sense of these empires." In these special cases the League of Nations, as the successor to the shattered empires,

will directly and without power of delegation watch over the relations *inter se* of the new independent States arising from the break-up of those Empires, and will regard as a very special task the duty of conciliating and composing differences between them with a view to the maintenance of good order and general peace. It is not improbable that this supervision of the new European States will impose the heaviest task of all on the League of Nations, at any rate, for this generation.

To all these territories he applies the principle that there should be no annexation of any of them to any of the victorious States, and that in their future government the rule of self-determination, or the consent by the governed to their form of government, should be fairly and reasonably applied. But the application of this principle varies considerably according to the stage of civilisation or capacity for government at which the particular countries are arrived. In the cases of Finland, Poland, Czecho-Slovakia and Yugoslavia, they would probably be found sufficiently capable of statehood to be recognised as independent States of the usual type from the beginning, but in the case of the Trans-Caucasian or Trans-Caspian provinces of Russia, Mesopotamia, Lebanon and Syria, it would "probably be found that they are as yet deficient in the qualities of statehood, and that, whereas they are perhaps capable of internal autonomy, they will in one degree or another require the guiding hand of some external authority to steady their administration." He then develops the theory of mandates and its application.

Palestine and Armenia he puts in a totally different category from the African colonies or from the islands of the South Seas or the Pacific. But they also are to be mandatory territories under the trusteeship of the League. He does so on the ground that, "owing chiefly to the heterogeneous character of the population and their incapacity for administrative co-operation, autonomy in any real sense would be out of the question, and the administration would have to be undertaken to a very large extent by some external authority."

As to the German Colonies, he places them in yet another category of mandates, on the ground that they "are inhabited by barbarians, who not only cannot possibly govern themselves, but to whom it would be impracticable to apply any ideas of political self-determination in the European sense."

He does not propose that any of these mandated countries should be controlled or governed direct by the League, but that the case should be met "not by the direct appointment of international officials, but by nominating a particular State to act for and on behalf of the League in the matter, so that, subject to the supervision and ultimate control of the League, the appointment of the necessary officials and the carrying on of the necessary administration should be done by this mandatory state."

His plan is differentiated from the other schemes worked out in Britain and France by the bold proposition he puts forward for the abolition of conscription.

This is the first scheme which advocates the incorporation in either the Treaty or the Covenant of the League of definite provisions for the abolition of conscription and of conscript armies, for the all-round limitation of armaments and for the nationalisation of munitions production. Of the three proposals which lead to general disarmament, Smuts attaches the most importance to the abolition of conscription. He calls it "the taproot of militarism; unless that is cut, all our labours will continually be in vain." For conscript armies he would in most countries substitute as an alternative a simple militia system, on a scale of numbers and service agreed upon by the League. He makes an exception in favour of countries where oversea possessions demand a long service and where an army so recruited would be more in accord with the need and with past traditions. But the League will have after enquiry to see to it that the voluntary army authorised by it will have no greater offensive power for foreign aggression than the militia authorised in other cases. He realises the difficulties which beset limitation of armaments, but he is convinced they can be overcome with the help of the experts of the League. He therefore proposes: "That while the limitation of armaments in the general sense is impracticable, the Council of the League shall determine what direct military equipment and armament is fair and reasonable in respect of the scale of forces laid down . . . ; and that the limits fixed by the Council shall not be exceeded without its permission."

In view of controversies which have arisen in many countries as to abolition of the private manufacture of arms, his views on this subject have a special interest:

The nationalisation of armament factories has been advocated on the ground that as long as the production of munitions of war remains a private commercial undertaking huge vested interests grow up around it which influence public opinion through the Press and otherwise in the direction of war. There is no doubt that the influence of Krupps has been harmful to the great peace interests of the world, and in a less degree the same could probably be said of most other similar undertakings. The very success of that sort of business depends on the stimulation of the war atmosphere among the peoples. The Press, influenced by the large profits and advertising enterprise of the armament firms, whip up public opinion on every imaginable occasion; small foreign incidents are written up and magnified into grave international situations affecting the pacific relations of States, and the war temperature is artificially raised and kept up.

This proposal is, in my opinion, a sound one, and should be adopted by the Conference or the League. Of course, difficulties have been urged against it. Where are the small States, who are dependent for supplies on the private munition factories in the countries of the Great Powers, going to get their armaments in future? I am not much impressed with this sort of argument. To keep up the high tension of the war atmosphere over the world for the sake of indulging the small Balkan and other States in their special form of sport will not appeal to the democracies of the world. It will materially assist the peace policy of the League to cut off the supply of arms and munitions from these small States, whose little fits of temper are too costly to the world and whose security could be more safely entrusted to the League.

His recommendation on the subject is: "That all factories for the production of direct weapons of war shall be nationalised and their production shall be subject to the inspection of the officers of the Council; and that the Council shall be furnished periodically with returns of imports and exports of munitions of war into or from the territories of its members, and as far as possible into or from other countries."

For the rest he largely follows the lines of the Bourgeois memorandum, except that he does not suggest the formation of an independent League army.

He sums up his view as to the status and power which the League must possess in the affairs of mankind in these words: "If the future peace of the world is to be maintained it will not be sufficient merely to erect an *ad hoc* institution for the purpose of settling international disputes after they have arisen; *it will be necessary to devise an instrument of government* which will deal with the causes and sources of disputes." Although General Smuts repudiates as emphatically as M. Léon Bourgeois or Lord Phillimore the conception of a super-state, there is no doubt that throughout this notable document his mind is stretching out in that direction.

On Christmas Eve the Imperial War Cabinet met to have a final review of the position in reference to the League of Nations. President Wilson was arriving from France on Boxing Day and I was desirous of equipping myself for the interview with the considered and final views of my British and Empire colleagues on the subject which specially interested the President. The Smuts and Phillimore memoranda and other papers prepared by the Foreign Office and Admiralty had been circulated before the meeting of the Cabinet. I invited Lord Robert Cecil, as a Minister who had always been concerned with the promotion of the idea of a League of Nations, to open the discussions. General Smuts was not present at the meeting, as he had not returned from Paris, where he had gone at President Wilson's request to discuss with him questions relating to the Treaty. The President always felt that he had in General Smuts a man whose views were in sympathy with his own and one to whose highly trained intellect he paid the homage of respectful attention. Lord Robert did not express any opinions on the respective merits of the various schemes and did not indicate any preference where they differed. He confined himself to general observations on the urgency of

the need, and did not go into any details as to constitution, functions and powers. He quoted the Supreme War Council at
Versailles and the Interallied Maritime Transport Council as examples of what might be accomplished by a well-organised international body: "Anyone who had dealt with these bodies must
know that there were great possibilities in them, provided there
were a genuine desire to co-operate, and a permanent secretariat
to keep the organisation alive in the intervals between formal
meetings." His suggestion was to establish in some neutral capital
a permanent organisation presided over by a man of the greatest
possible ability: a man, for instance, of the calibre of M. Veniselos. I have many a time since thought that if this proposal had
been acted upon, the story of the League would have been more
propitious and less disappointing. In an impressive passage at
the end of his statement he laid stress on the urgency of making
an effort now to save the world from the repetition of such a
catastrophe as that from which it had just emerged:

During the election he had become aware of a very strong state of
feeling in this country: and he had been impressed by the growth of
class bitterness. He was very much afraid that, unless the Government
showed that it was very seriously in earnest about this matter, the
view would grow that the present Governmental machinery was not
to be trusted to deal with serious questions. The feeling would grow
that the richer classes were not opposed to war, and that, indeed,
they regarded it as favourable to their class interests. The opinion, he
believed, was false, but it must be admitted that the Press organs of
the wealthier classes had shown the least enthusiasm for schemes to
put down war. He therefore urged that we should show ourselves to
be really in earnest about this question.

A discussion followed which revealed the fact that, although
there was complete agreement as to the desirability of setting up
the League of Nations for the purpose of exerting its influence in
the achievement of a peaceable settlement of disputes between
nations, some of the members were inclined to be cautious as to
the functions which the League could be called upon to discharge
and the limits of its authority and power. Two or three of those
who took part were not very hopeful as to the prospects of dis-

armament or even as to its desirability. In this connection it is worth quoting a very illuminating and prophetic statement made by Mr. Bonar Law. He said that:

Unless something definite was accomplished in regard to disarmament any discussion on the League of Nations would be in the main academic. Marshal Foch had some time ago expressed to him the view that the future European countries on the left bank of the Rhine should organise themselves into a combined force to meet any possible danger from Germany. This was a hopeless point of view, as far as the League of Nations was concerned. In his (Mr. Bonar Law's) view the question of safety was a relative one. If our Navy were reduced but retained the relative supremacy which it possessed at the present moment we should lose nothing. The same applied to France and her army.

Sir Joseph Cook, of Australia, a man of calm and balanced judgment, supported Mr. Bonar Law in his contention and laid great stress on the principle of relative armaments. In winding up the discussion, I said

that there appeared to be general agreement on certain points, firstly on the idea of a League of Nations, and, secondly in the main as to its framework. On the question, however, of the power of the League, there was, if not disagreement, at least considerable hesitation and doubt as to the extent to which it should be carried. On the question of the desirability of the League of Nations, he agreed with Lord Robert Cecil, that if it were not set up as the result of the Peace Conference, there would be profound disappointment in this country, and even profound anger. This, he felt sure, was the mind of a people who had suffered and endured in this war. They regarded with absolute horror the continuance of a state of affairs which might again degenerate into a similar tragedy. Hence any Government that dared to set up a League of Nations that was not real would be sternly dealt with by the people. If the League of Nations did not include some provision for disarmament it would be regarded as a sham. He advocated the abolition of conscription as one of the conditions of a real peace. Let them begin with Germany. If that were done, there would be no excuse for maintaining the system in enemy countries for defence against a shadow.

Disarmament would be regarded as the real test of whether the League of Nations was a farce, or whether business was meant. He did not agree with those who considered that the League of Nations would not stop war. In his own lifetime there had been three great European wars, namely those of 1870, 1878, and 1914. In his opinion all these would have been stopped if a League of Nations such as he contemplated had been in existence. . . . In the case of the present war, Lord Grey proposed a conference; Germany refused. If there had been in existence a regular permanent machinery, Germany could not have refused a summons to attend. The meeting would have been automatic. Could anyone imagine in those circumstances that the dispute would not have been settled?

MR. HUGHES said that the real dispute would never have been settled.

MR. BONAR LAW said that this depended on armaments.

MR. HUGHES said the real causes of the war were racial and economic.

MR. LLOYD GEORGE said that, at any rate, an obstacle and delay would have been interposed. In regard to the framework, he considered that the Imperial War Cabinet and Versailles would provide admirable precedents. The Imperial War Cabinet contained the representatives of the self-governing Dominions and India. When questions arose for consideration one of two things happened. Either before their arrival in this country the Prime Ministers had discussed the question with their colleagues, and therefore knew exactly how far they could go— in which case, when they assented to a proposition they knew that it would be agreed to by their own Government—or else they said that they must first discuss it with their colleagues. Exactly the same was true of Versailles. The decisions of the Supreme War Council had executive force, not because Versailles possessed executive authority but because its representatives carried the authority of their Governments. The authority was not vested in the Versailles Council, but was derived from the Governments represented there. This is what he took General Smuts to mean. This was why he said you must send Ministers with real authority who know the minds of their Governments, and this was the meaning of General Smuts' Articles 18 and 19. General Smuts made it quite clear that nothing would be decided by a majority. If Great Britain stood out she could not be compelled by a majority of other nations to agree. He himself had never seen a case at Versailles where the parties did not eventually come to some agreement. He quite agreed, however, that in the League of Nations it would be a mistake to attempt too much. It must not be constituted as a body with executive power. But on the basis of the Imperial War Cabinet and of the Supreme War Council you would get a body whose authority rested with the Governments. Failing this he feared the Peace Conference would be a failure.

MR. HUGHES asked Mr. Lloyd George to take note that, as the causes of most wars were ultimately economic, the question of the decisions of the League of Nations being binding on the British Empire would be a matter of difficulty.

MR. LLOYD GEORGE thought that Mr. Hughes was wrong in thinking that economic questions were the fundamental causes of wars. Racial feeling was one great cause, and this was quite separate from economic considerations, as the case of Ireland proved. You could not abolish it and it would be fatal to try to do so. You might as well try to abolish family feeling. He agreed with an observation of Sir Joseph Cook that in Wales national feeling was as strong as it had been a thousand years ago. Our aim was to utilise that feeling not for war but for the preservation of peace.

MR. HUGHES suggested that Mr. Lloyd George underrated the strength of the feeling of internationalism among the Bolsheviks and their sympathisers.

MR. LLOYD GEORGE said the Bolsheviks would be beaten if they tried to suppress racial feelings either in their own country or outside.

.   .   .   .   .

He said there was one point he had overlooked in his first statement, and that was that he attached great importance to movable meetings, that is to say that the meetings of the League of Nations should not necessarily always be held at the seat of the secretariat, but in different countries. He thought that if only the leaders of the different nations could meet it would make all the difference in international relations.

Were I now to indicate those members of the Imperial War Cabinet who were fervent believers in the desirability and feasibility as well as of a strong League of Nations, I should name Lord Robert Cecil, General Smuts, Mr. Bonar Law, Sir Robert Borden, Lord Milner, General Botha, Sir Joseph Cook, Mr. Barnes and myself. But even outside these names there were no out-and-out opponents. The rest accepted the principle and were willing and anxious to see the experiment tried, provided it did not go too far in the direction of committing us to the use of force or of a measure of disarmament which would impair the authority and influence of the British Empire. One or two members did not disguise their opinion that the League was doomed to disappoint the hopes of its devotees. Conspicuous amongst these was Mr. Hughes, the cynical and outspoken Premier of Australia.

But I must at this stage emphasise the fact that, of all the belligerent Powers, it was the Governments of the British Empire and of France alone who had during the War laboured at practical schemes for carrying out the ideal of a League of Nations to ensure peace between nations, and that the Covenant of the League was in substance the outcome of their joint efforts. I doubt whether any other Government except that of the British Empire had devoted two Cabinet meetings to an examination of plans. This disposes of the unjust legend that President Wilson's mission and supreme achievement in Europe was to force this noble project on nations imbued with the military mind and inspired by imperialistic aims, and that but for his high purpose and resolute spirit it would have been ignored altogether in the Peace Settlement. In America this fable was invented by the President's undiscriminating disciples to exalt their leader. In Europe it was taken up by persons whose sole purpose was to disparage and discredit all the President's colleagues at the Peace Congress. It is just as well that the real truth should be known, lest through sheer default history should accept the misrepresentations of faction for statements of fact. It is not a question of the prestige of rival statesmen, but of the honourable repute of great nations in the greatest test to which their people have ever been subjected.

In Europe the League received the unanimous support of all Governments and Parliaments. Not a voice was raised against it. And European nations have done their best to work it. It was the American Senate that threw it out. It was American Governments which refused to render any assistance to make it a success. It is rather hard that poor old Europe, with its tangled perplexities, should be blamed for the shortcomings of other continents more fortunately situated.

The influential commission which drafted the Covenant of the League of Nations was presided over by President Wilson. It held twelve full sittings and there were much more numerous meetings of sub-committees which dealt with special sections. The most prolonged discussion came over the French proposal to equip the League with an armed force over which it would have effective control and which would enable it to enforce its decisions against recalcitrant members. Monsieur Léon Bourgeois and his French colleagues pressed amendment after amendment with a view to establishing such a force. The opposition to the proposal was led by President Wilson. He resisted mainly on the ground that it was utterly incompatible with the Constitution of the United States. There was no support for the idea outside the French Delegation.

Baron Makino endeavoured to carry an amendment which would establish complete equality of status amongst all the races which belonged to nations who were members of the League. It was aimed at the restrictions and disabilities which were imposed by certain States against Japanese emigration and Japanese settlers already within their borders. This proposition was also turned down.

The effort made by the French to insist that the carrying out of disarmament proposals adopted by a majority of the members should be a condition of continued membership of the League, was also defeated.

An effort was made to abolish compulsory conscription. This was resisted strongly by the French, who not only considered that they could not rely on a voluntary army, but also on the ground that the defence of the country was an essential obligation of every citizen.

Ultimately a scheme was adopted which was an amalgam of all the proposals which were common ground in the Phillimore, Smuts and Bourgeois plans.

These are the outstanding provisions of the Covenant recommended by the Commission and finally incorporated in the Treaty:

THE COVENANT OF THE LEAGUE OF NATIONS

THE HIGH CONTRACTING PARTIES

In order to promote international co-operation and to achieve international peace and security

by the acceptance of obligations not to resort to war,

by the prescription of open, just and honourable relations between nations,

by the firm establishment of the understandings of international law as the actual rule of conduct among Governments, and

by the maintenance of justice and a scrupulous respect for all treaty obligations in the dealings of organised peoples with one another, Agree to this Covenant of the League of Nations.

ARTICLE 1

The original Members of the League of Nations shall be those of the Signatories which are named in the Annex to this Covenant and also such of those other States named in the Annex as shall accede without reservation to this Covenant.

ARTICLE 5

Except where otherwise expressly provided in this Covenant or by the terms of the present Treaty, decisions at any meeting of the Assembly or of the Council shall require the agreement of all the Members of the League represented at the meeting.

.   .   .   .   .

ARTICLE 8

The Members of the League recognise that the maintenance of peace requires the reduction of national armaments to the lowest point consistent with national safety and the enforcement by common action of international obligations.

The Council, taking account of the geographical situation and circumstances of each state, shall formulate plans for such reduction for the consideration and action of the several Governments.

Such plans shall be subject to reconsideration and revision at least every ten years.

After these plans shall have been adopted by the several Governments, the limits of armaments therein fixed shall not be exceeded without the concurrence of the Council.

The Members of the League agree that the manufacture by private enterprises of munitions and implements of war is open to grave objections. The Council shall advise how the evil effects attendant upon such manufacture can be prevented, due regard being had to the necessities of those Members of the League which are not able to manufacture the munitions and implements of war necessary for their safety.

The Members of the League undertake to interchange full and frank information as to the scale of their armaments, their military, naval and air programmes and the condition of such of their industries as are adaptable to war-like purposes.

ARTICLE 10

The Members of the League undertake to respect and preserve as against external aggression the territorial integrity and existing political independence of all Members of the League. In case of any such aggression or increase of any threat or danger of such aggression the Council shall advise upon the means by which this obligation shall be fulfilled.

ARTICLE 11

Any war or threat of war, whether immediately affecting any of the Members of the League or not, is hereby declared a matter of concern to the whole League, and the League shall take any action that may be deemed wise and effectual to safeguard the peace of nations. In case any such emergency should arise the Secretary-General shall on the request of any Member of the League forthwith summon a meeting of the Council.

ARTICLE 13

The Members of the League agree that whenever any dispute shall arise between them which they recognise to be suitable for submission to arbitration and which cannot be satisfactorily settled by diplomacy, they will submit the whole subject-matter to arbitration.

ARTICLE 14

The Council shall formulate and submit to the Members of the League for adoption plans for the establishment of a Permanent Court of International Justice. The Court shall be competent to hear and determine any dispute of an international character which the parties thereto submit to it.

ARTICLE 15

If there should arise between Members of the League any dispute likely to lead to a rupture, which is not submitted to arbitration in accordance with Article 13, the Members of the League agree that they will submit the matter to the Council. Any party to the dispute may effect such submission. . . .

. . . . .

The Council shall endeavour to effect a settlement of the dispute, and if such efforts are successful, a statement shall be made public giving such facts and explanations regarding the dispute and the terms of settlement thereof as the Council may deem appropriate.

If the dispute is not thus settled, the Council either unanimously or by a majority vote shall make and publish a report containing a statement of the facts of the dispute and the recommendations which are deemed just and proper in regard thereto.

ARTICLE 16

Should any Member of the League resort to war in disregard of its covenants under Articles 12, 13 or 15, it shall *ipso facto* be deemed to have committed an act of war against all other Members of the League, which hereby undertake immediately to subject it to the severance of all trade or financial relations, the prohibition of all intercourse between their nationals and the nationals of the covenant-breaking State, and the prevention of all financial, commercial or personal intercourse between the nationals of the covenant-breaking State and the nationals of any other State, whether a Member of the League or not.

It shall be the duty of the Council in such case to recommend to the several Governments concerned what effective military, naval or air force the Members of the League shall severally contribute to the armed forces to be used to protect the covenants of the League.

The Members of the League agree, further, that they will mutually support one another in the financial and economic measures which are taken under this Article, in order to minimise the loss and inconvenience resulting from the above measures, and that they will mutually support one another in resisting any special measures aimed at one of their number by the covenant-breaking State, and that they will take the necessary steps to afford passage through their territory to the forces of any of the Members of the League which are co-operating to protect the covenants of the League.

Any Member of the League which has violated any covenant of the League may be declared to be no longer a Member of the League by a vote of the Council concurred in by the Representatives of all the other Members of the League represented thereon.

ARTICLE 19

The Assembly may from time to time advise the reconsideration by Members of the League of treaties which have become inapplicable and the consideration of international conditions whose continuance might endanger the peace of the world.

ARTICLE 20

The Members of the League severally agree that this Covenant is accepted as abrogating all obligations or understandings *inter se* which are inconsistent with the terms thereof, and solemnly undertake that they will not hereafter enter into any engagements inconsistent with the terms thereof.

In case any Member of the League shall, before becoming a Member of the League, have undertaken any obligations inconsistent with the terms of this Covenant, it shall be the duty of such Member to take immediate steps to procure its release from such obligations.

CHAPTER XV

THE INTERNATIONAL LABOUR ORGANISATION

THE project of an international effort to ameliorate the conditions of the worker throughout the world owed its inception to a social reformer whose renown will grow with the ages—Robert Owen. Owen, who was a benevolent man of genius, was foremost amongst the real founders of modern ideas about the reconstruction of our economic and social system on humanitarian principles. Karl Marx subsequently worked out these ideas in ponderous treatises with a rigid framework of cast-iron logic. Robert Owen was the creator of the idea; Marx was the architect who built the structure on unattractive lines which gave the whole fabric the appearance of a well-ordered but repellent workhouse for all. Robert Owen had practical experience of the infamous conditions of the textile workers and the farm labourers in his own country. This impelled him to submit to the European Congress at Aix-la-Chapelle in 1818 two memoranda asking the Powers to introduce into every country measures for protecting the workers against the influence and exploitation to which they were exposed, and inviting them to appoint an International Commission to deal with the problem. Owen's appeal was dismissed with contempt as the cranky and crazy effusion of a "political lunatic," but his ideas were kept alive by public-spirited individuals in a number of countries.

Twenty years later Jérome Blanqui, the French social reformer, in a treatise on industrial economics, wrote:

There is only one way of accomplishing it (the reform) while avoiding its disastrous consequences: this would be to get it adopted simultaneously by all industrial nations which compete in the foreign market. Will people be willing to do this? Can it be done? Why not? Treaties have been concluded between one country and another by which they have bound themselves to kill men; why should they not be concluded to-day for the purpose of preserving men's lives and making them happier?

Then came the Alsatian manufacturer, Daniel Legrand, who from 1838 to the time of his death in 1859 bombarded not only the French but also the British and Prussian Governments with memoranda in the hope of inducing them to enact, in the terms in the title of one of his memoranda, dated 1847, "an international law to protect the working classes against premature and excessive labour, which is the prime and principal cause of their physical deterioration, their moral degradation and their being deprived of the blessings of family life."

These ideas, while having great propaganda value, could not be put into force, because at that date very little legislation for the protection of the workers had been enacted in any country. The point of view of French reformers was that competition between manufacturers in different countries was an obstacle in the way of the establishment of national legislation. This contention was by no means confined to France. It was the argument advanced by all those who resisted proposals for curtailing unconscionable hours of labour or any measures for improving factory conditions in the United Kingdom. It was urged that such proposals would place us at a fatal disadvantage in the markets of the world in competing with the goods of countries whose labour was cheaper and who had not to bear the heavy capital expenditure or improvement in building and machinery involved in the measures suggested. Many a bill introduced into the British Parliament by philanthropic legislators has been defeated or mutilated on this plausible ground. This argument has now lost a good deal of its force because it has been proved that the best workmen are produced by good conditions and that the best workmen turn out the best goods.

The theory of *laissez-faire*, which dominated industry and commerce and was treated with the reverence of an infallible religious dogma during the greater part of the nineteenth century, lost some of its power towards the second half of the century and legislation for the protection of workers in industrial countries became more frequent. Then the idea of international labour legislation received a fresh impulse. In France, Germany, Switzerland men of various shades of opinion argued that the progress made in the social sphere could be consolidated and further progress made by eliminating the disadvantages which such progress and the consequent rise in production costs would have for the industries of the more advanced countries in international competition.

It was the economic rather than the humanitarian justification for international labour legislation which led to the first practical results at the end of the century.

Colonel Frey, President of the Swiss Federal Council, referred in 1876 to the possibility that a diplomatic démarche would be made by Switzerland. His definite proposal was made in 1880 and was discussed in 1881. The replies of the Governments which were approached—Austria, Belgium, France, Great Britain and Italy—were by no means encouraging.

In 1889 the Swiss Federal Council sent the various foreign Governments an invitation to a "preparatory" Conference. In 1890 the young German Emperor, William II, who was then in the first flush of youthful idealism and scanned the skies for a vacant place amongst the stars of humanitarianism, ordered Bismarck to approach the foreign Governments and invite the Conference to meet in Berlin. Bismarck was opposed to the Conference although he himself had been responsible for measures of social amelioration which had added to the annual costs of industry. He had, however, no special interest in humanity outside Germany. He concentrated his whole thoughts on that portion of it that dwelt within the boundaries of Germany. An international conference to improve the state of French, British or Chinese workers did not interest him.

The Berlin Conference of 1890 lasted ten days and was attended by delegates from twelve chief industrial States of Europe. The programme of the Conference covered practically the whole field of the legislation in force in the countries represented.

But the Governments concerned and public opinion in their respective countries were both insufficiently prepared. The Conference merely adopted a certain number of resolutions on the limitation of the work of women and children, work in mines and the weekly rest. The results were limited and were not followed up.

The Conference, notwithstanding its failure, produced an immense moral effect. Everything tended to show that international Conventions, if suitably prepared and studied, were a possibility.

In 1900 a group of scholars and economists, profiting by the failure of the Berlin Conference, founded the International Association for the Protection of Workers in Paris, and undertook to convene International Labour Conferences, to prepare their agenda and, by constant propaganda, to have the texts adopted incorporated in national legislation.

An International Office was set up in Basle to centralise the research work and the circulation of information. The Association became known as the International Association for Labour Legislation. It founded an International Office at Basle which received considerable subsidies from all Governments. Conferences were held every two years down to the War. Profiting by the mistakes of the Berlin Conference, instead of trying to deal all at once with a wide programme, the Association preferred to select those subjects likely to call forth the least resistance and to have them studied thoroughly.

Thus, in 1901 two subjects were selected—the prohibition of night work by women, and the abolition of white phosphorus in manufacturing matches. These matters were carefully studied and a committee, which met at Basle in 1903, drew up two memoranda justifying proposals to be made to Governments.

The next Conference, at Berne, was held in two successive stages: (1) a preliminary Conference in 1905 consisted of a meeting of experts, delegates who were not plenipotentiaries, and (2) a Conference held in 1906 for the drafting of final Conventions which were drawn up by professional diplomats.

The 1905 Conference adopted drafts relating to white phosphorus and night work for women to serve as a basis for two Conventions. At the 1906 Conference only seven Powers signed a Convention prohibiting the use of white phosphorus. One recalls with shame the refusal of Great Britain to be one of the signatories. There was unanimity on the question of night work for women and the Convention was signed by the representatives of all the States except one.

Another preliminary Conference of experts met at Berne in 1913 and drew up bases for two new Conventions—one to limit the hours of work for women and young persons, and the other to prohibit night work for young persons. The conference of diplomats for voting final Conventions was to meet in September, 1914. It never met. Europe was aflame by September. Nations and Governments were concentrating their thoughts and energies on destroying not on saving lives.

During the War there were movements in Europe and in America for taking advantage of the Peace Settlement when it came, for a concerted effort amongst the nations of the world to improve the conditions of the wage-earners, and demands were made that terms of peace should "safeguard the working classes of all countries from the attacks of international combination and ensure a minimum guarantee of mutual material order, as regards legislation, trade union rights, migration, hours of work and industrial hygiene and safety."

When the War was approaching the end of its sanguinary course Mr. George Barnes who, as a member of the War Cabinet had been charged with the special mission of overlooking all labour questions, decided that the time had come for preparing the necessary measures to incorporate in the Peace Treaty the idea of international co-operation to raise the standard of living of the wage-earners in all countries.

Mr. Barnes was a fine specimen of the sturdy Northern artisan; shrewd, sensible, practical, straightforward: a man whose education did not stop when he left the primary school for the works. He and Arthur Henderson belonged to the same breed. They justify the confidence of the reformers who fought for the inclusion of the workers amongst the governing classes of their country. Barnes had two predominant characteristics—honesty and common sense. No words in the English language are more abused than these. Timidity is too often mistaken for common sense: shrinking in a dilemma from taking any course lest perchance you should take the wrong one is the overcautiousness which is con-

fused with wisdom. Honesty means more than that a person does
not peculate or pick pockets. An honest politician is not necessarily one who votes straight on the party ticket or who subordinates every consideration—except his own interest—to the success of his party. It implies, or ought to imply, that he never gives
a promise to induce support unless he means to implement it
and actually does his best to do so; that he does not designedly
use phrases which convey more than he intends in order to win
the adherence of individuals or sections of the community.
Whether in a politician or a Trade Union leader, honesty means
that he expresses an opinion or urges a course of action without
reference to its popularity but because he believes that it is right,
and that when he thinks so he stands by that conviction at all
hazards to himself. That is the type of man Mr. Barnes is. When
I first met him I was President of the Board of Trade and he was
Secretary of one of the most powerful Unions. He held a high
position in organised labour and enjoyed a big remuneration for a
Trade Union official. He resigned it because the Union rejected
his advice to take good terms offered to them by employers under
pressure from the Board of Trade and insisted on striking to their
detriment.

In the War Cabinet his counsel was eminently wise and always
straightforward. He spoke up fearlessly for the workers when he
thought they had a grievance that ought to be redressed, though
he never could persuade himself to subordinate his judgment to
the dictation of a caucus. Hence, although he was devoted to the
cause of Labour, he found no place in the Labour party. On the
other hand, when Labour Ministers were called out of the Coalition Government, and Barnes dissented from the resolution of
the majority of the party, he nevertheless gave up his office and
his £5,000 a year, because he would not have it supposed that
his disapproval of the decision was prompted by mercenary motives. At the same time he also gave up his party as a protest
against its action in withdrawing support from a Government
before they had a legitimate quarrel with its measures or policy
on a point of principles. He thus found himself without office,
without a seat in Parliament, without an official position in the

Trade Union movement and without a profession to maintain himself. But he never complained. He is not a man with a grumble. He has not soured. He is the same gentle and genial and level-headed personality whom I knew as a colleague in the War Cabinet, always modest, unassuming and entirely devoid of push and self-seeking. No thrust on his own part ever got him into office or procured him emolument. His own sterling abilities and character alone account for his advance into every position he ever held.

The contribution he made to our counsels during the War was of great service to us. He was one of the myriads to whom it brought a great sorrow, for he lost a promising son in action. In the Cabinet he was in a special sense a representative of the wage-earners. He knew the workers well and could discriminate between legitimate grievances and manufactured complaints. The first he urged us and helped us to redress. The latter he had no hesitation in recommending us to ignore and defy. He took a leading part in the grant of an eight-hour day for the railway workers before the Government parted with control of the railways—a concession by the Coalition Cabinet to the workers of this country which is conveniently forgotten by their official champions. It was he who took the principal initiative in the establishment of the International Labour Organisation and in the framing of its constitution. In his quiet persistent way, he piloted it safely through the committee as the principal delegate of Britain.

Mr. Barnes placed the whole scheme before me as Prime Minister before the War came to an end and I deputed him to enter into immediate consultation with the officials of the Labour Ministry, Trade Union leaders and representative employers, with a view to having his plans ready for the Peace Conference when it was reached. In an interview he gave on the project to the *Daily Chronicle* in September, 1918, he said: "What we want is some kind of international machinery. The Peace Conference should first be asked to agree to the principle . . . and then refer the matter to a Commission to consider and report on the measures to be taken. . . . The Commission would sit at the same time and place as the Peace Conference. Then the Congress would adopt recommendations." This course was subsequently followed.

The result was that when the Conference met the British Delegation alone were ready with a worked-out scheme and their plan became the basis on which the whole discussion proceeded. In substance it was finally adopted. As soon as the Peace Conference met, I proposed:

That a Commission be appointed to enquire into the question of international adjustment of conditions of employment, and to consider what forms of permanent international machinery should be established to enable the several countries to secure joint action on matters affecting conditions of employment, and to recommend what steps should be taken to set up an appropriate organisation.

The Commission was duly set up with Mr. Gompers, the famous American labour leader, in the Chair. Before its labours were concluded Gompers left for America. Samuel Gompers was a compact little man, radiating vitality. He was a born leader of the masses with great oratorical gifts. He had a resonant voice, a pleasant appearance and address and a fluent output of rousing generalities. Moreover, he was sagacious and had a great fund of intuitive common sense. He was an ideal leader for the stirring propaganda needed to create a new environment. But like most Trade Union leaders, he trusted to improvisation, experience and instinct, and was not accustomed to work out his problems on paper. There was no more forceful advocate of the general idea of international co-operation and his many orations from the Chair were convincing proofs of the ardour of his faith, but did not help the Commission in the building up of a plan. They were more stimulating than suggestive. He helped things along by his discovery that urgent business demanded his immediate return to the States.

Mr. Barnes, who was the only man on the Commission who had thought the matter out in practical detail, with the aid of very able experts such as Mr. (now Sir) Malcolm Delevigne and Mr. Harold Butler, had his plans ready. He was therefore elected

to the Chair and he directed the proceedings to a practical conclusion.

There was a good deal of division of opinion among Labour
leaders as to the nature of the institution which was to be set up.
The question of the powers which were to be granted to it was
the subject of a long battle between the delegations. The different
methods of approach to the problem can be clarified as follows:

(1) An attempt might be made to secure the insertion of a "labour
charter" in the Peace Treaty to provide for the immediate international application of a number of reforms such as the eight-hour day,
the institution of a minimum age for entry into industry, etc., and
set up a sort of international industrial Parliament.

(2) The alternative method was to obtain from the Peace Conference the setting up of some special machinery for dealing with labour
problems on an international basis.

The French Delegation were in favour of the former course.
They were anxious to use the Peace Treaty as a legislative enact-
ment to achieve the desired reforms at one leap. After a good deal
of discussion the delegates turned down this proposal. It was felt
that any attempt to force far-reaching changes in the industrial
and economic life of all the countries of the world, without giving
employers and workmen a full opportunity in each country to
discuss them and adapt themselves to the change, would end in a
complete failure of the whole scheme. The second alternative,
which was the British plan, decided in favour of one organisation,
that organisation to be permanent and to hold periodic meetings;
the delegates to be representatives of employers and workers, as
well as representatives of Governments. The American delegates
did not wish Government servants or politicians to be in the
organisation.

There were several controversial questions which arose in the
course of the discussions of the Drafting Commission which
some of the national delegations felt they were unable to settle
without authority from the Prime Ministers of their respective
countries. At that time the latter were immersed in a multitude
of difficult questions bearing on the functions of the League,
trouble in Russia and Central Europe, appeals from nations to

fix disputes as to boundaries, and many other intricate and absorbing problems. As the Foreign Secretaries were no longer members of the Supreme Drafting Commission the points raised by the Labour Commission were referred to them. I had been kept fully informed by Mr. Barnes as to the issues and differences and I communicated my views to Mr. Balfour and had no difficulty in securing his interest and sympathy in the whole project. The other Foreign Secretaries did not function. They had no special interest in Labour problems and clearly thought it was none of their business to attend to them.

On the 2nd of April Mr. Barnes wrote me a letter calling attention to the general attitude of the Foreign Ministers:

British Delegation,
Paris.
2.4.1919.

My dear Prime Minister,
I am getting very uneasy at the way things are going. I was summoned yesterday to a meeting of the Foreign Secretaries to put the case of the Labour Commission for an early meeting of the Plenary Conference to accept our report. The case briefly is: (1) that the Commission thought unanimously that the subject of the regulation of Labour was of such importance as to justify a meeting of the Plenary Conference so that the scheme of Labour organisation could be launched in such a way as to mark it as one of the important matters of the Peace Conference and thereby to have an effect in easing the Labour situation; (2) We propose a Conference this year and we ask leave to set up an international Committee to make the arrangements; and, in order to get arrangements made in time, the Committee should be at work now. We are ready to begin. Until the scheme is passed by someone with the necessary authority and a Committee set up nothing can be done. The Secretaries yesterday shunted the whole thing on to the Prime Ministers so that you will have it before you in a day or two and the matter is still open. So far so good.

But what struck me yesterday was the attitude of the Foreign Secretaries. Except for Mr. Balfour no one appeared to regard Labour settlement as of any importance. One of the Secretaries said that, in his judgment, it was not Labour but Territory which was agitating the minds of peoples. I combated this idea as well as I could. I feel sure it is an idea which, if paramount here, will lead us all into the ditch. I noted in the proceedings, as reported in the Bulletin relating to Poland, that you had to combat it last week. I have heard of it in connection with the Saar Valley. I know that Labour is relentlessly hostile to annexation or to leaving numbers of Germans, after our proceedings, under French or other rule. And, if it gets abroad that the Peace plenipotentiaries are only taking a languid interest in Labour adjustment, then Labour will be very wroth and will have reason to be so.

For my part I must of course keep in mind that I am here to advise you on Labour feeling when necessary. This is my justification for writing you this long letter. I know that Labour cares nothing about Territory except to see such adjustment made as to leave no rankling sore for the future; and, I know further that Labour does care about getting on with those things that concern the daily life of working folk.

It is because of that that I want our scheme through and our Committee at work.

Yours faithfully,
(*Sd.*) GEO. N. BARNES.

At last all the differences were adjusted. I saw President Wilson and Signor Orlando, who were sympathetic, and M. Clemenceau, who was indifferent but not obstructive.

The British plan was finally adopted and with some not very material amendments was incorporated in the Treaty. The most important amendment was the insertion of what is known as the Labour Charter, the ideal for which the new international body was to strive. Here are the points of this revolutionary charter:

Right of lawful association.
Payment of a reasonable wage.
The eight-hour day and forty-eight hour week.
Weekly rest.
Abolition of child labour and restriction of juvenile labour.
Equal pay for equal work.
Legal conditions of labour in each country to have regard to the equitable economic treatment of all workers lawfully resident therein.
Proper inspection, in which women should take part.

In submitting the Constitution to the Assembly of the Allied and Associated Nations at Paris, Mr. Barnes delivered one of his lucid, practical and matter-of-fact speeches:

We have issued, along with our report, two separate and distinct drafts, one being the text of a scheme of international organisation, the other a collection of nine resolutions for insertion in the Peace

Treaty or issued therewith. Before dealing with the documents, however, perhaps I may be allowed to say a few words in regard to our conception of the task entrusted to us.

First of all, I want to say that we approached our work, as I am sure you would have had us do, in a sympathetic spirit and from a humane standpoint. Some of us knew our labour world at first hand, and we knew that there were many in it condemned to lives of toil relieved only by spells of compulsory idleness. In the old times, before the war, labour conditions were largely the outcome of blind chance. Age and want, that ill-matched pair, haunted the mind of the average workman in his working life, and we must remember that the labourer still lives in pre-war memories and is determined not to return to pre-war conditions. Those pre-war experiences of labour have laid upon the world a heavy burden and a great danger. They have produced a man who is class-centred, who regards work as a blessing, and who has been deluded into the belief that the less work he does the more there is left for his mates to do. This feeling, and the practice based upon it, is demoralizing to the individual and harmful to the community, but it is based on the fear of want, and can be eradicated only by security of employment under improved conditions.

In saying that, I am not casting stones at any class for existing conditions—it has not been conscious of cruelty—but rather the long arm of circumstance that has cast a devil's chain around the lives of some workers in some countries. I do not deny that some may rise to share in the pleasure of life, but, nevertheless, it is true to say that the mass remain a misfit in their present condition, a source of concern to all lovers of their kind and a menace to the peace of the world.

It is this last aspect of the matter which makes labour regulations and improvement an integral part of the work of a Peace Conference. The question we had, therefore, to consider was how to provide the means whereby to promote a better mental atmosphere, as well as to produce improved material conditions.

Hitherto, it has sometimes been found that efforts at improvement in a country have been checked by the fear, or the plea, of competition from other lower-wage countries. I do not enter into the question as to the validity of that plea, although in parenthesis it may here be said that the highest-wage countries are not the least successful in world competition. I merely mention it as a factor in sometimes preventing improvements in countries of a relatively high standard of life.

For the first time in history, we are now seeking to get the co-operation of all concerned. States, employers, and workers are engaged in a common cause and animated by a common desire to raise the standard of life everywhere.

At the threshold of our proceedings, however, we were met by two real obstacles—first, the difference in industrial development as between countries; and, second, the limitations of States in regard to acceptance of international decrees. We had perforce to give up the idea of uniformity or coercion, and to rely mainly on the good will of States to accept or reject advice and guidance as might be decided by their own competent authorities. I freely confess that at one time I was in favour of penalties. Closer inspection, however, led me to the conclusion that penalties must be kept well in the background, and imposed then only through the agency and with the authority of the League of Nations. That provision is now embodied in our organisation. But, while my mind was driven from one channel, it was at the same time attracted to the possibility of another. Publicity and agreement presented themselves in clearer and better colours. After all, it is not coercion which is needed, so much as knowledge and good will.

We have, therefore, provided for conferences of States, employers, and workers to be held in the light of day, to be representative of all concerned, and to be armed with the fullest possible information. It will be the business of the organisation which we propose to establish to collect and distribute information, to stimulate healthy public opinion, and to let light into dark places, wherever such may be found to exist. This, then, may be said to be the fundamental, and as we believe the effective, idea in our organisation, the creation and mobilisation of humane public opinion.

Regarding the provisions of the document. First of all, its boundaries are made to coincide with those of the League of Nations. There are two reasons for that—first, because thereby the League of Nations is invested with duties of a positive character and associated with the everyday work of the world; and, secondly, because it brings all the nations in the League into world co-operation for industrial improvement and thereby conveys to Labour the impression that labour improvement is regarded seriously by the Peace Conference as a matter of world importance.

Secondly, it provides for an annual conference, to be held, unless otherwise provided, at the seat of the League of Nations. The Conference will consist of four members from each State, two being representatives of the State and one each of workmen and employers respectively. Each delegate will be allowed to vote separately, so that we may promote the spirit of internationality.

Thirdly, there will be a permanent office, also situated at the capital of the League of Nations, whose business it will be to collect and distribute information, and which will be under the control of a governing body constituted in like manner to the Conference itself—half of Government and half of non-Government elements.

I now come to procedure. The most important article connected therewith is No. 19. It has been the chief obstacle to the agreement, ultimately, I am glad to say, reached. It now provides that if the proposals are endorsed by a conference, they are to be in the form of a draft convention or, alternatively, in the form of a recommendation. In either case, if supported by two-thirds of the votes cast at a conference, they become the finding of that conference and are deposited with the Secretary-General of the League of Nations. Each high contracting party then comes under the obligation to submit the convention or recommendation, as the case may be, within 12 months to its competent authority, and, unless such competent authority endorses or accepts the recommendation or convention, as the case may be, that is the only obligation resting upon the affiliated States, subject to a proviso, however, in the following clause, of which I shall say a word in a moment. The State comes under the obligation if its competent authority accepts the recommendation or convention to carry it out.

Here, however, we come upon the difficulty of Federal States. There are States which are prevented by their Constitutions from making treaties in regard to labour matters. There are States, such as the United States of America, which include numbers of competent authorities which must be left free to decide for themselves. It was because of that that we decided to allow of a convention being cast in the form of a recommendation, and then if cast in the form of a convention it should still be regarded by a Federal State as a recommendation only. If a Federal State adopted it, it would do so in its own way. The net result of all this is that there is a less degree of obligation resting upon a Federal State, than upon other States. That is regrettable but, as we found, unavoidable.

Now I come to the two suggested additions to Article 19. It will be remembered that I said a few moments ago that a State was bound to put a convention or recommendation to its competent authorities within 12 months. It has been pointed out, however, that there might be exceptional and unforeseen circumstances which would make that impossible, such as a general election in a country, and it has been suggested that after the words "12 months after the meeting of the conference" there should be inserted, "or if it is impossible, owing to exceptional circumstances to do so within a period of one year, then at the earliest possible moment, and in no case later than 18 months from the end of the conference."

Speaking now as a representative rather of the British Delegation than of the Commission, I can say that I have no objection to the insertion of these words. Then another addition is proposed as a protocol to Article 19 to make the meaning clearer. The words are simply declaratory and do not alter the sense. It will be remembered that I said we had to give up ideas of uniformity in consequence of different degrees of industrial development in different countries. Of course, every State is free to reject, and therefore it may be said that there is a sufficient safeguard against coercion or non-elasticity. It has been pointed out, however, that States might be charged with insincerity if they came into the organisation and repeatedly rejected its recommendations. In order, therefore, that it should be made clear that there is an obligation resting upon the conference itself to have regard to undeveloped countries, it is proposed that the following words should be added to our document as a protocol to this Article 19:

"In framing any recommendation or draft convention of general application, the Conference shall have due regard to those countries in which climatic conditions, the imperfect development of industrial organisation, or other special circumstances make the industrial conditions substantially different and shall suggest modifications, if any, which it considers may be required to meet the case of such countries."

This makes no difference to the scheme of organization and may be accepted as part of it.

The provision of Article 20 is that, in the event of a State adopting a convention, it shall be bound to it, subject only to conditions in the convention itself. What we had in mind there was that it might be subject to the proviso that the convention had to be accepted by a certain number or proportion of all States.

A word only about the Enforcement Clauses. It will be noted that although the machinery of organization is brought into play, reliance is placed on publicity and inquiry, with an appeal in the last resort to the League of Nations. The governing body can initiate proceedings, but the inquiry is made by persons selected by the Secretary-General of the League of Nations, and the International Court of the League may affirm, vary, or reverse any decision reached.

I pass over some comparatively unimportant provisions and come to the transitory articles. We propose a conference being held this year at Washington, provided that the United States Government is willing to co-operate with an International Committee which we propose should be set up and consist of seven representatives of seven States, including one from Switzerland as representing neutral States. We are most anxious to begin the preparations for this conference as soon as possible.

Just a few words now about the resolutions. It was felt by the Commission that its work would not be complete if it were confined to setting up machinery. Great hopes have been raised of something of a direct nature being done by the Peace Conference itself through some terms in the Peace Treaty. It was not within our competence to deal in detail with specific questions of industrial improvement. It is not even within the competence of this august body to impose industrial changes on affiliated States. At the same time, the Commissioners were so impressed with the need for recognizing some principles that they decided to submit some principles to the Conference. It will be noticed that the high contracting parties are not asked to give immediate effect to them, but only to endorse them generally. Nine such proposals were adopted by the Commission, each of them getting the support of a two-thirds majority which was a condition of their adoption. That, Sir, is the completed work of the Commission, of which you have a full report in your possession. Provided you give us the necessary authority, we are ready to start forthwith in preparing for our first Conference.

Sir, I need scarcely remind you of the urgency of the work of labour amelioration, for it is known to all that new thoughts are surging up among us and about us and that the world as a result is in a ferment. Nor need I dwell on its importance, an importance second only to the prevention of war, to which we have already given our hand and seal. Our scheme will, we think, give strength to the League of Nations by enabling it to take root in the daily life of peoples. It will, we believe, give hope and health to those whose lives are scarred by toil and sorrow, and on behalf of the Commission I commend it to your favourable consideration.

There is no part of the Treaty which has functioned more smoothly or more successfully than the section which deals with international labour problems. There is no section of the Treaty which so far has brought such unmixed blessings to the lot of untold millions of the humblest workers in many lands. It has already achieved incalculable advantages for the wage-earners of the world. By the middle of 1938, the International Labour Conference had adopted 62 International Labour Conventions. A total of 771 ratifications had been received from 53 countries, and in many other cases, legislation is being prepared which will make further ratifications possible. All these Conventions represent a definite improvement—some great, some small—in labour conditions throughout the world.

The subjects of the Conventions cover nearly all the main industrial problems of to-day. The first Convention of all was the "Washington Hours Convention," establishing the eight-hour day and forty-eight hour week. This Convention applies to workers in industry, including mines and transport. A similar Convention dealing with workers in commerce and offices was adopted in 1930, and a special Convention for coal-mines in 1931. Recommendations cover the cases of workers in the fishing industry and inland navigation. One Convention lays down the principle of a weekly rest of at least twenty-four consecutive hours in industry, and a Recommendation asks that the same rest shall be enjoyed by workers in commerce and offices. In 1935 the principle of the forty-hour week was adopted, and is being applied successfully to industry. France has recently given it a sweeping and comprehensive application.

Not only is the protection of children a question of the very first humanitarian interest, but it is economically important; for men and women cannot command a living wage when children can be employed at half their rates in their stead.

The International Labour Conference has concluded a series of Conventions, covering the whole field of employment, and laying down a minimum age below which children are not to be employed. The standard for entry into industry is fourteen; for sea the same age, or eighteen for trimmers and stokers; for agriculture fourteen, or an earlier age outside school hours; and for work in commerce, offices, etc., fourteen, except that some kinds of light work are allowed after the age of twelve. Young persons under eighteen may not be employed on night work in industry nor in bakeries, nor in processes involving the use of white lead, nor at sea, unless a medical certificate is produced showing that they are fit for the work. In 1935 the Conference recommended that the minimum age for leaving school and entering employment should be raised to fifteen as soon as circumstances permit.

There are three Conventions and three Recommendations specially dealing with women. Of the former, one prohibits the employment of women on night work in industry, the other provides that women employed in industry shall enjoy a rest period before and after confinement, with free medical attendance and safeguards against dismissal from their posts. Two of the Recommendations deal with the extension of these Conventions to cover women employed in agriculture; the third with the protection of emigrant women and girls on board ship. Women may not be employed in processes involving the use of white lead, and native women are not to be called up for forced or compulsory labour. The third Convention prohibits the work of women in underground mines of all sorts.

The transformation which the International Labour Organisation has brought about in many countries is incredible when one recalls pre-war conditions. Here are a few examples:

In China, it was stated in a British Consular report of 1924 that the normal duration of a shift in the British-owned and Japanese-owned cotton mills in Shanghai was twelve hours; in the Chinese-owned, fourteen hours. In another town an eighteen-hour day was common. In some places only four days' holiday were kept in the year. The filth was such that 70 per cent. of the match workers in some factories were "advanced consumptives at an age at which many young people have scarcely completed their studies." In the carpet factories, in which children of seven and eight were employed, abscesses of the face and scalp were common, and often resulted in early blindness. Wages were at "starvation rates," and safety devices lacking. Women and children were employed all night, and children taken to the cotton mills "as soon as they were old enough to be useful."

China has now worked out a most advanced Factory Act. Hours of work for adults in large factories are limited to eight a day; children under fourteen may not be employed at all, and neither women nor young persons may be employed on night work. A weekly rest for all workers is laid down. A factory inspection service has been organised with the help of the International Labour Office which sent a special mission to China for that purpose. It is true that owing to the absence of any very real central authority in China, the system is not yet working perfectly, but millions of workers have benefited by the changes, and the country will certainly never go back to the old conditions.

Japan warmly acknowledges her debt to the International Labour Organisation. She has ratified twelve Conventions, including nearly all the minimum age series. She has also brought her legislation into line with the International Labour Office standards in many other respects. A special Bureau of Social Affairs has been set up, which keeps in close and permanent contact with the International Labour Office. Incidentally, it was the insistence shown by the International Labour Office on the appointment of a properly representative workers' delegate at Geneva which brought about the unification of the Japanese workers' movement, and the recognition of it by the Government.

In Persia the carpet factories employed children of five, who sat all day weaving in stuffy, crowded rooms, seated on a narrow plank without a back, and hung up in the air so that they could not get down until they were lifted. This constant work in one position from which they could not move caused the children to become deformed; their legs were permanently bent, for no surgical operation could straighten them. If they lived to be adults—and too often they died in early childhood—they were permanently deformed. This state of affairs was reported to the International Labour Office, which intervened, and, as a result, Persia has made regulations setting a limit of eight hours to children's work, forbidding the employment of children under ten, and introducing healthy conditions.

Up to a few years ago, white phosphorus was largely employed in the making of matches. It is cheaper to use than red phosphorus, but produces burns, coughs, etc., and chronic poisoning in two forms; a general condition ending in fragility of the bones, anaemia, fever, mental dullness, insomnia and languor; and the disease known as "phossy-jaw" in which the jaw becomes ulcerated and rots away, assuming a "coral-like appearance." Unless quickly operated, the cases usually end fatally, and often produce pain so severe as to drive the sufferer to madness and suicide. To-day thirty-one countries have agreed not to use white phosphorus. The International Labour Office has done similar work in connection with other industrial diseases, and has in every way done an immense work in preventing industrial disease, encouraging and making known the results of research into its causes and prevention, and enforcing the principle of compensation for the sufferers.

Countries in which industrialisation is still young are coming to the International Labour Office for help and advice in framing measures in advance, to prevent abuses arising in the future. Turkey and Mexico are two countries which have recently called on the International Labour Office in this way.

The success of the International Labour Organisation has been one of the most amazing and gratifying miracles of the post-war period. This bare recital of some of its triumphs will give an idea of the beneficence of this humane and healing institution. No organisation has ever in the course of nineteen years spared mankind as much misery, torture and degradation which was awaiting it.

Will the critics of the Versailles Treaty have the decency to acknowledge that this humanitarian organisation was set up by that Treaty and that it was promoted by the Governments and statesmen who have to bear the brunt of the critical scurrility of the assailants of Versailles?

The success of the International Labour Organisation was due in no small degree to two men. One, as I have said, was Mr. George Barnes, who was responsible for the preparation of the scheme and for steering it through the Peace Congress; and the other M. Albert Thomas, the man who made this Constitution march. I have always speculated what would have happened if M. Thomas' dynamic energy, his gift of organisation, his bonhomie and his charm of manner had been transferred to the League of Nations—that machine which never had a chauffeur but was expected to go of its own volition, through the perfection of its mechanism and the amount of petrol in its tank, with a competing shuffle of feet for the accelerator and a mere scramble of hands for the wheel.

During the years of the War, the making of the Peace, and afterwards during two years of conference, I transacted business with a considerable number of the leading men of divers nationalities. On the whole I got on quite well with them personally. For some of them I acquired a great liking—e.g. Clemenceau,

Briand, Wilson and Veniselos. But with Albert Thomas I had a sense of personal friendship. To the end of his days he never visited London without calling at my house for a long breakfast chat. I had a great respect for his abilities. He was one of the most efficient organisers thrown up by the War. He was moreover a man of broad culture, a powerful speaker and a good writer. I remember a visit to Paris during the War to discuss some munition problems with Albert Thomas. Sir Frederick Maurice accompanied me as representative of the General Staff. That evening Thomas invited Maurice and myself to dinner at a well-known restaurant on the Versailles road. After dinner the conversation turned upon the Franco-Prussian War. Thomas quoted an opinion on the siege of Paris from a chapter in a volume of the Cambridge Modern History dealing with the Third Empire. Maurice said: "I wrote the military chapters in that volume." Thomas replied: "And I wrote the political chapters." One would not have thought that his academic qualifications and political experiences were the best training for the production of munitions in a great war. There were many such surprises in this war. Who would have imagined that a land agent's desk in Australia and another in Canada would have turned out two of the ablest generals in the British Army?

Albert Thomas, the professor and Socialist orator, was one of the great organisers of the War. This academic Socialist, who had always preached the brotherhood of nations and as such worked earnestly for international peace and goodwill, became one of the most formidable human instruments for waging deadly war. He manufactured terrible guns by the thousands and shells by the millions for the destruction of his fellow men whom he loved. And he did it with a fierce eagerness that never slumbered or slacked. I saw this gentle and genuine believer in the brotherhood of man gloat over the number and power of the engines of destruction which he had turned out, and his sonorous voice would roll out with diabolical glee the statistics of his contrivances for human slaughter. Such is the demoniac power of war to suppress the benevolence of human nature and to arouse its savagery.

But many a time, even in these hours of frenzy, he turned with a wistful longing to his dreams of a better world. I remember, when in 1916 we visited the battlefields of the War together from Verdun to the Somme, we talked for hours about plans for the regeneration of the world and the amelioration of human conditions which must follow this orgy of barbarism. He was a delightful companion with his keen sense of humour, his gaiety, his infectious laugh and his genuine idealism.

His appointment as Director of the International Labour Office was a real inspiration. No other man I can think of could have given it such a start and kept it going despite obstacles which seemed at the time insuperable, until it had reached a height of success where it was beyond the reach of the malignity of detractors, or the mischief of wreckers.

The International Labour Office was fortunate in his successor, Mr. Harold Butler: a man whose capacity for intelligent work, and whose genuine sympathy with that work were a guarantee that Thomas' great achievement would continue to prosper in its beneficent task of improving the condition of the worker in every continent. But Mr. Butler would be the first man to own that without Albert Thomas' colossal pioneering labours his efforts might have been in vain. There is no man of this century to whom the workers of the world owe more, if as much, for the improvements in their conditions which have been effected since the Great War.

Albert Thomas travelled far and near to persuade, to stimulate and to remove obstacles. He interviewed Ministers, employers, workmen's leaders and the Press in every land. Whilst at Geneva he worked early and late. He threw heart and soul, body and mind into his immense enterprise and by doing it added to the greatness of the undertaking. He gave his life for it and fell prematurely exhausted by the superhuman strain of his incomparable toil. Had he survived the progressive forces in France might have at last secured a leader who would have placed France at the head of the democratic states of Europe, at a juncture when European democracy is failing through lack of strong direction. A man who combined great oratorical gifts with exceptional capacity as an administrator and had withal the prestige of two triumphant achievements—one in war and the other in peace— might well have energised the democracy of France to greater things than it has ever yet attained in its glorious past.

CHAPTER XVI

THE PRESENTATION OF THE TREATY

THE meeting with the German delegates took place at the Trianon Hôtel at Versailles, where the Allied Supreme Council had held its anxious meetings less than a year before to the continuous sound of the throb and thud of the German guns at Château Thierry. The camouflage, which had given the lakes in the adjoining park the appearance of green meadows in order to mislead the German aeroplanes, had not yet been removed. The men who ruled Germany then had now either fled the country or were in retirement, dethroned and discredited. The German Delegation which confronted us to-day was drawn from amongst the German workers who had no previous experience in Government. Every opportunity to acquire that experience had been denied them by the old régime. There was one exception—the head of the delegation, Count Brockdorff-Rantzau. He was a civilian who belonged to the official classes. But none of them had the haughtiness of demeanour which characterised the men of the ancient régime. This first meeting between victor and vanquished offered the latter an excellent opportunity for softening the stern mood that still possessed the Allies without any grovèlling inconsistent with the pride of a great people.

An unfortunate incident, however, which occurred in the delivery of the German reply gave us the impression that Brockdorff-Rantzau not only belonged to the Junker class, but had come there to exhibit deliberately their rudest manners. Clemenceau, in opening the proceedings, stood up and in a few short but perfectly courteous sentences addressed the German delegates and said that the representatives of the Allied and Associated Powers had assembled to hear their reply to our peace terms. When he sat down it was expected that Count Brockdorff-Rantzau would follow the President's example and rise in his place to reply. Instead of which he leisurely or nervously unfolded a manuscript document and, after a painful interval of strained silence, proceeded from his seat to read it page by page in a loud, harsh and defiant voice. His conduct was regarded as an insult to the Assembly and especially to its aged President. It created the worst impression and there was a perceptible hardening in the faces of the Allied representatives present. Whatever sympathy might have been felt for a valiant enemy, hopelessly vanquished after four and a half years of unsurpassed courage, was completely chilled by this one exhibition of inexcusable boorishness. It added to the difficulties in the way of those who were anxious to give a tolerant hearing to the German plea for modification of features in the Treaty which savoured of inequity or undue severity.

The effect on President Wilson's mind was to close it with a snap. He turned to me and said: "Isn't it just like them?" It was only years afterwards that I heard the real explanation. It was given me by one of the German delegates who sat near Brockdorff-Rantzau. The poor man was so nervous that he was physically incapable of standing up. He made an effort to do so. But he trembled at the knees and could not rise. It was a terrible ordeal for a man who had been given an unaccustomed task. It was no reflexion on his innate courage, but he had never faced any audience before and here was a hostile assembly of men who had fought Germans to the death. I have seen many brave men quail and quiver before such an experience. It was too much for him. Hence his collapse. It was an unfortunate episode or rather accident, because it fitted in perfectly with our notions of the Prussian temper which we had fought for years and, as we thought, battered into a more becoming recognition of equality with other races. The trained speakers before him could not appreciate his predicament and set down to arrogance what was attributable to stage fright.*

This appearance of arrogance was not reflected in the speech

* This account however has been contradicted by one (Dr. Stern-Rubarth) who claims to have been a "friend and biographer of the late Count Brockdorff-Rantzau." He says that the action was "intentional and deliberate." (Vide Daily Telegraph, Aug. 10th, 1938.)

itself, which, although it contained a protest, was characterised rather by dignity than defiance. He spoke as follows:

Gentlemen,

We are deeply impressed with the lofty character of the task which has brought us together with you, namely, to give the world a speedy and enduring peace. We cherish no illusions as to the extent of our defeat—the degree of our impotence. We know that the might of German arms is broken. We know the force of hatred which confronts us here, and we have heard the passionate demand that the victors should both make us pay as vanquished and punish us as guilty.

We are required to admit that we alone are war-guilty; such an admission on my lips would be a lie. We are far from seeking to exonerate Germany from all responsibility for the fact that this world war broke out and was waged as it was. The attitude of the former German Government at the Hague Peace Conferences, their action and omissions in the tragic twelve days of July, may have contributed to the calamity, but we emphatically combat the idea that Germany, whose people were convinced that they were waging a defensive war, should alone be laden with the guilt.

None of us will wish to assert that the calamity dates only from the fateful moment when the Heir to the throne of Austria-Hungary fell a victim to the assassin's hand. During the last fifty years the imperialism of all European States has chronically poisoned the international situation. The policy of retaliation and that of expansion, as well as disregard of the right of peoples to self-determination contributed to the disease of Europe, which reached its crisis in the world war. The Russian mobilisation deprived statesmen of the possibility of effecting a cure and placed the decision in the hands of the military authorities.

Public opinion in all the countries of our adversaries is echoing with the crimes which Germany is alleged to have committed during the war. Here again we are ready to acknowledge wrong has been done. We have not come here to belittle the responsibility of the men who conducted the war politically and economically, and to disown breaches of international law which have been actually committed. We repeat the declaration which was made in the German Reichstag at the beginning of the war. Belgium has been wronged and we will make this good.

Moreover as regards the method of conducting the war Germany was not alone at fault. Every European nation knows of deeds and persons on whose memory their best citizens are reluctant to dwell. I do not wish to answer reproaches with reproaches, but if it is from us that penance is demanded, then the Armistice must not be forgotten.

Six weeks passed before we obtained it, and six months before we learnt your conditions of peace. Crimes in war may not be excusable, but they are committed in the struggle for victory, in anxiety to preserve national existence, in a heat of passion which blunts the conscience of nations. The hundreds of thousands of non-combatants who have perished since the 11th of November through the blockade were killed with cold deliberation, after victory had been won and assured to our adversaries. Think of that, when you speak of guilt and atonement.

The measure of the guilt of all participants can only be determined by an impartial enquiry by a neutral Commission, before which all the principal actors in the tragedy should have their say and to which all records should be disclosed. We have demanded such an enquiry and we repeat the demand.

Though we stand alone at this Conference, without Allies, and confronted by our numerous adversaries yet we are not defenceless. You yourselves have brought us an Ally:—Justice, which was guaranteed to us by the agreement relating to the bases of peace.

Between the 5th October and 5th November 1918, the Allied and Associated Governments abandoned the idea of a peace of violence and inscribed the words "Peace of Justice" on their banner. On 5th October 1918, the German Government put forward the principles of the President of the United States of America as a basis of peace, and was informed on 5th November by Mr. Lansing, Secretary of State, that the Allied and Associated Powers had accepted this basis with two specific reservations. President Wilson's Principles therefore became binding upon both belligerent parties—upon you as well as upon us, and also upon our former Allies.

These principles taken individually demand of us grievous national and economic sacrifices; but the sacred and fundamental rights of all nations are protected by this agreement. The conscience of the world is behind it; no nation will be permitted to violate it with impunity.

On this basis you will find us prepared to examine the Peace Preliminaries which you lay before us, with the fixed purpose of sharing with you the common task of rebuilding that which has been destroyed, of righting the wrongs that have been done, first and foremost the wrong done to Belgium, and of pointing mankind to new goals of political and social progress. In view of the bewildering number of the problems which beset the fulfilment of our common purpose, we ought to refer the principal questions individually at the earliest possible moment to a special Commission of experts, for discussion on the basis of the draft presented by you. In this connection it will be our chief task to build up anew the shattered human energy of the nations concerned, by international protection of the life, health and liberty of the working classes.

I consider our next aim to be the restoration of the territory of Belgium and Northern France which were occupied by us and devastated by the war. We solemnly accepted the obligation to do this and are determined to carry it out to such extent as may be agreed upon between us. To do this we are thrown back on the co-operation of our former adversaries. We cannot complete the task without the technical and financial participation of the victors; you can only carry it through with our aid. It must be the desire of impoverished Europe that reconstruction should be carried out as successfully and economically as possible. This desire, however, can only be fulfilled by means of a clear and businesslike understanding with regard to the best methods. The worst method would be to continue to have the work done by German prisoners of war. Such labour is certainly cheap. It would, however, cost the world dear, if hate and despair were aroused in the German people at the thought of their captive sons, brothers and fathers continuing to languish in their former bondage after the Peace Preliminaries. We can attain to no enduring peace without the immediate settlement of this question which has dragged on far too long already.

Our experts on both sides will have to study how the German people can best meet its obligation of financial reparation without breaking down under the heavy load. Such a collapse would deprive those entitled to compensation of the advantages to which they have a claim, and would entail irreparable confusion in European economic existence as a whole. Both victors and vanquished must be on their guard against this threatening danger and its incalculable consequences. There is only one way of warding it off:—unreserved recognition of the economic and social solidarity of peoples, of a free and comprehensive League of Nations.

Gentlemen, the lofty conception that the most terrible calamity in the history of the world should bring about the greatest advance in human progress, has been formulated and will be realised. If the goal is to be attained, if the slain in this war are not to have died in vain, then the portals of the League of Nations must be thrown open to all peoples of good will.

The German nation is earnestly prepared to accommodate itself to its hard lot, provided the foundations agreed upon for peace remain unshaken. A peace, which cannot be defended in the name of justice before the whole world, would continually call forth fresh resistance. No one could sign it with a clear conscience, for it would be impossible

of fulfilment. No one could undertake the guarantee of fulfilment
which its signature would imply.

We will examine the document submitted to us with all good will,
and in the hope that the final result of our meeting can be subscribed
by us all.

On May 29th, the German Peace Delegation sent in their
memorandum to the Allied Peace delegates replying to the conditions of the Draft Peace Treaty.

After denouncing the harsh exactions of the Treaty the document went on to explain what Germany was willing to do. As
regards disarmament, Germany offered to "proceed with her
own disarmament in advance of all other peoples." She was
willing to give up compulsory service and reduce her army to
100,000. "She stipulates, however, that (1) all other Powers who
are parties to the Treaty should also abolish conscription and reduce their armaments in the same proportion; and that (2) she
shall be admitted forthwith as a State with equal rights into the
League of Nations." She was also ready to subject all her colonies
to administration by the community of the League of Nations,
if she was recognised as its mandatory. But in territorial questions she took up her position on the ground of Wilson's programme:

> She renounces her sovereign right in Alsace-Lorraine, but wishes a
> free plebiscite to be taken there. She gives up the greater part of the
> province of Posen the districts incontestably Polish in population to-
> gether with the capital. She is prepared to grant to Poland, under in-
> ternational guarantees, free and secure access to the sea by ceding
> free ports at Danzig, Königsberg and Memel, by an agreement regu-
> lating the navigation of the Vistula and by special railway conven-
> tions.

As regards Upper Silesia, however, Germany declared that she
could not cede this region if she was to pay her debts. "Germany
cannot dispense with Upper Silesia. Poland does not need it."
The protest against the cession of this province was long and
vehement, and every kind of argument was brought forward in
support of Germany's refusal to hand over this territory.

Nor would Germany agree to the handing over of East Prussia to the Poles.

As regards the reparation terms of the Treaty, the German delegates made counter-suggestions in detail. Germany was prepared to make payments up to a maximum sum of 100 milliards of gold marks—20 milliards by May 1st, 1926, and the balance (80 milliards) in annual payments without interest. These payments to be equal in principle to a fixed percentage of the German Imperial and State revenues. For the first 10 years the annual payment should not exceed "one milliard of gold marks a year." She further proposed contributions in kind by way of reparation in coal, benzol, dye-stuffs, etc. There was also a lengthy repudiation of war guilt and a demand for a neutral enquiry into the responsibility for the War.

As soon as the reply of the German Ministers reached the British Delegation, Mr. Balfour and I examined it carefully with the expert assistance available. We did our best to weigh impartially the arguments and appeals it urged in favour of an alteration in the main clauses of the Treaty.

As to its challenge of the war guilt of Germany, I could not accept the German point of view without giving away the whole of our case for entering into the War. I considered the reasons addressed by the German Note utterly inadequate to shake conviction on the issue which had carried Britain reluctantly into a war that had cost her so much. But once more I reviewed the considerations which had impelled us to throw in our lot with Belgium, Serbia, France and Russia and I had not one wavering of doubt as to the culpability of the Central Powers. I am still of the same opinion.

I also considered the claim made by the German Delegation that the fact of the repudiation by the German people themselves of the rulers who had the supreme responsibility for making war absolved them from liability for the actions of these rulers. Should this consideration weigh with the Allies to the extent of inducing them to effect any changes in the Treaty in the direction of greater leniency? It had no bearing on the readjustment of boundaries. Those changes were justifiable, apart from any question of war guilt, on the grounds of national liberty and independence. They constituted a restoration of freedom to the nations that had been deprived of it by force. But when one came to the questions of reparations, the colonies and German disarmament, one could not forget that the German people were not in a position to repudiate responsibility for the War and its consequences, for they had without distinction of class or party enthusiastically applauded the action of their rulers in declaring war and in the invasion of Belgium, and given them wholehearted support in their most aggressive and indefensible actions during the War. And had they won, they would have acclaimed the victory and all the demands for annexation of foreign territory in the East and the West which would have inevitably followed. To quote from the reply given by the Allies on this point:

. . . Throughout the war, as before the war, the German people and their representatives supported the war, voted the credits, subscribed to the war loans, obeyed every order, however savage, of their government. They shared the responsibility for the policy of their government, for at any moment, had they willed it, they could have reversed it. Had that policy succeeded they would have acclaimed it with the same enthusiasm with which they welcomed the outbreak of the war. They cannot now pretend, having changed their rulers after the war was lost, that it is justice that they should escape the consequences of their deeds.

As to the appeal for restoration of the German Colonies, the considerations that moved us to deprive Germany of all these possessions until the League of Nations had established its authority in all future disputes between nations were overwhelming. It would be asking too much from us to give back Germany such formidable naval and aerial bases to attack our lines of communications, until international peace had been assured on a basis that could not be shaken by the ambition or greed of any aggressive or ambitious States. Reparations followed inevitably from the decision as to Germany's responsibility for the War that had caused such devastation. As to Brockdorff-Rantzau's protest against depriving Germany of some of her provinces on her Eastern frontiers, such a readjustment was imperative, once

that principle of national right which we had adopted throughout
the War was accepted as a just criterion for the rearrangement of
boundaries in Europe and Asia. Our reply said:

There can be no doubt as to the intentions of the Allied and Associated Powers to base the settlement of Europe on the principle of
freeing oppressed peoples, and re-drawing national boundaries as far
as possible in accordance with the will of the peoples concerned, while
giving to each facilities for living an independent national and economic life.

The only question was whether we had departed from this principle or applied it unfairly in some of the territories of which we
proposed to deprive Germany. On a re-examination of all the
relevant facts in our possession, supplemented by those given in
the German reply, I came to the conclusion that the boundaries
on the new Eastern frontier of Germany ought to be altered in
her favour in one or two cases, and that we were not justified on
any ground of principle in tearing Upper Silesia out of Germany
and handing it over to Poland, without taking a plebiscite to
ascertain the wishes of the inhabitants.

Another point where I felt a concession might be made was
over reparation. Were it possible, I thought it extremely desirable to arrive at an agreed figure with Germany. The mere fact
that she had accepted that figure would make it worth our while
to agree to a reduction in our estimate. I therefore was in favour
of giving the Germans time and opportunity to examine for
themselves the damage done, and to make a definite offer to the
Allies upon the basis of their own assessment of the injuries
effected and their own estimate of their financial capacity to meet
the charge.

On the paramount question of disarmament, I considered the
German plea to be irrefutable. The Allies could not in fairness
impose permanent disarmament on Germany whilst all her neighbours across the frontiers glistened with weapons which on the
slightest dispute could be turned on a defenceless Germany. I
felt we must make it abundantly clear that German disarmament would be followed by a general reduction in armaments
operated on the same principle as we applied to Germany. I

came to the conclusion that the Allies ought to give a solemn pledge to that effect.

I summoned a meeting of British Ministers and Dominion Premiers in Paris to consider the reply we should make to the German Note. It met in my flat in the rue Nitot on Sunday, June the 1st, 1919. It lasted with a short interval for lunch until late that evening. It then adjourned to the following day and continued the whole of the morning. It was one of the most remarkable Cabinet Councils ever held by the British Empire. It consisted of nine of the principal members of the British Government. Every Dominion was represented by its chief political leaders. We had assembled to sit in judgment upon the reply given to the terms of peace offered by the Allies to an enemy that had fought us for four and a half years, and inflicted incalculable losses and injuries upon us in the course of the most destructive war ever waged in this world. We were all convinced that this devastating conflict had been deliberately provoked by the enemy that was now suing for more lenient terms, and we each represented nations that had suffered cruelly from the hurts wantonly inflicted upon them. Nevertheless the meeting was specially notable for the calm and impartial spirit displayed by every speaker. There was a complete absence of bitterness or vindictiveness in the observations made. As far as the temper that prevailed was concerned, it might have been a meeting of the official representatives of a benevolent neutral called upon to adjudicate upon the points in dispute between the parties.

The spirit of the meeting was exemplified by a dramatic incident that happened. Lord Milner and General Botha had taken their seats next to each other round the table. When General Botha's turn came to speak, in pleading that one of the provisions of the Treaty should be softened, he turned round to Milner, patted him on the knee and remarked: "This is the seventeenth anniversary of the Peace of Vereeniging—as my friend, Milner, will remember."

I opened the proceedings and said

that the experts of the British Empire Delegation had been engaged in examining the various parts of the German Observations.

The experts on indemnities (Lord Sumner and Lord Cunliffe) were not disposed to make any concessions. They were of opinion that Germany had not made out a case on the subject.

The experts on the Eastern boundaries had recommended a series of concessions. . . . In Northern Silesia they suggested a plebiscite, and further north, where the Germans claimed that the population was solidly German, they recommended that a concession should be made. In other regions the case was not so strong, but in some districts the Germans were very numerous and concessions might be made even without a plebiscite. He reminded the Delegation that some of those districts had been included within Poland only because of railway facilities.

There was a small piece of territory to the west of Danzig which was also German, and a concession was recommended there.

As to Memel, the position was doubtful. The country behind Memel was Lithuanian, though the city was German. It might be possible to make Memel a free port. Without Memel, Lithuania had no outlet to the sea.

MR. BARNES asked whether the result of the concessions suggested would be to make a connection between East and West Prussia.

MR. LLOYD GEORGE replied in the negative. He added that the experts had pointed out that the Germans thought a road across foreign territory good enough to satisfy the requirements of the Poles, and therefore it was impossible for them to contend that a similar road across between East and West Prussia would not be sufficient for the needs of these provinces. The population was overwhelmingly Polish in the corridor to Danzig.

He further pointed out that the traffic from East Prussia was mainly by sea. The traffic by land, East and West, was almost negligible. The disadvantages as between East and West Prussia were not comparable with the disadvantages to Poland if Poland were cut off from the sea. . . .

MR. LLOYD GEORGE said that he wished to put two questions to each individual member of the Delegation:

1. Was he in favour of standing on the terms proposed in the present Draft Treaty, or was he in favour of making some concessions, the nature of which could be considered at a later stage?

2. If any concessions should be made, should they be communicated in a written statement, naming a period within which the Germans must reply, or should verbal negotiations be encouraged?

MR. MASSEY said that he experienced a difficulty in answering "yes" or "no" on the whole subject of the Peace Treaty, and suggested that the important points should be taken one by one.

MR. LLOYD GEORGE said that the first question was whether the British Delegation was prepared to make any concessions at all.

(In reply to the first question put by Mr. Lloyd George, each member said that he was in favour of making some concessions on the present Draft Treaty.)

MR. LLOYD GEORGE then raised the question of procedure.

.   .   .   .   .

MR. LLOYD GEORGE said that he thought that it would be desirable in the first place to have a general discussion.

MR. BALFOUR said that he hoped that everybody would remember that what was decided by the Delegation would thereafter be discussed by the Council of Four. He was satisfied that the French would strenuously oppose the removal from the Treaty of some features which the British regarded as indefensible. It was highly important that the Delegation should not bind Mr. Lloyd George too tightly, as he must have liberty to negotiate.

MR. LLOYD GEORGE said that he wanted to know generally the position which he would have to adopt, but it was necessary for him to have a certain latitude.

The discussion which followed occupied the best part of two days. General Smuts led off with a severe criticism of the Treaty. When he came to details, he confined his adverse comments to, first of all, the proposed military occupation. In his opinion: "The military occupation of a large and rich part of industrial Germany for fifteen years was indefensible from every point of view. Military occupation and industrial conditions were incompatible ideas, and military occupation was quite unnecessary."

With this criticism I was in entire sympathy. I opposed this provision and only accepted it under pressure from President Wilson because it represented a compromise he had arranged with Clemenceau. When I asked General Smuts whether he had any specific proposals to make regarding the size of the army or the length of the time of the occupation, he replied

that in the first place he preferred that there should be no Army of Occupation at all, considering, as he did, that the other provisions of the Treaty were sufficient safeguard for what was required. But if there were to be armies of occupation, they should be set down at certain points and should not be allowed to interfere in any way with the civil administration. He thought that if this proposal were put

to the French and the nature of the other safeguards fully explained
to them, it was quite possible that they would accept it. . . . If an
Army of Occupation were absolutely unavoidable, he would limit it
to the number necessary to deal with German aggression—in view
of the small forces left to Germany.

His second point was "that Germany should become a Member of the League of Nations as soon as the Treaty was signed, it
being essential to carry her with us and remove the possibility of
another combination through Germany and Russia joining hands
in misfortune."

His third objection was that "some parts of the Draft Treaty
should be scrapped altogether," but when pressed, he only mentioned one part: "The internationalisation of German rivers and
their subjection to an alien or foreign administration was a great
mistake. It was not covered by the Wilson terms. They could not
expect any country to accept such invasion of its internal sovereignty." Then the Eastern settlement was thoroughly bad:

He was glad to know that it was generally agreed that the Eastern
provisions must be modified. Poland was an historic failure, and always
would be a failure, and in this Treaty we were trying to reverse the
verdict of history. He asked that the Allies should hesitate before
guaranteeing frontiers for Poland such as were now proposed. These
frontiers required careful reconsideration. Perhaps a plebiscite would
afford a solution.

As regards reparation, "he thought that the provision should be
altered by fixing a definite sum which Germany undertook to
pay, say, £5,000,000,000, though that was probably not enough."

In the subsequent discussion there was a good deal of support
given to General Smuts' view that it would be better to agree to a
fixed sum if that were possible, although it was quite clear from
the various suggestions made in the course of our deliberations
that if we had attempted at that gathering to obtain agreement
as to the actual amount of that sum, we should have failed entirely to do so. There was also some assent to General Smuts'
comment about quartering a large army of occupation on Germany for fifteen years. All agreed that it would be desirable to
bring Germany into the League at the earliest possible moment,

but no Minister took General Smuts' view that Germany should come in immediately on the signature of the Treaty.

All agreed that Germany had made a case for revision of the Eastern boundaries fixed in the Draft.

It could be seen from the observations made by many, if not most of the speakers, that there was a real apprehension lest the Germans should refuse to sign the Treaty and that as a consequence we should have to march to Berlin. Some speakers went so far as to insinuate that such was the French hatred of Germany, that they were hoping that such a refusal would be provoked by the harshness of the Treaty in order to justify a military occupation of the German capital. I was convinced at the time—and still am—that no responsible Frenchman had that thought in his mind. France was tired of war, and all her soldiers were yearning to get back to their homes and to substitute the daily vocations to which they had been accustomed before the War for the misery and the squalor and the alternate peril and boredom of trench life. Not even Marshal Foch wished for a renewal of war—certainly not war in its most inglorious form. I recollect that during the Armistice, when someone was urging him to insert harsher terms in the Allied conditions for a cessation of hostilities, he replied that he would not sacrifice the life of a single French soldier to achieve any of the proposed additional stipulations. But the apprehension of a refusal to sign undoubtedly influenced some of the speakers at this Cabinet Conference.

The general character of the discussion can best be inferred from the speeches delivered by Mr. Balfour and myself at the end of the debate. It is clear that the summary which I attempted of the comments, criticisms and suggestions put forward by the various Ministers was at the time regarded as being perfectly fair, from the fact that there was no correction made by any of those present of my representation of their views.

Mr. Balfour said that he did not propose to survey the whole debate, but he thought it would be generally admitted that the attack made by General Smuts on the Draft Treaty was most impressive and important. He could not help thinking, however, that General Smuts treated the matter in rather too legal a manner. He asked the Delegation to remember how it came about that the Fourteen Points were accepted. The Prime Minister and he suddenly found themselves faced with the Fourteen Points and the time was too short to discuss them. There was really no question whether there should be an Armistice or not. There had to be an Armistice. Time was the essence of the matter. They had no option but to take the Fourteen Points. They made some corrections in them, and they were supplemented by some perorations. He agreed that if the Fourteen Points were pressed from a legal point of view, it was possible to make out an awkward case, but it was only necessary to read the Fourteen Points to see that they were incapable of being treated in that strictly legal manner. For example, one point dealt with Russia, and by it all the Allies pledged themselves to welcome her into the League of Free Nations and to give her assistance of any kind which she might need or desire. It was impossible to interpret these words literally and to make a contract out of them. The point dealing with Italy afforded another example. It provided that a readjustment of the frontiers of Italy should be effected along recognisable lines of nationality.

President Wilson himself, not at the prompting of Great Britain, but in accordance with the desire of Italy, has assented to a frontier which utterly violated "easily recognisable lines of nationality." These examples were sufficient to show that it was impossible to interpret the Fourteen Points and the supplementary speeches as if they constituted a contract between two litigants.

With regard to Poland, he believed that all members of the Delegation were really agreed. The Prime Minister had made a suggestion which, in the opinion of all present, met the case fairly. He wished to add that it was impudent for the Germans to speak of purely German areas being included in Poland. The Allies had again and again been forced in the case of the new States which they were setting up to leave pockets absolutely opposed in nationality to the States in which they were included. That was inevitable in some cases.

The Germans themselves in their own document asked for a land connection between East and West Prussia across what was purely Polish territory. He did not see that the Germans could make a case before the League of Nations.

He agreed that Poland had behaved quite abominably and had mismanaged her affairs, but he wished to point out that in discussion it had apparently been assumed that Germany was repentant, that her soul had undergone a conversion and that she was now absolutely a different nation from the Germany which in the past had built up armaments and had caused the war. But why should there be faith in Germany altering her course, and no hope of—he would not go so far as to say confidence in—Poland behaving as a reasonably civilised State? He had no sympathy whatever with the attacks on the Eastern frontier. It was a very difficult problem and on the whole it had been well handled.

If the Prime Minister's suggestions in respect of Silesia were adopted, he thought Germany would have nothing to complain of.

With respect to the Army of Occupation, all his inclinations were in favour of the critics of the Draft Treaty. The army was not only very costly, but the cost was thrown on the British taxpayer and really on him alone. In fact, the British taxpayer was asked to support the French Army.

He was ready to do a good deal for France, but the terms in respect to the Army of Occupation were not reasonable.

The results which he had mentioned followed from the provision that the cost of the army was to be the first charge on the reparation fund. He agreed that the less French soldiers were allowed to manage affairs in Germany the better. He agreed that there was a real danger that the French might drive inhabitants to acts of reprisal and then summon the British forces to support them. He thought that the time of occupation and the size of the Army of Occupation should be reduced as far as possible. He did not feel well qualified to deal with the financial clauses, but he thought that one line of argument had been unduly pressed. This argument was that if heavy taxation was imposed on Germany, all the results of German labour would be taken and the Germans would not work. But was this true?

The answer was that Germany could only pay by exports, and these represented only a small fraction of what Germany could do. It was only the people who were engaged in the production of exports who would really be working for the foreigner. Thus, if a man were occupied in building houses in Germany and supplying goods for internal consumption, he would not in any sense be working for a foreigner.

MR. CHURCHILL said that surely the country was all one, and that there was one basis for the whole industry of Germany.

MR. CHAMBERLAIN asked whether Mr. Balfour had not misunderstood the argument. The argument was that an uncertain liability deprived Germany of all incentive.

MR. BALFOUR replied that he was answering the argument that the whole German people would become slaves to the Allies. He entirely sympathised with the argument that if Germany could not get credit she could not get raw material and therefore could not manufacture goods and that consequently she could not pay. But it was not only the credit of Germany which would have to be considered. It was a mistake to concentrate attention on Germany. How would Poland, Belgium, Italy, and the Balkan States get on in the future? It had been said that Belgium was rich. He could not forget that, while Germany was going on manufacturing, Belgium was not, because Germany had looted her factories.

They were facing a world in which tragedy was universal. It was a wrong attitude to fix the mind on the lamentations of the Germans, upon their misfortunes, when in fact the Germans were responsible to the whole world. Still, it was necessary to set up again the industry of the world, and he was anxious to get credit for Germany. Germany was no unhappy victim of circumstances; she was suffering, and ought to suffer, for her crimes; and there was no sign whatever that Germany was repentant, either in Rantzau's documents or in the German newspapers. If the Germans were to be given an army to-morrow, he thought that they would immediately begin a war of revenge. He did not differ from many of the conclusions which had been reached by other members of the Delegation and agreed with many of their suggestions, but he was not sure that some members had not come to the discussion of this question in a temper produced by Rantzau's pathetic appeals, without sufficiently remembering the other side of the case. He recognised also that the British Representatives had been driven into a peculiar state of mind by the greed of France, Belgium and Italy, but it was necessary to get into a more normal condition in order to deal with the problems before them.

MR. LLOYD GEORGE said that he would sum up the result of the discussion and would conclude with some practical suggestions for the Plenipotentiaries.

In the first place, he wished to say that he thought the discussion was very creditable to the British Empire.

The members of the Delegation represented a great victorious Power with a most formidable enemy at their mercy after long and cruel fighting. The whole discussion had taken the form of an earnest and sometimes a passionate plea for justice for the fallen enemy. He thought that they erred rather on the side of consideration for the enemy.

There was no note of vengeance. He thought it an extraordinary tribute to the temper of the British Empire that in such circumstances there could be a discussion in such a spirit. He was sure that the Germans would not have believed it possible.

Three of his colleagues had said to him that he must not imagine that when they criticised the Draft Terms of the Peace they were criticising the action of the Plenipotentiaries. (Hear, Hear.) He could assure the Delegation that such a view had never entered the minds of their Representatives. After all, he and his colleagues had acted on such evidence as they had. One story held good until another was told. Their information was *ex parte*.

They had presented their demands and now they heard the criticism. The question had been asked that morning why it was only at this late stage that mistakes were discovered. The answer was that they now had fresh information from the Germans, and that on the whole they found that it required investigation. He had no fear of changing his view if he was shown that the information on which he had acted in the first instance was proved afterwards not to be in accordance with the actual conditions.

The first thing was to have an absolutely just Peace, and that standard must be applied to the whole Peace.

They must have no hesitation in admitting that they were wrong, if they were wrong, and in modifying the terms accordingly. But they must also see that the terms imposed were expedient as well as just.

Justice was a question which the Germans were at liberty to raise, but expediency was a matter for the Allies to consider and not the Germans. The Allies were entitled to go to the limit of justice so far as Germany was concerned.

He thought that the Allies had gone too far in two or three directions.

First, regarding the Eastern frontiers, he thought that the Allies had gone too far and that the matter should be put right. Regarding the Army of Occupation, that was rather a question of expediency than of justice. There were several points on which he would like to make suggestions for a departure from the original terms and for an attempt to meet the Germans. On the question of German rivers, he did not think that General Smuts had done justice to the considerations influencing the Committee which made the recommendations on the question. All these rivers were international. They were not like the Thames or Severn. The Rhine and the Oder, for example, were international rivers.

The Allies were creating two new countries with no sea frontiers. They must have access to the sea. The Oder ran from Czecho-Slovakia through Poland to the Baltic.

It was necessary for Czecho-Slovakia to have access along the Oder to the sea. It was therefore quite right to have international control of the Oder. So also in the case of the Rhine. The industries of Alsace-Lorraine must have access to the sea, and the Rhine was practically the only means by which material could be got cheaply to the manufacturing towns. He was told that the same principle applied to all the other rivers in Germany for which an international régime was proposed. Whether the representation of Germany on the Commission of Control was sufficient was a different matter, and perhaps might be reconsidered.

He thought that it was better for Germany that there should be Allied Representatives on the Commission besides Czecho-Slovaks and Poles. He did not think that there was any injustice to Germany in the provisions relating to rivers. The Germans had made no representations on the subject.

As regards the Eastern frontiers, his views were apparently accepted by his colleagues.

MR. MONTAGU asked whether the Prime Minister suggested a plebiscite in all the areas of the Eastern frontier to which he referred.

MR. LLOYD GEORGE replied in the negative, and said that he only suggested a plebiscite in certain cases.

Referring to a map, and pointing out particular areas, Mr. Lloyd George said that in certain cases where the territory was preponderantly German in nationality, and in a case, for example, where territory had been added to Poland only on account of the existence of a railway, he thought that no plebiscite was required. In each of these cases they ought to be restored to Germany.

There should be a plebiscite for the coal-field in Silesia. In other cases, if the Poles challenged the facts alleged by the Germans there could be plebiscites. In most cases no very considerable populations were involved, but in Silesia one of about two millions was concerned. It must be remembered that Prussia had built up the Eastern portion of the Empire to a large extent by successful wars—for example, in the case of Silesia and Poland. They had no right to found an argument on the contention that she had held these areas by force of arms for two or three hundred years.

MR. HUGHES said that Rantzau had alleged that these districts had for eight hundred years been part of Germany.

In fact, for the greater part of that period they had belonged to Bohemia. They had been Prussian only since 1742. The election results showed that the Poles were numerically very strong.

MR. LLOYD GEORGE said that a plebiscite would determine all questions of numerical strength and nationality.

The proposals with reference to the Saar Valley could not be defended upon any definite principle. They were acknowledged to be a compromise. France would have liked to take the left bank of the Rhine. All the French military advisers pressed M. Clemenceau for this very hard. On the whole, he thought that they had done the best for Germany that reasonably could be achieved.

Another alternative was to give to France the 1814 frontier. He would have thought that Germany would have preferred a chance of getting the whole back instead of permanently losing two-thirds. It might be said that the Commission controlling the Saar Valley could be improved by introducing elected representatives. If the people of the Saar Valley were really German, fifteen years would not make any difference. He did not believe that the Germans would refuse to sign merely because a lease for fifteen years of the Saar mines was given to France and the control of the area handed over to the League of Nations. Within five years Germany would be represented on the League of Nations.

As the British representatives had so many questions on which they had to press the French, he asked that he should not be required to place the Saar Valley among them.

LORD MILNER enquired about the provision for buying back the mines at the end of fifteen years.

MR. LLOYD GEORGE said that he did not think that that provision mattered much, because any payment made under it was credited to the reparation account.

What did matter was that the plebiscite should be honest and that it should be acted on.

MR. HUGHES enquired whether there was anything to prevent the Saar Valley coal being sold to Germany.

MR. LLOYD GEORGE said that this would never be done, because it would involve carrying the coal through the Westphalian coal-fields. The Saar Valley provisions only caused a money loss to Germany and did not affect German internal economy.

He had had an interview with a British officer at Versailles, who was formerly at Berlin, and who had already furnished most useful information to the British authorities. He said that he had talked a good deal with the Germans at Versailles and found that they were most concerned about the two questions of Silesia and the League of Nations.

They were very sensitive on the latter subject, because they felt they were being driven out of the community of nations. They attached even more importance to that than to Silesia. They were convinced that such harsh conditions were not insisted upon because the British wished to be unjust and that they were satisfied that if they were only able to state their case on equal terms before the League of Nations, they would get alleviation from Great Britain.

Some months ago, he (Mr. Lloyd George) had circulated his views about the Terms of Peace, and had proposed that the Germans should join the League of Nations at once. Now, however, he had modified those views. He did not think that the Germans could be admitted until the Allies had settled their own differences. Lord Robert Cecil concurred in this view. Take, for example, the protest made by M. Bratiano at the last meeting of the Peace Conference. To admit the Germans would enable them to take advantage of the differences between the Allies. He thought that the Allies should settle down first. He did not see why the period of exclusion should be longer than twelve months.

SIR GEORGE FOSTER asked how long it would be before the League of Nations got into working order.

MR. LLOYD GEORGE replied that it would not be as long as twelve months. He thought that the Germans would be satisfied if they were brought in within two years. If making such a concession to them would induce them to sign, it would be well worth while.

MR. HUGHES said that it must be subject to the condition that, in the meanwhile, they had carried out their obligations.

MR. LLOYD GEORGE said that the condition should be that they had made their best effort to carry out their obligations.

MR. HUGHES said that he suggested a period of five years, the Germans to have a right at the end of two years to come before the League of Nations and show cause why they should be admitted. He thought that, if this were done, the Government would have a good position before the British public.

MR. LLOYD GEORGE said that if he thought that early admission to the League would make the difference of whether the Germans signed or not, he would take an indulgent view on the matter.

He had found the subject of compensation the most baffling and perplexing of all. He did not say that the Germans could pay a particular sum or could not pay it. He did not think that, for the time being, this aspect mattered much. Most experts had told him that it was impossible to be quite sure that Germany could pay any particular sum. He did not think that the time had quite come for letting Germany off anything. There were provisions in the Treaty which enabled the Allies to reconsider the matter if they came to the conclusion that it was quite impossible for Germany to pay. She could appeal to the Commission for a postponement and the Commission had power to adjudicate on the request. The Commission could reduce the amount of payments and, though postponed amounts nominally rolled up, they did not really. Further, the Commission had the power, with the sanction of the Governments behind it, to reduce the actual payment to be made. Those provisions were in the Treaty, and he should have thought that the general character of the provisions would not have prevented the Germans from signing. He would have thought that they would have realised that this was not an appropriate moment for them to show what they could or could not pay.

The Germans had inflicted on the Allies a loss which, in cash, amounted to something like £30,000,000,000. If loss of trade were included as well as war debts, he doubted whether that sum would cover the Allied loss. By every principle of justice, by the principles of justice which were recognised as applicable between individuals, the Germans were liable for the whole of the damages and the cost of recovering them. The Allies were not doing anything which was unjust in their demand for reparation. They had not presented a bill for the whole sum, which might amount to £10,000,000,000 or £11,000,000,000. The Germans would say that it was idle to ask for such an amount. The Commission would say that the first instalment should be, say, £500,000,000, due on such and such a date. The Germans would then say what they could pay and what their case was for modification of the demands. The Commission would then examine the question on its merits. He hoped that a strong Commission would be appointed. Germany could then demonstrate before the Commission her position regarding grade, raw materials, etc. The time would come when the Commission would have to recommend postponement and perhaps ultimately the surrender of a portion of the sum claimed.

MR. BARNES said that he looked at the reparation clauses from the point of view of international Labour and of the effect which they would produce upon the Labour world.

MR. LLOYD GEORGE said that it was possible to attach too much importance to the resolutions of associations. The British workingman would have to pay more if Germany did not.

He would be glad to receive suggestions from members of the Delegation regarding how much and in what manner Germany should pay. A great deal of criticism was founded upon the fact that the amount of Germany's liability was undefined. He agreed that it would be better to define it, but, in the first place, it was impossible to settle the exact capacity of Germany to pay; in the second place, it was impossible to estimate the cost of repairing the devastated areas; and, in the third place, the Germans could not tell the Allies how much reparation work they were themselves prepared to undertake. It was therefore impossible to fix the liability under these conditions.

As a solution, he would like the Germans to make an offer on the following lines: "We recognise that you (the Allies) cannot now tell us what reparations will cost. We will undertake the whole job of restoration as a contract; we will undertake to do it ourselves and we will pay for it." The Germans would have an idea of what it would cost and could reckon it out roughly, but it was quite impossible for us to arrive at any agreement with the French on the amount. £3,500,000,000 was their minimum.

As far as the ships were concerned, their value was really a small item in the whole bill. Six million tons at £40 per ton only amounted to £240,000,000. There was no difficulty on this item. If the Germans said that they would rather undertake the whole task of restoration, the amount for pensions could be fixed by means of actuarial calculations. Then the Allies would be in a position to agree to the Germans' undertaking the work of restoration and paying, say, £3,000,000,000 to cover the whole of the rest. That was one suggestion which he made for a solution.

Another suggestion was this: that the Allies should insist on the Germans signing the Treaty and then give them three months within which they could make a cash offer as a commutation for their whole liability, including both restoration and compensation.

He preferred the former alternative, because it avoided all dispute with the French.

He had discussed the question of the Army of Occupation with the Chief of the Imperial General Staff that day. Sir Henry Wilson was opposed to the proposal for occupation for fifteen years. He had said that it was not a military proposition at all. The French wanted a thirty or forty years' occupation: that is, practically permanent occupation. That was the desire of Marshal Foch. All the French Military experts said that the true boundary of France was the Rhine. Mr. Balfour had made it clear that the proposals for the Army of Occupation were likely to be a disturbing element in Europe, and also that the cost of the Army of Occupation practically fell upon the British taxpayer, inasmuch as the cost of the Army reduced the Reparations Fund and therefore the amount to be paid by Germany to meet Allied pensions. As pensions were payable by all parts of the Empire, the burden of the Army of Occupation really fell upon the British Empire taxpayers.

We were confronted by a very grave issue. The French would give up nothing unless they were forced. As had already been remarked, the hatred of the French for the Germans was something inconceivable —it was savage—and he did not blame them for it. He had seen most of the devastated areas, and if that devastation had happened in England he doubted whether the British would examine proposals for peace with any idea of justice, but he did not think that the British Empire would allow the future peace of the world to be tied to the chariot of French fury—legitimate and justified though it might be. When, in his speech at Versailles, Rantzau spoke of an atmosphere of hatred, he said a thing that was terrible but true.

The French would not concede anything unless we could say to them that unless they agreed to the proposed concessions (1) no British troops would advance to Berlin; (2) no British ships would be employed to starve the Germans.

It was sometimes necessary to starve women and children as an operation of war, but it was a poor business at best. We were entitled to say that we would not inflict these horrors on the population to enforce anything which we thought unjust or unfair.

Was the British Delegation prepared to adopt that attitude? Would his colleagues support him if he said that he could not ask the British Parliament to sanction the necessary measures for an enforcement of the Treaty unless the French would make concessions in the direction mentioned? It was no use for him to go on the following day to the Council of Four and merely say that his colleagues said so and so. If he merely did that, M. Clemenceau would say that he could not help it and that he was going on.

MR. CHURCHILL said that it appeared to him that it followed from all that had been said that the Delegation should give to the Prime. Minister the assurance which would enable him to take the strong line proposed. It was idle to suppose that Germany could be induced to sign unless we offended France—though not mortally offended her. The Foreign Secretary had said that the members of the Delegation had been influenced by Rantzau's eloquence. He thought that they were inclined to underrate the enormous work which had already been achieved. The Germans had given up their fleet and their army, they were prepared to dismantle fortresses and to give up their guns, they were giving up their colonies, Poland had been carved out of their territory, they had offered to pay five thousand million pounds, there was the Kiel Canal, and Heligoland, and similar things. Already it was the greatest triumph in the history of the world. He felt the greatest confidence that he could justify the Treaty to his own constituents as fulfilling everything that he had ever led them to anticipate.

MR. LLOYD GEORGE asked whether he was authorised to press to the extent mentioned the views of the British Delegation. He would be much strengthened and have much greater influence from the fact that he was authorised by the Delegation, especially if the authority were given unanimously.

MR. HUGHES said that he agreed that the Prime Minister must have this authority, but desired to know the point at which he proposed to deliver the ultimatum.

MR. LLOYD GEORGE said that it was a question of tactics which he wished to think out.

Mr. BALFOUR said that he begged the Delegation to leave absolute discretion to the Prime Minister.

Mr. LLOYD GEORGE said that he would say to the Council of Four that he had had a very serious meeting of the British Delegation. He could say that the Delegation had stated that they might not be able to see their way to use force to enforce the provisions of the Treaty as it now stood.

He wanted to get M. Clemenceau to discuss questions. He would not enter upon any discussion unless he was forced. M. Clemenceau was a man with a sense of justice, but he was in a position of very great difficulty in view of the opinion which was behind him. Still, if he knew that he had either to face his own extremists or to march forward without the British Empire he would be willing to discuss.

GENERAL BOTHA said that France had a feeling that she must occupy Berlin. Such an act would really mean the defeat of the Allied war aims. France no doubt wanted to occupy Germany, but she must be told that such a course was impossible. The whole world was behind the Prime Minister in trying to secure Peace, and if he took the lead he would be leading, not only the British Empire, but the whole world out of a very great difficulty. They had now reached the turning-point. If the Germans refused to sign, what would be the position of the Allies? It had been said that morning, "take less and settle soon." He endorsed that line of action, although he wanted the Germans to pay as much as possible. We held the Germans in the hollow of our hands by having all their guns, their fleet, etc. It was most important that Germany should sign. If the Germans refused to sign they would be getting towards the position in which they would be able to dictate to the Allies. He understood the position and feelings of the Germans because he also had had to make a peace.

Lord Milner would remember that it was exactly 17 years on that very day that Peace was signed in South Africa. On that occasion it was moderation which had saved South Africa for the British Empire, and he hoped on this occasion that it would be moderation which would save the world.

Mr. MASSEY said that he did not go back on one word which he had said that morning, but was prepared to take his share of responsibility in authorising the Prime Minister to do what had been suggested.

He further expressed the hope that there was no question of going back on the decisions reached in regard to the German Colonies.

Mr. LLOYD GEORGE said "No!"

Mr. MASSEY said that he hoped also there was no suggestion of going back on the proposals relating to those guilty of atrocities.

Mr. Lloyd George said that he would like to state the points which he would press. They were the following:

(1) Eastern frontiers.

(2) Some sort of promise regarding the League of Nations which would give the Germans the hope of coming in if it was found they were making a real effort to fulfil their obligations.

(3) The Army of Occupation. He thought that he could take a pretty strong stand on that. (Hear, hear.)

(4) Reparations—some means of fixing the figure on the lines which he had mentioned.

Lord Milner asked whether there was any chance of making comparatively minor revisions to which the Allies did not attach much importance but which the Germans regarded as important. It appeared to him that collectively the Allies were putting the Germans at such an enormous number of disadvantages that they were crippling their power of recovering and therefore of paying any sum for reparation.

Mr. Lloyd George said that he had heard that contention in the abstract, but had never been given it in detail. He had obtained a report on the matter from Sir H. Llewellyn Smith, and he did not expect any difficulty with France on these points. M. Clemenceau was too big a man to insist on petty annoyances. If any member of the Delegation would give him a list of these points he would look into them.

Lord Milner said that collectively they appeared to him to prevent Germany from ever being able to pay a very large sum. If these or some of these restrictions were removed they might pay a great deal more.

Mr. Lloyd George said that the present time was the best opportunity for the Germans to say so.

Lord Milner said that one of their difficulties was that of getting raw materials. When admitted to the League of Nations they could get raw materials from the mandated territories, but not before.

Mr. Lloyd George said that at the worst they would have to employ foreign agents, and by this means would be able to get all the raw materials they wanted.

Mr. Chamberlain said that the Germans' capacity to pay would be greatly assisted if the Prime Minister's suggestion that restoration in kind should be carried out were adopted.

Mr. Fisher said that while Sir H. Llewellyn Smith made a fairly plausible case on each detail, he did not meet the case of the collective effect of the restrictions. These restrictions collectively, would paralyse German industry.

LORD MILNER said that, according to the Treaty, there was not a single thing in the whole world outside Germany which the Germans were to be entitled to keep.

MR. BARNES said that, in his opinion, the three big things were:

(1) Occupation for fifteen years. He thought that as Great Britain and America were giving France a guarantee, France was going too far in asking for occupation for fifteen years. It was sufficient to have an Army of Occupation for a period necessary to carry out the razing of fortifications, etc. On the 3rd December last the Imperial War Cabinet had discussed the question of the period of occupation. Marshal Foch had suggested twelve months.

(2) Membership of the League of Nations. He saw no reason why Germany should be kept out for two years. There was a positive danger in keeping the Germans out. They were trying to enlist the support of the democracies of the world, of Labour and Socialist movements, and they were relying upon the decisions of the Berne Conference. If the Germans were not soon admitted into the League they would be setting up another League of Nations with Russia. He urged that the proposal for the admission of Germany should be placed before the League of Nations in October next.

(3) Reparations. He was still of the opinion that the idea of claiming an indefinite amount was wrong. He had not been converted on that point by Mr. Balfour. On the literal interpretation of the Treaty the Reparations Commission could impose all kinds of restrictions on the Germans, even limiting them in boots, tobacco, and beer.

MR. HUGHES said that in agreeing to give the Prime Minister the authority he asked for he wished it to be clearly understood that the limits of that authority were as stated by the Prime Minister himself and not by Mr. Barnes and Lord Milner and others. He was opposed to their views altogether.

MR. LLOYD GEORGE asked whether the Delegation was content to leave it to him to consider the best method of presenting the case. He would go to the Council of Four and state that the British Empire could not engage its forces to compel Germany to sign the Treaty unless the modifications mentioned were made, modifications, that is to say, regarding the Eastern frontiers, reparation, the Army of Occupation, and Germany's admission into the League of Nations.

LORD BIRKENHEAD said that it appeared to be the unanimous opinion of the Delegation that the Prime Minister should be armed with the large powers which he suggested, and also that the members should submit to him any observations on other points which they wished to make.

MR. FISHER suggested that there should be a certain amount of elasticity in relation to the Eastern frontiers, and urged that the Germans were likely to attach the greatest importance to the geographical connection between East Prussia and Brandenburg, that a reconsideration of this question should not be excluded, and that a big Poland was necessarily a weak Poland.

MR. LLOYD GEORGE said that he wished to thank his colleagues in London for the loyal way in which they had stood by their colleagues in Paris.

It was resolved that the Prime Minister, in his negotiations at the Council of the Allied and Associated Powers, should press for concessions to be made to the enemy in the Treaty of Peace in the following respects:

(a) A modification of the clauses dealing with the Eastern frontiers in the direction of (i) leaving to Germany the districts where the population was predominantly German in cases where there was no overwhelming reason for transferring such districts to Poland, and (ii) providing for plebiscites being held in doubtful cases.

(b) The extension to Germany of some promise that she should enter the League of Nations at an earlier date than at present arranged in the Treaty, subject to the condition that Germany was making a real effort to perform her obligations.

(c) A modification of the clauses dealing with the Army of Occupation in the direction of (i) reducing the numerical strength, having regard to the reductions made and about to be made in the German forces, and (ii) making the period of occupation as short as possible.

(d) A modification of the Reparation Clauses in the direction of fixing the liability of the Germans to the Allies at a definite amount, by one or other of the following methods:

(i) The Germans to undertake the whole task of restoration and, in addition, to pay at as early a date as possible a fixed sum to be divided between the Allies in proportions to be agreed upon between them.

(ii) The Germans to sign the Reparation Clauses as they stand, but, within three months, to make an offer of a fixed sum in cash, or in cash and kind, in discharge of their total liabilities for reparations; in the event of the Germans making no satisfactory offer the present Reparation Clauses to stand.

The Delegation authorised the Prime Minister, in the event of any resistance on the part of any of his colleagues on the Council, to use the full weight of the entire British Empire even to the point of refusing:

(1) The services of the British Army to advance into Germany.

(2) The services of the British Navy to enforce the Blockade of Germany.

The Delegation agreed that in his negotiations on the four points mentioned above, the Prime Minister should not be confined to any set limits, but should be allowed a certain latitude.

It was further agreed that members of the Delegation should submit to the Prime Minister for his consideration any modifications relating to other points, which, in their opinion, might with advantage be conceded.

(The Meeting adjourned.)

When the decision of the British Ministers was conveyed to our Allies, Clemenceau was annoyed and President Wilson was righteously indignant. He had come to terms with the French as to the conditions of peace. The Draft Treaty represented to him the compromise he had reached with Clemenceau in return, partly for a surrender of the idea of a Rhine frontier, and partly in consideration of a pledge to suppress personal attacks in the French Press, and he had no desire to depart from his bargain. Moreover, the most important concession for which we were stipulating was at the expense of the Poles, who were by way of being the President's protégés. He liked them as much as he detested the Italians. The line he took was that after prolonged discussions we had prepared an agreed document which in many particulars represented a compromise of conflicting views. To alter it now in deference to German criticisms and protests was to run the risk of the whole fabric falling to pieces and of our having to build it up again from the foundations.

This, of course, was a complete reversal of his original view when he came to France, that we must hear the Germans before we came to any final decision as to the terms of the Treaty.

Despite French and American protests I decided to stand by the resolution adopted by the rue Nitot meeting, even if it were necessary to withhold our signature to the Treaty. I felt more than ever convinced that the handing over of Upper Silesia to Poland would be a great wrong and that it would endanger the peace of Europe by creating a new Alsace-Lorraine grievance in Middle Europe.

When our amendment on the subject came up for discussion at

the Council of Four there was a certain acerbity in the proceedings which had been almost entirely absent from our previous consultations. In support of my demand for a plebiscite, I pleaded President Wilson's principle of self-determination. Upper Silesia had not been Polish for 800 years, and according to my information had no desire to become Polish now. To quote from a note of my protest:

There was no resemblance between the case of Upper Silesia and and Alsace-Lorraine. It was proposed to tear something from Germany that had been in the same combination as the other States of the German Empire for 800 years. In these circumstances I considered that the people must have some voice.

The President urged that the majority of the population of Upper Silesia was Polish and not German, and ought therefore to be given to Poland. His experts had so advised him. I replied that it was not a question of what Mr. Lord (his somewhat fanatical pro-Polish expert) wished, but what the inhabitants of Upper Silesia themselves desired. The President's contention was that this could not be ascertained, because the land mainly belonged to a few great German landowners and they would exercise intimidation on their tenants and workers. I pointed out to him that the majority of the population was industrial and dwelt in the towns, that our workmen resented any attempt by employers to bully them into voting against their convictions.

President Wilson said that Mr. Lloyd George spoke of England. The same was not the case elsewhere. Even in the United States of America there was a great deal of domination at elections by employers in the great industrial districts. He himself had done much to overcome it and would be disappointed if he did not succeed in doing so in the end.

I suggested that before the plebiscite was taken all German troops should be withdrawn from the area and that American troops should occupy it until the voting had decided its future destiny. This would be a guarantee that no intimidation would be permitted. After a prolonged debate, in which President Wilson displayed the greatest reluctance to accept the proposal, and after a vehement protest from M. Clemenceau, the Silesian plebiscite was accepted. The other rectifications of a minor character which I proposed in the Pomeranian frontier of Germany were also agreed to without any difficulty.

The result of the plebiscite was an overwhelming vote in favour of restoring a substantial part of Upper Silesia to Germany. The British stand in this question was thus completely justified.

When the Four came to consider the German reply on reparations I put forward the amendment which had been agreed to by British Ministers. It was in favour of alternative suggestions. The first was:

"The Germans to undertake as a contract the whole task of Reparation, and that a sum should be fixed in the Treaty of Peace for all other items in the category of damage."

The second alternative was:

"In the alternative, the Germans to sign the Reparation Clauses as they stand, but that three months should be given them to endeavour to effect an arrangement for the fixing of a definite sum in cash as a commutation for all the claims. In the event of the Germans making no satisfactory offer, the present Reparation clauses would stand."

There was much to be said for the first plan had the French been agreeable. But they felt a strong objection to having a large contingent of German workmen quartered for two or three years in the North of France. It might lead to friction and perhaps riots, having regard to the intensity of the feeling against the Germans which existed amongst the French population, more particularly in the devastated area. The only part of this proposal that was acceptable to the French was the idea that the Germans should be called upon to furnish such material for reconstruction as the French required and that its value should be credited to Germany in the reparation account.

The French did not object to the second alternative. They went so far as to propose that the Germans should be given an extra month to examine the damage and estimate the cost of repairing it. President Wilson still adhered to the American proposal for a fixed sum. He was prepared to insert as high a figure as £6,000,000,000 in the Treaty. Ultimately the British amendment was agreed to and was incorporated in the reply sent to the German Delegation.

The questions of the German criticisms of the Draft Treaty in respect of ports and waterways, of the military occupation, Germany's demand for immediate admission into the League of Nations and her demand that the reduction of her armaments should be conditional on a similar measure of general disarmament applicable to the Allies as well as herself, were the subject of informal conversations between President Wilson, M. Clemenceau and myself. M. Clemenceau referred the questions of waterways and the army of occupation to the Ministers who had charge of those particular sections of the Treaty. On the whole these talks resulted in substantial modifications in favour of Germany. The agreement we reached with regard to the vital matter of general disarmament was embodied in two separate clauses of the Allied reply to the Brockdorff-Rantzau memorandum which I have already quoted in full in the Chapter on Disarmament.

As to the time when Germany should be permitted to enter the League, the following answer was given:

. . . Any State whose government shall have given clear proofs of its stability as well as of its intention to observe its international obligations—particularly those obligations which arise out of the Treaty of Peace—will find the Principal Allied and Associated Powers disposed to support its candidature for admission to the League.

In the case of Germany, it is hardly necessary to say that the record of the last five years is not of a character to justify an exception, at the present time, to the general rule to which reference has just been made. Her case demands a definite test. The length of this period will largely depend upon the acts of the German Government, and it is within the choice of that Government, by its attitude towards the Treaty of Peace, to shorten the period of delay which the League of Nations, without any intention of prolonging it unduly, shall consider it necessary to fix.

Provided these necessary conditions are assured, they see no reason why Germany should not become a member of the League in the early future.

With regard to waterways, it was decided to send the following reply:

Such are the principles which underlie and explain the texts referring to the general régime of traffic on ways of communications. The Allied and Associated Powers have in no case attempted to prevent the legitimate use by Germany of her economic independence, but have merely proposed to prevent the abusive use thereof. Above all, they have aimed at securing freedom of communications and transit to or from young landlocked States, which, in the absence of definite guarantees, would have regained their political independence only to fall once again under the economic tutelage of Germany.

But it was decided to introduce the following amendments:

The freedom of transit between East Prussia and the rest of Germany is more clearly defined.

The number of representatives from Germany on the Commission for the Oder is increased from one to three.

Measures are taken to ensure the representation of Germany at the Conference which will be charged with the duty of establishing a definitive statute for the Danube.

The (future) Rhine-Danube canal is to be subjected merely to the régime applicable to waterways declared to be international.

The provisions relating to the possibility of an International Commission being required for the Kiel Canal, and a large part of the provisions relating to railways to be constructed on German territory are deleted.

As to the military occupation of the Rhineland, the Military raised several difficulties in the way of giving effective guarantees that the civil administration should not be unduly interfered with, but ultimately an arrangement was come to by which guarantees were given that there should be no undue interference by the Military with the ordinary administration of the civil authorities. Another very considerable concession in this respect was the result of prolonged discussions between M. Loucheur and myself. I urged that the garrison should be reduced to the lowest possible figures compatible with safety and that the costs of the occupation should be limited to an agreed maximum. Ultimately M. Loucheur and I drew up the following document:

I. The High Powers concerned are in agreement for the greatest possible reduction in the numbers of the troops of occupation. They consider the maximum to be a figure fixed by the military experts in their Note of the 8th June, and which the latter indicate as being liable to reduction from the moment that the disarmament of Germany becomes an accomplished fact. They reckon that at that moment the reduction should be effected to the figure of about 110,000 men.

II. The High Powers concerned are agreed as to the reduction to a minimum of the expenses of occupation with a view to using the maximum at their disposal for the payment of reparation. With this object the revision of the basis of payment of the expenses of occupation provided for in the Treaty ought to be effected and from the moment that the reduction of the above-mentioned number of troops is carried out the amount of the sum to be demanded from Germany ought not to exceed 240 million golden marks a year.

III. The High Powers concerned are agreed to suppress from the moment when the Treaty of Peace is ratified, all the measures of censure or others which are likely to hinder free trade between German countries on the left bank of the Rhine and on the right bank. The solution of all these questions concerning occupation will be entrusted to a civil organisation composed of one representative from each of the four nations interested.

The terms of reference of this organisation are actually in process of being drawn up.

On June 10th I reported these proposed alterations to a meeting of the British Empire Delegation, with a further proposal that a general undertaking should be given to Germany that every facility would be offered to start her industry again. Those amendments were accepted by the British Empire Delegation and were embodied in the considered reply sent by M. Clemenceau to the German emissaries.

CHAPTER XVII

RECEPTION OF THE TREATY IN BRITAIN

THE terms of peace were well received in all the Allied countries. In Britain there was no condemnation of the Treaty as a whole. The general view is expressed in a phrase used by a speaker in the debate in the House of Commons on the second reading of the Treaty—"severe but just." That debate fairly represents the attitude of the general public towards the provisions of the Treaty. Sir Donald Maclean, the leader of the Liberal Opposition, in his opening sentences said:

. . . We have controversy with the Prime Minister, but no controversy which in the slightest degree prevents us from gladly affording to him all the laurels which were accorded to him by his fellow countrymen on the occasion of the celebration of Peace. He has exhibited a skill, an energy, and an indomitable optimism in the darkest days for which we are all very grateful. . . . Democracy has won this War. Are we getting or likely to get a democratic peace? That naturally is a question which I have addressed to myself in asking whether or not I will vote for the Second Reading of this Bill. I have no hesitation in answering that question. Of course I intend to vote for the Second Reading, but I have had to put to myself one or two questions, and the first is this: Who signed the Peace? After all, Democracy has signed it. The Prime Minister signed it, and I am not sure I am not right in saying that he is Prime Minister of the most democratic nation in the world. Then we have the President of the United States— the latest expression of democracy on the greatest scale by means of a settled written constitution which the world has known. I will only mention two more names, those of General Botha and General Smuts, in addition to the Premiers of our own self-governing Dominions. I mention those two names especially because not so many years ago both these men were our enemies in the field, and they, having gone through the whole of these long and toilsome days came to the conclusion that it was their duty to sign this Peace. There are many points of gloom, as well as, I am thankful to say, of brightness in this document. I am quite sure that one of the best of them is Clause 13, dealing with the question of labour. For the first time in the history of the world we have had laid down by the solemn consent of responsible representatives of the powerful nations who have signed this document, conditions to which they have pledged themselves, and which if only partially, and to some extent substantially carried out, will change the face and conditions of international labour all the world over.

Mr. Clynes, the spokesman of the Labour party, whilst criticising one or two of the terms, said:

. . . We must balance the great gains now enjoyed—which I hope will be perpetuated for the benefit of mankind—as expressed in the Treaty, against the defects that we may consider are within that Treaty. . . . I said at the beginning that we have had to balance considerations in relation to this Treaty. Our view is that with all its defects, with all its blemishes, it is the work of men who, in the circumstances which surrounded it, must have acted with motives of the highest patriotism and with the highest and noblest considerations for human government.

Lord Robert Cecil's view on the Treaty as a whole was expressed in this sentence: ". . . We are all prepared to say with the utmost confidence that the broad lines of the Treaty are right."

There were criticisms on details. For instance, no member from any party objected to the demand for reparations, but two or three were of opinion that it would have been better to fix a sum, and there was just an echo of the famous telegram which accused the peace delegates of letting the Germans off too easily. Not one objected to putting the Kaiser on his trial for the crime of initiating the War, but one member suggested that he ought to be tried by the League of Nations. No one complained that boundaries had been rearranged on ethnical principals, but Mr. Clynes objected that in doing so millions of Germans had been thrown into Poland and he gave as an illustration the case of a town called Birnbaum, whose population was mainly German but had nevertheless been assigned to Poland. As Labour was inclined to make much of this allegation and Birnbaum afforded an excellent illustration of our difficulties, I dealt with it in my reply:

. . . If my right hon. Friend means to say that you must have no Germans inside Poland and no Poles inside Germany, that was impossible physically. But that is largely due to the German policy. Germany had been setting up little colonies here and there, with a view to the Prussianising of Poland. I will tell him about Birnbaum. Birnbaum is a district in the province of Posnania. The town of Birnbaum is German. The whole district is Polish, and if you took a plebiscite of the whole of that area the majority would be decisively Polish. Now I ask him what he would have done in those circumstances? Birnbaum is a very good illustration of some of the most difficult problems with which we were confronted. He could not have said: "We will take that little town in the middle of a great wide area. We will declare that to be German; all the surrounding area must be Poland." That would be an impossible limitation . . . as if you had an Irish colony in this country, like the Scotland Division of Liverpool, where you have got an overwhelming Irish population. My hon. Friend [Mr. T. P. O'Connor] is a great Irish Nationalist and a distinguished Irish patriot, but not even in his most intense moments has he ever claimed that the Scotland Division of Liverpool should be added to Ireland. . . . But that is a comparable case, and you have many cases of that kind. The Germans had the habit of settling in industrial districts in towns where the whole of the surrounding population is Polish. The country is traditionally Polish. Birnbaum is one of these cases. . . .

Something—but not much—was said about the Polish Corridor, but having pointed out how Polish the population was, I then asked:

. . . Will they (my hon. Friends who criticise our severance of Prussia by the handing over of a population which is purely Pole to the Republic of Poland—and I put this as a challenge—) now say that we ought to have forced this Polish population, this population which is overwhelmingly Polish in tongue, spirit, tradition, and aspiration, under the dominion of Prussia against their will, merely in order to unite East and West Prussia? If not, there is no sense in their protest about the Polish corridor. . . .

There was no response to this challenge. After listening carefully to the speeches delivered from every point of view I felt I was entitled to sum up my impression of the discussion in the following words:

. . . There has been no fundamental criticism. There have been suggestions made; there have been one or two sections of the Clauses of this gigantic document which have been subjected to some slight criticism, but, in the main, it has struck me that the House as a whole—I do not know that I can make any exception—has accepted this Treaty. . . . May I say, in conclusion, about the Treaty, that it was a gigantic task; it was certainly one which was complicated. I do not claim that the Treaty is perfect in all respects. Where it is not perfect, I look forward to the organisation of the League of Nations to remedy, to repair, and to redress.

And that undoubtedly represented the general opinion of the country on the terms of the Treaty.

The House accorded a second reading to the bill ratifying the Treaty without a division. The only hostile motion came from Mr. Bottomley who wished to record his opinion that we had not exacted a sufficient indemnity. He had only one supporter and he did not challenge a division.

The section of the Labour party which opposed the War, at a meeting held some weeks after the publication of the Treaty, condemned some of its terms. But Mr. Ramsay MacDonald, who moved the resolution of censure, did not condescend to any detailed criticism and confined himself to vague denunciation. Here is a characteristic sample of his well-known oratorical style extracted from that speech:

Their nation, the nations of Europe, had no confidence in the conquering power of great personality. They clenched their little fists, they pirouetted round their enemy and challenged him to take his coat off. That was the weakest of human weaknesses. The great man, the great individual, the great personality was the person who went through the raving crowd surrounded with that dignity which made it impossible for the blackguard to touch him, even though he talked behind his back. Translate that power of great personality, give it a national value and a national expression, that was the thing that was going to secure them for ever. . . .

Very impressive, no doubt, delivered in his sonorous voice, but not helpful in enabling the Ministers concerned to comprehend his real objections to the details of the Treaty.